MW01199851

The History of Mandeville:

From the American Revolution
to Bernard de Marigny de Mandeville

by
Anita R. Campeau & Donald J. Sharp
Foreword by
Clayton J. Borne, III

The History of Mandeville:
From the American Revolution
to Bernard de Marigny de Mandeville

A Cornerstone Book
Published by Cornerstone Book Publishers
An Imprint of Michael Poll Publishing
in Association with Clayton J. Borne, III
Copyright © 2014 by Anita R. Campeau & Donald J. Sharp

Front cover images:
(left) Antoine de Marigny de Mandeville, artist unknown, oil on canvas, c. 1795. Courtesy of the Louisiana State Museum, loaned by Gaspar Cusachs. Used by permission.
(right) Pierre Enguerrand Philippe de Marigny de Mandeville, artist unknown, oil on canvas, c. 1820. Courtesy of the Louisiana State Museum, loaned by Gaspar Cusachs. Used by permission.

Back Cover image:
Bernard de Marigny de Mandeville at 31 years old. Litographed on paper by Henri Fontallard, Paris, France. Courtesy of the Louisiana State Museum, loaned by Gaspar Cusachs. Used by permission.

Cover design by Michael R. Poll

Cornerstone Book Publishers
New Orleans, LA
www.cornerstonepublishers.com

First Cornerstone Edition - 2014

ISBN: 1613421761
ISBN-13: 978-1-61342-176-5

MADE IN THE USA

iv

DEDICATION

To our spouses John and Kathleen

This book is affectionately inscribed
by Anita and Donald.

The authors would also like to dedicate this
book to the brave souls who fought in the
Battle of New Orleans
defending the city from the British.

Table of Contents

ACKNOWLEDGEMENTS

Donald J. Sharp, co-author, always had a love of history, but a turning point occurred in the early 1960s when his father Clarence kept showing him their old Sharp family Bible, and asking questions. After procrastinating for a couple of summers, he decided to look into his family history. The trail led to St. Tammany Parish with stops to meet Zachariah "Cutsie" Sharp owner of Mandeville's Ford Agency, and Edgar "Old Pelican" Sharp, his first contacts, and then on to the lake front to the home of Dr. Harvey and Melba Colvin, at the suggestion of Edgar Sharp. He then ventured to the archives at the Covington Court House where he was directed by the St. Tammany Parish Clerk of Court Robert Fitzmorris to the basement archives. Down the steep steps, careful not to stumble, a quick glance around brought a feeling of disappointment since he had expected to see a neat, well-organized room with rows of filing cabinets, tables and chairs to do research.

The view was a partially empty basement room with several long tables in the middle, old stained cardboard boxes on one of the tables and underneath over a dozen boxes lined up, some filled to capacity causing their sides to bulge. Around the room near the walls were several old large cabinets ready for future filing. Records had been moved several times over the years whenever a new courthouse was built and the location was changed. The present location was the fourth time in its history. On the opposite end of the room, facing the stairs, was a pleasant looking, gray haired lady seated at a desk busily sorting and arranging a stack of old records. This was a first meeting with Mrs. Bertha Perreand Neff, archivist, historian and genealogist who would open doors for this amateur researcher and later furnish some of the raw material for *Court Case No. 225, Letchworth and Wife vs Bartle and Wife* of the Eighth District Court of St. Tammany Parish.

Mrs. Neff, whose family had lived in Madisonville for years, had been hired by Clerk of Court Robert Fitzmorris and was given the job of sorting and cataloging the large amount of records collected over the years, some of them going back to the very beginning of the Parish in the late 1700s. After explaining to Mrs. Neff that he was seeking information on the Sharp and Spell families, as he recalls, she took him over to one of the tables and with delight displayed what she had come across in one of the cardboard boxes, files on Court Case No. 225. As she took out items from the folders, original surveys and maps done prior to 1825, affidavits, marriage licenses, land confirmation certificates issued by the land commissioners to carry out the land laws enacted by Congress, he knew instantly that this was a once in a lifetime opportunity for a researcher, doing his family history, and realized that a family is a deeply rooted tree with branches of different strengths, and that archives and libraries are havens where societies are preserved. She went beyond the call of duty, introduced Mr. Sharp to a voyage of discovery, by giving him an insight on his family through various documents.

Most interesting was when Mrs. Neff took out of a box and held in her hands a large brown seal attached to an old land survey that was literally disintegrating to pieces. The seal was the Great Deputed Seal of West Florida used in the process of issuing land grants in the time of the British Colonial Period. The land survey had been done by Elias Durnford, Surveyor General of West Florida, in 1777, for the land grant of William O'Brien, a key piece of evidence, as we will learn during the trial of 1825. The Seal made of paper and wax has deteriorated much since the nineteenth century, the edges are badly worn and roughly about one-eighth of the lower portion is missing.

Respects are due to the late Dr. Robert R. Rae, noted author on the history of British West Florida and Professor of History at the University of Auburn, whose enthusiasm kindled interests on the subject of seals. After searching both in the United States and London for several years, Dr. Rae could not find a surviving copy of the seal.

During a trip to England during the summer of 1979, Mr. Sharp went to the Public Records Office in Kew Gardens, London, to find information on early British settlers in the Bayou Castein area. There, information was abstracted from Photostats of the British Public Records. The forty-plus land grants examined cover an area from Bayou Castein to the Tchefuncte River. No impressions of the Great Seal of West Florida have survived in the Public Records Office of London, although there is a unique guarded example of the East Florida Seal.

Most of the people, first encountered in starting the research, are now deceased. They need not be forgotten as Mr. Sharp has them recorded on voice cassette tapes telling their interesting stories. These tapes are deposited in the Donald J. Sharp Collection at the Center for South East Studies at Southeastern University, Hammond, Louisiana.

It is impossible to name all the contributors, but appreciation goes to Mrs. Bertha Neff and Norma Core of the Covington Court House. Greatly appreciated was Adrian Schwartz, a Covington lawyer, and the first known St. Tammany historian whom Mr. Sharp met and got him started on the history of Bayou Castein, which we tend to forget started with complacent Indians, then as a French enclave in the Western wilderness, followed by a handful of British settlers who remained on their land and maintained ownership through the Spanish Colonial period, followed by ambitious Americans.

Respects are due to deceased cousins Zachariah "Cutsie" Sharp, who at the time had the oldest Ford Agency of the United States and Edgar Sharp, a crabber on Lake Pontchartrain, who had a keen mind and was an excellent story teller of family anecdotes. His bright spirit whose enthusiasm and reminiscences told with ready wit kindled Mr. Sharp's interest in Mandeville's local history. Gratitude is also owed to Mrs. Alma Armstrong, a resident of New Orleans, whose mother saved the Tom Spell Cemetery, an 1815 family cemetery located on the property of Thomas Spell and Elizabeth Goodby.

Thanks to Jeremy Sharp who helped his father through his computer skills, and to Robin Perkins, clerk at the Covington Court House, on the Joseph Letchworth information, and to Angela Pope Reid for providing information on her Cooper and Sticker ancestors.

Writing a book is solitary work but the research which goes into a manuscript requires the help of many. Sincere thanks to all the persons involved.

FOREWORD

In an attempt to embrace and adequately describe the City of Mandeville, the words of King Arthur in describing his Mythical Kingdom came to mind. "In short, there's simply not, a more congenial spot, for happily-ever-aftering, than here in Camelot." To those of us that call Mandeville home, the reality is truly Camelot.

The fantasy is further enhanced by the charm of its enigmatic visionary name sake Bernard de Marigny de Mandeville of the noble French aristocrat Phillippe de Marigny family. This mega wealthy, larger than life, extremely well educated legend traveled in elite social circles, was involved in the creation of famous gaming endeavors, was identified with curious political alliances and assumed leadership roles in dynamic charitable and fraternal activities with lodges of Freemasons. All of which had him close friends with such historical legends as the Marquis de Lafayette, Andrew Jackson, Sam Houston, Zachary Taylor, and Jean Lafitte and many more. His footprints across the decades of Mandeville's history have added to the city's mystic, making Mandeville truly a noble Kingdom. Fantasy leads to intense curiosity and that mystique creates the intrigue which leads to the research to discover how this mythical Kingdom came to be.

The dynamic dedication of seasoned historian and researcher, Donald Sharp, combined with the unique writing talents of Anita Campeau take us into the mysteries of yesterday by examining the early families, their lives, their labors and the legal disputes that shaped the city's geography subsequent to the Concession periods of English and Spanish Rule and prior to the masterful subdivisions of our City of Mandeville. The real life legends that shaped the personality of our charming city suddenly take on new meaning. As Don Sharp's research clearly shows, it was not all harmonious with the early family involved in acrimony for years establishing the parameters and boundaries of the city's beginning.

Come with us now on a wonderful journey made possible by these two dynamic historians as they academically unravel the "Mystery of Mandeville."

Clayton J. Borne, III
Mandeville City Prosecutor
2014

PREFACE

The roots of present-day America go deep down into the European past. The first settlers on the North American continent came out of Western Europe and brought with them their differing cultural patterns and their prejudices. The history of the American people can be roughly divided into three periods: the colonial where they adjusted to the American environment and thereby, slowly and surely, evolved into a new nation. The second is the national period, in which the young United States turned its back on Europe, and marched westward across the American continent transforming it, region by region, from a wilderness into a land of farms and towns, as they sharpened and modified their own national characteristics to emerge as a powerful nation. The third is the one in which we find ourselves at the present time.

At first, unconnected with the East, were the French in Louisiana and the Spanish in the Southwest. Both were Catholic in religion, and each gave the dominant color to life in the regions which they occupied. Both exerted a strong and permanent influence on later American architecture. The Roman law, modified by French and Spanish influences, permanently shaped the legal code of Louisiana. The contributions of the Negro slaves are hard to measure. Their labor helped open the way for the production of the great staples necessary to trade. The successful slave sales which financed the James Willing raid convinced Oliver Pollock that additional profits could come to the American cause by raiding British slave holders in West Florida. The taking and selling of slaves became a primary motivation to purchase goods and supplies needed for the war effort.

Many were lured to the New World by hopes of a better life for themselves and their children. England was foremost in sending the greatest amount of settlers, but Germany, Holland, France, Spain, furnished enough to make the American colonies the children of Europe. All of these early groups were augmented during colonial and in early national days, by new arrivals of the same stock.

From 1765 to 1775, Americans tried to reform the British Empire with their conception of law and liberty, not break it up. A Continental Congress was called in September 1774 to secure colonial unity. This congress became the battleground between colonial conservatives and extremists on the question of relations with England. As long as the dispute was on this basis, most Americans supported the colonial cause. After 1775 when the idea of independence was put forth, the colonists divided into pro-British and pro-American camps.

Following the Declaration of Independence, America was far from united in the struggle with England. Many loyalists left the colonies to escape the ravages of the war, relocating either to Canada, East Florida, or West Florida where some obtained land grants on the north shore of Lake Pontchartrain, at Bayou Castein.

At the close of the American Revolution, inhabitants living near Bayou Castein found themselves under Spanish rule for Spain had recovered old Spanish West Florida from Britain under the terms of the 1783 Treaty of Paris. Life of the settlers remained much the same, undisturbed. Their forest and cattle produce found ready markets in New Orleans. A number of Spanish land grants were given in the vicinity of Lake Pontchartrain between the years 1779 and 1810.

The greater influence of frontier living and the steady advance into the wilderness came in the years after the second war with England, in 1812. Emigrants poured in westward in greater numbers. But after 1830, they were again increased by people from wider areas.

The Eighth District Court Case titled *Court Case No. 225, Joseph Letchworth and Wife vs Jacob Bartle and Wife* covers the years 1825 to 1829. It bridges the pre-history of Mandeville between the British Period when the first settlers arrived and the American Revolution to Bernard de Marigny when he starts to buy up land on the north shore with the idea of making it a resort town.

The case is important because early historical documents and maps dealing with the history of St. Tammany Parish have been preserved for posterity, and we are to use several as primary sources in recording the early history of Castein Bayou and Bayou Chinchuba. It is also of interest because of the human element that involves two families, neighbors living side by side, who test the court system in order to determine the rightful owners of land in an area which five years later became known as Mandeville, Louisiana. The trial is valuable in content and will be used to illustrate the theme covering Land Grants that passed the Great Seal of the Province of British West Florida during the period 1772-1779, followed by the Spanish who inherited the large plantations that the British had cultivated, and then redistributing the land, remaining so until 1810. Land grants will be used as primary sources material in covering the local history of pre-Mandeville, a focus in this study.

Court Case No. 225 is the story of rightful ownership, trespassing, cutting of timber, fraud, stubbornness, lies, deceit, and the triumph and vindication of Martha Richardson, the plaintiff, the daughter of George Richardson, an early settler. She was the widow of Zachariah Faircloth, the wife of Joseph Letchworth in a second marriage, and a woman who would not be intimidated. It is also the story of Elizabeth Goodby, the defendant, widow of Thomas Spell, whose father John Spell had been granted a British grant, and whose family remained in the area. Her second marriage was to Jacob Bartle. A proud, arrogant, and defiant woman, Elizabeth Bartle does not accept the verdict of the court and makes an appeal to the Louisiana Supreme Court, even though it was not in her best interest.

Except for the writings of André Pénicaut who first described the Indians on the north shore, the 1825 trial documented by the court recorder, is the beginning of the written history of Bayou Castein. We do not know of any diaries or collections of letters in private hands for that period of history in St. Tammany Parish. The case generated over 160 pages of hand-written testimony, from old-timers who had lived in the area between Bayou Castein and Chinchuba, either called up by the plaintiff or the defendant to testify. Some reminisced for pages, mostly about times and people long gone by. The case becomes a lively guide to a little-known part of Lake Pontchartrain. Documents and official records, used as evidence, shed light on the early settlement of the north shore thus connecting every day life to the events that emerged as historical turning points in the life of those early settlers.

The main historical events that took place after 1760 on the north shore to 1850 will be the subject of this book titled *The History of Mandeville: from the American Revolution to Bernard de Marigny de Mandeville*. Land tenure on the north shore endured for six families across the shifting eras of domination by Great Britain, Spain and the United States. Our research in land records has provided us with some individual stories and a demographic pattern of these Anglo settlers who came to Bayou Castein because of the Revolutionary War. They remained, intermarried, whether they had been loyalists, patriots or neutrals or surrendered to Captain Pickles in 1779. As a group they have been largely forgotten by history.

In our research an attempt was made to understand the life and times of these ancestors. Efforts were made to learn of the circumstances in which they lived and to appreciate the conditions that defined their tribulations and their hopes for the future. These people are worthy to be remembered since their stories become tapestries of kinship woven over two hundred years. Their flaws, their virtues, their endurance, their genetic and moral imprint make them worthy of our esteem. We do not intend to glamorize or glorify these forbears, but we hope to understand their times, view their accomplishments in a good light, and forgive whatever failings they may have had.

The settlement began in turbulent times, during the British Period (1763-1783), when the first settlers fleeing the violence on the East Coast remove to British West Florida to hack out homes and fields from the forest. We learn more on the settlement through the witnesses who took the stand in Court Case No. 225, for they were the children of those settlers. It continues through the Spanish Period. Witnesses identify original settlers who died or left the area and the new ones who came to take their place. They explain how some settlers acquired ownership of their land when the United States took over West Florida.

The case presents an insight as to who pioneered the settlement. As we move from one witness to another, a picture emerges of two headstrong frontier women, who lived as neighbors for years. Because of their dispute, we have the impression that they tore up the little community on the north shore of Lake Pontchartrain between bayous Castein and Chinchuba. The 30 witnesses called to testify recalled at length some of the first settlers at Bayou Castein during the British and Spanish Colonial periods. A few describe how surveys were made for the reconfirmation of land grants. Because of this legal drama, almost two hundred years later we are given the opportunity to read about the people who first settled the area in order to learn about their social life and their conflicts. In part, this dispute and estate settlements put in motion forces that would ultimately change the ownership of the land on the lake-front. As a result of the case, family feuds and a divided village open the way for William Bowman and Bernard Xavier Marigny de Mandeville to purchase the land which became Mandeville in 1834.

PROLOGUE

The Acolapissa's earliest known location was on Pearl River about eleven miles above its mouth. In 1702, in search of food and religious freedom from white Christian zealots, they migrated from Bay St. Louis to settle on a bayou on the north side of Lake Pontchartrain called "Castembayouque" later known as Castine Bayou. A first mention was found in a description by the young cabin boy, André Pénicaut who, with eleven Frenchmen, lived with the Acolapissa Indians from May 1706 to February 1707. Governor Jean-Baptiste Bienville sent most of his men to live with the Indians because of a shortage of supplies. In 1718, according to André Pénicaut, the tribe moved over to the Mississippi River and settled on the east side about thirteen leagues from New Orleans. The Acolapissa traded with New Orleans settlers as early as 1725.

The Treaty of Paris marked the end of France as a great power in America. In the Proclamation of 1763, King George III of England consolidated much of the new territorial in three colonies of North America – Canada (Quebec), East Florida and West Florida. Lake Pontchartrain became an international boundary separating British West Florida to the north from the Spanish Isle of *Orléans* to the South. Spain gave Florida to England in return for the restoration of Cuba and the Philippines. France compensated Spain for the loss of Florida by giving her that part of Louisiana that lay west of the Mississippi and a small strip of land east of the mouth of the river. The rest of the expanded British territory was left to Native Americans. The British arrived in 1764 at Mobile to take possession. The frontier provinces were immediately organized as English Colonies and named East and West Florida, whose capital was Pensacola. The population grew steadily.

Louisiana was a part of the British possessions in America from the time of the treaty in 1763 until, as a result of the Revolutionary War, the American colonies wrested from Great Britain all the American territory she possessed.

Taking advantage of the English's weakness, Don Bernardo Galvez, Spanish Governor of Louisiana, recruited troops to capture the British forts in 1779, including Fort Bute, the one at Baton Rouge, and Natchez that soon capitulated. Mobile fell to him in 1780 and Pensacola in 1781, thus extending the Spanish government over West Florida. By 1783, Spain and the young United States would fight for the control of the Lower Mississippi Valley. It would take another fifteen years before the United States could claim victory.

France reacquired Louisiana from Spain in 1800. In 1803, Napoleon sold it to the United States as the Louisiana Purchase. Americans took over in 1804. The Florida Parishes were not part of the Purchase. Florida became Spanish again, remaining so until 1810.

The United States did recognize the land claims of actual settlers between 1803 and 1810, regardless of the Spanish titles or lack of one. It would take many years before the final chapter of land disputes would be closed.

CHRONOLOGY

Historical timeline of Bayou Castein and the Tchefuncte River beginning with the British Colonial Period:

1767   John Jones receives a British land grant on the Tchefuncte River.

1774   Settlers begin to arrive at Bayou Castein and the Tchefuncte River.

1775   John Perry receives a British land grant at the mouth of Bayou Castein.

December 4: Jacob and Sarah Ambrose have warrant issued for land on shore of Lake Pontchartrain.

December 4: John, Joseph and Mager Spell apply for warrant on Bayou Castein and Lake Pontchartrain.

1776   William O'Brien has warrants for grants on Lake Shore and Tchefuncte approved.

John, Joseph and Mager Spell reapply for warrants because King George III had put a hold on issuing land grants.

The formal Declaration of Independence, written by Thomas Jefferson, was adopted on July 4.

1777   Morris Smith, Rebecca Ambrose, Paul Labyteau, John and Thomas Loofbarrow, Samuel Ferguson received confirmation of their land grants on Lake Pontchartrain near Bayou Castein.

1778   France provides military support to the Thirteen Colonies.

February: James Willing and American Raiders from the East Coast burn and plunder plantations from Natchez to the Amite River.

1779   Spain enters war against Great Britain, attacks fort at Baton Rouge.

September 12: William Pickles coming back through the Rigolets from the Gulf spots the *West Florida* to the southwest and closed in for the battle.

The American ship *Morris Tender*, commanded by Captain William Pickles and the *Sloop of War West Florida* commanded by John Payne fought a naval battle on September 10, 1779.

October 16: Captain William Pickles of the American Forces lands at Bayou Castein and demands that settlers sign an Oath of Allegiance. Nineteen settlers signed the Oath, received by Oliver Pollock, then sent up to the Continental Congress. President John Jay read the Oath to the members of the Continental Congress.

1781   Pensacola falls to Spain. The British lose all of West Florida.

1783   Treaty of Versailles: recognition of the independence of the United States. Settlers have 18 months to sign allegiance to His Catholic Majesty or leave their land in West Florida.

Morgan Edwards gets a Spanish grant from Governor Miro on Bayou Castein that included the old British grants of John Perry and Alexander McCullough.

1790   James Goodby and his sister Elizabeth settle on vacant abandoned land on Bayou Chinchuba.

Joseph Rabassa abandons his improvement between lands of Thomas Spell and Joseph Lorreins and receives a new one on the east bank of Bayou Castein.

1791   George Sharp and Zachariah Faircloth, flat boatmen from Kentucky, settle "high up" on Bayou Castein. George Sharp receives a Spanish land grant.

February 20: James Goodby assigns his improvement to Thomas Spell who marries his sister Elizabeth.

1796   George Richardson, moving down from Natchez, settles on abandoned Loofbarrow and Ambrose land grants.

1798   Peter Labyteau, son of Paul, improves abandoned grant next to his father's grant and obtains possession from the Spanish government.

Gilberto Guillemard, officer in the Spanish service, aide major of New Orleans, architect, builder of the Cabildo, St. Louis Cathedral and *Presbytère*, makes confirmation survey for Smith, Spells, and Morgan Edwards.

1801   Zachariah Faircloth buys George Richardson's land improvement for "a cow and a calf" and he takes his daughter Martha as his common-law wife.

1803   Napoleon sells Louisiana to the United States as the Louisiana Purchase.

1804   Charles Parent, Spanish commandant of the North Shore and Tchefuncte River dies.

1806   Mary O'Brien tract is surveyed and reconfirmed by Deputy Surveyor Ira C. Kneeland.

First U.S. Gunboats appear on the lakes.

1808   Lt. Colonel Gilberto Guillemard dies at Pensacola in 1808.

1810   Heirs of Samuel Ferguson sell British grant to William Dewees of New Orleans.

Heirs of Paul Labyteau sell grant to William Dewees.

William Dewees hires William McDermott as caretaker.

1811   Dorothy O'Brien Sanderson, daughter of William O'Brien, sells grant on Lake Pontchartrain to Jacob Bartle.

1812	War of 1812 with Great Britain.
1813	William McDermott tries to claim Dewees' property.

1812　War of 1812 with Great Britain.

1813　William McDermott tries to claim Dewees' property.

Thomas Spell is seen cutting timber west of the O'Brien tract.

Land Act of 1813 passed by the United States Congress.

The U.S. Navy facility started in January on the Tchefuncte River and block ship built.

Jacques Lorreins gives U.S. government a 10 year lease at $20.00 a year.

Fort Oak built on the Tchefuncte River, opposite Madisonville, for the protection of the Navy workers and the people of Madisonville.

1815　Thomas Spell dies at the U.S. Navy facility on Tchefuncte.

1818　Widow Elizabeth Spell marries Jacob Bartle on August 11, 1818.

1819　Land Act passed by Congress that entitles settlers who had occupied and proven land claim before 1813 to 640 acres of land. This entitles Zachariah Faircloth to full amount and starts into motion land dispute that will bring on Court Case 225.

1820　April 8: Jacob Bartle receives Certificate from United States Land Commissioners Charles S. Cosby and Fulwar Skipwith of the Greensburg District.

1821　Elizabeth Goodby starts her slaves cutting wood on disputed land. Zachariah Faircloth legally marries Martha Richardson on August 14, 1821.

1823　Zachariah Faircloth becomes ill. On August 6, 1823, he makes deed of gift to wife of land with 200 acres going to his nephew Joseph Sharp.

Zachariah Faircloth dies.

Elizabeth Bartle continues having her slaves cutting trees on disputed land even after being warned to stop. On September 5, the widow Martha Faircloth becomes legal owner of land.

1824　Widow Martha Faircloth marries Joseph Letchworth.

Elizabeth Bartle forewarns Martha Letchworth that the disputed land is hers and she will continue cutting wood. Martha Letchworth "forewarns" her neighbor that unless she stops trespassing and cutting wood on her land she will sue.

1825　On May 21, Joseph Letchworth and wife file suit against Jacob Bartle and wife. The plaintiffs hire Branch W. Miller as their lawyer. The defendants hire the up-and-coming lawyer Alfred E. Hennan. Case is scheduled for the second week of October. June 8, Zachariah Faircloth's estate goes before probate judge. Martha Letchworth assumes full control by law of Zachariah Faircloth's succession.

October 1, 1825, Jacob Bartle dies.

October 12, 1825: nephew Joseph Sharp sells his 200 acre donation of land to Joseph Letchworth and wife for $200 dollars. Sharp was living on the land that was part of the dispute.

1826 Probate of Jacob Bartle's succession. The O'Brien (Bartle) tract is sold to William Bowman, of Madisonville, to satisfy claims of the Bartle heirs.

1826 The verdict of Case No. 225 is appealed by defendants to the Louisiana Supreme Court.

1828 The second trial between Letchworth and Bartle begins.

1829 Heavy damages imposed on Elizabeth Goodby, and some of her slaves were seized by the local sheriff.

Bernard Marigny purchases land from the heirs of Morgan Edwards at Bayou Castein.

Bernard Marigny purchases land from William Bowman on the lake-front.

1830 July 12: Bernard Marigny purchases land from widow of Zachariah Faircloth. Joseph and Martha Letchworth move to Strawberry Bluff on the Bogue Chitto River.

December 24: Bernard Marigny purchased land from the heirs of Samuel Smith.

1832 John, Thomas, and Aaron Spell give power of attorney to their brother-in-law Joseph Sharp to sell to Bernard de Marigny the 640 acres bought by their father John Spell from John Knight.

1834 Mandeville founded by Bernard Xavier de Marigny de Mandeville. It was not a real boom town until the late 1800s, when it became a popular spot for New Orleanians.

1837 Economic depression in the United States.

1844 Elizabeth Goodby, widow Spell/Bartle dies January 10, 1844, and was buried in the Spell family cemetery on the banks of Bayou Chinchuba.

1844 Martha Faircloth Letchworth dies November 14, 1844, at Strawberry Bluff. She gave her husband Joseph a usufruct to enjoy and reside at the place for the remainder of his life. After his death the property was to go to her nephews and nieces.

LIST OF MAPS

The History of Mandeville:

From the American Revolution
to Bernard de Marigny de Mandeville

CHAPTER 1

THE ENGLISH COLONIAL PERIOD

The long-drawn-out struggle between the French and the English colonists for the possession of New France has provided posterity with a wealth of events and personalities. As we look upon this period in retrospect we see emerging from the indistinct mass of explorers, soldiers, pioneers, certain figures that rise above others, thanks to their achievements and force of character.

History recognizes the Canadian soldier, sailor, and explorer, Pierre Lemoyne d'Iberville, better known to writers of history simply as Iberville, as the man who established the first French Colony in the southern United States and, who was the first governor of Louisiana.

The Acolapissa Indians were not mentioned among the tribes that came to Iberville in 1699 to form an alliance with him. But after his departure for France, his brother Jean Baptiste Lemoyne, better known as Bienville, visited them and was well received. The Indians were terrified at first because of a slave raid upon them two days before by the English and Chickasaw. In 1705 they moved from Pearl River and settled on a bayou on the north side of Lake Pontchartrain called "Castembayouque" (Castine Bayou). Bayou Castine was once the home of Choctaw Indians, whose word "caste" meant fleas, thus Bayou Castine was originally the Bayou of fleas. They called Lake Pontchartrain *Okwa-ta*, the Wide Water.

Six months after their meeting with Bienville, the Natchitoches Indians descended to the French fort on the Mississippi from their town on Red River to ask assistance from Juchereau de St. Denis, the commandant at Fort de la Boulaye on the lower Mississippi, because their crops had been ruined by a flood. St. Denis sent them under the charge of André Pénicaut to the Acolapissa who welcomed them and assigned a place for them to settle close to their village.[1] *In Fleur de Lys and Calumet*, Pénicaut left a vivid account of the life-style of the Acolapissa Indians, from their method of fishing and hunting, their religious rites, the way they prepared and cooked their food, even on how they lit a fire. As for fruits, there were peaches in season, strawberries, plums and grapes. Nuts were pound into flour, using it with water to make pap for their children or mixing it with corn meal to make sagamite or bread.

By 1725 a regular commerce in foodstuffs, mostly meat, had developed between the Acolapissas in St. Tammany and the emerging city of New Orleans. Their later history is one with that of the Houma.

1

Under the French regime, the north shore of Lake Pontchartrain was exploited for its natural resources, and very little development took place. There is hardly any mention made of the north shore in the French records after 1750. Events in Europe and in the northeast United States would bring a series of changes.

The frontier skirmishes of 1754 prompted France and Great Britain to secure Continental allies. With Europe divided into two camps, conflict was inevitable! Two great empires would soon collide. The Seven Year War, a war for the conquest of an empire, familiar to the Americans as the French and Indian War (1754-1763) pitted Great Britain and her Continental Ally Prussia against the power of France, Austria and Russia.

At the time of the French and Indian War, there were thirteen British colonies in North America ranging along the Atlantic coast, they were: Massachusetts, New Hampshire, Connecticut, Rhode Island, New York, New Jersey, Pennsylvania, Maryland, Delaware, Virginia, North Carolina, South Carolina, and Georgia. They were not homogeneous groups and their governments were decentralized. They ranged from the Quakers in Pennsylvania who had come to America to find religious freedom, while New York had a sizable Dutch population and various traditions. Virginia was most important depending largely on its many plantations that gave its society a very distinctive class structure with large estates and important social elite.

After a series of initial defeats, Britain rallied her strength under the strong and able leadership of the War Minister William Pitt and, in 1759, the Royal navy swept the French battle fleets from the seas. Quebec, the citadel of New France, fell to British arms, and the French overseas empire lay helpless, waiting for the surrender. By 1761, the French and Indian War had ceased in America but the French and English continued it upon the ocean and the West Indies with an almost success among the latter. Spain was lured into the war in 1762 by the desperate French diplomacy, only to see her prized possessions, Havana and Manila fall to the conquering British.

The contest between the two great powers had been inevitable for each had aspirations of extensive empire, and one could not grow without hampering the other. It was a long struggle, but in the end His Majesty George III had led the English to success. The War ended by a treaty of peace negotiated in 1762, and signed in Paris on February 10, 1763.

The climax of the war was the defeat of the French, in 1763, when the British Crown emerged victorious with Canada as the chief prize, except for the islands of *St. Pierre et Miquelon* located south of

Newfoundland. These have remained French to this day. France received Guadeloupe and Martinique which had been lost during the fighting.

By the terms of the treaty, France ceded to Great Britain all her claimed territory in America eastward of the Mississippi River north of the latitude of the Iberville River, a little below Baton Rouge. Britain now held undisputed control of North America east of the Mississippi. In an effort to strengthen Bourbon family ties, France gave to Spain all of Louisiana west of the Mississippi River, and in the pre-negotiations she saved for Spain the city of New Orleans and that adjacent territory denoted by lakes and rivers, and known as the isle of Orléans. Spain with whom the English had been at war was forced to relinquish Florida which was to be divided into two new colonies, East and West Florida. The capital of the new province was established at Pensacola. The British arrived in 1764 at Mobile to take possession. Commodore George Johnstone was appointed colonial governor of West Florida in November 1763 and served for a period of four years.

The Treaty provided that none of the Spaniards who remained in Florida should be disturbed in the exercise of the Catholic religion, and that all private property should be respected. But, the Spanish inhabitants were not pleased with the change of government and everyone from Pensacola and all but five from St. Augustine left on the transports provided to take them to Cuba or Mexico. The few French who were living on the north shore of Lake Pontchartrain at Bayou Lacombe, Bayou Liberty, and the mouth of the Tangipahoa River remained. This part of West Florida was a great distance from the capital of Pensacola.

Throughout the occupation of the Louisiana Territory, the French had succeeded to maintain positive relations with the local Indian tribes. When these territories were transferred to the British, the question of European-Indian relations was a major concern. French diplomats worried for two reasons: first should the Choctaws, their long term allies, rise up against the British, the latter would blame the French. On the other hand, if the Choctaws attacked the French, they would need to partner with the British to be safe against Indian attacks. The local Indians were still a force to contend with and merited logistical respect. To this end the French diplomats explained in great detail their limited ability to control the Choctaws and other tribes who did not understand what being "transferred" to another "king" meant in terms of behavior.

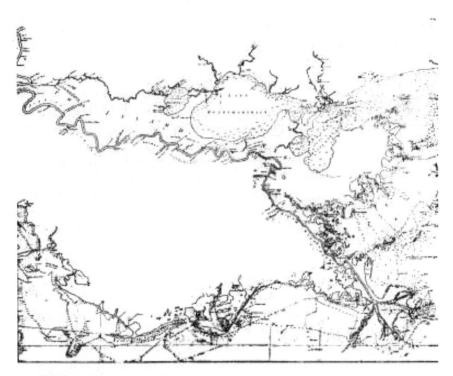

1768: *Portion of the great Chart of the West Florida Coast and the Coast of Louisiana* was published by Faden in 1803, and by the Admiralty in 1823. It depicts George Gauld's work as naval surveyor on the Gulf Coast. (Courtesy of the Library of Congress).

George Gauld's Map of 1768, Lake Pontchartrain

Prior to the French and Indian War or the Seven Years' War, the British controlled the Atlantic seaboard colonies while the land beyond the Appalachian Mountains was in the hands of the French and their Indian allies. At the conclusion of the war in 1763, England emerged victorious with a vast territory that brought nearly all of North America into the British Empire. The successful conclusion of the long war brought some pressing needs to facilitate the administration of the newly acquired territory. Prior to the war, the British possessed few detailed maps of the interior of North America. To facilitate the development of the western territory topographical and hydrographic surveys were initiated. British colonial expansion and military operations led to mapping expeditions in the form of reconnaissance and route maps and fortification plans.

In 1764, the northern boundary of West Florida was shifted north to 32 degrees 30 minute north latitude, which was approximately the mouth of the Yazoo River. The English now held undisputed possession of the whole continent, except Indian land. The new colonies were to operate under English law. France had been nullified as an adversary in North America. This expansion of an empire helped lay the foundation for a global empire which eventually would provide the wealth and resources to fuel the industrial revolution and transform the world.

The main activity by the British in the western portion of the Province was centered on the Iberville River which connected Lake Maurepas with the Mississippi. They were attracted to the idea of using the waterway as the main route to their possessions in the Illinois country by the Mississippi. In 1765, Philip Pittman surveyed the Mississippi and Iberville River (now known as Manchac). Several plans were proposed by British engineers to clear debris, make a cut off and lower the Iberville River to permit small boats clear passage. None of the plans in the next ten years succeeded.

The British had ambitious plans for the Floridas. Between 1764 and 1781, the British Admiralty assigned George Gauld, a British military engineer, cartographer and artist, geographer and surveyor, to map the landscape and chart the waters off the coast of the British colonies of West Florida and East Florida. At the same time their mission was to develop relations with the Indians.

In the year 1781, George Gauld was taken prisoner at the siege of Pensacola. He was taken to Cuba and then to New York, and later repatriated to England where he died shortly afterwards in London on June 8, 1782, aged 50 years.

The Royal Proclamation of October 7, 1763, stated that reduced military Men who had served in the French and Indian War, according to their rank and service, would receive grants if they resided in the colony. The amounts to be granted were as follows: field officer, 5,000 acres; captain, 3,000 acres; subaltern or staff officer, 2,000 acres; non-commissioned officer, 200 acres; private, 50 acres.[2]

Monfort Browne, Lieutenant Governor of West Florida, reported on his tour of inspection through the new province in 1766 and demonstrated a somewhat shaky knowledge of the geography of the province. In August 1770, Peter Chester became the fifth and last governor of the province, and British West Florida began to enjoy some stability. During his tenure, he redirected the province's focus from commerce to agriculture.

The scramble for land began after Surveyor Elias Durnford brought back his survey of the Amite River in the spring of 1771 and showed it to Governor Chester.[3] Durnford had reported on the depth of the rivers, the rise and fall with rain, the condition of the soil and what crops could be grown, that a town could be built between the forks of the Iberville and Amite River with Post and Church, and that it was only fifteen miles from Baton Rouge. The British believed that the Iberville could be made navigable from the lakes to the Mississippi River, an easy route to the north. The western part of the province was still unknown. Reports of the country's natural wealth and advantages were published on the East Coast and in the *London Gazette*. It was expected to attract new settlers. By 1773, surveyors were working more than thirty miles up from the mouth of the Amite on land grants.

Elias Durnford, Lieutenant Governor and Royal Surveyor of West Florida, was requested to report on the affairs of the Colony. He wrote his report from London, England, dated January 15, 1774, for the Secretary of the American Colonies.[4] In his description of West Florida titled, *The State of Its Settlements*, he mentions "…some English families lately settled thereon…," meaning that in 1772/1773 settlement had begun on the Tchefuncte. What he probably implied was that he saw settlers when he passed by in the summer of 1773. Few land grants were given on Lake Pontchartrain since the early settlers preferred grants closer to Pensacola or on the fertile tracts of the Mississippi River.

Following the French and Indian War in America, the British had to devise a policy for the orderly distribution and a systematic scheme of settlement. A number of grants were issued for thousand of acres to reward government officials and friends of the court and to military men according to their ranks. Unfortunately, most of the early land grant recipients were more interested in speculation than settlement. Attractive to those who were interested in settling the land were the less generous grants of land made under "family" and "purchase" rights.

On the eve of the American Revolution, in order to escape the upheaval and ravages of the rebellion along the Atlantic seaboard, English-stock settlers from the eastern colonies, loyal to the British Crown, relocated to West Florida that was established as a loyalist haven, receiving refugees from all the colonies in rebellion. Land on the Amite, on the north shore of Lake Pontchartrain, at Bayou Castein was granted to British loyalists fleeing the fighting on the Eastern Shore during and after the American Revolution. After 1775, West Florida enjoyed its greatest period of growth.

The governor and council administered the following affidavit to the refugee who petitioned for land: "_____ maketh oath that he came from the colony of_____ in order to avoid the troubles then prevailing in that colony and to seek an asylum in West Florida; that he is well attached to His Majesty's government and disapproves of the present rebellion in the northern colonies."[5]

The procedure in securing a grant in West Florida was complicated, slow, and expensive because there was no land office. The office of the provincial secretary at Pensacola was the headquarters for land business. The cumbersome process was the subject of much complaint, especially because of the expenses that were encountered at every step. There was a fee for the preparation of the petition and another for reading it in council. A payment had to be made for making out the warrant of survey and the governor was remunerated for signing it. The fee of the surveyor was determined by the size of the grant and its distance from Pensacola, plus there was an additional charge for the plat which accompanied the return. The provincial secretary was paid for preparing the grant and passing it through his office, and the governor was again rewarded for signing the grant and attaching the great seal, plus the fee to the attorney general for his examination of the patent. No wonder that provincial officials encouraged the granting of land when one considers the lucrative returns they enjoyed.[6] The spirit of speculation as elsewhere, so characteristic of the period, was much in evidence in West Florida. A number of provincial officials promoted looseness in administration, and granted lands with a prodigal hand.

The head of a family (or mistress) that came to West Florida was entitled to one hundred acres for himself and fifty acres for every white or black man, woman or child in his establishment actually present at the time of making the grant. This was known as "head right" or "family right" on the authorization of royal *mandamuses* (Orders in council), the Proclamation of 1763, or the royal instructions to the governor.[7]

Head right was a Virginia system of land patents prevalent in the seventeenth century in which immigrants, including minor children, were entitled to fifty acres of land apiece. It was customary for the person paying the passage of the immigrant to claim the head right, though the right appears to belong to the immigrant. Head rights, or importation rights, could be sold or assigned to others. If one desired to take up more land that he was entitled to by family right, that person could do so in amounts up to one thousand acres if the governor deemed that he was able to cultivate and improve it. Grantee had to pay to the receiver-general of quit-rents, on the day of the grant, five shillings for every fifty acres. Land acquired in this way was by purchase right.[8]

Who were the first British settlers to occupy land from Bayou Castang to the Tchefuncte? The grantee listings from the British records made it possible to draw a map showing the approximate locations of the settlers who first received land grants from 1775 to 1778 in the Bayou Castang area.[9]

There were about twenty families living at Castang Bayou (as it appears in the petitions) during the peak of settlement between 1776 and 1779. Due to limited records, it is difficult to come up with statistics as to the number of people who settled at Bayou Castein. Some of the grants were given to people who did not settle on the land, while others did not have their families with them. By January 1777, there were at least forty registered British Land Grants issued to individuals and their families from the east side of Bayou Castang to both banks of the Tchefuncte. The distance from the mouth of Bayou Castang to the mouth of Bayou Chinchuba, to the Farrell land grant, is about three miles.

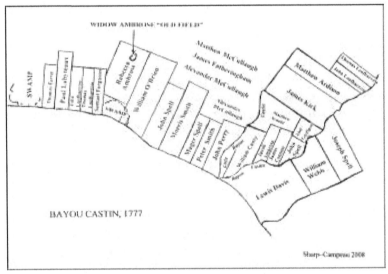

Sharp-Campeau: Bayou Castin map, 1777

The Tchefuncte River, about 48 miles (77km) in length, rises in northeastern Tangipahoa Parish and flows southward. The river defines part of the eastern boundary of Tangipahoa Parish and part of the western boundaries of Washington and St. Tammany Parishes, then turns southeastward into St. Tammany Parish, where it passes Covington and the town of Madisonville, then drains into Lake Pontchartrain. The Bogue Falaya, its largest tributary, and the nearby Abita River flow into the Tchefuncte which then flows into Lake Pontchartrain about 2 miles (3.2 km) south of Madisonville near the northern extremity of the lake. Important to the southern Louisiana trade, it became a major trade route.[10]

The settlers that did bring their families averaged about six to a family, plus slaves. We estimate, including children and slaves, a population ranging from 350 to 400 in the Bayou Castein and Tchefuncte area around the end of 1779.

On the map going east from the swamp, Thomas Farrell received on July 26, 1776, 100 acres at Bayou Castang.[11] We have no knowledge of this settler after 1781.

Paul Labyteau obtained 100 acres on family right and 100 acres on bounty on Bayou Castein to adjoin Widow Ambrose or near said tract as can be found vacant. A carpenter with wife and five children, he was an artificer (craftsman) from New York who declared his loyalty to Britain.[12] He obtained his grant after completing his term for working with the military at Pensacola in 1775. It was impossible for him to return to New York due to the fighting. He had no other choice but to accept a land grant and stay in West Florida. His son Peter acquired a Spanish grant next to his father in 1798. Today, the land makes up a large part of Lewisburg.[13] He went to Pensacola when the hostilities broke out but returned to the Lake Pontchartrain area, where he remained after 1781.

John Loofbarrow on March 23, 1776, was granted 100 acres on family right, and 100 acres on bounty on Bayou Castein.[14] An artificer with wife and five children, he had been hired by the military in 1775 to work on the Fort, barracks, and other military projects at Pensacola. When his term was completed he was unable to return to New York because of the fighting. He probably returned to Pennsylvania after 1781.

Thomas Loofbarrow, John's brother, an artificer from New York, who had no family, declared his loyalty to Britain. He was granted 100 acres on family right, and 100 acres purchase on Bayou Castein. The two brothers abandoned their grants on the lake front when the fighting broke out with the Spanish in August of 1779. Since the two brothers did not confirm their land under Spanish authorities, the land, under law, reverted to the King. Their location is unknown after 1781. He probably returned to Pennsylvania with his brother John.

Samuel Ferguson was granted 100 acres on Lake Pontchartrain on March 4, 1777. The Fergusons, which were located next to the Labyteau and Ambrose grants at Bayou Castein, left when the fighting started but retained possession until 1810. Samuel died intestate, and the land was inherited by his son, Thomas, who sold it in 1810.

According to Governor Peter Chester's ledger, the page for January of 1777 shows that Jacob and Rebecca Ambrose, John and Mager Spell, and Morris Smith were in West Florida as early as December 1775 but due to the prohibition by King George III for Governor Chester to issue grants, they had to wait for their applications to be approved.

Following the 1774 moratorium, Governor Chester renewed their applications. It was a year later, in 1776, that the ban was lifted, but it took several months for Surveyor Elias Durnford to process the list, and the year 1777 was the date of issue.

Jacob and Rebecca Ambrose had applied for two separate land grants, one on the west bank of Bayou Castein and, one by its mouth, between the "Forks". On August 11, 1777, Jacob Ambrose received 100 acres near the entrance to Castang Bayou. Unable to get land on the lake-front, he had to take further inland. On the map, you will notice that the bayou has a small branch to the west and the main stream is to the east.[15]

Rebecca Ambrose listed as "widow", on August 15, 1777, received 200 acres on Lake Pontchartrain. Under English law a woman could not own land in her own name. The English common law system of "dower rights" for a widow was followed in the American colonies. English probate law entitled her to one-third of her husband's real estate upon his death. "Her thirds" was a phrase used for this. The dower rights and early land deeds, along with the inherited land, mention the name of a man's wife because she had a legal interest in any land being sold or purchased. She had "veto power" of the land sale by her husband and she could veto the sale of the land. Many early deeds include an affidavit in which a wife was interviewed privately by the court clerk to determine whether or not she was in favor of the sale. In the United States it was common for a woman to formally relinquish her dower claim on land sold by the husband. This guaranteed that the property was clear of all obligations. In some areas, the lack of a dower relinquishment at the time of sale was proof that the man was single or widowed.[16]

Widow Ambrose remained on her land at least until 1786. She moved to Natchez with the Davis and Webb families where she obtained a Spanish land grant. She did not confirm her land on the lake-front with the Spanish authorities, and under the law it reverted to the King, and became vacant land. The estimated location according to General Morgan's map of 1827 would be present-day Mandeville town Hall.[17]

William Bryan (O'Brien), born *circa* 1720, a native of Ireland, migrated first to Virginia, then to North Carolina. He married Mary Knowles, daughter of John Knowles of Virginia. He and his wife settled on land at Tarboro, Edgecombe County, in North Carolina. William and Mary had at least two children born there prior to the Florida move, possibly St. Augustine. The O'Brien family was in New Orleans as early as 1769. There, he met John Fitzpatrick, a British merchant, who had come down from Canada a year or two earlier. John Fitzpatrick hired Williams as a clerk and bookkeeper, forming an association that would last from 1768 to 1776.[18] General O'Reilly banned all British merchants from New Orleans in 1770, forcing Fitzpatrick to move up the river to Manchac and set up business there. O'Brien drowned crossing a small bayou, above the Fort at Baton Rouge in the latter part of August or early September of 1780 while going to collect a debt from one John Campbell, a native of Scotland, and the owner of one of the "floating warehouse" seized by Governor Galvez on the Mississippi river at New Orleans.

O'Brien's tract of land, which he never occupied, was located on the lake front next to John Spell and Rebecca Ambrose. His grant on the Tchefuncte and the one on the lake-front next to John Spell at Bayou Castein were later destined to play an important part in the history of Mandeville. The official surveyor's plat attached with the Great Deputed Seal of West Florida was an important piece of evidence in Court Case No. 225. There is no evidence that William O'Brien or any of his children ever lived at Bayou Castein. Witnesses at the Letchworth Trial stated that they never knew or met William O'Brien, although they knew that the grant belonged to the family. The O'Brien land deed with the official surveyor's plat has been preserved in the Covington Court Archives.[19]

John Spell, heir at law to the deceased Joseph Spell Sr., reported to the government in Pensacola to renew his warrant for land on December 4, 1775. Recorded January 21, 1777, he was granted "200 acres situated on Lake Pontchartrain, one Mile West from Castine Bayou bounded on the South by Lake Pontchartrain, on the East by Land Surveyed unto Morris Smith on the West and North by vacant land", and 350 acres on Bayou Castang recorded January 20, 1777.[20] John and Joseph Spell did not get the number of acres for which they had applied. There was only so much good land going down the lake. The O'Brien tract was the last piece of land and to the west, for a mile, was a small swamp before high ground was reached. When the surveyor came to Bayou Castein he learned that the mouth of the bayou was already taken by John Perry, possibly the first to have obtained land in that area. John Spell, who had applied for two tracts of land of 150 and 200 acres, could get the 200 but had to take the other 150 further inland. John and his wife Celia (Seely) McLemore were deceased according to the Sacramental Records when John Spell Jr., age 19, married Rosalie Sarah Wescott, age 20, at the Catholic Church in Galveztown in 1786.

11

John Spell Jr. was fifty years old in 1817 when his children Aaron, John and Thomas left the Bayou Castein area. They relocated to the northern part of St. Tammany that became Washington Parish.

Morris Smith, on September 10, 1779, received 200 acres "on the North side of Lake Pontchartrain Bounded on the South by said Lake on the East by Major Spells Land on the West by John Spells land and on the North by vacant land distant westward from the Entrance into Castang Bayou about three quarter of a mile."[21]

Maurice/Morris Smith (used interchangeably both in New York and Louisiana) was the son of a Samuel Smith. On May 29 1762, he married Mary Smith, daughter of Isaac and Margaret Platt. She was born on October 20, 1744, and baptized at St. George's Church, Hempstead, on May 29, 1745. She died January 8, 1799, at Castan Bayou on the other side of the lake. (SLC, F4, 62). Their eldest daughter Margaret "Peggy" Smith was baptized at St. George's Church in Hemstead on October 13, 1765. The church record says, they were living, in Chester, Connecticut.[22] The exact date of their move to Louisiana is not known, but land for Morris Smith, next to Mager Spell, was surveyed in 1777, and the grant was made official on September 10, 1779. His son Uriah Smith testified in 1819 that it was granted by the British to his father in 1779. They are considered residents of the Pontchartrain Post about the time of the American Revolution.

We know of four children: Margaret who married first Morgan Edward-Huett *circa* 1780 and second to Hugh Sheridan. Isaac Smith baptized August 12, 1769, at Christ Church, Poughkeepsie; apparently died young. Samuel Smith, baptized July 21, 1771, Christ Church, died single, before December 1830. Uriah Smith, baptized January 16, 1774, Christ Church, died 1838; married about 1807 to Frances George and lived in St. Helena Parish.

After the lifting of the moratorium, Mager Spell reported to the government in Pensacola to renew the warrant for land on December 4, 1775. He was granted on January 20, 1777, "one hundred acres situated on the North side of Lake Pontchartrain bounded on the West by land surveyed for Morris Smith, Easterly and Northerly by vacant land and Southerly by the Lake Pontchartrain."[23] Mager Spell had a sister named Margaret who married a Skofield at Baton Rouge. In a 1792 sales transaction, she stated that she had obtained the Negro slave from her brother's estate, "who died about ten or eleven years ago." His death occurred about 1783. He had been in West Florida for about ten years.

Peter Smith received a land grant dated September 10, 1776, for 100 acres on Lake Pontchartrain.[24] After 1781, he relocated to Natchez. No further record was found.

John Perry stated in his petition that he had come into the Province in 1774 and was granted 200 acres in 1775. He settled on Bayou Castein with his wife and three children on land grant dated September 16, 1777. Perry then requested permission to change location to the east side of the Pascagoula River and the north side of the Chickasahay River in the forks of the two rivers, but his petition was rejected.[25]

Thomas Westcott and his brother-in-law Captain William Canty, with their families, were in British West Florida early. They brought a group of settlers from Carolina to the Natchez area about 1770. When the land on the Amite River opened for settlement in 1772, they were among the first to apply. William Canty who had a wife and eight children, on July 24, 1772, received 300 acres by family right in part on the Amite River and 400 on the Iberville River.[26] He received an additional 200 acres on family right on Bayou Castein. He died in Galveztown in 1778. The administrator for his estate was Thomas Westcott.[27] The Canty, Westcott and McCullaugh families were related as indicated at the marriage of John Spell and Rosalie Westcott in 1788 at St. Gabriel Church in Galveztown where it is stated that they were "uncles of the bride."

James Connett, an artificer from New York, on March 23, 1776, received 100 acres on family right and 100 acres by bounty.[28]

Joseph Spell was granted 300 acres on Bayou Castein. The relationship between Mager, John and Joseph has not been established. Originally from Tarboro, North Carolina, they came by trail from Charleston to St. Augustine, stayed a year or two and then on to Pensacola arriving in 1774. There was a Joseph Spell listed in the 1812 Tax list living with 1 woman, 2 children, and 0 slaves, but we were unable to verify if it is the same person.[29]

Robert Davis came from Georgia seeking asylum with his wife and child and 13 slaves. On July 10, 1777, he was granted 1,000 acres on family right and 500 acres bounty with a part on Lake Pontchartrain.[30] Robert Davis, the planter from Georgia, made out his Will at Natchez on September 5, 1771. In his Testament, he left his slaves and property to three sons, Lewis, Landon and Hugh, and other children (probably in Georgia) a portion of his estate in money. Hugh Davis, being younger, was left in the care of his mother, Grace. Lewis Davis married Martha Webb, daughter of William Webb who came to West Florida about the same time as the Davis family.

William Webb, on July 10, 1776, received 450 acres by family right, and 250 acres bounty in part north of Lake Pontchartrain bounded on the Southeast by 774 arpents of Lewis Davis.[31] He came from Augusta, Georgia, with wife, Susanna Reed, one son of age (William Jr.), one daughter (Martha) and 5 Negro slaves. William Webb Sr. moved to Manchac where he died a few years later. Antoine Bonnabel, a merchant at New Orleans, purchased the old British grants of Davis and Webb.

Matthew Arnold, on March 23, 1776, received 100 acres on bounty, north side of Lake Pontchartrain on Bayou Castein.[32] He was an artificer from New York of whom we have no knowledge after 1781.

Nathan Gamble received 100 acres at Castang Bayou on January 6, 1777.[33]

Abel Geoffigon (Geoghegan) was given a small grant of 100 acres along the north shore of Bayou Castein, the minimum amount for a grant under British West Florida land laws. Abel married Christina Weeks, born in Falmouth, Massachusetts, issued from the second marriage of Benjamin Weeks and Mary Chase, in Swansboro, previously known as Weeks Wharf.

Prior to the family's move in North Carolina, Benjamin Weeks had operated the ferry between Falmouth and Martha's Vineyard. As more settlers flocked to the Bay area, arable land grew scarcer, forcing the children of the original colonists to look elsewhere for means to provide their families. The answer was the established Carolinas which offered land and a gentler climate. Benjamin and his wife Mary, their children, and relatives were among those from the Falmouth region who migrated together to the White Oak River area of eastern North Carolina. The land Weeks obtained was located at Carteret County on Hadnots Creek as its confluence with White Oak River. By 1760, the Weeks descendants owned most of the land bordering the White Oak River. The French and Indian Wars, ending in 1763, changed the lives and fortunes of the Weeks family. The British Crown was offering land from their recent acquisition to settlers who wanted to homestead in British West Florida. Spurred on by population pressures, like their Falmouth forebears, members and neighbors of the Weeks family responded to the call by trekking off to the Floridas to seek their fortunes.[34]

Abel and Christina's daughter Maria Antonia was likely only a few years old when they arrived at Bayou Castein. Francesca and Leah were born after their arrival in the area. Abel, a native of Ireland and a Catholic, lived long enough to sign Captain William Pickle's Oath of Allegiance in 1779. By 1785, the land belonged to his widow Christina Weeks.

From the Spanish West Florida Archives were found the statements of William McDermott, John Edwards, John Wood, and Samuel Sims attesting that Christina died a natural death at 1:00 o'clock in the afternoon on January 21, 1806. Nicholas Ducre, officially referred to as "Alcade of the Tchefuncta" and Syndic of Bayou Lacombe and its Dependencies", heard about it on the 27 and came over from Bayou

Lacombe to gather the facts. The priest who buried her (Spanish West Florida Archives) stated that there was no consecrated ground on the north shore, so it is not known if she was buried on her property. Today their descendants reside from coast to coast.

James Kirk on January 6, 1776, was granted 500 acres on family right, and 500 acres bounty on Bayou Castein. He arrived from New York with his wife in July 172, and took oath.[35]

The petition reads:

> That your petitioner came out from the Province of New York some time since as a contracted artificer in the Engineer Department, as appears by a certificate hereto annexed. That the works carrying on at this place having been lately discontinued your petitioner has been discharged and through his contract he was to be sent back to New York at the expense of his Majesty. Yet on account of the increasing troubles in that and the rest of the Northern Province your Petitioner rather chooses to settle in this Province provided he could get Lands for that purpose. That his family consists of himself, his wife, six negroes and one apprentice and is desirous of obtaining the Bounty and Encouragement mentioned in your Excellency Proclamation of the eleventh of November last (1775). Therefore prays for an account of 1500 acres on Castang Bayou to adjoin land settled by Morriss Smith or as near as Smith on the Bayou as can be found vacant and your petitioner as is Duty bound shall ever pray.

It was advised that 500 acres be given on family right and 500 acres on bounty.[36] He did not sign the Oath in 1779 and we have no knowledge of this settler after 1779.

Alexander McCullaugh was a staunch loyalist from South Carolina who came to Pensacola where he was appointed Provost Marshall. Like several of his compatriots, he was involved in land speculation before the hostilities broke out with Spain. He was granted on February 4, 1772, 1,000 acres near Baton Rouge. In 1776, he purchased over 5,000 acres in the same area from various individuals. On April 6, 1778, his petition for 200 acres on the Tombigbee River was rejected.[37] He received two grants off Bayou Castein. Alexander died at Pensacola prior to April 30, 1805. His nephew Matthew tried for many years under American authority to recover his uncle's claims, but with no result. He maintained ties with some of the settlers at Bayou Castein.

James Fatheringham was an artificer from New York who desired to stay in the Province because of the Rebellion.[38] He declared his Loyalty to the British Crown. He was given on March 23, 1776, 100 acres on family right and 200 acres bounty on the east side of the Amite River plus land at Bayou Castein located between Matthew and Alexander McCullough.

With the outbreak of the American Revolution, in 1775, the British had quickly converted both Florida Provinces into sanctuaries for Loyalists who wanted to continue living under the rule of His British Majesty, George III. During the years of English rule, Anglo-Saxon families came into the region from the Carolinas, Virginia, Tennessee, and Kentucky. Soldiers who had served in the British army were given the opportunity to accept land grants instead of money payments. They were, therefore, reluctant to fight against England in the American Revolution.

With the use of land grants, we were able to identify the British settlers who received tracts of land between Bayou Castein and the Tchefuncte. The two Floridas did not join the Revolutionary War but the effects of the war had a profound impact on West Florida who, under Governor Chester, had enjoyed some stability, and in the process attracted sturdy pioneer stock of loyal Englishmen, Scots and Irish. Efforts to induce the French west of the Mississippi to migrate to British West Florida were generally unsuccessful.

Pioneer life at Bayou Castein was drawn largely from early colonial Anglo-Saxons. British soldiers who had served in the British army during the French and Indian Wars were given the opportunity to accept land grants instead of money. The recipients were the descendants of the British settlers who had first settled in the thirteen colonies.

The fundamental problems faced by these early pioneers involved the day to day struggle with the clearing of the land, and the struggle with the elements. The land that was more wilderness than anything else needed a bit of optimism to make the going possible. The area around Bayou Castein was either forest or swamps. The settlers could clear small patches to grow vegetables and family crops but the land was not suited for large scale farming. They raised cattle, hogs, and horses which they sold in New Orleans or traded to travelers. The economy of the north shore was based more on agriculture than on exploitation of the natural resources.

The lumber business on the north shore started on the day when the first settlers built a cabin. Like the French had done, the forest was used to make pitch and tar. Later, as settlements grew and as the nineteenth century passed into a period of great expansion, sawmills were erected in many locations; but for the most part, the production of these mills was for local consumption.

Settlers had come to West Florida to escape the Revolutionary War, but their respite was to be short lived. On the horizon, there were signs that the war would come to them.

NOTES

1. André Pénicaut, a youth of eighteen, was a ship's carpenter who left for posterity an account, written from personal knowledge, of the first voyages to Louisiana in the early years of the colony. For an English translation see *Fleur de Lys and Calumet*, edited by R. G. McWilliams, Baton Rouge, 1953.

2. For a discussion on land policy and settlement in West Florida one may refer to Cecil S. Johnson, "Distribution of Land in British West Florida," *Louisiana Historical Quarterly*, Volume16, No. 4. (Oct. 1933): 115-149.

3. Elias Durnford was a reduced aide de camp to Lord Albermarle. He was Deputy Surveyor and served as Lieutenant Governor. He was granted land on the Amite and Comite rivers, and Thompson Creek.

4. A British engineering lieutenant, Elias Durnford served with distinction during The Seven Years (French and Indian) War. Because of strong family connections, he gained for himself a place in the New World as an engineer officer, administrator, and surveyor to British West Florida. He arrived in Pensacola in 1764 with a commission to create a new plan for the city. After the Spanish forces defeated the British, he was paroled and returned to the north of England with his family.

5. Minutes of the Council, 26 February 1776, British Colonial Office 5/634, (hereafter cited as C.O.)

6. Cecil S. Johnson, "The Distribution of Land in British West Florida," *The Louisiana Historical Quarterly*, Volume 16, No. 4. (Oct. 1933): 548.

7. Governor Johnstone's instructions are found in C.O. 5: 201, 131-177; numbers 44 to 56 relate to the granting of land. Refer to article by Cecil S. Johnson, "The Distribution of Land in British West Florida," *Louisiana Historical Quarterly*, Volume 16, No. 4. (Oct. 1933): 539-553.

8. Ibid. 545.

9. The 1777 Bayou Castein map and the names of the grantees were published in an article written by Anita R. Campeau and Donald J. Sharp titled "British and Spanish Land Grants: From Bayou Castein to the Tchefuncte," *New Orleans Genesis*, Volume XLVII, No. 186. (Apr. 2009): 101-141.

10. Ibid. 103.

11. Mary E. Peterson, "British West Florida Abstracts," (hereafter cited as BWF Abstracts). *Genealogical Register*, (March 1972): 86.

12. Mary E. Peterson, "BWF Abstracts," *Genealogical Register*, (June 1972): 164.

13. British Colonial Office, 5/607: 133.

14. Mary E. Peterson, "BWF Abstracts," *Genealogical Register*, (June 1972): 164.

15. Anita R. Campeau and Donald J. Sharp, "British and Spanish Land Grants: From Bayou Castein to the Tchefuncte," *New Orleans Genesis*, Volume XLVII, No. 186. (April 2009): 101-141.

16. Coverture restrictions (status a woman acquires under common law) prevented most married American women from the colonial period through a good part of the nineteenth century from acting as their own agents at law or to have an independent property rights. Married Women Property Act partially remedied some of these legal disabilities, but others lingered well into the twentieth century.

17. In the trial known as Court Case No. 225, it was referred to as Ambrose Old Field.

18. Margaret Fisher Dalrymple, ed., *The Merchant of Manchac: The Letter book of John Fitzpatrick 1768-1790* (Published for the Baton Rouge Bicentennial Corporation, Louisiana State University Press, 1978), 362.

19. *Circa* 2001, the New Orleans Historical Collection purchased a "West Florida Seal" at an antique show in Charleston, South Carolina. There are at this time only two known seals in existence.

20. British Colonial Office 5/608.

21. Mary E. Peterson, "BWF Abstracts," *Genealogical Register*, (Dec. 1972): 341. Public Record Office, London, Colonial Office 5, Volume 608.

22. Notes taken from Yahoo [on-line] site: "Ismith Liptrsp Chess Chemistry." Accessed April 2012.

23. Colonial Office 5/608.

24. Ibid.

25. Mary E. Peterson, "BWF Abstracts," *Genealogical Register*, (Sept. 1972): 341.

26. Mary E., Peterson, "BFW Abstracts," *Genealogical Register*, (Dec. 1971): 330.

27. *The Merchant of Manchac, Letter book of John Fitzpatrick, 1768-1790*, edited with an Introduction by Margaret Fisher Dalrymple, published for the Baton Rouge Bicentennial Corporation, Louisiana State University Press, 1978.

28. Mary E. Peterson, "BWF Abstracts," *Genealogical Register*, (Dec. 1971): 333.

29. Mary Elizabeth Sanders, *An Index to the 1820 Census of Louisiana's Florida Parishes and 1812 St. Tammany Parish Tax List*, 1972, xii.

30. Mary E., Peterson, "BFW Abstracts," *Genealogical Register*, (Dec. 1971): 335.

31. Mary E. Peterson, "BFW Abstracts," *Genealogical Register*, (Dec. 1971): 4.

32. Ibid. 322.

33. Mary E. Peterson, "BFW Abstracts," *Genealogical Register*, (March 1972): 87.

34. "Founding Florida Pioneer Settlers and Their Descendants," Roots Web's World Connect Project.

35. Mary E Peterson, "BFW Abstracts," *Genealogical Register*, (June 1972): 164.

36. Colonial Office 5/608.

37. Mary E. Peterson, "BFW Abstracts," *Genealogical Register*, (June 1972): 165.

38. Mary E. Peterson, "BFW Abstracts," *Genealogical Register*, (Dec. 1971): 86.

CHAPTER 2

THE REVOLUTIONARY WAR: UPHEAVAL IN BRITISH WEST FLORIDA

The seeds of the American Revolution existed in the colonies from the outset because of the British Colonial Policies. The different groups that settled the parent states and the distance between the mother country and the colonies scattered along the Atlantic seaboard made it impossible for England to establish a unified government during the age of colonization. Each colony operated as separate units and had been permitted to exercise certain governmental powers, which eventually led to the development of a sense of independence.

The French and Indian War highlighted existing tensions between the British government and the Thirteen Colonies, and added new ones. The numerous grievances harbored by the Thirteen Colonies had developed by 1775 into open rebellion against the British crown. In winning the French and Indian War, the British government had amassed considerable debt, and the continued military presence in North America was stretching funds further. The Thirteen Colonies did not feel it was their responsibility to pay for the war, and they had no intention of contributing funds for the upkeep of security along the frontier, which they felt was solely there to stop the westward movement of settlers.

The American Revolution was an event of singular historic importance. During the period, two events took place: the Revolution, a social and political struggle; and the War of Independence (1775-1783), a fight between the Colonies and England. Soon followed by the French Revolution, forces had been unleashed that were to shape world history in the nineteenth century. It not only broke the unity of the British Empire, but heralded a period of change. On the eve of the Revolution, the thirteen English colonies contained about two and a half million people, compared with the eight million in England. They were mostly a rural people, and by this time many had caught the vision of a democratic America, where an ordinary citizen could shape his own destiny. After 1775, when the idea of independence was put forth, the colonists divided into pro-British and pro-American camps, and Neutrals.

When British King George III and his Parliament refused to recognize the Declaration of Independence issued in 1776 by the Continental Congress, those who firmly believed in a united British Empire were labeled "Tories" and rebel attitude towards them became harsh. They were treated as traitors and many lost their homes and businesses and had to flee either in Canada or the British Floridas.

The British quickly converted the two Florida provinces into sanctuaries for Loyalists escaping the ravages of the rebellion or wishing to continue living under the rule of "His Britannic Majesty." East and West Florida did not join the American Revolution, but the conflict had a profound impact on West Florida who, under Governor Peter Chester, had begun to enjoy some stability.

Many historians play down the American Revolution in West Florida, but it had an impact on the people for years to come. Granted it was less violent than in the east where the slogan was either "Join or Die." You may have heard in a Revolutionary history class of the Gadsden flag "Don't Tread on Me," the first flag carried into battle by the U.S. Marines during the American Revolution. It was a symbol of patriotism in support of civil liberties - that is, libertarian ideas. Yet there was much apathy in America making it difficult for Congress in keeping an army in the field and supplying it. Instead of winning a quick victory, the struggle lasted for years. Ultimate independence could have been lost had it not been for French aid.

Secretary to Governor Chester, Philippe Livingston, known as "Gentleman Phil" left West Florida in early 1774 to go back to New York to visit his family. His father, a prominent wealthy merchant in New York, was a leader of the movement against taxes put on by Great Britain. His father and his uncle Philippe Livingston Jr. signed the Declaration of Independence in 1776. While in New York "Gentleman Phil" advised his father of the opportunity to invest in land in West Florida, which he did through his son, the Secretary. While in New York, he witnessed the hostilities and violence which broke out. His observations were relayed to Governor Peter Chester. On his return, his young brother William left with him to be an overseer on his main plantation on the Amite River. Land and profits were on Livingston's mind. William remained a year and returned to New York by way of the Mississippi River.

The north shore of Lake Pontchartrain from Bayou Castein to the Tchefuncte, like the rest of East and West Florida, attracted Loyalists who wanted to escape persecution in the Thirteen Colonies. Land grants were issued to these people by royal mandamuses, or direct orders of the King and Council.

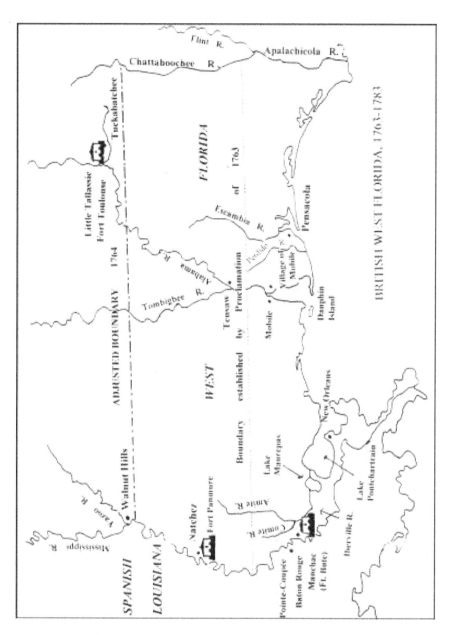

Map of British West Florida, 1763-1783 – showing boundaries.

The British province of West Florida extended from the Mississippi River in the west to the Apalachicola River in the east. Prior to the signing of the Declaration of Independence, and as early as the spring of 1776, there had been trouble between Britain and American ships on the Mississippi River at New Orleans. American privateers were using the "river" under the threat of British capture. Under the command of George Burdon, the British maintained the HMS *West Florida*, the only armed sloop, on patrol in the lakes and in Mississippi Sound. Burdon's duty was to stop and search all manner of shipping, including Spanish merchants destined for New Orleans, much to the annoyance of the Spanish.

The British controlled the lines of communication between Pensacola and the settlements on the Mississippi River. Trade was openly carried on by the British and Spanish at Fort Bute, the British post situated at the point where Bayou Manchac meets the Mississippi River. The English controlled the entire trade of the colony, and Manchac had acquired a very important place in international affairs. It was the center of English aggression, of smuggling, and illegal commerce. It was a danger point for the Spanish because the English could reach the Mississippi at Manchac through the lakes and the Iberville River without their knowledge as the latter had no establishment on the banks of the lakes except at Bayou St. John.

In April 1777, the *West Florida* captured three boats on Lake Pontchartrain. The British contended that they were American boats smuggling tar to New Orleans from the north shore while Governor Galvez contested that the captured boats were Spanish and not American and immediately retaliated.

In May of 1777, England seized several Spanish boats on Lake Pontchartrain. Governor Galvez retaliated by capturing eleven British ships or "floating warehouse" engaged in illicit trade on the Mississippi, claiming that they, too, were smuggling. Among the vessels taken was the *Norton*, of British registry, owned and commanded by William Pickles, a Philadelphian. Lengthy discussions took place between Governor Bernardo de Galvez and Governor Peter Chester of West Florida.

A warship was dispatched to New Orleans by the British who demanded the return of their property and threatened the city's destruction if the Spaniards did not comply. Governor Galvez held his ground and immediately issued a plea for assistance. Troops were sent from Cuba to reinforce the tiny garrison at New Orleans. While the British poured in more troops in West Florida, the Spanish Crown started a slow build up of soldiers, artillery, and munitions in Louisiana. Preparation for war was evident as each side built up their strength in the area by fortifying their forts, bringing in artillery, ammunition, and troops.

The territory South of Bayou Manchac to the Gulf of Mexico belonged to the Spanish while the British owned the lands north of Bayou Manchac to Canada. The little bayou was the international boundary line between the two foes. The fight was on as to which would control the waterway in order to define ownership of the land.

Spanish attitude under Governor Bernardo de Galvez was pro-American. Charles III of Spain to whom Louisiana was ceded by Louis XV of France in 1762 instructed Bernardo de Galvez to give aid to George Washington during the American Revolution. Taking the Revolutionary War to the Old Southwest and seizing control of the Mississippi River was a sound strategic and feasible plan for the rebel forces in the east.

The American Revolution was in its infancy when the Continental Congress gave orders "to build, with all expedition, as many gallies and armed vessels as...shall be sufficient to make us indisputably masters of lakes Champlain and George."[1] Skenesborough (now Whitehall, New York) became the "Birthplace of the American Navy" when, in the summer of 1776, General Philip Schuyler chose this location for its two sawmills and iron forge. The fleet construction was under the direction of Benedict Arnold. His success as a merchant ship owner and master made him the ideal choice for this endeavor. Construction began at a slow pace but within two months craftsmen completed eight 54-foot gondolas.

The gondolas were known by other names: gundalow, gun'low, gondola, gunlo, or simply gunboat. The gunboat, easy and quick to build, was an armed ship of shallow draft, also described as a flat-bottomed rowing craft with square sails that enabled them to sail before the wind. Gunboats, effective along a coast, have also been described as "tiny-men-of war" extremely over gunned in proportion to size. In order for them to be stable on the open sea, their crews had to stow the cannons below deck.

In the late summer/early fall of 1776, American Captain George Gibson, with "eighteen men and a boy" departed Fort Pitt, descended the Ohio and Mississippi rivers and disguised as traders arrived in New Orleans carrying the American Declaration of Independence and letters of introduction from General Charles Lee, Commanding Officer of the Southern District, and the Virginia Committee of Safety – all American Rebels.[2]

The Gibson party had stopped briefly in Walnut Hills (Vicksburg today), and several of its members declared openly that they had dispatches from the Continental Congress in Philadelphia for the Court of Spain and Luis de Unzaga, the Spanish Governor of Louisiana. Unconcerned, Captain Gibson hoisted the "Rebel" colors as he passed Natchez. On hearing the news, Peter Chester, the Governor of British West Florida, raised the proverbial flag. Gibson's instructions had been to contact Oliver Pollock, who immediately enlisted as an American supporter. Pollock had the Declaration published in New Orleans and introduced Captain Gibson to Governor Unzaga whose plea was for 9,000 pounds of gunpowder urgently needed at Fort Pitt.[3]

Governor Unzaga supported the American cause, and its threat to British power in North America. He was aware that Madrid did not want Spain embroiled in this recent New World conflict.

Oliver Pollock, an influential merchant in New Orleans, paid for the gunpowder. It appears that he took it upon himself to finance the Colonies with the necessary supplies for conducting the war. Governor Unzaga put Gibson's Lieutenant Linn and the powder on a boat flying Spanish colors. With a Spanish master at the helm, the boat secretly made its way up the Mississippi for relief of the Western Country against the Indians. At the same time, to cover up, Unzaga had Gibson submit to arrest – a ruse to quell the British protest, in case it would forthcoming.

Oliver Pollock was the man greatly responsible for the successful waging of the American Revolution in the West. But, who was Oliver Pollock? To escape poverty and seek his fortune in the American colonies, he migrated from Coleraine, Ireland, to Pennsylvania. By the late 1750s, he moved to Havana, Cuba, where he represented the firm of William and Robert Morris. He became fluent in Spanish and attained success as he ventured into the Spanish speaking regions of the West Indies. He became involved with other merchants in the slave trade, a commerce permitted to foreign merchants by the laws of Spain.[4]

He removed to New Orleans in 1769 following the military expedition sent from Cuba to assert Spain's control of Louisiana. France had just ceded its Louisiana province to Spain. The news in New Orleans caused the Creoles to revolt. General Alejandro O'Reilly, a friend of Pollock, was to quell the opposition to the cession with a force that doubled the city's population to 3,000. O'Reilly's commercial needs were met by Pollock, and the two men became very close friends

A famine threatened, but fortunately a ship of Pollock's made it into port with a cargo of flour which he generously offered to O'Reilly. In gratitude for his benevolence, Pollock was awarded the privilege of trading in Louisiana free of all taxes and licenses. As a result he became a rich, successful, and respected merchant who was also an intimate friend of Governor Galvez. By the time of the American Revolution, Pollock was considered a wealthy man with limitless credit, and a sincere Patriot. His role as the congressional agent at New Orleans earned him the title as "The Financier of the Revolution in the West."[5]

The American Revolution began, was fought, and won in the Thirteen Colonies, but little is said about the bitter conflicts and wars that were waged from Ohio to the Great Lakes, to the Illinois country and the provinces of British West and East Florida.

In 1777, Oliver Pollock was made American agent in Spanish New Orleans by his friends Robert Morris and Benjamin Franklin, of the "Secret Committee" of the Continental Congress. Their confidence in him was no secret nor was it misplaced. Pollock had arranged for shipments of gun powder from Spain and Cuba to George Washington's army in 1776 and 1777. He gave them the financial support that was needed and complied with every request for financial aid, until his own funds and credits were exhausted.

British commerce on the Mississippi River decreased significantly in the last half of 1777, while American trade under the protection of the Spanish flag increased. The American Revolution had an impact on the lower Mississippi Valley because of the proximity of British West Florida to Spanish Louisiana.

Pollock actively aided George Rogers Clark who received permission from Governor Patrick Henry of Virginia to lead a small force into the Western wilderness and drive out the British before it was too late. With 200 Virginians, in 1778, Clark conquered and held lands now comprising the states of Illinois, Indiana and Ohio. He testified that he was successful because Oliver Pollock provided the necessary material. It was Pollock who also convinced Governor Galvez that the best defense for Spanish New Orleans in 1779 would be an offense against British West Florida. Pollock was proven right!

In the summer of 1771, James Willing, the son of merchant Charles Willing, twice mayor of Philadelphia, and Anne Shippen, granddaughter of Philadelphia's first mayor, arrived in British West Florida in the hope of becoming one of the area's leading planters and merchants. Prior to the outbreak of the Revolution, James Willing was a personal associate of Pollock. It was he who encouraged him to remove to Natchez. James Willing acquired 1,250 acres of land on the east bank of the Mississippi just north of Baton Rouge and later acquired property near Natchez and became a trader in the tiny settlement of Natchez.

Business wise, James Willing was not successful nor had he won the affection of his fellow traders who were chiefly of the loyalist persuasion and supporters of King George III in the eventual contest to follow.[6]

At the start of the Revolt James Willing returned to York, Pennsylvania, his hometown of Philadelphia, then in British hands. He informed the expedition planners that British West Florida grew more Tory every day; that a substantial number of people were either American or neutral and if an American expedition sailed down the river, these people would flock to it. The Commerce Committee bestowed a Continental Navy Captaincy on Willing and put him in charge of executing the attack against British West Florida. Thus, James Willing was one of the first captains of the United States Navy. He had no sea experience but through his brother, Thomas Willing, the partner of patriot-financier Robert Morris, and their banking firm, he was considered a member of the most respectable families in Philadelphia. Robert Morris was a good friend of Pollock and he had interests in New Orleans.

The objective was to bring the War to the British Loyalists who were settled along the lower Mississippi River. At Pittsburg, previously known as Fort Pitt, already being called the Gateway to the West, Willing with the handful of enlisted seamen he had brought from Philadelphia supervised the construction of a stout high-sided river boat, a sort of galley, equipped with a mast. The vessel could not be designated by its rig, for she had only one stumpy mast and a square sail that might be hoisted upon it. "Gunboat" was the best word to describe it, for she did carry a few weapons.[7] Christened *Rattletrap* (for reasons that have not survived) she was duly-commissioned, the first United States Navy vessel ever to be seen in western waters.[8]

Rattletrap sailed from Pittsburg January 11, 1778, having on board twenty-four enlisted men, two sergeants, and Thomas McIntyre, newly released from a British prison camp, as second in command, who was bestowed the rank of lieutenant. Members of the volunteer crew were the following men: Capt. Thomas Love, Sgt. John Marney, Levin Spriggs, John Walker, Richard Murray, Mark Foley, John Ash, Daniel Whittaker, Lazarus Ryan, Philip Hupp, John Gouldin, Lawrence Kana, Samuel Taylor, John Hanwood, and James Taylor from Captain Harrison's Company of the 13th Virginia Regiment. Greenbury Shores, Nathan Henderson, Richard Rody, Henry Haut and Tobrar Haut of Capt. Sullivan's Company. Sgt. Thomas Beard, Nathaniel Down, James King, Alexander Chambers, William White, and John Rowland of Capt. O'Hara's Company. James Ryan, Reuben Hamilton and James Cordonis of Capt. Heth's Company.[9]

Willing's instructions were to deliver some dispatches to New Orleans, to bring up the Ohio and Mississippi part of the stores Spain had agreed to deliver at New Orleans for the use of the United States, and to "capture whatever British property he might meet with."

Captain Willing, the former resident of Natchez, led an American raid on the pro-British settlements along the Mississippi River in the hope of obtaining supplies for American forces in the area of New Orleans. To help him in his mission, Captain Willing enlisted all the ruffians he could find on his way down the river. The estimated number of marauders in his command numbered over a hundred when he disembarked at Natchez on the afternoon of Friday, February 19.

Orders were sent to all residents to convene the next morning. They were to be made prisoners of war and that he, Captain Willing, was taking possession of the jurisdiction. Aware of their remoteness, the residents proposed that they would not take arms against the United States, nor assist its enemies if their persons, slaves and property would be left secure. Having captured the settlement and obtained neutrality oaths from the settlers, they continued on down the river looting and burning British plantations.

His force embarked on a "career of confiscation and cruelty" as they moved south beyond Natchez. The Americans went on to raid plantations on the Mississippi, Thompson Creek and Amite. Wanton destruction accompanied the seizures: animals were slaughtered, dwellings burned, slaves were seized, businesses and indigo works destroyed. These raids took the loyalists and neutral settlers by surprise. After having reached Manchac, Willing sent his Lieutenants up the Amite and Tickfaw rivers. When word of the attack reached them, all of the settlers fled in panic. In the words of Thomas Westcott to merchant John Fitzpatrick: "There is no one left. It is too dangerous to go back." The attack did not reach the Tchefuncte or Bayou Castein area in 1778. During this period when authority was preoccupied with treason and rebellion, the Indians did take advantage of the situation by attacking and sacking plantations.

Willing's expedition captured Fort Bute and an advance party at Manchac captured a British ship, the *Rebecca*, "mounted with sixteen guns, four pounders, beside swivel. He did not capture Manchac or Baton Rouge, he raided them. He left before the Loyalists could raise a force to fight him. He fled for protection to New Orleans, where he was welcomed and given asylum by the Spanish. A detachment of his, sent back up the river after he was in New Orleans, was ambushed, several killed including one of his lieutenants and several captured.

Willing did not occupy the areas he raided. He had a post set up opposite Galveztown but it was destroyed by Loyalist forces.

While Willing had wished to further the American cause, his raid had the opposite effect for it turned most of the inhabitants against the United States, and it exposed the vulnerability of British West Florida to foreign assault.

According to John Caughey, *Louisiana Historical Quarterly*, January 1932, the "raid" was a legitimate and duly commissioned martial enterprise. However, this American presence in the Spanish owned New Orleans became a problem for Governor Galvez. The British protested Willing's plundering on the lower Mississippi claiming it was Spanish territory. Adam Chrystie and Captain Richard Pearis was the British response to the attack by Captain James Willing and his rebels on the Iberville and Amite rivers.

British war ships were sent to New Orleans to reclaim their property and defend British subjects. British reinforcement of West Florida and the establishment of a virtual blockade of the river stopped Willing from sending supplies upstream to the revolution and the English bank of the Mississippi were lost back to England.

It was Oliver Pollock who interceded with Galvez to have Willing lodge his troops and to sell his loot in New Orleans, despite the protests that rose from Pensacola. On April 6 and 8, 1778, Pollock sponsored a public auction at which the Americans disposed of the majority of the slaves taken during the Willing raid. Some 74 slaves crossed the block, raising a total of 16,518 *pesos* for Pollock and Willing. Leading citizens of Spanish Louisiana, including Antonio de Marigny, Philippe de Mandeville, Gilbert Antonio St. Maxent, all purchased slaves, although in many cases cash money was not on hand to complete the sales. Pollock met this lack of specie by financing most of the transactions on promissory notes due the following January first.[10]

When the goods captured by Willing's expedition were auctioned in New Orleans, Pollock bought the *Rebecca* for the account of the United States; renamed it the *Morris*, in honor of his Philadelphia associate and outfitted her as a man-of-war. Agent Pollock, using a blank commission sent him by Congress gave the command to an old Pennsylvania merchant ship's captain by the name of William Pickles who had settled on the Mississippi River. The young French national Pierre George Rousseau, a lieutenant in the U.S. Navy, was named as second in command.[11]

Willing quarreled with Oliver Pollock, became a pain for Bernard de Galvez, and quarreled with almost everybody he met. Yet, the purpose had been a firm strike for liberty. But he had not endeared himself to the Creoles of New Orleans. First hailed as heroes, they over stayed and left a bad impression.

Pollock had seen enough of Willing's annoyances, and wrote to Congress expressing his concerns about Willing's poor judgment. Pollock's plans were to send Willing and his men to return north, part by land and part by water through Spanish Territories. Governor Galvez issued a letter to Spanish commanders along the Mississippi to allow Willing and his 25 Americans to pass. With the settlers being so angry, the route north was too hazardous, and not followed through. A month later Lieutenant Robert George requested permission to lead the men through. On their solemn oath that they would not offend English subjects, Galvez gave his permission. They traveled north via Opelousas, Natchitoches, and the Arkansas to St. Louis where they were placed under the command of George Rogers Clark.

Willing finally got away by sloop for Philadelphia. The vessel was captured and he was taken prisoner to New York. At the end of 1779, he was exchanged for British Colonel Henry Hamilton.[12]

Was Willing's trip a success? First we have to face the fact that his plan to take West Florida could not be put in effect once the British had been warned. Oliver Pollock had been a great help, boatloads of war supplies had been shipped up the Mississippi and it had cost little, though it frightened the Loyalists of Natchez and the neighborhood. Willing's raid also hurt Pollock's abilities to function as the official agent in New Orleans, and drained some of his resources. It failed to open the great river to United States traffic, but succeeded in blocking Great Britain from making a flank attack by way of the west. Complaints were made against Willing and his men from colonists who saw in him a bad-tempered bandit. He sold his loot for a good price in New Orleans, but the damage done was much greater than the profits he secured.

NOTES

1. Journal of the Continental Congress, June 17, 1776, in Clark, Morgan, and Crawford, *Naval Documents of the American Revolution*, 5:589.
2. By Captain is meant a commissioned officer in the navy ranking above a commander and below a commodore. It is also used in the sense of a naval officer who is master or commander of a ship.
3. Thompson Ray, "Unsung Hero the American Revolution," *Times-Picayune*, New Orleans, Volume 7, No. 3, December 14, 1972, 11.

4. Hayden, Horace E., *A Biographical Sketch of Oliver Pollock*, Harrisburg, Pennsylvania, 1883, 4-6.

5. Mulloney, William F., "Oliver Pollock: Catholic Patriot and Financier of the American Revolution," *Historical Records and Studies of the U.S. Catholic Historical Society*, (1937), 164-236.

6. Campeau, Anita R., and Sharp, Donald J., "The United States Navy and the Naval Station at New Orleans, 1804-1826," *New Orleans Genesis*, Volume XLVIII, April 2009, 243-245.

7. Chidsey, Donald Barr, *Louisiana Purchase*, Crown Publishers Inc., New York, 1972, 2.

8. Ibid., 2.

9. Thwaites Rueben Golden, LLD, and Kellogg Phelps Louise, editor, *Frontier Defense on the Upper Ohio*, 1777-1778, 1993, 302-303.

10 Orleans Notary Archives, Acts of Juan Batista Garic, Volume 9, April 6-8, 1778, ff. 202-224.

11. Ellis, Frederick S., *St. Tammany Parish: LAutre Côté du Lac*, A Firebird Press Book, Pelican Publishing Company, Gretna, 1998, 51.

12. The return of Willing and his men is based on an article by John Caughey published in *The Louisiana Historical Quarterly* entitled "Willing's Expedition down the Mississippi," January 1932.

CHAPTER 3

THE BATTLE OF LAKE PONTCHARTRAIN:
SEPTEMBER 10, 1779
(Between the *Tender Morris* and the British Sloop *West Florida*)

The British Sloop of War *West Florida* had been cruising Lakes Pontchartrain and Maurepas since 1776 under the command of George Burdon. Unsuccessful in tracking down Captain Willing during his 1778 raid, he returned late that year to Pensacola, for refit and repair.

Governor Peter Chester and Council met on March 3, 1778, and requested Lt. Colonel William Stiel to detach an officer and twenty-five men to Lt. George Burdon and the armed sloop *West Florida* on Lake Pontchartrain to defend the lakes. In January 1779 Burdon was replaced at her helm by Lt. John Payne who was familiar with the Gulf Coast and Lake Pontchartrain having assisted George Gauld when he surveyed the area ten years before.

On April 27, 1779, the Council decided it would be imperative to protect British subjects in the western part of the Province. It unanimously recommended the establishment of a military post at Manchac. Lt. Colonel Stiel, present at the meeting, agreed to send one Captain, one lieutenant, one ensign, three sergeants, one drummer and forty rank and files for the proposed garrison. Lt. Colonel Stiel ordered the twenty-five men who had gone to reinforce Lt. Burdon on board the *West Florida* to take post at Manchac.

That year, Oliver Pollock kept coordinating efforts between Governor Galvez and George Rogers Clark to keep the American cause armed and supplied through smuggled supplies up the Mississippi River. During that time Galvez kept the appearance of neutrality by making occasional showy prearranged arrest of American smugglers. But he met with British ire by seizing British ships in similar activities.

Neutrality fell away when Spain declared war on England on June 21, 1779, and entered into a treaty with France. Word of the declaration was sent to the colonies prior to its being made known to the British. Governor Galvez knew of the war in August 1779, before the word had reached West Florida. He had already prepared for war even before the official declaration was made. He described his preparations as purely defensive.

Lt. Payne patrolled the West Florida waters uneventfully until August 1779. On the 27th of August he sent a boat with a few men to make contact with a detachment of Lt. Colonel Alexander Dickson's men at Manchac. The boat was captured by Bernardo the Galvez, the governor of Spanish

Louisiana, who would soon launch an expedition to gain control of the British military posts on the Mississippi. Galvez took the Manchac garrison on September 7, and negotiated the surrender of Dickson and the remaining British forces on the Mississippi after the Battle of Baton Rouge on September 21. Lt. Payne was unaware of the military activities.

In 1779 Pierre George Rousseau, who descended from an old Huguenot family of France, was ordered by George Washington to report at New Orleans to assist Galvez in routing the British from the Gulf of Mexico, from Lake Pontchartrain to West Florida.[1]

Oliver Pollock used the commissioning authority he had been granted by Congress to give command of the *Morris* to Continental Navy Captain William Pickles. However she was destroyed on August 18, 1779, by a terrible hurricane that hit New Orleans and sank all of the boats and ships in the river, including the *Morris* (*ex Rebecca*), which was fully outfitted and ready for sea. Galvez's expedition was also delayed. But within the next few days, he provided another ship for Pickles called Morris or "Morris's Tender." Second in command to Captain Pickles was Lt. Peter George Rousseau (Pierre for the French, Peter for the English, and Pedro for the Spanish) who described the *Morris Tender* as a schooner armed with five small (2.5 pound or less) cannons and ten swivel guns, and that it lacked barricades to protect the men on deck from gunfire. The crew lacked axes, lances, and other tools useful for boarding action.[2]

On August 27, 1779, Governor Galvez set out on foot for Fort Manchac with a company of 667 men, while a handful of ships moved up the Mississippi River. He picked up an additional 600 to 800 men at the German Coast. By the time he arrived at Manchac he had over 1,400 men, though many were sick.

When in sight of Manchac on September 6, Galvez informed his men of the declaration of war. A surprise attack was launched on Fort Bute. He met very little resistance, the English suspicious of Spanish activities had withdrawn their main forces to Baton Rouge.

On receiving his orders from Pollock in early September, Captain Pickles set sail for Ship Island where the *West Florida* was last sighted. Not finding the enemy frigate, the *Tender Morris* turned around and headed for Lake Pontchartrain.[3] Captain Pickles entered the Rigolets and after passing through headed southwest toward Bayou St. John. Almost immediately, after entering Lake Pontchartrain, they sighted a sail on the horizon. Getting closer they could make out it was the *West Florida*, supposedly commanded by Lt. John Payne. He had been appointed its Captain seven months prior and as luck would have it, part of his crew was at Manchac. The *West Florida* was down to thirty men and was waiting for 15 officers and crew to return to the ship. Some short biographies of John Willett Payne claim that he commanded the *West Florida*. Lengthier biographies place him in European waters at the time of this action.[4]

According to Lt. Rousseau who wrote a detailed report, "the *Morris Tender* arrived on the lake on Tuesday, September 10, at one o'clock in the afternoon, "discovered the boat the *West Florida* and gave chase to him, and he gave chase to us at the same time" Captain Pickles gave the orders for everyone to hear, and ordered Lt. Rousseau to be ready to board and the swivel guns ready to fire."[5]

The *Morris Tender*, a smaller ship, numbered 51 men and six cabin boys. To hide his intentions, Pickles flew a British ensign as a false flag. The two ships closed, and Lt. Payne hailed the *Morris* to discover her intentions. Within shouting range, Lt. Payne asked "Whose ship are you and where are you from?" Captain Pickles playing for time to get closer, yelled back, "I'm a British merchant out of Pensacola on my way to Galveston." Lt. Payne then answered that he was satisfied and to pass on. Captain Pickles now close enough shouted back "you won't be" as the false colors were hauled down and replaced with the American flag. Each ship immediately prepared for battle.

Captain Pickles ordered the *Morris* in close to the *West Florida* and for Lt. Rousseau to board. The Americans then threw grappling hooks to bring the ships together and opened fire with their swivel guns while Lt. Rousseau prepared the boarding party. The *West Florida* had nets set up to prevent boarding which made it difficult for Lt. Rousseau and the boarding party. Lt. Rousseau was first repulsed by his first attempt, receiving a slight wound on the hand. Captain Pickles, seeing this, ordered Rousseau to try again and he, Pickles, led his own boarding party. Lt. Rousseau immediately led his own men again in the second attempt. Payne's small crew put up spirited resistance, and twice repulsed the boarders. Payne went down in the third attempt having received a mortal wound in a battle described as "very violent."

When Captain Pickles got to the bridge of the *West Florida*, it was all over. Lt. Payne lay on the deck dying from his wounds, with three other men, and the British sailors crying for mercy. This was granted by Pickles and Rousseau and the fighting was over.

Captain Pickles finding himself in command of the West Florida, made Lt. Rousseau Captain. They landed and anchored at the Fort at Bayou St. John and put ashore the dead and wounded. The boarders had successfully overwhelmed the British wounding two men in addition to Lt. Payne, while suffering 6-8 killed and several wounded.[6]

Captain William Pickles and Lt. Rousseau who wrote their reports on September 12, 1779, from Fort St. John stated that they had defeated the British war ship *West Florida*.

Lt. Rousseau described the *West Florida* as "a boat armed with two cannons of six and two of four pounds, barricades the height of a man, with a siege barricade nine and a half inches thick, and with ten swivel guns mounted on the bridge at the same height, which made them tower over us, giving them considerable advantage; further they had lances, battle axes and many other implements of war. The number of men they had on board was twenty-eight or thirty, among who were found several Americans who had been forced to serve."[7]

The capture of the *West Florida* eliminated the major British presence on the lake, thus weakening British control over the western reaches of West Florida.

Aboard the schooner *Morris*, September 12, 1779, Captain Pickles reported to Pedro Piernas, the acting commandant in New Orleans, that at Ship Island he found a small ship which he captured, and brought with him, in a battle which lasted about 20 minutes and with many injuries on both sides. One of his corsairs was leaving to guard the Rigolets. The aim was to prevent any aid coming from Pensacola. It also prevented any British inhabitants from fleeing the lakes by boat to Pensacola or Mobile. He then continued to patrol the lake and the Mississippi Sound, where he captured a small British vessel which was carrying a number of slaves.

Captain Pickles did not mention Rousseau in his report of September 12. But Galvez in a letter dated April 29, 1783 states clearly that Rousseau captured the *West Florida* and does not mention Captain Pickles. Rousseau himself stated in his petition for a pension after the Louisiana Purchase addressed to the King of Spain (with documents of proof attached) that he captured the West Florida, he does not mention Captain Pickles.[8]

In the aftermath of the battle, Captain Pickles took his prize the *West Florida* back to New Orleans, where Pollock had her fitted out. He then cruised with her in West Florida's waters and later assisted Galvez in the Battle of Fort Charlotte, which resulted in the capture of Mobile, before sailing her to Philadelphia for sale.

Captain Pickles landed on the north shore on September 21, 1779, with some of his People and accepted the capitulation of the Inhabitants of the Settlements on Lake Pontchartrain. Most of the settlers on the Tchefuncte and Bayou Castein had fled and only a handful remained.[9] With the threat of an Indian attack and British forces, Captain Pickles put on shore a detachment of men for the remaining settlers' protection. They stayed at Bayou Castein from September 21 until Pickles return on October 16, with his "Oath of Allegiance" to the American Colonies.[10]

Nineteen persons signed allegiance on October 16, 1779. Most were not inhabitants as the document says "from the Tanghiphoa River to Bayou Lacombe."

At the time Governor Galvez and Oliver Pollock were attacking the little post at Manchac, William Stiel, the high British officer, and four men who later signed the Oath at Bayou Castein had escaped across the Iberville canal and headed down the Amite River to Lake Maurepas where they had a boat, attempting to get back to Pensacola. Right after the battle, Captain Pickles sent an armed corvette to the Rigolets to prevent any British barges or small ships from getting to Pensacola or bringing in supplies. This action prevented Lt. Colonel Stiel, Deputy Provost Alexander McCullough and his brother Matthew, Jerard Brandon, and Frederick Spell from getting back to Pensacola. They could not go to Bayou Lacombe or Bayou Liberty since the French were there. Their only option was to seek shelter at Bayou Castein, the English settlement. This is how and why they were there on October 16, 1779, when Captain Pickles, of the navy in the United Independent States of America, docked his ship at Bayou Castein and took the Oath of nineteen British West Florida inhabitants.

The Oath of Allegiance document dated October 16, 1779, is transcribed as follows:

"We whose Names or Marks are hereunto Set and Subscribed being Settlers and Inhabitants on Lake Pontchartrain between the Bayou LaCombe and the River Tangipaho, do hereby, Acknowledge ourselves to be Natives as well as true and faithful Subjects to the United Independent States of North America.

And whereas on the Tenth Day of last Month William Pickles Captain in the navy of the said States did arrive in this lake and make Prize of the English armed Sloop West Florida who had kept possession of the Lake for near two years before, and the said William Pickles, Esquire, did on the Twenty first of the same month land some of his People and take Possession of this Settlement and gave us all the Protection and others that His Force would admit of, and suffered us to remain on our possessions till further Orders; We therefore consider ourselves belonging to the said States, and are willing to remain here and enjoy our Property and Privileges under the said States."

October 16th, 1779

Paul Pigg
James Farro
Daniel Tuttle
Abel Goffigon
Matthew McCullough
Edward Torriman
Francis Fisher
William Dickinson
John Spell
William Stiel

Jacob Ambrose
Alex^n McCullough
Fred^k Spell
James Mosley
Benjn Curftis
Mary Smith
Willm Fisher
Samuel [his X mark] Smith
Jerard Brandon

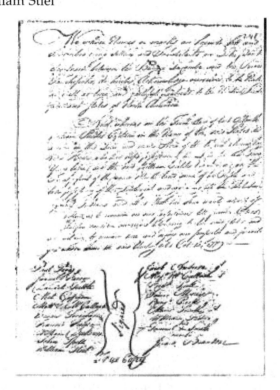

Eighteen men and one woman signed the document as "true and faithful subjects" of the United Independent States of North America. Why were there only nineteen signatures when there were many more who had settled in the area in the past four years? Who were the British settlers that remained in the area? We found no land grants assigned to the following persons who signed the oath: Daniel Tuttle, Paul Pigg, James Farro (Farrell), William Dickinson, James Mosely and Benjamin

Curtis. A possible explanation as to why they had not been granted land was that it often took time after a settler applied for a land grant to have it processed and for the land to be surveyed with Seal. There were fees to be paid and permission had to be given by the Governor and Council. It is possible that these people had just "squatted" on some location or had recently arrived in the colony, had applied, and were waiting for a reply.

Seven of the signers actually had land grants on Bayou Castein, but only five lived on their concession. Frederick Spell and Jerard Brandon had evidence of living at Manchac in 1779. Three had reasons for moving around the western part of the province: Lt. Colonel William Stiel had troops stationed at Manchac and the McCullough brothers had land purchases all over the western part of the Province and were looking for more. The signers of the surrender who had been recipients of British land grants were Jacob Ambrose, Francis Fisher, William Fisher,[11] John Spell, Frederick Spell, and Abel Geofigon, who died at Bayou Castein prior to 1781.

Geofigon's widow, Christina Weeks stayed on and had a second marriage to Jacob Miller. She died January 21, 1806, leaving him a widower.

Edward Foreman, a relative of John Perry, was one of the first settlers at the mouth of Bayou Castein. He removed to the Attakapas area in 1785 (Bayou Chicot).

Mary Smith, widow of Morris Smith, was the only woman who signed the surrender. The Samuel Smith, who made his mark, could not have been Mary's son since he was born in 1771.[12] No record was found on Samuel Smith. He could possibly have been a presumed brother of Morris Smith, or the son of Peter Smith who had 100 acres on Castang Bayou. The Smith family stayed on the lake-front until they sold the property to Bernard Marigny in 1830.

Matthew McCullough had a son named Alexander who was the main heir of his uncle Alexander who died intestate in Pensacola *circa* 1805. Alexander claimed his uncle's British land grants after 1810 when West Florida came under American authority. He also claimed 400 acres at Manchac as the sole heir. The two brothers, Matthew and Alexander McCullaugh, were at Bayou Castein when Captain Pickles landed and required them to sign the Oath. Alexander McCullaugh owned several thousand acres all over West Florida.

Did Captain William Pickles realize the importance of two of the signees, Alexander McCullaugh and William Stiel?[13] We are left with the impression that Captain Pickles was unaware of whom he had in the gathered inhabitants since William Stiel did not put his military title when signing and nothing is mentioned of Alexander McCullaugh as being a high official in the Pensacola Government. Signee Jerard later relocated to the Mississippi territory. His son Jerard Brandon, born near Natchez (1788-1850), was twice Governor of Mississippi.

By signing the Oath, these early residents of Bayou Castein were the first to swear allegiance to the new United States. The British fort at Baton Rouge and Natchez surrendered to Governor Galvez. He had little difficulty in seizing Natchez in 1779 and Pensacola fell in 1781 with considerable fighting encouraged by Bernardo de Galvez. By 1783, Spain and the young United States were taking a fighting stance for control of the lower Mississippi valley. It would take another fifteen years before the United States controlled the mighty Mississippi.

From the time of Willing's raid in February 1778 until evidence of American settlers coming to the area, several petitions were made by the Loyalists to the British government for compensation for the destruction of their plantations. Governor Chester in his claim stated that the Indians would not allow anyone to return to their plantations. What Willling's raiders did not destroy, the Indians did. Thomas Westcott told John Fitzpatrick that all the settlements on the Forks of the River were burned. No one remained and it was too dangerous to venture into the territory.

Spain allowed British inhabitants 18 months in which to dispose of their property but, according to a statement signed by Elias Durnford, James Bruce, David Taitt, and more than forty planters, merchants and others, there were no purchasers. Their plantations and settlements "... late so valuable had all been destroyed by Indians soon after the final reduction of the province, ...nor will the Indians ever suffer them to be reposed by their Owners while the country is under the Dominion of Spain."[14]

The British government treated the claims of the Loyalists of West Florida differently than those on the east coast. Evidence suggests that at least a majority and perhaps as many as two-thirds of the Loyalists remained in West Florida after the Spanish conquest. Thirty-eight as West Floridians had petitioned Lord North, asserting that they were "equally entitled to a compensation for their losses, as their other fellow sufferers on the same continent." Again, in 1787, the loyalists attempted to obtain compensation for their losses to Spanish arms. In that year, a sixteen-page pamphlet was printed entitled *The Case and Petition of His Majesty's Loyal Subjects, late of West Florida*. Their Loyalist effort was in vain!

Within a year and half after the Commission started meeting, it began considering claims from West Florida for losses caused by the Americans. In West Florida this meant compensation for losses occasioned by Willing's raid. The Commission did grant small annual pensions to eight West Floridians for property lost to the Americans during Willing's raid.

Many West Floridians had already petitioned the Commission before this change in policy became public, and the decision of their claims simply read, "Does not come within the scope of this enquiry," or "not admitted." There were at least ten West Florida loyalists who suffered losses to Spain and losses because of the American raid, and consequently the Commission disallowed their claims. Only two of these loyalists re-petitioned the Commission after making the necessary distinctions.

At the same time, many West Florida loyalists suffered almost total destruction of their personal fortunes. England failed to grant them some kind of relief through direct compensation or annual pensions. They continued for over thirty years to seek compensation or confirmation by the United States of their British land grants in West Florida. Their efforts were largely in vain![15] This is a reason why the West Florida grants and seals have not survived because the British Claims Commission for the American Revolution did not consider the hostilities with Spain in West Florida as part of the American Revolution War and, consequently, did not accept claims from West Florida Loyalists. East Florida did, and as a result they kept the turned in grants and Seals.

A 1978 issue of the *The Alabama Historical Quarterly* contained an article describing the official seal of British West Florida and noted the author's unsuccessful search for a surviving specimen of the artifact.[16] Shortly thereafter, Professor Dr. Robert R. Rae had the pleasure of meeting Mr. Don Sharp of Metairie, Louisiana, who had also searched widely, but in vain for a copy of the seal. Mr. Sharp's association with the *St. Tammany Historical Society* led to information regarding an extant copy of the seal, and a picture of it was published in *The St. Tammany Historical Society Gazette*.

About 2001, the *New Orleans Historical Collection* purchased a "West Florida Seal" at an antique show in Charleston, South Carolina. It appears to be from the Eli Hall Bay's Collection. Mr. Bay had purchased from Alexander McCullough several grants of land on the Mississippi River near Natchez around 1778. He settled in Charleston after the Revolutionary War. It appears that one of the seals survived and appeared at the Antique Show. We know of two known seals in existence.[17] According to Dr. Robert Rae, the original metal mould for the West Florida Seal was destroyed, and original grants and Seals were lost to posterity, except the old O'Brien grant that surfaced during Court Case No. 225, and the Bay one.

During his business career, Oliver Pollock, received land grants from the West Florida authorities and operated plantations in English territory. He did everything in his power to aid the American cause while serving as a loyal subject of Spain. After the revolt, his British titles were confirmed by the Spanish. It was he who convinced Governor Galvez that the best defense of Spanish New Orleans in 1779 would be an offense against the British. Galvez became a military ally who took up arms against the British a thousand miles removed from the main theaters of war.

In the *Journals of Congress* the committee, to whom were referred the letters from Governor Galvez and O. Pollock, brought in a report that was read: Whereupon,

The Committee to whom were referred the letter of his Excellency Bernardo de Galvez of the 8th of May last, together with the letter of Oliver Pollock of the 20th of January last with the papers enclosed have considered thereof and agreed to report –

That it appears to your Committee Captain Wm Pickles Commanding a Schooner in the service of the United States in the Month of Sept: 1779 entered the lake Pontchartrain and Captured the British Armed Sloop West Florida, which had been in possession and command of the Lake near two years before, and after taking the Sloop landed part of his men in the district of Country on Lake Pontchartrain between the Bayou le Combe and the river Tanchipaho and obtained from the inhabitants of that district a submission in writing, acknowledging their subjection to the United States, a copy whereof (the original being in his possession) hath been transmitted to Congress by the said Oliver Pollock.

That it also appears to your Committee by the letters of the Governor of Louisiana that Capt Pickles in the Sloop West Florida by joining the force of those States under his command with that of Spain greatly facilitated the reduction of *West Florida*, which acknowledgement on the part of his Excellency Governor Galvez together with the submission of the inhabitants on Lake Pontchartrain may in the opinion of your Committee serve to strengthen and support the claim of the United States to the free Navigation of the river Mississippi, and to a port or ports on the said river, the Committee therefore submit the following Resolution:

Resolved, That a copy of the capitulation of the inhabitants on the Lake Pontchartrain, dated 16 October, 1779, and the copies of the letters of his Excellency Bernardo de Galvez, governor of Louisiana; the one to the President of Congress, dated 8 May, last, and the other to Oliver Pollock dated 21 October last, be transmitted to the honorable John Jay."[18]

John Jay (1745-1829) was delegate and elected President of Continental Congress in 1778, and Minister to Spain in 1779 in order to seek recognition of Colonial Independence, financial aid, and commercial treaties.

Heavily in debt, financially ruined, Pollock, the largest single financial contributor to the American Revolution, tried for years to recover the money he loaned while agent at New Orleans. In late April 1782 Pollock requested a passport from Governor Estevan Miro in order to leave Louisiana and return to Philadelphia so he could convince Congress to pay the loans he had negotiated in New Orleans on its behalf. It would not be the end of his financial troubles.

The Legislature of Virginia did authorize a certificate of indebtedness which promised payments to be made over a period of four years. Assured, he accepted the job as Consul to Havana in the hope that could make a come back to pay his creditors. Hardly there, Virginia cancelled the certificate and stopped payments on vouchers already issued. His absence would last for six years. It was four years after the war was won and over that Virginia again officially recognized Pollock's claims and began paying off.

In 1798, Pollock was still seeking compensation. He drew a rough map of where the battle of Lake Pontchartrain was fought for the members of the Virginia Committee he was addressing. Titled "Sketch of the Isle of New Orleans by Oliver Pollock, April 1798," Pollock indicates that Lake Pontchartrain is 7 leagues broad.

Written by Pollock underneath his rough sketch "Where the British Sloop of War West Florida commanded the Lakes and was taken by the U.S. Schooner Sloop Morris Tender by order of Oliver Pollock the American Agent and directed by Capt Wm. Pickles in the month of

Oct^er 1779 which prevented General Campbell then at Pensacola from coming through the lakes to attack New Orleans. At the time General Galvez was on his way with his army to attack the British posts up the Mississippi. This capture was thought ... to be one of the principal events that bound this country to the Spanish arms."

In Pollock's handwriting on the first page: "The schooner was of superior force...the fight lasted about 15 minutes in which the British captain was killed and seven mortally wounded. Captain Pickles had one officer....the wounded were all landed at the Spanish Fort of which this capture was made...which was about one league from New Orleans."

The Surrender is commemorated by a historic marker in Mandeville, Louisiana, which reads: On October 16, 1779, the British living between "Bayou Lacombe and the River Tanchipaho," surrendered to Captain William Pickles who had won a naval battle off the shore on September 10, 1779, and thereby ended the Revolutionary War in Louisiana.[19]

The Revolutionary War players still had work to do. Spain and Galvez still had a vital role in determining the war's outcome. True, starting in 1776, Spain provided substantial aid to the American colonists fighting up and down the East Coast, with much shipping activity moving through New Orleans. After Spain declared open war on Britain in June 1779, Galvez lost no time in attacking forts on the east bank of the Mississippi River and along the Gulf Coast. Galvez had a final victory at Pensacola, capital of British West Florida, in May 1781 after a two month siege. His feats gave the Spanish control of all of West Florida and so ended all possibilities of any British offensive up the Mississippi River. Galvez did not return to New Orleans. He died in Mexico City in 1786, aged 40.

In 1803, when Louisiana became American and the Spanish relinquished the reins of power, Pollock was still petitioning Congress for recognition of his claims. But he held no rancor for his personal disastrous role in the winning of his adopted nation's independence.

Anglo-Saxon settlers came to the north shore of Lake Pontchartrain to escape the Revolutionary War, but at the close of the American Revolution those settlers at Bayou Castein found themselves subjects of the King of Spain. The families that maintained ownership through the British period were the Labyteau, O'Brien, Spell, Smith, Geoffigon, Ambrose, the Webb and Davis families on the east bank of Bayou Castein. According to the *American State Papers*, the American government recognized only seven English grants of land that antedated the Spanish period.[20] The map of Lt. Colonel Gilberto

Guillemard is important for its connection with the original British grants. He used the old British lines of Elias Durnford when he surveyed the Spell, O'Brien, and Smith grants. After some eighteen years of English rule, British West Florida ceased to exist, but its legacy would endure for some time.

The winning of independence from England in 1783 was a political, diplomatic, and military achievement for the American colonies. The new nation had won a great victory in the peace treaty. In the treaties between Spain, France, and England, Spain recovered Minorca and Florida, and now held all the land west of the Mississippi and Florida, and would not be dislodged from this area until the nineteenth century. France, who now had a bankrupt treasury, received a few West Indian islands, the hope of an American market, and a future ally in the United States. The United States gained not only its independence but also the territory east of the Mississippi River between the Great Lakes and the thirty-first parallel of north latitude. Spain refused to recognize America's claim to the thirty-first parallel. Consequently, the southern boundary of the United States remained in dispute until finally settled in the Pinckney Treaty of 1795.[21]

The greatest change was the change in land ownership. The abandoned lands of the loyalists who had fled to join the English cause were confiscated. The acquisition of all this land put the state governments into the real estate business. Some of the land was given as bounties to the soldiers or sold at extremely low prices. This greatly increased the number of property-holders, hence the number of voters. Meanwhile the United States government would sweep across the American continent promoting its ideologies. The setbacks were short-lived.

To the new nation, Spanish territory and interests were now seen as a threat since without free navigation on the Mississippi and a port of deposit at its mouth they felt "destined to remain a nation in want". It would take another fifteen years before the United States controlled the Mississippi. By 1783, Spain and the young United States were squaring it out.

NOTES

1. Martinez, Raymond J., Rousseau: *The Last Days of Spanish New Orleans*, copyright 1964, Pelican Publishing Company, 2003, 14.
2. Account of Pierre Rousseau, American First Lieutenant, Fort St. John, 12 September, 1779, in Frederick S. Ellis, *St. Tammany Parish*, 54.

3. Report of Captain Pickles to Pedro Piedras after the battle on Lake Pontchartrain, September 12, 1779.

4. Cocks, Randolph, "Payne, John Willett,"http://www.oxforddnb.com/view/article/21648; *Oxford Dictionary of National Biography:* http://www.oxforddnb.com/view/article/21648.

5. Report of Lt. Rousseau written from Fort St. John, September 12, 1779.

6. Rae, Robert, "Florida and the Royal Navy's Floridas," *Florida Historical Quarterly,* 1981, 200.

7. Report of Lt. Pierre Rousseau dated September 12, 1779, Fort St. John.

8. Martinez, Raymond J., Rousseau: *The Last Days of Spanish New Orleans*, Pelican Publishing Company, 2002, copyright 1964, 14.

9. A.G.I. Cuba, Lego 701.

10. October 16, 1779, Records and papers of the Continental Congress, supra; Claiborne; Jackson Powers and Barksdale, 1880, *Mississippi as a Province, Territory and State.* Reprint Baton Rouge, Louisiana State University Press, 1964, 122.

11. William Fisher was listed as having received a land grant on the Tombaghee River under Spanish rule in the 1780s.

12. Samuel Smith's baptism was recorded on 21 July 1771 at Christ Church, Poughkeepsie, New York.

13. Lieutenant Colonel William Stiel strengthened the defenses of West Florida on Lake Pontchartrain and Natchez. He did not indicate his title when he signed the Oath.

14. C.O. 5/595, Memorial of Proprietors of Land, Planters, Merchants—undated.

15. Cotterwill, R.S., *The National Land System in the South, 1803-1812*, 495-499.

16. Rea, Robert R., "A Better Fate! The British West Florida Seal," *Alabama Historical Quarterly*, Winter 1981, 289.

17. Note by Donald Sharp to Anita Campeau dated November 30, 2007.

18. A Century of Lawmaking for a New Nation: U.S. Congressional Documents and Debates, 1774-1875, *Journal of the Continental Congress*, Volume 17, 600.

19. McLellan, Tara, "Group restores marker dedicated to Battle of Lake Pontchartrain," *The Times-Picayune*, 14 November 2008.

20. Starr, J. Barton, *Tories, Dons and Rebels*, University of Florida Presses, 1976, 239-240.

21. Pinckney's Treaty, also known as the Treaty of San Lorenzo, or the Treaty of Madrid was signed in San Lorenzo de El Escorial on October 17, 1795 and established intentions of friendship between the United States and Spain. The treaty defined the boundaries of the U.S. with the Spanish colonies and guaranteed U.S. navigation on the Mississippi River. The treaty's full title is Treaty of Friendship, Limits, and Navigation between Spain and the United States. Thomas Pinckey negotiated for the United States and Don Manuel de Gody represented Spain.

CHAPTER 4

THE SPANISH COLONIAL PERIOD, 1779-1803

East and West Florida became problematic for His Majesty, King George III, as the Revolutionary War dragged on. The Spanish governor, Don Bernardo de Galvez, sympathized with the American colonists in their struggle for independence. As a result of Galvez's successful conquest of Baton Rouge in 1779, Mobile in 1780, and Pensacola in 1781, the British surrendered East and West Florida to Spain on April 10, 1781. British loyalists who flocked to Florida during the Revolution were then forced to leave if they did not submit to the new rules. The Spanish inherited several large plantations that the British had worked hard to cultivate.

When the Spaniards evacuated St. Augustine in 1763, practically the entire civilian populace had sailed away. But in 1783, a sizable minority of the British loyalists elected to remain in West Florida under Spanish rule. Spain encouraged this because of the difficulty of settling the Floridas and because of the growing rift with the United States over boundaries and Mississippi navigation.

Spanish territory and interests on the west threatened the United States even more than did those of the British on the north. In possession of the Mississippi River and the great Louisiana territory beyond, Spain controlled the destiny of all those who dwelt west of the Alleghenies.

With Spanish approval, Tories in the Natchez district, and even those out of reach in the Indian country remained on their property and continued trading with the Indians. Nor did Spain press the issue of conversion to Catholicism. Should she mistreat these loyalists, they were likely to move northward out of Spanish reach to join the American frontiersmen who made no secret about their designs on the Mississippi. It was preferable to keep the Tories in West Florida rather than see them become restless neighbors. Furthermore, pioneers of the interior of the continent had left behind them the comforts of an older society and had staked their hopes on regaining those comforts by their ability to produce a surplus in the new West and finding markets for them, and the way to markets where their goods could be exchanged lay down the rivers which drained into the Mississippi.

After the Spanish takeover, seventy-seven grants were given in St. Tammany Parish, based either on Spanish patents or on occupancy that commenced from 1779 until 1810.[1]

NORTH AMERICA

1783

*Map of North America in 1783 showing areas owned by England,
Spain and United States.*

A handful of British settlers remained on their land at Bayou Castein and maintained ownership through the Spanish Colonial period. Many grants were found to be unoccupied and unimproved thus violating the terms of their grants. Spanish officials legally dispossessed many of the grantees and then reassigned such lands to valid settlers.

Of the original grantees, it was found that John Spell, Mary Smith, Paul Labyteau, Lewis Davis, William Webb, and Christina Geoffigon remained on the land adjacent to Bayou Castein. William O'Brien and his family never occupied the land as they lived near Manchac but kept ownership through the British, Spanish and American periods of domination. Widow O'Brien had the Lake Pontchartrain grant resurveyed by Ira C. Kneeland on June 15, 1806. She gave the grant as a donation to her daughter Dorothy, probably as a wedding present when she married the New Orleans merchant John Travis Sanderson. Dorothy kept the land until 1811, and then sold it to Jacob Bartle. She passed on the original British land grant with its survey and attached with the Great Deputed Seal of West Florida.

A number of Spanish land grants were executed at the Bayou Castein vicinity between 1779 and 1810. The first to come in during the new regime and obtain some abandoned land was Morgan Edwards in 1781.[2] There were whispers that Morgan had been a "pirate", that he had sailed with Jean Lafitte, and that he gave a fictitious name to hide his true identity.

The first evidence that Morgan Edwards was in Louisiana came from the Spanish census of New Orleans in June 1778. Governor Galvez ordered the census in order to identify the inhabitants that flooded the city caused by the raid of Captain James Willing in late February of that year. The census shows an English tenant by the name of Mr. Morgan Eduerdo on St. Louis Street. Two doors away, Mr. Willing (no first name) shared his lodging with five men: Mr. Francois, Mr. Harrison, Mr. Mactintere, Mr. Jorge, and Mr. Gooding, two of which were identified as James McIntyre and Reuben Harrison. Willing is listed as "English Tenant –Voyager").[3]

There is no written evidence that Morgan Edwards participated in Willing's raids, nor was he officially listed in the company of Captain William Pickles or an agent of Oliver Pollock. What is known is that he was a good friend of Governor Galvez and the Almonester.

A controversial and mysterious figure, the baptismal records of Morgan Edwards' two daughters is a first clue to his true identity. In 1793, the Edwards and Geoffigon families journeyed across Lake Pontchartrain for the baptismal ceremony to be held in temporary quarters as the new church (the old one having been destroyed by the fire of 1788) being built through the generosity of the godfather, the Almonester.

Morgan Edwards identified himself as Huet/Hewit, (Heruet) son of David Heruet and Margarete or Margaret Bradley (spelled Bradle in the Church of St. Louis Records) of Dublin, Ireland, as recorded by the priest Father Joseph de Villaprovido, at the baptism of two of his children on Friday, the fifth day of April, 1793. The entry reads:

> ...a daughter who was born the thirtieth day of July in the year one thousand seven hundred eighty-nine to whom was given

the name Margarita, natural daughter of Morgan Edwardo Heruet Smitte, native of Ireland and of Margarita Smitte, native of New York, married only with the usual marriage ceremony of the Protestant Religion, but who promises to instruct her child in the Catholic Religion in order to perform the administration of the Catholic Catachism in her language. Her Paternal Grandparents are David Heruet and Margarita Bradle, natives of Dublin, in Ireland. Her Maternal Grandparents, Mauricio Smitte and Maria Smitte, Natives of New York. Her godfather is the sainted Don Andres Almonaster, Colonel of the Royal Militia; Governor, and Royal Lieutenant. At the baptismal font I name Don Joseph Capotillo and Maria Irene Luisa Goffigon who agree to advise on the spiritual relationship and the administration of this sacrament to this girl child, to the two forefathers and to follow with the sister of this one for the other natural children of these parents until all are here instructed....

The second daughter was born the "first of February of the year just pass...and to whom was given the name Maria Luisa, natural daughter of Morgan Edwardo Heruet Smitte, resident of the Pontchartrain Post[4] belonging to the Parish district of St. Luis, native of Ireland, and of Margarita Smitte, Native of New York. Her godparents are Don Luis Estevan, Nicolas Dreux, Master of Music, for the Ruling Council of Louisiana, and Maria Antonia Goffigon, who will advise about the spiritual relationship and the sacred obligation of this girl.... ".

Why the name Morgan Edwards? Could it imply that he had been adopted? Why would a person, whose name was Hewitt (or any other name), call himself by another name unless adopted?

With baptismal sponsors like Don Andres Almonaster y Rojas, Luis Estevan, and Nicolas Dreux, it appears that Morgan Edwards submitted his children to this religious rite to cultivate friendship among the political elite in New Orleans for political gain rather than spiritual motives.

Morgan was connected in some way to a William Hewit, who had predeceased Mrs. Geoffigon (Christina Weeks), and had referred to her as his cousin in his will.[5] In 1761 in Onslow County, North Carolina, Abel lived next door to John and Mary Hewitt who begot Sarah Hewitt (b. 1747) who married Benjamin Weeks in 1766, the nephew of Christina. It is not known if there was a connection between Piere Hewit and Hendriet Hewit, inhabitants of Mobile, who took the oath of allegiance to the British King George III, and forwarded by Major Robert Farmer by his letter on October 2, 1764.[6] There were obvious misspellings or misreading by the English scribe.

Morgan Edwards, a well-educated man, had influence with the highest authority of the Spanish Government in New Orleans. As a reward, he became the owner of a large section of land. A first grant was given by the Spanish Governor in the fall of 1783 when the Treaty of Peace took effect. Edwards occupied the Perry and Alexander McCullaugh claims, an area that covered about 700 acres. Jacob Ambrose died prior to 1783. His British land grant in the "forks" of Bayou Castein became part of Morgan's first grant dated June 2, 1783, "25 arpents deep to the north and 40 arpents frontage." The second grant was given by Governor Estevan Miro in 1785. The third piece was the British grant of Mager Spell who died in 1783, of which Morgan purchased the 100 acres from the Spell heirs. The land was located next to the land of Mary Smith, his mother-in-law. The total area of his land was in three different pieces for a total of about 1800 acres. Refer to map T8S – R11. Of interest make a copy of the Bayou Castin map of 1777 and superimpose on T8S – R11 map so as to identify the original settlers.[7]

On April 17, 1795, Morgan Edwards surveyed his plantation with the help of three local residents to assist him: Jonathan Meekes, who had settled on the O'Brien tract and later found out that the O'Brien's owned it, Jonathan Rabassa and Uriah Smith. Note their attestation to the survey: "*Do hereby certifie that at the Request of Morgan Edwards I did*

aid the said Edwards to survey his plantation and do hereby Depose that the same is executed with accuracy and agreeable to His Directions from His Honor D^n Carlos Trudeau-Esquire Surveyor General Of the province – Witnessed My Hand this Seventeenth Day of April 1795." Signed Uriah Smith

Morgan Edwards must have been a qualified surveyor as Carlos Trudeau, the Surveyor General of Louisiana, accepted the survey dated April 17, 1795, as accurate and accepted it for his files. His house, about one mile from the lake-shore, can be located on the Guillemard map of 1798. It was on the trail or road that connected Bayou Castein to the home of James Goodby at Bayou Chinchuba.

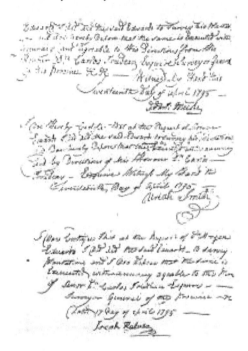

Copy of attestation by Meekes, Smith and Rabasa, dated April 17, 1795

Henry Richardson and his brother George, from Natchez, came in and settled in 1796. Henry settled in the forks of Bayou Castein but found out that it was owned by Morgan Edwards. After a dispute of both parties, Henry Richardson and family pulled up stakes and removed to Manchac below Baton Rouge. George Richardson settled on the abandoned British land grant of Rebecca Ambrose and Thomas Loofbarrow. He enclosed about twenty acres for his livestock and cultivated the "Ambrose old field". Widow Ambrose abandoned her land around 1785 and removed to the Natchez area where there were many English families. She did not reconfirm her title under the Spanish and did not have it resurveyed. George Richardson lived there with his daughters Nancy, Martha, and sons Amos and John. He did not apply for a Spanish grant. On leaving a few years later to move to Manchac he sold his improvement to Zachariah Faircloth for a cow and a calf. Zachariah and Martha Richardson, although they were not legally married, continued to live on the land and improved it for over twenty years.

Dated May 11, 1798, a Spanish document written in French states that "Morgan Edwards appears to have died a few days ago" and directs Charles Parent, the first commandant of the District of Chifoncte (*sic*), to administer his estate. It is not known if he died at sea since he ran schooners and barges across Lake Pontchartrain, or on his plantation. If so, his house and grave marker were washed into Lake Pontchartrain by a hurricane in 1810.

Morgan Edwards and Margaret Smith had seven children. Widow Edwards has a second marriage to Hugh Sheridan on November 1, 1800 at St. Bernard's Church in old Galveztown. She raised a second family.

Jacob Miller, of German origins, the son of Jacob and Anna Maria Theighen, was listed as two years of age (passenger list) when the English schooner *La Bretana* set sail from Maryland on the fifth day of January 1769. The ship carried one hundred passengers of German, Acadian and British settlers destined for New Orleans.[8] The family settled in the Baton Rouge area. Jacob Miller, listed in the records as the son of Jacob and Anna Maria Deyen of Maryland, married Catherine Adams, daughter of Americus and Catherina Keleinpeter (*sic*) of Mansack (*sic*), on November 23, 1795 (SJO-13, 13).[9]

Miller had been around for some time in the area of Bayou Castein as he was a witness to Maria Antonia Geoffigon's wedding to William Owens on July 6, 1792. His second marriage was to Christina Wilkes, widow of Abel Geoffigon.

Governor Carondelet was eager to have brick making facilities in operation to rebuild New Orleans after the great fires of 1788 and 1794. Ordinances were passed by the Cabildo that all buildings were to be of brick. Jacob Miller, interested in a brick making operation, sought the tract located south and west by the lands of Morgan Edwards and to the north by that of George Sharp at Bayou Castein.

In 1796, the 29 year-old Miller went to New Orleans to petition Governor Carondelet for land:

"I, Jacob Miller, a bricklayer, have found vacant lands on the other side of the Lake suitable for a brick kiln and, desirous of erecting buildings for that purpose, I supplicate your Excellency to grant me 10 arpents of land front with the ordinary depth of 40 arpents in said place, bounded on one side by the lands of Morgan Edwards and by the other side on the domain of His Majesty."

Dated at New Orleans on 9 May 1796 and signed by Jacob Miller.[10]

Written in French, New Orleans, LA., dated May 10, 1796 "Parent will inform me if the land claimed by said Miller is of the domain of the King." (Signed) Le Baron de Carondelet.[11]

The 1796 Miller grant caused problems for Morgan Edwards until the day he died. Miller complained to Governor Carondelet: "I, Jacob Miller, have the honor to present to you the respect which is due you, and say that Morgan Edwards sees and wants the plantation of the suppliant, it having been abandoned for more than 10 years, and since he has cleaned out the Bayou to make it navigable. I appeal to you to render him the certificate and plan." (Signed Jacob Miller).

On January 31, 1797, signed by Le Baron de Carondelet: "Parent will inform me if requests and ordinances have been presented to Morgan Edwards with the titles."[12]

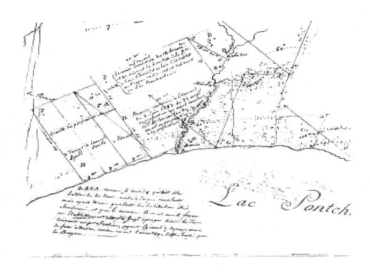

Guillemard map of 1798

Carondelet wrote to Commandant Charles Parent, telling him to investigate Edwards, and for him to bring his proof of ownership to New Orleans. Morgan contacted his friend Almonester Roxas, an influential man in the Spanish government who sent Gilberto Guillemard to survey the tracts in the winter of 1797/1798. The Guillemard map is important not only to the pre-history of Mandeville but it shows three of the British grants resurveyed by the Spanish under their laws.

Soon after the survey was made a series of mishaps occurred. Morgan Edwards died, and a few weeks later Almonester Roxas passed away. Baron Louis Hector de Carondelet left office suddenly before the issue was solved since he was assigned to Central America. Manuel Gayoso Lemos, took the oath of office in late August 1797, but was too busy with other matters to attend to the Edwards/Miller dispute. To add to the confusion, before he could rule on the petition, the newly installed Governor died of yellow fever on July 18, 1799. Before proper action could be ruled on by the by the Spanish officials, word of the transfer of West Florida back to France, then to the United States was received.

Due to several unforeseen events, Jacob Miller still claimed the land in 1808 when he tried to sell the land to Jacob Bartell (*sic*). In a letter to James O. Cosby, the Land Commissioner West of Pearl River, Jacob Bartell wrote:

> Take notice that I claim as much land as the Government may think proper to grant, in virtue of two separate Spanish papers given by the Baron de Carondelet to Jacob Miller. The date of the first, 1796, the date of the second, 1797 and by him (Miller) inhabited and cultivated until the 23rd of August 1808 –HWF, when it was transferred by said Miller to Jacob Bartell. Since the date of the transfer, the said land has not been inhabited and cultivated. The Spanish papers referred to accompany this notice. (Signed Jacob Bartell.)

Petition and decree for 400 Arpents dated May 10, 1796.

Written in English: This is to certify that I, Jacob Miller, have made over all my rights and claim to the land written and improvements thereon, this 23d day of August 1808. (Signed Jacob Miller.) Witnesses present: Joseph Rabossa and Ramon Lisano.

Since Miller did not have a clear title, the deal fell through. After 1808, Miller who had spent 16 years at Bayou Castein and the Geoffigon family disappear from the area.

Joseph Rabassa was directly across Bayou Castein from Morgan Edwards. He was the son of Joseph and Catarina Co (Quo), natives of Cabella in the diocese of Gerona, in Catalonia. He married Juana Simon Laurent *dite* Durio, daughter of Simon (Lorenzo) and Margarita Derbin, of the parish of New Orleans on June 1, 1784 (SLC, M5, 28). At the time of her marriage, Juana was eighteen years old. Shortly after 1784, Joseph and his wife moved across the lake and occupied vacant land between James Goodby and Jacques Lorreins *dit* Tarascon Senior. He did not remain long on his first settlement, as on February 13, 1790, he petitioned Spanish Governor Carondelet that "wishing to establish myself on the Bayou named Castin, there is an abandoned tract of land of 30 arpents front and on the other side by lands of Joseph Laurent and on the other side by the land of Thomas Spell. I beseech your honor to grant me this tract in order to cultivate the same." The patent for the claim was issued for a 10 arpents front by the ordinary depth of 40 arpents from Carondelet to Rabassa.

Joseph Rabassa died at 61 years of age on August 8, 1811 (SLC F7, 169). On March 12, 1830, the Rabassa heirs sold the entire tract to the Frenchman named Toussaint Letourneau, who was married to Marie Plauche (Blanche) Rabassa, daughter of Joseph Rabassa, for the sum of $1,695,00 (STRC #1764, COB C-1, page 186, Conveyance of March 12, 1830).

Pascalis de la Barre, a Spanish official, son of François, "the Muscateer of France" as the record states, tried to obtain the Webb land in 1787. The land was located on the eastern side of Bayou Castein. Lewis Davis died in 1784 and his widow removed to the Natchez area in 1785. There was a lawsuit brought against de la Barre in New Orleans by Martha Davis and William Webb. Jean Joseph de Forrest, Judge in the city of New Orleans, acknowledged the grant given to Lewis Davis by Peter Chester, which was 774 arpents of land on the south side of Bayou Castein and adjacent to lands of Nathan Gamble, Joseph Spell and Thomas Farrell. It was given the 24th day of July 1777.[13] It happened that the Webb had registered with the Spanish, so the Judge admonished De La Barre for trying to claim the plantation.

Martha Webb sold her British plantation to Santiago Constant (Spanish inhabitant): "Be known that I, Martha Webb, widow of Lewis Davis, a resident of this province, depose that I really sell to Santiago Constant, of the neighborhood, a tract of land situated on the other side of the lake, composed of 774 arpents square, south of Bayou Castin...Dated April 4, 1789.

Constant died within three years of this purchase: "September 19, 1793, Santiago Constant, deceased, Isabel and Estevan Lumones, also guardian *ad litern* of Lus and Luisa Constanza, natural daughters, and heiress of the said Santiago Constant. Auction of said land, 387 square arpents, bounded by Castein Bayou, bounded on one side by Joseph Durio and on the eastern part by William Webb. The company of Liauteau Angelin and Morateau made the highest bid (360 pesos) and obtained the Webb grant. Year 1792. *Number 62 Testamentoria* de Santiago Constant."[14]

Within a few years, the two entrepreneurs were deceased. Dated 20 October 1796, New Orleans (written in Spanish): "Public sale of property belonging to the Company composed of the deceased Augustin Favre, Joseph Angelin and the said Espiritu Lioteau who was present with Pedro Jeridan testamentary executor for the named Augustin Favre, and Antonio Bonnabel, formerly attorney and now testamentary executor for the named Joseph Angelin."[15]

Antoine/Antonio Bonnabel, the New Orleans merchant and brother-in-law of Morateau, was the highest bidder. The amount of 400 pesos was to be paid in cash. Bonnabel, a native of Chateauroux in the diocese of Embrun in Dauphiné, a department of Hautes-Alpes, France, was married to Celeste Morateau, a native of New Orleans. He came to the Bayou Castein area in 1789.

On August 5, 1797, Feliciana Morateau, widow of Joseph Angelin, agreed to sell to Antonio Bonnabel a plantation, Negroes (Betty) and two slaves named Felipe and Tisa (slaves being purchased from Espiritu Lioteau) for the sum of 1,000 pesos.[16]

The *Lago Pontchartrain* map of 1799 reproduced shows the grant of 4,020 *arpents* made by Governor de Lemos to Antonio Bonnabel on January 25, 1799.

Plan of the Bonnabel grant

This tract lies in Section 42 of T. 8S. R. 12E., Greensburg District, Louisiana and Section 54 of T. 8S., R. 11E. A Translation of the Bonnabel grant is as follows:

"I, Don Carlos Trudeau, royal and private surveyor of the Province of Louisiana, etc...certified in favor and in the presence of Antonio Bonnabel, a merchant of this city, and with the assistance of the owner of the adjoining land, a certain land measuring four thousand and twenty arpents (old French measure of an acre each arpent) of surface, measured with the perch (rod) of the city of Paris, consisting of eighteen lengths of the King's foot, a land measure used in this colony, said land being situated on the northeast of Lake Pontchartrain, known as the "Punta Verde" suburb, about one and a half miles southeast of Bayou Castain, bound on the southwestern side by the shores of Lake Pontchartrain; on the northwestern side by the lands of Pedro Piquery, and on the other side by vacant lands belonging to His Majesty. This survey was made in compliance with the following three decrees: The first, dated February 22, 1790; the second dated June 2, 1797, and the third and last, dated December 20 of last year (1798). Said lands are joined together according to the attached plan and the boundaries are fixed according to the red lines (A, B, C, D, E, F, G,) on said plan to wit: Line A to B shows the road that separates and fixes the common limits between said lands and the lands of Pedro Piquery; said road has been agreed upon by said interested parties as the boundary line between both properties. Point A, beginning from the shores of Lake Pontchartrain on the western side of the road, has been marked with a sharp-pointed dividing post of cypress, five feet eight inches high by seven by eight inches square, with the bottom end buried three feet in the ground and four squares of bricks around its base. On point B, was placed a similar landmark, measuring seven feet high by seven inches square, with its bottom end buried three feet in the ground and two squares of bricks around its base. From point B to Point C, a distance of forty-one arpents eight and half perchs, the line of demarcation was directed to the north, seventy degrees east up to point C on which it was placed another similar land-mark seven feet high by six inches square with its bottom end buried three feet in the ground and four squares of bricks around its base. From point C the line of demarcation was directed to the north, forty degrees east up to point D, a distance of fifty arpents; on said point D was placed another similar landmark five and a half feet high by seven and a half by four and a half inches square with its bottom end buried three feet in the ground and four squares of bricks around its base. The line D to E measures twenty arpents long directed to the south, fifty degrees east, indicating the limits of the depth of said lands, and on said point E was placed another similar landmark five and a half feet high by five and a half inches square with the bottom end buried three feet in the ground as the others. The line from E to F measures forty-six arpents directed to the south, forty degrees up to and parallel with line C to D; on point F was placed another similar landmark five and a half feet high by four inches square with its bottom buried three feet in the ground etc. From point F, fifteen fathoms on the other side of the "Ravine de las Canas", another similar landmark was placed for the purpose of showing that said ravine is to serve as the natural boundary of said lands from point F to point G where said ravine flows into Lake Pontchartrain, all of which is clearly shown in the attached plan. In witness whereof I issue the fore-going description with the attached explanatory plan, on this fifteenth day of January of the year one thousand seven hundred and ninety-nine." (Signed) Carlos Trudeau, Surveyor

The Bonnabel grant having been examined by Don Manuel Gayoso de Lemos by the power granted him by the King approved the said survey and those present signed and sealed with our coat of arms etc. (Signed) Manuel Gayoso de Lemos by order of His Lordship.

Bonnabel died in 1800 leaving a large succession. He owned several ships, some with large cannons. He also had a special ship to cross the lake to his plantation. The Bonnabel heirs sold the property to Bernard de Marigny in 1829, now the present site of Fontainebleau State Park.

Hugh and Landon Davis, brothers of Lewis who died in 1784, settled on lower Bayou Chinchuba next to Widow Ambrose and family in 1785. After the death of their mother (1784) Landon and Hugh took over the 13 slaves instead of dividing them with the widow of Lewis.[17] The land became vacant again for a few years, and this is when James Goodby with his wife, Diana Ross, and younger sister Elizabeth Goodby arrived and settled north of the O'Brien and Spell tracts.

Edward Ross, brother-in-law of James Goodby, was a Lieutenant in the Spanish militia when he arrived at Bayou Chinchuba. He settled on abandoned land between James Goodby and Morgan Edwards on the east, and was given a Spanish grant in 1798.

Edward's parents and a brother lived at Galveztown. He pulled up from Bayou Chinchuba *circa* 1805 after helping the Spanish Governor Vincente Folch to build a road to Baton Rouge to attend to the Kemper Brothers' disturbance. Afterwards, Lt. Edward Ross and family left for the Amite River Crossing where he obtained a new Spanish grant of 1,200 acres. The crossing was about six miles from Galveztown. The area was developed in 1804 when the Syndics at Baton Rouge committed to the building of a new road from Baton Rouge to the Amite Crossing that would connect to the road to Springfield (Bookter's Landing) and then on to Baham Village on the Tchefuncte. The land that had been devastated by Willing in 1778 was now slowly being settled. Inland, the Indians were still hostile to settlement. The Ross grant at Bayou Chinchuba was divided and sold to Samuel Lloyd and John Knight in 1806.

Pierre Piquery (Piedro), from an old New Orleans family, had land located next to Bonnabel. On December 11, 1797, Bonnabel sold him the Lewis Davis plantation, "a plantation of my property consisting of 774 arpents squared, being bounded on one side by the lands of mine and on the other side by Joseph Rabassa...also two Negresses, named Betty and Sire, and eight or nine animals found on the marked G. D." The land in question had been purchased from Feliciana Morateau, widow of Joseph Angelin, by the act of sale under the date of 5 August 1796. Piquery was unable to make the payments on the notes owed and Bonnabel retrieved his property. He attempted to make it a workable and profitable plantation. He hired Barthelemy Martin as the overseer, built a new wharf for his ship that Martin sailed back and forth from Bayou St. John to the north shore. Improvements were made on the buildings and he put his slaves to work making pitch and tar and cutting timber.

Charles de Reggio obtained a Spanish grant on the west side of the Labyteau family. He did not settle or use the land. He passed it on to Pierre Denis de La Ronde in 1806. The United State Commissioner later denied the claim. It was Amos Richardson who qualified and received the 640 acres. Amos married Mary Sodon; widowed she married Thomas Spell Jr. after selling the land in 1836 to Armand Marigny, son of Bernard and Mathilde Morales.

George Sharp was the grandson of a Scotch-Irish man who migrated from Northern Ireland. The family tradition is that three Sharp brothers left Belfast in the great migration to America to seek a better life. They followed the Great Valley Road into Western Virginia beginning at the Shenandoah Valley. After the Revolutionary War, they crossed the Cumberland Gap settling near Boonesborough, Kentucky. In 1789, Captain John Halley, one of the first large tobacco growers in the Boonesborough area, made the first of two trips down the rivers to New Orleans. George Sharp and Zachariah Faircloth, were two of the young men hired by Halley to man his four flatboats.

Sharp, the "Boatman from Kentucky" settled "high up" on Bayou Castein, receiving 640 acres in 1792. Sharp appeared to have had the favor of Spanish Governor Estevan Miro and didn't have to wait four years, the required time under Spanish law. Miro was mentioned in an article taking a "kickback" of the tobacco coming in from Kentucky that was set up by General Wilkinson in 1787. A possible reason for George Sharp to rapidly obtaining a grant of land was either that or Governor Miro's appreciation and friendship to Captain John Halley for having brought supplies after the great fire that devastated New Orleans.[18]

In 1796, George Sharp sold his grant to his friend Zachariah Faircloth and returned to Kentucky. At Natchez, he stopped to see his two younger brothers, Joseph and James Sharp, who had settled at Coles Creek, sixteen miles north of the Fort of Natchez. There, Joseph Sharp married Elizabeth Richardson, daughter of George, in 1793. Joseph Sharp Sr. was murdered in 1805. His sons, Joseph Sharp Jr. and William Sharp, came to live with their uncle Zachariah Faircloth and their aunt Martha Richardson at Bayou Castein. Martha Richardson, a daughter of George, stated in several documents that Joseph and William Sharp were her nephews and were named as such in her Will. The Sharps and their descendants have been a part of St. Tammany Parish for more than 200 years.

The official correspondence between the Spanish governors and Charles Parent, the commandant of the Tchefuncte offers insight in the lives of the settlers. In 1788, while Miro was Governor, Parent was called upon to investigate the purchase of some local residents, including himself, of horses and sheep illegally stolen by the Indians in other localities.[19] In 1790 Parent was asked to locate two Negro slaves held by the Choctaws. Another duty was to settle disputes over money matters of the local inhabitants. Morgan Edwards had a dispute over money with his neighbor Daniel Coyle in 1790, the same Coyle who helped him survey Mary Smith's property in 1785. There is a mention of a Thomas Rees having died and leaving his possessions to Daniel Coyle. George Callwell claimed that Paul Labatut owed him for back wages. In 1792, George Sharp, newly settled on Bayou Castein also claimed that John Spell Jr. owed him for work done. John Spell was sued on his note for 100 barrels of resin and 25 barrels of tar, an indication that the tar works were still functioning on the north shore in 1794 when the suit was filed.[20]

After the Peace Treaty of 1783, American settlers came in looking for good land and game to feed their families. They first came to Natchez in a trickle, then almost in a flood by 1790. A majority did not especially like the Dons, but the pressure for new land moved them on. The Spanish had difficulty in getting their own people to settle except for the Canary Islanders. Then as more settlers came in, they made it harder by adding religion as a prerequisite. Most settlers did not give up on their religious convictions. There were a few travelling ministers, under cover, that performed marriages and baptisms. When a Protestant minister was not available, they would wait until later when one would travel to their area.

Spain was unable to hold on to its possessions in Louisiana for very long. The importance of the free navigation of the Mississippi River to Western men and the desire of France to restore her empire on the American continent took a new turn with Napoleon Bonaparte whose rise to power and his vision of Louisiana as the center of a great French-American Empire brought pressure on Spain to cede all of her North American possessions to France and, Napoleon began preparations for the re conquest of Santo Domingo as a base for French activities. Don Carlos IV, the Spanish king, was a weak man who gave most of his attention to hunting and toiling at his forge, leaving the affairs of the state to his minister, Manuel de Godoy. For the promise of a kingdom in Italy for his daughter, Don Carlos readily agreed to Napoleon's demands, but Godoy had enough vigor and common sense to reduce the grant to the territory of Louisiana alone. The order of transfer was signed on October 15, 1802.

Spain returned Louisiana to France. The slave revolt in Haiti, under the command of the genius named Toussaint l'Ouverture so frustrated Napoleon that he abandoned his plans for North America. Between them and yellow fever the French lost seventeen thousand men, including fifteen generals, one of them being Leclerc himself who was married to Pauline, Bonaparte's sister. The second expedition, originally designed to go to New Orleans, was diverted as reinforcements to the island of Santo Domingo, where the same thing happened all over again.[21]

In early 1802, Thomas Jefferson, President of the United States, made a proposal to the French. The United States offered to buy *la Nouvelle-Orléans* and the territory to the north and east of the Mississippi for two million dollars in compensation. France would retain the area west of the Mississippi, between Arkansas, the Mexican frontier and the sea and the Mississippi River would separate the territories of the U.S. and France.

60

Jefferson's envoy arrived in Paris on April 12 with this proposal, only to find that Bonaparte had a deal of his own: *"Take it all or nothing!"* It was a transaction that would quadruple the size of America.

The result of the Louisiana Purchase in 1803 was that New Orleans and the vast Louisiana Territory became American property. This vast land purchase led to America's assuming control of the Mississippi River – the back door to the United States of the 1800. This monumental deal would affect the economy and ultimately the unity of the shaky young republic.

The United States claimed that West Florida was included in the Purchase but Spain contended otherwise. West Florida had been acquired by conquest from the British, therefore it formed no part of the property it had received from France in 1763, and which had been transferred back to France in 1803. The respective claims would remain items of contention between the two countries. Spain remained in control of West Florida and maintained a major base at Baton Rouge. This is where the records pertaining to the District of Tchefuncte were kept after 1803.

NOTES

1. Ellis, Frederick, S., *St. Tammany Parish L'Autre Côté du Lac*, Pelican Publishing Company, Gretna, Louisiana, 1998, 58.
2. Ibid., 63.
3. Robichaux, Albert J., Jr., *Louisiana Census and Militants*, Volume 1: 1770-1789, Polyanthos, New Orleans, 1977, 30.
4. During the Spanish Regime, Bayou Castein was referred to by the Spanish as Pontchartrain Post.
5. Ellis, Frederick S., *St. Tammany Parish*, Pelican Publishing Company, Gretna, 1998, 70.
6. The "List of the French taking the Oaths of Allegiance" is found at Dunbar Rowland, *Mississippi Provincial Archives 1763-1766. English Dominion*, Volume 1, Nashville, 1911, 121-122.
7. Campeau, Anita R., and Sharp, Donald J., "British and Spanish Land Grants: From Bayou Castin to the Tchefuncte," *New Orleans Genesis*, Volume XLVII, April 2009, No. 186, 127-128.
8. *La Voix des Prairies No. 5*, " An Episode in the History of the Emigration of the Acadians to Louisiana". It includes a list of some German families who were on board the Bretana.
9. Hebert, Donald J. Rev., *Southwest Louisiana Records 1770-1893*, Volume 2, 545.
10. Pintado Papers, Microfilm Reel # SARS-2, Survey of Federal Archives, in the New Orleans Public Library, 71.

11. Ibid., 72.

12. Book A No. 2, 79-83, Greensburg.

13. British Florida Land Claims, Book 2, Part 2, 226. Special Collection, Tulane Library.

14. Ibid., 237.

15. Ibid., 238.

16. Ibid., 241.

17. McBee Papers, Natchez Court Records.

18. John Halley's Journal...of His Trip to New Orleans...1789 and 1791 is taken from Judge Samuel Wilson's photo static copy, collection number 49W31 copied from the original journal. Manuscript Collections & Archives, Service Center, Margaret I. King Library, University of Kentucky, Lexington, Kentucky.

19. Ellis, Frederick S., *St. Tammany Parish*, 60.

20. Ibid., 60.

21. Chidsey, Donald Barr, *Louisiana Purchase*, Crown Publishers, Inc., New York, 1972, 133.

CHAPTER 5

A DECADE OF TURMOIL, 1800-1810

In 1800, Napoleon Bonaparte compelled Carlos IV, King of Spain, to retrocede the colony of Louisiana to France by the secret treaty of San Ildefonso stipulating that it had to remain under Spanish control as long as France wished to postpone the transfer of power. Pierre Clément Laussat, authorized the transfer to France in early October, 1802, and gave authority to Governor Juan Manuel Salcedo, the tenth Spanish governor of Louisiana, and the Marques de Caso Calvo de Yrujo, where it was handed back to the French on November 30, 1801. Together with Salcedo, Caso delivered Louisiana to the French on April 10, 1803, but he remained in New Orleans after the American flag was raised.[1] The French prefect, Pierre Clément de Laussat arrived in New Orleans on March 23, 1803 and formally took control of Louisiana for France on November 30, only to hand it over to the United States on December 20.

Encouraged by President Jefferson, the Virginia gentleman and intellectual, who had won the trust of the westerners was elected president in a period of deep internal dissent, maneuvered the scheming behind the real estate deal that would affect the economy and ultimately bring unity to the shaky young republic.

The United States Commissioners in Paris signed an agreement to purchase the entire area originally claimed by France and ceded over to Spain in 1763. Since the Spanish already occupied the contested area of West Florida, the United States would not insist on its rights by means of military force, but would be patient and wait for the political atmosphere to change. Jefferson always hated the thought of war; he planned to get these provinces without recourse to it.

The Spanish officials at New Orleans were unhappy at Spain turning over control of Louisiana to France and then having France turn right around and selling to the United States. Some, like Intendant Juan Morales, did everything in their power to undercut the terms of the Treaty.

Americans watched the developments with genuine alarm. Spain in Louisiana was one thing – but France in Louisiana was another matter. President Jefferson expressed it best when he said: "The day that France takes possession of New Orleans…we must marry ourselves to the British fleet and nation." On another occasion he declared that "the inevitable consequences of their taking possession of Louisiana would be a war that would annihilate France on the ocean and place England in the control of the seas," a development he foresaw as dangerous for the United States. His fears were justified when on

October 16, 1802 Juan Ventura Morales performed his most controversial acts as Intendant of Louisiana. On the secret orders of his sovereign, he suspended the American right to deposit their merchandise at New Orleans. His "worst fears" were justified when on October 29, 1802, Governor Claiborne of the Mississippi Territory, informed him that the Mississippi River had been closed. Through Pinckney's Treaty signed on October 27, 1795, Spain had granted the United States "Right of Deposit" in New Orleans, allowing Americans to use the city's port facilities for only three years, but when the time expired, in 1798, the grant was not renewed, but the shipments kept rolling on as though good times had come to stay.

For Napoleon "the very last of his constructions was the sale of Louisiana. He needed the purchase-money; he selected his purchaser and forced it on him, with a view to up-building a giant rival to the gigantic power of Great Britain."[2] The peace of 1763 that ended the Seven Year's War was considered a bad peace because Great Britain, the victor, had been voracious in grabbing huge chunks of territory all over the world at the expense of France, the loser. France never forgave! It was not for attachment to the rebels that France agreed to help the thirteen colonies in their struggle against Great Britain. France's help made victory certain, and in the process Spain had been dragged into the contest.

Western and eastern men were back where they were in 1794. This brought the United States and Spain to the brink of war and the end of the Louisiana Purchase. Under bitter protest the right of deposit was restored after a five month's interval. Nevertheless reactions in Ohio, Kentucky, and Tennessee had been violent enough to cause President Jefferson to send James Monroe to France as minister extraordinary with instructions to join with Robert Livingston in an effort to purchase the Isle of Orleans and West Florida.

In the final agreement, the United States was to have Louisiana with the boundaries "that it now has in the hands of Spain and that it had when France possessed it." Not only had the United States bought a large territory, it had also purchased a boundary dispute. In colonial days, in the various wars between France, England and Spain surveys had never been made and definite boundaries fixed in the various treaties. Claims were advanced, but where were the exact lines between British Canada and Spanish Louisiana on the north? Was Texas included on the west, or whether West Florida was part of it, or included in the east? The expansionists under Jefferson wanted to make the best of the bargain, but there would be consequences for the future. It was to be one of the causes of the Mexican War of 1846-48 with the United States making the extraordinary claim that the Louisiana Purchase included all of Texas, its southwestern boundary being the Rio Grande, whereas Mexico citing the Neutral Ground Treaty, insisted that the boundary was the Sabine.

The Louisiana Purchase can be seen as the biggest real estate deal in history. The territory that changed hands, though the exact limits had not been established, was to be almost four times as large as the original thirteen colonies, more than seven times as Great Britain and Ireland put together, and about three times as big as Italy. It was learned eventually that the Purchase comprised 875,025 square miles. All the United States east of the Mississippi at that time contained 909,050 square miles. The annexation of Louisiana gave a new face to politics, and in the field of diplomacy it was unparalleled, because it had cost almost nothing, about four cents a square mile.

"An event so portentous as to defy measurement" the purchase of Louisiana removed the threat of European aggressions and restrictions which had greatly affected the United States, up to this time, were in large part removed. For Spain it would be little more than temptation and as for England it would not matter until English and American settlers met in Oregon. The Mississippi River would now run undisturbed from its source to its mouth through United States territory. The young nation had been given the freedom to expand in what would have been in the Old World half a dozen kingdoms.

Map: The Louisiana Purchase Territory- 1803

Juan Ventura Morales Hidalgo did not want to leave New Orleans after the ceremony of December 20, 1803. He had made a fortune as

65

Spanish Intendant of Louisiana and wanted to protect his wealth and continue as a Spanish official. It did not take long for some American merchants and land speculators to realize that money could be made with this "changing of the guard." Once again, as was the practice beginning in the 1760s, when England took the almost inhabited land of the two Floridas as her price for getting out of Cuba, the nations of Europe, as they had done after each war, tossed foreign lands back and forth across the bargaining table as if they were playing an international poker game. The lust for land was a national characteristic already imbedded when the young nation came into being. People responded to the lure of strange land. Soldiers and officers had been paid with land, but they had to travel far to get a glimpse of their property. But the land lay there to be tamed and settled. Soon there was a migration that is hard to explain. They knew that it would be a life of hardship, of toil, peril and loneliness. Nevertheless, they came carrying the frontier with them.

Don Manuel de Salcedo and the Marques de Caso Calvo published an edict on May 18, 1803, concerning the fact that the cession of Louisiana to the French Republic would not include West Florida. That the land from the Iberville River to the American line north and to the east of Pensacola and beyond would remain Spanish. This edict was founded on the right of conquest by which Spain took the settlements of Natchez and Baton Rouge from the British in the War of 1780. It wasn't long after the Edict that requests started to come into New Orleans to purchase large tracts of land in West Florida. It was assumed that after the transfer of Louisiana and New Orleans to the French Republic that the Spanish Officials would be pulling out of Pensacola.

The Louisiana Purchase brought some changes to West Florida: the old northern boundary, through the lakes, was once again an international boundary. There was less government by the Spanish since it was a relatively minor province.[3] With time, between the years 1803 and 1810 as more and more Americans moved into the Florida Parishes, the Spanish administrative control became weaker and weaker.

It will be recalled that many English speaking people who had desired to remain loyal subjects of His British Majesty had moved from the colonies along the Atlantic to West Florida, the English territory in the south. It was natural that they would be alarmed and disappointed over becoming Spanish subjects. However, Spain with its liberal policies, had allowed them to retain their lands and to a certain extent their life had not been too affected by this change.

In the tale of the two treaties, when news reached them that Spain had secretly transferred Louisiana to France, they were not too alarmed thinking that they would not be involved. But, when Napoleon Bonaparte broke his promise to Spain and offered to sell all of Louisiana to the United States for $15,000,000, they were overjoyed. They thought that West Florida would be annexed and, once again, would be under the rule of English-speaking people.

The boundaries of West Florida had never been clearly defined, and it now seemed that no one cared just where this vast territory began or ended. The citizens of West Florida were not alone in their disappointment nor were the residents of New Orleans, and those located west of the Mississippi who had expected immediate statehood. There was concern as to the restrictions placed upon them and requirements needed for admission to the United States. Promise had been received that they would be made a state when the population reached 60,000, but how long would they have to wait before a census would be taken? On March 26, 1804, Congress divided the newly acquired areas into two territories: The area north of 33° latitude became the Territory of Louisiana; the area south of this latitude (the boundary now between Arkansas and the state of Louisiana) was designated as the Territory of Orleans.[4]

The potential for both progress and disaster soon proved apparent during the Spanish period. The character of the economic base, on "the other side of the lake", although still based on cattle began to change slightly and growth of settlement to the north in the Mississippi territory proved an impetus for development. Early transportation was horseback or wagon and buggy. Products sent to Covington went over rough roads or if sent to New Orleans by schooner. Market trails, many built upon older Native American trade paths, soon traversed St. Tammany to the South's metropolis at New Orleans and another having its terminus near present day Covington and Baham Village, Madisonville after 1814. Development proved promising as probate records indicate that Juan Batiste Baham *dit* Gentil raised a large number of cattle, an area which emerged as an important terminus for cattle drives and other commodities transported overland and loaded onto schooners for transport to New Orleans. The increase in commerce led to an increase in the number of settlers desirous of establishing commercial enterprises along the market trails.

In the treaty discussions boundaries were not discussed nor were there talks about mines, or other amassments of materials, as if they did not exist in the territory. Nobody foresaw that cotton would become king in the south; that slavery as it was could not survive. In 1803 slavery did not loom as a menace, but who foresaw that it could not survive being an archaic and a disgusting institution that would bring a movement to bring about the greatest of all civil wars?

Politically, the ownership of the land north of the lakes called West Florida was in dispute between the United States and Spain. The U.S. claimed the land as included in the Louisiana Purchase and Spain claimed the land by conquest from Great Britain. These ambiguities made officials in Washington realize that they needed the United States Navy presence in New Orleans for security. United States Naval facilities at New Orleans were established during the years 1804 to 1826. The Spanish ruled the land, however sparsely with military personnel and could not defend it against the United States military action. Relationships were strained and fights broke out between Spanish and American seamen at different times.

There were gunboats on the Tchefuncte River some time between late October and December 1, 1806 when two United State's ship-or-war called "Jefferson Gun Boats" entered the mouth of the river and sailed up the three miles and anchored on the west bank opposite a little settlement which consisted of a few log cabins and huts built by Juan Baham and his sons. Baham had obtained his Spanish land grant about 1783 and had relocated from Mobile. The facts are in a statement by Carlos Trudeau, the Spanish surveyor who states that "he had found the Baham family living on their grant as of April 24, 1783." This means that they started living on the abandoned British grants before the Treaty of Peace signed in Paris on September 4, 1783.

The Spanish problem was a legacy of the Louisiana Purchase. It appears that in the final terms of that treaty, France had purposely left the boundaries of Louisiana ill-defined and despite repeated efforts by the American diplomats the French had refused to clarify them. Ambiguous wording implied: the Spanish boundaries of Louisiana were the same as when France possessed it prior to 1760. Spain later divided the Floridas into two administrative districts. It became clear to the Spanish that the United States coveted West Florida more than Upper Louisiana.

Spanish control was problematic in St. Tammany since they exercised no realistic authority over the territory. There was no police force in the region, although they tried to keep a small garrison on the north shore. By the eve of the Louisiana Purchase a condition of near anarchy prevailed in St. Tammany where thieves and desperadoes roamed the territory virtually free from molestation by the law. These circumstances led William C.C. Claiborne, the first American governor of Louisiana, to comment, "Civil authority remains weak and lax in West Florida especially in the region of Pearl River, where the influence of the law is scarcely felt."

The Spanish were meticulous at keeping records, and we are fortunate to be able to reconstruct activities from documents in the Spanish West Florida papers held in the Louisiana archives. Violence was rampant! The following anecdote is about a clamorous group of seven who crashed in on a "log rolling" event.[5]

When Alexander Bookter arrived in Spanish West Florida, *circa* 1798, he settled at a place called Wolf's Landing. He must have made a favorable impression of Governor Don Carlos de Grand-Pré in Baton Rouge because the Governor selected him to be Alcalde of the St. Helena District which included most of present day St. Helena, Livingston, Washington, Tangipahoa, and St. Tammany Parishes. An Alcalde (Al-cal'-de) was the Mayor or senior judicial official of a Spanish town, so Alexander represented the Spanish government in his area. Shortly after being selected as Alcalde probably the third of April in 1800, Alexander Bookter invited some of his neighbors to his plantation to dine and collect some timber from his land. He called it a "log rolling". In addition to his invited guest, Gabriel Burris and six of his friends came as uninvited guests. From Alexander's version and two of his invited guests, this is what happened that evening.

Alexander Bookter knew Gabriel Burris who had been brought up among the Choctaw Indians and was known to be a "master among blackguards". He definitely was not within Alexander's circle of friends. Gabriel soon became intoxicated and attacked one of the invited guests, a Mr. Joseph Sharp, but was restrained. (Mr. Sharp was later murdered by the alleged Irishman named William Flanagan.) Later, Burris attacked another guest, a Mr. Samuel Long, and had him down biting him on the finger and trying to gouge his eyes out. Alexander heard this disturbance and, as the Alcalde, ordered those around to separate the two. When his order was ignored, he ran to the house and asked his nephew to help him rescue Samuel Long. They were able to do this with considerable difficulty and brought Long back to the house.

According to the other two guests, Kay Hutchinson and Anna Spillars, Long was bloody and his finger had been bitten off. They heard Burris outside cursing and calling for Mink, Bookter's nephew, to come outside so he could whip him and Bookter and all of Bookter's protectors. Although Alexander Bookter and Mary Dawkins, his wife, told Mink to stay inside he ventured too close to the door. Burris dragged him out into the yard by his hair and began beating him. Alexander tried to get the other guests to help, but half of them were against Mink and the others were afraid to get involved. Alexander Bookter tried to jump into the fight but was beaten, dragged down and trampled on. He called on his slaves to help, and by the time he was able to get Mink into the house, Mink's eyes were swollen shut, some of his hair was torn out, and he had bite marks on his arm. Burris was then running after the slaves cursing and yelling that he would kill them and their dammed masters now that they were "free of Spanish law."

Evidently, there was an unconfirmed rumor that France had taken control of West Florida. The next morning Burris came to tell Mink he was sorry and to ask Mink to forgive him. However the Alcalde had other ideas. Burris was arrested and spent the next two years jailed at Fort San Carlos in Baton Rouge. Undoubtedly, Alexander Bookter was one of the most important men in Spanish West Florida and he seemed to have a knack at keeping his name in the news. In August of 1803 a petition was signed by friends of Burris asking for his release after two years and three months of confinement.

Another petition in October of 1804 was signed by fifty-one citizens of St. Helena District and charged that Bookter was disloyal to the Spanish government and cruel and unjust to the community at large. The petition asked that Bookter be expelled from Spanish West Florida. Alexander Bookter responded in a letter to the Governor that stated in part, "God knows I have been a true friend of the government and have acted with honor and truth."

During the investigation into this affair in February of 1805 disposition from four signers of this petition was taken. John Glasscock, William Bell, Daniel Raner, and William Bickham all stated that the signatures on the petition was not their own. Only William Bickham knew how to write. William Bell stated that, "Alexander Bookter had told the government that all the residents of St. Helena wanted to rise in rebellion." Bookter was not expelled and in October of 1807 he was selling town lots in Bookter's Landing.

In a letter to Governor Grand-Pré dated the thirteenth of March 1805, he refers to himself as "a resident and previously Alcalde of St. Helena," so his term may have been terminated after the investigation. In this letter, he asked the Governor to free a slave named Nelly. This request seems out of character for Bookter since he was one of the major slaveholders in Spanish West Florida. Perhaps this shows as a softer side of Bookter that was not always evident. Nelly had been sold by Joseph Bradford to Samuel Long and then stolen from Long by Bradford. According to several dispositions recorded in the Spanish West Florida papers, Bradford had been apprehended and along with Nelly was being taken to New Orleans in January of 1803 on a schooner that belonged to Bookter when they were allowed to escape. It appears that when Long tried to recover Nelly, Alexander appealed to the

Governor on her behalf. He stated that Long had left the Dominion and was living with the Indians.

The Gulf Coast served as a sanctuary and foraging ground for outlaws, political refugees, military deserters, fortune hunters, and a great variety of misfits and malcontents, and according to author Stanley Clisby Athur, "even more numerous...were the ruffians, thieves, and small-scale land speculators who loomed large among the frontiersmen spilling down from Kentucky and Tennessee."[6] William C. C. Claiborne, the first and only governor of Orleans Territory and later the first governor of the state of Louisiana, once described the people of Louisiana's "Florida parishes," which lie in old West Florida between the Mississippi River and the Pearl River, by saying that "a more heterogeneous mass of good and evil was never before met in the same extent of territory."[7]

There was a pattern to violence by those who fled to the region in order to avoid the more established system of justice in neighboring American controlled regions. The Spanish did not set up courts to handle disputes, and the forts only had small garrisons. It happened just a few weeks before the Kempers' abduction, a small detachment of "12 Spanish Light Horse" crossed into southeastern Wilkinson County near Ticksaw Creek in search of William Flanagan, an alleged murderer of Joseph Sharp, in order to extradite him. Joseph Sharp had settled at Cole's Creek, sixteen miles north of the Fort of Natchez where he married Elizabeth Richardson, daughter of George Richardson, in 1793. Their two children, Joseph and William Sharp, were sent to Bayou Castein to live with their uncle Zachariah Faircloth and his wife Martha Richardson.

According to a report by Thomas Holden, a local resident, the soldiers came to his house, inquired about the whereabouts of Flanagan, to which Holden reported "that he had not seen him for six months." After Holden kept insisting that he had not seen Flanagan, the soldiers, "at the point of a sword," angrily ordered him to accompany them. Luckily for Holden, friends appeared causing the Spaniards to scatter.

Shortly after this incident, Governor Grand-Pré requested Governor Williams to extradite Flanagan for the premeditated murder of Joseph Sharp. Williams refused to comply, but the Spanish later caught the elusive Flanagan, took him to the international boundary, and there threatened to imprison him indefinitely unless he would agree to surrender his horse, saddle and bridle on the spot. Not surprisingly, Flanagan gladly returned home on foot.[8] Sharp notes of protests were sent by Williams to Grand-Pré who then placed the territorial militia in alert. Lt. Colonel John Ellis of the Fifth Militia Regiment was ordered to place two companies along the border; one at Ticksaw, the other at Pinckneyville. The guards had been ordered to "examine all equivocal characters passing the line from below and especially if at night."[9] These precautions gave rise to a false rumor, supposedly spread by Colonel Henry Hunter that the governor planned to take Baton Rouge.[10]

By leaving the eastern boundary indefinite, the French had subtly prepared the ground for conflict, and not surprisingly trouble came in 1804 when unrest broke out along two of the territory's southern borders. The first was the area of Baton Rouge (Feliciana District) which stretched along the eastern bank of the Mississippi River, just below the international boundary. The second was the Mobile-Tensaw District. Between the years 1801-1803, Louisiana had changed rulers three times creating a climate ripe for intrigue and unrest.

Settlers were not as patient as diplomats abroad or at home, and local agitators were unwilling to wait for Jefferson's peaceful tactics. His strategy with respect to West Florida was "amicable negotiations." He would do it by migration, and was eager to transform the Tombigbee District (Washington County) into a haven for industrious settlers. Given these circumstances it was only a matter of time before disturbances erupted. Conflagrations occurred not in the Bigbee District where grievances were particularly pronounced but in the western part of West Florida at Feliciana. There were advantages: the area was a hotbed of land speculation with several absentee claimants who planned to dispose of their claims by selling them to the flow of expected settlers who would be eager to buy with ready cash. Then came land speculators who were much more than real estate agents, for they played a part in advertising the West for American settlement. They stirred up Western indignation against Spain and discontent with the Union. And it was these speculators who forced the issue of controversy between their government and Spain, for the success of their speculative schemes depended upon the free use of the Mississippi.[11]

Born in Fauquier County, Virginia, The Kemper brothers, Reuben, Samuel, and Nathan had moved to Feliciana about 1802 as agents of Senator John Smith of Ohio who, three years before the Louisiana Purchase, acquired 750 acres in Feliciana Parish near the village of St. Francisville located equidistant between Baton Rouge and the international border. The Kempers owned land in both the Feliciana District of Spanish West Florida and nearby Pinckneyville, Mississippi. They were expelled from the province by the Spanish authorities in a dispute over land titles.

The brothers were among the most prominent troublemakers in West Florida. The uncouth, boozing and violent trio was once described by a Spanish official in the area as "white Indians and river pirates".[12] The Kemper "raids" or the Kemper "rebellion" has long been interpreted by American historians as a symptom of growing Anglo American dissatisfaction with Spanish rule in the late colonial period. The thinking was that Spain maintained an ineffective presence. The Kemper brothers helped shape much of this thinking through their efforts to proclaim West Florida a republic in 1804 - one complete with flag and declaration of independence authored by Edmond Randolph. They attempted to capture Baton Rouge in 1804, but were defeated, having failed to gain the support of local Anglo-Americans, mostly satisfied with Spanish rule on account of Spain's liberal policy of land grants and its protection of slavery.

From 1804 to 1810 they engaged in attempts to expel the Spanish from West Florida and actively sought Anglo-Americans to engage in their filibuster. Beginning in June, their gang of ruffians terrorized the area for several months, crossing and re-crossing the border into United States territory, using the border as a means of escaping the Anglo-American-staffed Spanish militia avowing that their aim was to overthrow the Spanish colonial regime by the district residents and invite what they termed "a more stable American government in the area." Similar to the James Willing expedition, the raiders stole slaves and other property and left burning buildings, and injured residents. The Spanish government was determined to run the Kempers to ground.

The following year they were captured by Spanish forces while on U.S. soil, but were rescued by U. S. forces as they were being taken down the Mississippi River. American officials publicly deplored the exploits of the Kemper brothers and cautioned others against engaging in rebellious activities. In fact Jefferson found them useful in furthering his strategy of annexation, both he and the Kemper brothers had similar grievances and common objectives, but they differed in the methods for redressing the complaints and securing the desired goods. In 1804, urged by President Jefferson, Congress passed the Mobile Act to solidify their claim that the Louisiana Purchase included West Florida, but under the protests of Spain's minister to the United States, rather than risk war with Spain, Jefferson held the course, anticipating that with his policies for migration it would eventually tilt the balance in favor of the United States.[13]

In 1810 during the rebellion against Spanish rule by the British and American settlers, who made up the majority of inhabitants, Reuben Kemper and Joseph White were authorized to invite the inhabitants of Mobile and Pensacola to join in the revolt. Kemper crossed into Mississippi Territory but U.S. forces, not wishing to provoke Spain into war, and fearing Kemper's intentions, arrested him. He was more fortunate than his colleagues, who were seized by the Spanish and sent as prisoners to Havana, Cuba. The Kemper attempts to win independence, although unsuccessful, was only a temporary delay, because four years later in 1810 the rebellion of West Florida overthrew Spanish rule and established the Republic of Florida.

NOTES

1. The Cuban born Casa Calvo (1751-?) participated in the re-conquest of Louisiana by Spain in 1769. He fought in the campaign at Mobile in 1780, but a hurricane prevented him from fighting at Pensacola. Manuel Gayoso de Lemos died in 1799, and was replaced by Casa Calvo sent by the captain general of Cuba to take the military command of Louisiana which he did on September 18. The following June, he was succeeded by Juan Manuel de Salcedo. Together with Salcedo, he delivered Louisiana to the French on April 10, 1803, but he remained in New Orleans after the American flag was raised. He led an expedition in 1805-1806 with Nicolas de Finiels into western Louisiana and Texas. After an analysis of his mission and presidial records at Nacogdoches and survey of the jurisdiction of Los Adaes, he was convinced of the just claims of Spain to territory as far east as Arroyo Hondo, which formed the boundary between Louisiana and Texas. Upon his return to New Orleans, Governor Claiborne expelled him from Louisiana. In March 1806 he asked permission to lead a military expedition against Louisiana. To him, it was the only hope of saving Spanish North America from the rapacious conquest by Anglo-Americans. (Charles Gayarré, A History of Louisiana (4 volumes, New York: Widdleton, 1866.)
2. Sloane, William M., "The World Aspects of the Louisiana Purchase," *American Historical Review*, Volume 9, 1903-04.
3. Ellis, Frederick S., *St. Tammany Parish*, Pelican Publishing Company, Gretna, 1998, 65.
4. McGinty, Garnie Williams, *A History of Louisiana*, pub. Exposition Press, New York City, 1949, 88-111.
5. Email communication between Don Sharp and Anita Campeau dated Tuesday, July 29, 2008.
6. Arthur, Stanley Clisby, *The Story of the West Florida Rebellion*, St. Francisville, LA., St. Francisville Democrat,
7. Cox, Isaac Joslin, *The West Florida Controversy, 1798-1818: A Study in American Diplomacy*, Baltimore, John Hopkins Press, 1918, 507.
8. Haynes, V. Robert, *The Mississippi Territory and the South West Frontier: 1795-1817*, University Press of Kentucky, 2010, 29.
9. Ibid., 114.
10. Ibid., 114.

11. Whitaker, Arthur Preston, *The Spanish-American Frontier: 1783-1795. The Westward Movement and the Spanish Retreat in the Mississippi Valley*, Boston:Houghton Mifflin Co., 1927, 48-49.

12. Cox, Isaac Joslin, *The West Florida Controversy, 1798-1818*, 154.

13. Smith, Gene A., "Our Flag Was Displayed Within Their Works": The Treaty of Ghent and the Conquest of Mobile, *Alabama Review* 52, January 1999, 3-20.

CHAPTER 6

THE WEST FLORIDA REBELLION OF 1810

When the United States made the purchase of Louisiana, in 1803, it was for French Louisiana and the Isle of Orleans. In 1810, Spanish West Florida was still a sparsely settled area lying between the Pearl and Mississippi rivers, and North and East of Lake Pontchartrain. Its boundary lines, indefinite, were therefore vulnerable and in dispute. The Florida Parishes of Louisiana: Livingston, East Baton Rouge, St. Tammany, Tangipahoa, Washington and West Feliciana were not a part of the Louisiana Purchase. The region remained a part of Spanish West Florida. The designation of the region as the "Florida Parishes" was derived from the area's time as a distinct and separate entity known as "West Florida". Though most of Louisiana and a large part of the United States were acquired through complicated negotiations and diplomatic means of buying it from France, the history of the Florida Parishes was far more violent and convoluted.

With the land filling up with Americans from the east, mostly farmers and tradesmen of Scottish and English descent, many of whom were still instilled with the spirit and dreams from the Revolutionary days, with their land still under the domination of the Spanish king, resented the European manner of conducting government. The planters had expected to become a part of the American territory with the Louisiana Purchase. In the failure of the United States to annex the territory, they were frustrated because they had been excluded. A Spanish argument was that Napoleon could not sell what he did not own. President Jefferson's reasoning was that "navigation of the Mississippi could not be secure as long as West Florida remained under Spanish rule."

The years between 1803 and 1810 saw an influx in the population of West Florida as more Anglo-Americans removed to the area since the Spanish were fairly generous in granting land to settlers. Some came to establish new homes while others to engage in conspiracies against the weak Spanish government. West Florida was multicultural. It had a strange population of traders, land speculators, fleeing debtors, fugitives and others of infamous backgrounds.

Those who resided on significant Spanish land grants that American control could have threatened remained loyal to Spain. For those who enjoyed the absence of taxation and the *laissez-faire* attitude practiced by the Spanish government, had no objections to Spanish rule. The Spanish administration made concessions to the inhabitants, but the more made, the greater became the demands for a voice in their government. As a result, Spanish administrative control grew weaker.

Thomas Lilley, a syndic of the Plains area wrote a letter dated December 4, 1808, to Governor Grand-Pré, citing "prevalent unrest" of the people. West Florida could be compared to a colony of angry ants. Lilley suggested to the Governor that he should call a meeting of the syndics and alcaldes at some central place to discuss "the best means of quieting the public mind."[1] The residence tavern of John Murdock on Thompson's Creek was chosen. Mr. Murdock was known to be a loyal Spanish citizen who was quite satisfied with conditions as they existed. At the appointed day and time the syndics and alcaldes met, and nominated William Harris as presiding officer. He declined in "favor of Thomas Lilley, the syndic from Feliciana", who seems to have been the prime mover."[2]

After endless discussions, it was agreed by the assembly that a petition would be drawn and presented to the officials at Pensacola. Among their request, Grand-Pré should be allowed to remain as Governor because he had the confidence of the people and it was unanimously felt that a new governor would not be accepted by the people. Request signed, the meeting was adjourned until December 21 when they would again meet.

The Spanish officials did not appreciate the repeated requests, and in the spring of 1809 Don Carlos de Lassus replaced Governor Grand-Pré who was removed to Havana where he died of a broken heart before he stood trial for his French sympathies.[3]

Not a popular figure, Governor Lassus was disliked mainly because he delegated his authority to men who were not responsible officials. The measures attempted to secure to a degree some traditional English liberties, within the framework of their Spanish government, culminated in a convention of the people meeting in June 1810 to press for some constitutional guarantees. It was not a vintage year for Spain! The added turmoil of the Napoleonic Wars sparked revolt in Spanish possessions throughout the Western Hemisphere from Texas to South America.

Most of the support for the West Florida rebels was concentrated in the wealthy Feliciana District near the border of the Mississippi Territory. In the districts of Tangipahoa and Chifoncte, which included St. Tammany, there was little overt evidence of support for the rebels. Bayou Castein was not the theatre of action during the West Florida Rebellion, but its citizens could identify with most of the grievances, especially the lawlessness that created so much havoc.

The West and East Florida Boundaries, the theatre of action, gleaned from Arthur Clisby Stanley, *The Story of the West Florida Rebellion*, St. Francisville Democrat, 1935, text in the public domain.

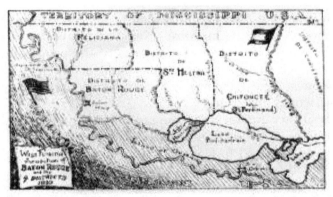

The West Florida Jurisdiction of Baton Rouge and its four districts in 1810. (Courtesy of the Louisiana Collection, State Library, Louisiana, U.S.)

On Saturday, June 23, 1810 the planters of West Feliciana took matters in their own hands by calling a meeting at the farm of Mr. Sterling. His plantation was known as "Egypt" Plantation, and is known as "Rosalie" today.[4] The "secret meeting" was no secret since about 500 Spanish citizens had heard word of it. News reached Governor de Lassus who sent two trusted friends, Philip Hickey and George Mather Sr., to attend the meeting and report. Over 500 citizens attended the meeting at Mr. Sterling's. After much discussion on grievances, John Hunter Johnson, William Barrow, John Mills and John Rhea were duly elected to attend a general council that would include representatives from the districts of Baton Rouge, St. Helena, and Chifoneté (*sic*).

Hickey and Mather, after hearing the various grievances brought forward, were won over to the side of those who fomented independence from Spain, but kept their attitudes to themselves and reported to Governor Lassus that "he had nothing to fear" for they were loyal to him, but wanted a greater voice in government.

On July 25, 1810, a convention of men, who at this time did not anticipate revolution, from the various districts of West Florida, was held to list their grievances. William Cooper, a staunch Spanish loyalist, represented the "District of Tanchipaho and Chifuncte."[5] The main grievances brought forward were: that the country was a place of refuge for deserters and fugitives from Justice of the neighboring States and Territories; another was the neglect of laws respecting roads, slaves, and livestock. It was ordered that a committee of five members be appointed to plan a draft for the redress of the existing grievances, and that the said elected committee would report to the convention by Bill or otherwise. Duly elected were the following men: John H. Johnson, Thomas Lilley, John W. Leonard, Philip Hicky and John Mills.[6]

These grievances plus others related to methods of taxation, neglect of petitions filed by the citizens, inability of settlers to obtain land titles from the government, and the failure to prescribe punishments for assault and battery and slander, and several other demands resulted in concessions by Lassus, but in doing so he placed himself at the mercy of the Convention.[7]

Shepherd Brown, representing the District of St. Helena, was not keen on these meetings because he had received many favors from the Governor, therefore was completely loyal to the Spanish. William Cooper, a former British loyalist from North Carolina and Georgia, and now a faithful supporter of the Spanish King, represented the District of Tangipahao and Chifuncte. He accepted the responsibility because as an alcalde he had often been frustrated by the difficulties he had faced in administering justice. Cooper later refused to go along with the more extravagant demands of the convention, and at some point, when it appeared that the members were about to declare independence from Spain, he excused himself from the convention and returned to his home on the Tangipahoa River.

A small group of rebels now secretly organized to overthrow Spanish rule to carve out a tiny, independent nation. Its leaders would deal harshly with opponents to either Independence or U.S. annexation. The rebels were aware that if they were not successful, they faced the hangman's noose or incarceration at Morro Castle in Havana, Cuba, if accused of treason.

On September 12, 1810, William Cooper dictated a letter to Spanish Governor Folch in Pensacola.[8] The letter was delivered by Captain Luis Piernas who returned to Pensacola and personally delivered the letter to Governor Folch in early October.[9] Cooper's letter begins: "At this dangerous time it is my duty to give you information of the dangerous situation of the jurisdiction of Baton Rouge,"[10] He then explained to the Governor that he had served as a delegate to the convention but being in the minority in support for the Spanish Crown, he now believed that the convention was on the verge of declaring independence from Spain. He asked Folch to quickly send troops immediately to thwart the impending rebellion.[11]

Awaiting Spanish reinforcement from Pensacola, on the Natalbany River, he and Shephard Brown with a group of Spanish loyalists from the Tangipahoa District began the construction of a fort near today's Springfield in the hope of holding out until the requested troops arrived. Cooper also organized a militia company to support the Spanish. At Springfield, John Ballinger who had recently emigrated there from Kentucky, was told that Michael Jones and William Cooper were "erecting a fort on the Nictalbany under the instructions of Shephard Brown" [as a base for troops expected from Pensacola]. Ballinger related this information to Colonel Philemon Thomas and urged prompt action.[12] It was in 1805 that Philemon Thomson, a native of Virginia, moved his family to what was then Spanish Florida where he purchased land and operated a store at Baton Rouge. He had joined the Revolutionary War at the age of thirteen, and at the end of the conflict, the once child soldier was discharged as an officer. During the summer of 1810, he was made local militia commander.

On Saturday, September 22, 1810, Colonel Philemon Thomas went to Springfield and, assisted by John Ballinger, mustered a "grenadier company" of 44 men. They returned to Baton Rouge and were joined by some 21 mounted men from Feliciana. That night General Thomas led the forces in revolt against the Spanish authority. This little "army" attacked Fort San Carlos at Baton Rouge, killed the commandant and imprisoned the governor and other Spanish officials.[13] They lowered the Spanish flag and raised the Bonnie Blue Flag, a single white star on a blue field, that had been adopted for the new nation they called West Florida. Four days later, on September 26, 1810, John Rhae, president of the West Florida convention, signed a Declaration of Independence and set up a government for the new nation that historians say included about 4,000 people.

Cooper's prediction of "an impending rebellion" proved true when in September the Spanish fort at Baton Rouge was taken by the rebels of West Florida. Philemon Thomas continued with his forces through the countryside to secure control from Spanish loyalists.

On September 30th, fearing local opposition to the revolution in the districts of St. Helena and Chifuncte, the convention ordered Philemon Thomas, the Brigadier General, to take a detachment to those areas. His orders read that he could "resort to force chiefly for the purpose of securing designing and unprincipled men who have attempted to mislead those inhabitants. Under suspicion was a member of our body, and one of the judges of the Supreme Court, William Cooper and Shephard Brown who could be of the number."[14] The Brigadier was advised to be prudent and was to use the proper measures to take them into custody so they could be brought to answer the charges to be laid upon them. General Thomas was to carry a copy of their declaration of the Independence of this Commonwealth, and receive the signatures of such as may choose to support it. General Thomas was given the following proclamation to use in enticing the people to join the revolution:

"Inhabitants of St. Helena & St. Ferdinand! The Convention call on you for the last time to unbosom yourselves to Genl. Will abandon you at the hour of danger, by a man who accepted, meaning to betray, an appointment from the Convention of the highest trust & importance to the People, you will no longer suffer yourselves to be misled by the Cameleon, Brown; & much less by the Traitor from our own Bosom, whose Murderous cruelties, even at an age when the youth of his Beard might have taught the most criminal in lieu of the most innocent Captives, to expect mercy, will not allow him to remain quiet.- Cooper! After approving, & sanctioning with his signature all our Ordinances, endeavored with Brown to stir your bloods to anarchy & discord."[15]

Shepherd Brown, penned the "Cameleon" by the rebels, was born April 16, 1776, the son of William Brown, early property owner and developer of Shepherdstown, Virginia, and Elizabeth, daughter of Thomas Shepherd and Elizabeth Van Metre. Shepherd Brown's maternal grandfather, Thomas, was an early American settler and patriot whose five sons served in the Revolutionary War. In memory of these heroes, a bronze plaque on the fence at the Shepherd Family Cemetery was placed by the Lafayette Chapter, Sons of the American Revolution, Akron, Ohio.

Brown arrived in New Orleans in 1800 as an associate of Baltimore merchant William Taylor. He associated with two other Taylor colleagues, William O. Payne and John McDonough. The Brown Company pursued the newly developing western trade, purchasing agricultural products from up river for eventual transshipment to eastern markets. The relationship of McDonough and Brown with William Taylor broke down in early 1805. In February of that year Shephard Brown and Company was dissolved, possibly due to Brown's ill health. In 1805 Brown retired to his plantation in St. Helena, where he was appointed commandant and alcalde by the Spanish rulers of

West Florida. It was Brown who greased Spanish palms to secure for McDonough "worthless" lands in the cypress swamps along the Iberville, Amite and Comite rivers. William Cooper was an adherent of Shephard Brown.

Thomas Brown was captured by the Rebels in 1775. The real fighting in Georgia started in 1776. The violence and animosities were kindled by a revolutionary fervor that resulted in a struggle that resembled more a civil war than a revolution. It takes some research before you can place an ancestor in a specific regiment and ultimately at a specific battle, especially during a rebellion. Historical accounts state that Henry Cooper Sr. and his young sons William and Henry Cason Cooper, and their probable uncle, Samuel Cooper, of Effingham County, Georgia, served in Major James Wright's Corps, also known as the Georgia Loyalists Regiment. This regiment later became a part of King's Carolina Rangers which was commanded by Thomas Brown.

The Coopers fought against their Patriot neighbors for the cause of George III. More than thirty years later, the stories of William Cooper's Loyalist activities when he was a youth were used to incite anger against him among the citizens of West Florida. They were reminded of the young Cooper's "... Murderous cruelties, even at an age when the youth of his Beard might have taught the most criminal...to expect mercy..."[16] Strong assertions that need clarification! Who was this William Cooper? Why labeled a "traitor"? What monstrous cruelties could he have committed at such an early age?

Briefly, what follows is the story of the Cooper family's journey from North Carolina to Georgia, their involvement in the Revolutionary War, their banishment, their escape to St. Augustine, and their relocation to Natchez, West Florida, where they received land grants from the Spanish.

Henry Couper Sr., in 1770, sold his property in Pitt County, North Carolina, and moved his wife and five children to the area now called Effingham, Georgia. Here he received a headright. The Cooper family settled in the Bark Camp community near the Ogeechee River. Called Bark Camp community because the Indians had shown the settlers how to build houses by using round trees with the bark left on. Freely translated, the Ogeechee would be the "River of the Uchees". The Ogeechee referred to a sub-tribe of the Creek Confederation. The British settlers called the stream "Hogeechee".

When the American Revolution began, Henry Couper Sr., and his two eldest sons: William C. and Henry Cason Cooper, and their possible uncle, Samuel Cooper, became embroiled in the violent civil war-like fervor, which was inspired by the bad blood between the Loyalists and the Patriots of Georgia. Unlike many Georgians, who traded loyalties to suit their needs, the Coopers were staunch Loyalists and remained faithful to their King, George III.

A December 1781 deposition from a soldier named Mark King is the only known Revolutionary-era document known that sheds light on the activities of the Cooper brothers as soldiers. King, a captured Loyalist deserter from Savannah, informed his captors that he was not a willing Loyalist. He swore that he was captured or kidnapped on the Ogeechee River, just below Horse Creek, by William and Henry Cooper. He testified that he was led to believe that if he did not join them he would be put aboard a prison ship and taken to the West Indies. But most important, he gave valuable information to his patriot captors concerning Loyalist strategy and weapons and said that he had fought with Major Wright's Corps.[17]

The regiment was commanded by Colonel Thomas Brown, an early outspoken loyalist from Yorkshire, England, who with a group of colonists migrated to Georgia in 1774 and established the community of Brownsborough northeast of present day Augusta. He was soon engaged in the coming revolution when on August 2, 1775, a crowd of Sons of Liberty confronted him at his house. Brown requested the liberty to hold his own opinions, and finally met their demands with pistol and sword. He was taken prisoner with a fractured skull, tied to a tree where he was roasted by fire, scalped, tarred and feathered. He survived, and this mistreatment resulted in the loss of two toes and lifelong headaches. He then lived a turbulent and combative career.

In September 1780, Colonel Brown succeeded in maintaining a stout defense against Elijah Clarke's attack at First Battle of Augusta, holding fortified Mackay House until the arrival of a relief force. It appears that Brown captured twelve rebels, plus the young son of the American rebel leader Captain McKay. The order to hang the rebels came from British General Lord Cornwallis. When American Colonel Elijah Clarke beat a hasty retreat back to North Carolina, he was hounded by Indians and loyalists. Cornwallis dispatched a force of loyalists under the command of Lt. Colonel Patrick Ferguson to cut off Clarke's band. Instead, his friends from the mountains swarmed down under their own leaders, caught Ferguson on King's Mountain, and scored a decisive victory on October 7, 1780. Clarke's raid upon Augusta triggered the events that led to King's Mountain and Cooper was remembered for the part he played in the hanging of the thirteen Rebel prisoners.

McKay's mother came to the camp and tried to plead with Colonel Thomas Brown for her son's life. Her pleas were not heard. She was escorted out of the camp. Brown's career was later vilified, and according to Joan E. Cashin's research there is no historical evidence that Brown did anything beyond his duty according to the recognized rules of war. It is unlikely that he hanged the thirteen prisoners, one a thirteen year old boy, at the Mackay House "with savage relish". What part the young William Cooper played in this affair is not known, but this possibly could be the incident referred to when the activities of his youth were used to incite anger against him among the citizens of West Florida. There is no proof that the Coopers were in on the hangings of the rebels, but it is known that they would stop at nothing to defeat the Patriots.

In another incident, Captain Henry Cooper along with Captain Johnson and their troops attacked the Lt. Governor of Georgia's home and took all of the Lt. Governor's slaves into South Carolina and sold them to raise money for the loyalist forces. Because of this bold attack, the Governor of Georgia put bounties on the heads of all the Coopers. At one point it would appear that the Coopers planned to kill the Governor of Georgia. It has not been established if the Coopers were at the siege of Savannah. When the war ended, they did not surrender, and continued to create problems for the fledgling Georgia government. They even intercepted Governor Martin's letters and messages when his soldiers stopped for dinner one evening at a home near Brier Creek, Georgia.

The British surrender in the fall of 1781 should have brought peace to the Georgia backcountry, but there were just too many unhealed wounds. Laws were passed by the new state of Georgia and the names of all men judged as traitors to the Patriot cause were listed county by county and published in Georgia newspapers and were ordered to leave within sixty days. Should one decide to return to Georgia, he would be tried and executed. All their property and livestock were to be confiscated and sold. Henry Couper Senior, his two sons, and Samuel, the probable uncle, were listed among the traitors from Effingham County, Georgia. The Cooper cattle was also tallied and sold.[18]

The Georgia backcountry was a dangerous place where desperate Loyalists with nothing left to lose were plundering boats, and stealing horses and cattle as a means to support their families. There were other outlaws in the territory taking advantage of the lawlessness in the countryside.

The Coopers were driven out of Georgia by Major Patrick Carr, whose job it was to rid the Georgia backcountry of all die-hard Loyalists. Ultimately, Carr found the Coopers in the fall of 1783 at Rocky Ford, Georgia, and ultimately gave chase. The Cooper family and their group were pursued all the way to St. Mary's River, the border of Georgia and East Florida where Carr gave up the chase due to the fact that East Florida was not a part of the United States.[19]

Just prior to their arrival, St. Augustine had been turned over to Spain by the British. The Spanish Crown ordered the evacuation of all British Loyalists. The Cooper refugees learned that they had just been expelled from yet another country.

Enticed by the news that the Spanish Crown was giving out Spanish land grants in the Natchez District, the Coopers, who had nothing left to lose, pinned their hopes on Natchez and Spain. They pledged their loyalty to Spain in order to receive those land grants. This oath of loyalty was something that the Coopers did not take lightly. William and Henry Cason Cooper remained loyal to Spain, as a result of this. Henry Couper Sr. died in Natchez about 1792. He had lived long enough to see his sons prosper in their new home.

William C. Cooper obtained two Spanish land grants and Henry Cason Cooper obtained one. When Spain turned over Natchez to the United States around 1798, William and Henry Cooper demonstrated their disdain for the United States by selling out their land grants and moving to West Florida. Their younger brother, Samuel, bought one of William's land grants on Sandy Creek outside of Natchez. Samuel remained in Natchez.[20]

In 1800, Henry Cason Cooper purchased 640 acres on the west side of Tangipahao River from Jeremiah and Elizabeth Strickland. In 1801, he was granted 640 acres directly from the Spanish Crown, by settlement, on Black River, now called Black Creek, just outside of Madisonville. Henry moved his family to this grant and made it his permanent home. He named his plantation, Cooper's Oaks.[21]

In 1810, some American rebels from Feliciana remembered events that took place in Georgia nearly 30 years earlier. At Baton Rouge, the new government issued orders for the arrest of Brown, Jones and William Cooper. Meanwhile, at Springfield, Brown and Michael Jones continued to recruit settlers favorable to the Spanish regime to assist Governor Folch in putting down the rebellion. Shepherd Brown had succeeded in enlisting about eighty men, sixteen of which were left in the stockade at Springfield, while he used the others to reconnoiter the country. After four or five days, he returned, dispirited at his failure to raise his boasted five hundred loyalists. Brown and Cooper held the small Spanish fort on the Natalbany River until they realized the rebel force was near and defeat was inevitable. Brown advised his followers to disperse and save themselves. He set them the example, by taking a boat for New Orleans, but was later captured and suffered a brief imprisonment.[22] Captain Michael Jones, earlier called a Loyalist, made common cause with the rebels.

The aftermath of the attack of the fort at Springfield illustrates how the rebels felt toward William Cooper. He had abandoned the convention with probably a few choice words about what he thought about their plans.[23] From the many Cooper documents that exist today, it is evident that William Cooper was a diligent and hard-working individual who had earned the trust and respect of his superiors and neighbors in the Tangipahao District. A final vote of trust for William Cooper was when he was chosen by the citizens of his district to represent at the west Florida Convention. This trust propelled Cooper toward his "ultimate downfall". They later caught up with William Cooper near the Tchefuncte River. He was captured and purportedly killed as he tried to escape. His home was burned, and his cattle were slaughtered by the rebels.[24] Noted historians of the West Florida Rebellion, Isaac Joslin Cox and Stanley Clisby Arthur, appear to agree that William Cooper was captured and killed by the rebels in early October 1810. It is historically evident that Cooper was despised by the rebels for his efforts to derail their rebellion.

For the second time in his life, William Cooper had fought on the losing side and was now judged as the "bad guy". Lest we forget, atrocities happened on both sides of the American Revolution. We have to view each side for what they were, soldiers in a terrible war. They did what they did either for the British Crown or for the Americans. It appears that the effects of the American Revolution were still felt or used as propaganda twenty-seven years later in West Florida with the killing of the former loyalist William Cooper whom they associated with horrible deeds.

The independent nation of West Florida became known as the "Original Lone Star Republic." The residents of the new nation created an assembly, proclaimed St. Francisville as their capital, and elected Fulwar Skipwith as their president before being forcibly annexed by the Americans in December 1810.

The West Florida Government was formally inaugurated by November 26, 1810. A month earlier on October 27, 1810, President James Madison issued a proclamation declaring that the lands lying south of the Mississippi River to the Perdido belonged to United States under the terms of the Treaty of Paris dated April 30, 1803. The president directed Governor William C.C. Claiborne, of the Orleans Territory, to take possession of the new nation.

Governor Claiborne left for Natchez on December 1, 1810, to work out arrangements for the occupation of West Florida. Captain John Shaw who was returning down the Mississippi River by way of

Pittsburg for his second tour of duty at the New Orleans Station joined Governor Claiborne at St. Francisville on December 8. Governor Claiborne had received the proclamation from President Madison who had declared West Florida United States Territory. The president had ordered the Governor to take control of the disputed territory and raise the American flag, by force if necessary.

When Captain Shaw met Governor Claiborne, at St. Francisville, he found out that the Governor had raised the flag the previous day. The Governor continued down the river to Baton Rouge accompanied by Captain Shaw and five gunboats of the River Division, stationed at Natchez, under the command of Lt. Daniel Patterson, to transport the troops downriver. The gunboats first transported the 400 American troops to about two miles above the Fort. There they met Governor Claiborne supported by a force under the command of Colonel Leonard Covington coming down the river road with the Mississippi mounted Dragoons.

After the soldiers were landed, the gunboats dropped down the river and anchored in a line opposite the fort. Their heavy 32 pound cannons pointed on the fort were primed and ready to fire. It was an enormous force to contend with! Fulwar Skipwith who had been elected Governor of the newly declared Lone Star Republic by the Legislature on November 22, 1810, realized that it was useless to resist and ordered the gate to the fort to be opened. With the gunboats covering the landing of the troops, the American flag was quickly raised, and the short life of that nation came to an end. The 15-starred flag of the U.S. became the sixth flag to fly over the Florida Parishes and St. Tammany.[25]

Captain Shaw then proceeded down the river to New Orleans. A letter dated December 24, 1810, written by Lt. Merrill from the Tchefuncte River awaited Shaw's answer. The Tchefuncte River had been a main port and repair facility, next to Bayou St. John, for the gun vessels on the lakes and Gulf Coast since 1807. In his letter Lt. Merrill related to the Captain of the "lawlessness" and "depredations" going on the Tchefuncte and asked for his responsibilities. He was reminded that as an officer in the navy, it was his duty to give protection to any citizen that asked for it, and he was to assist any officer of the law appointed by the Governor to restore and keep order. A reason the people were in such a hostile mood was because of the treatment given to William Cooper and his family.

As for Shepherd Brown, he was captured on October 5 and taken to Baton Rouge where he joined ex-governor de Lassus in the "jug". The two were released on December 8. Brown returned to his plantation on the Amite River and quietly became an American citizen. After the

Florida parishes were annexed by the United States, he was appointed a parish judge. He died in Baltimore in January 1818.

De Lassus was repatriated to Havana where officials arrested him and put him on trial for his loss of the colony of West Florida.[26]

The rise and fall of the Republic of West Florida presents us with few genuine heroes. Of those who took action at the scene, all the leaders with the possible exception of Fulwar Skipwith, the republic's president, seem to have been land grabbers, adventurers, or job-seekers."[27] Early on the revolutionaries revealed their ulterior motives in an early October convention, they laid claim to all the unoccupied lands in the territory, because they had "wrested the Government and country from Spain at the risk of their lives and fortunes."[28]

Fulwar Skipwith, who had lost his position as a U.S. diplomat in Paris, was now seeking to recover his political career and financial standing in West Florida ended up as registrar of the U.S. government land office in charge of filings on lands between the Pearl River and the Mississippi.[29]

Philemon Thomas who had led the attack on the Spanish garrison at Baton Rouge declared after the U.S. takeover that "the great object he had in view was now accomplished, and that he approved of the taking."[30] After the annexation of the West Florida Republic on December 10, Louisiana territory governor described Philemon Thomas as "the ajax of the late revolution, who [has] always been esteemed an honest man." He was a hero to the people of the Baton Rouge and Feliciana Parish, a man whom they could compare to George Washington.

The history of the breakaway of the West Florida Republic is rather complicated, but unique. It is the only region in the United States which can identify with every major European government that ruled the area. The Parish has seen more flags flying than most other U.S. territories: The Royal Spanish flag, the French *Fleur de lis*, the British Union Jack, the Spanish National Flag, the U.S. flag, the flag of the West Florida Republic, the Louisiana Secession flag, the Confederate National flag, and the Louisiana State flag, for a total of nine different flags. St. Tammany had been a part of the 72 day Republic. Very few nations have such a disputed heritage!

NOTES

1. Cox, Isaac Joslin, *The West Florida Controversy 1798-1813*, The John Hopkins Press, Baltimore, 1918, 318.
2. Ibid., 318.

3. Arthur, Clisby Stanley, *The Story of the West Florida Rebellion*, St. Francisville Democrat, 1935, 29.

4. Ibid., 34.

5. Cox, Isaac Joslin, *The West Florida Controversy, 1798-1823*, The John Hopkins Press, Baltimore, 1918, 346.

6. Padgett, James A., ed., "The Official Records of the West Florida Revolution and Republic," *Louisiana Historical Quarterly*, Volume 21, 1938, 688.

7. Ibid., 690-691.

8. Cooper to Folch, Legaho 1568, Papeles de Cuba.

9. Cox, Isaac Joslin, *The West Florida Controversy, 1798-1823*, 386.

10. Cooper to Folch, Legaho 1568, Papeles de Cuba.

11. Ibid. Cooper to Folch.

12. Clisby, Arthur Stanley, *The Story of the West Florida Rebellion*, 100.

13. Ibid., 102.

14. Ellis, Frederick S., *St. Tammany Parish, L'Autre Côté du Lac*, Pelican Publishing Company, 1998, 74.

15. Padgett, James A., "Official Records of the West Florida Revolution and Republic," *Louisiana Historical Quarterly*, Volume 21, 720.

16. Padgett, James A., The Official Records of the West Florida Revolution and Republic," *Louisiana Historical Quarterly*, Volume 21, 688.

17. Mark King Papers, MS 462, Georgia Historical Society, Savannah, Georgia.

18. Candler, Allen D., *Colonial Records of the State of Georgia*, Volume 11, Atlanta, Georgia, The Franklin Printing and Publishing Company, 1904, 389-90.

19. E-mail communication between Angela Reid and Don Sharp, November 19, 2011.

20. E-mail communication between Angela Reid and Don Sharp, January 14, 2012.

21. E-mail communication between Don Sharp and Angela Reid, Friday, January 6, 2012.

22. Cox, Isaac Joslin, *The West Florida Controversy, 1798-1823*, 411.

23. Ibid., 411.

24. Ibid., 412.

25. Campeau, Anita R. and Sharp, Donald J., "The United States navy and the Naval Station at New Orleans, 1804-1826," *New Orleans Genesis*, Volume 49, July 2011, No. 195, 263-264.

26. McMichael, Andrew, *Americans in Spanish West Florida: 1785-1810*, University of Georgia press, 2008, 167.

27. John Rhea to James Madison, October 10, 1810, quoted in Arthur 1935, 123.

28. Ibid., 123.

29. Ibid., 644.

30. Sterks, Henry E. and Brooks, Thompson E., *Philemon Thomas & the West Florida Rebellion*, 1961, 361.

CHAPTER 7

CONFIRMATION OF FOREIGN LAND TITLES

"The incomplete Purchase was complete," wrote Clisby Stanley Arthur. Governor William Charles Coles Claiborne faced many administrative tasks in order to set up the government of the newly acquired lands. Three days before Christmas, on December 22, 1810, he established the boundaries of the Florida Parishes, including the parishes of Feliciana, East Baton Rouge, and St. Helena between the Mississippi and Pearl rivers. He gave the name of St. Tammany to the fourth parish created from St. Helena and Orleans Parishes, the area that had been called Chifoncte and then St. Ferdinand.[1] It lay east of the Tanchipao, to Pearl River and south of the Mississippi Territory.

Governor Claiborne gave no explanations as to why he picked the name, but it is assumed that it was because of Tamanend, a renowned Delaware Indian chief, who was reputed to have been a great friend to the white men in the early days of colonization of the east coast. His name was attached to the political society called the Sons of St. Tammany which eventually gave its name to Tammany Hall in New York City. The Protestant American governor then tacked on "saint" in the fashion of the French and Spanish regimes, who had named parishes after Catholic saints.[2]

The Spanish still held Pensacola, in East Florida, obviously weakened and indecisive, but there was apprehension that they might retaliate against the United States, and attempt to recapture the territory they had lost in West Florida. As early as December 25, 1810, Governor Claiborne wrote to Colonel Covington about the information he had received at the exposed situation of the newly acquired settlements on Lake Pontchartrain, and the description of its inhabitants. He was impressed at the expediency of the establishment of a military post somewhere on that Lake or its waters. His orders to Covington were: "...therefore Sir request of you to detail for duty under the command of a proper officer about one hundred men with orders to the commanding officer, to proceed from hence by way of New Orleans to the Fort on the Bayou St. John, and there to await my instructions as to the Position he is to occupy."[3] Shortly, thereafter, a cantonment was constructed a few miles north of Covington, but the extent of its occupation by troops is not certain. In addition, a navy yard was constructed near Madisonville, about two miles upstream of the present site of the town.

Not without some difficulties, Governor Claiborne also turned his attention to appointing officials for the new parishes. On December 24, 1810, he wrote to Robert Smith, the Secretary of State of the United States, stating: "Judges for the parishes of St. Helena and St. Tammany have not yet been named; - there is in that quarter a great scarcity of talent, and the number of virtuous men too, (I fear) is not as great as I could wish."[4] Governor Claiborne offered Fulwar Skipwith a post, but he declined.

Joseph Spell was appointed to the office of justice of the peace on February 1, 1811, being the first man named to hold office in the new American regime. He was the son of the original British land grantee John Spell Sr. and Cecilia McLemore at Bayou Castein. Baptiste Baham, son of old Juan Baptiste Baham dit Gentil, first settler at Madisonville on 1783, was named to the position on March 2, 1811. He and his five sons settled on a 1000-arpent Spanish land grant on the left side of the Tchefuncte River in 1782. It was on April 24, 1783, that Surveyor Charles Trudeau noticed them on their property. The Bahams are considered as the earliest permanent settlers of the present-day settlement of Madisonville.

In August 1811, a proclamation called for the election of one representative from the Parishes of St. Helena and St. Tammany, the election to be held on the first Monday of October 1811, and on the two following days. These appointments completed the political organization until statehood.

Louisiana was admitted to statehood on April 8, 1812, as the eighteenth state, the first to be admitted outside the original boundaries of the U.S. as established by the Treaty of Paris in 1783. There were very sharp opinions among the citizens of the Florida Parishes as whether they wished to be included. People were generally favorable in Baton Rouge and Feliciana to be a part of Louisiana while the people in St. Tammany petitioned Congress to be made a part of the Mississippi Territory. Their requests were not heard and, despite the resistance, they were included when on August 4, 1812, the State Legislature accepted the Florida Parishes, and St. Tammany became a part of the State of Louisiana.

This would not be the last time that the people of St. Tammany would be opposed to their political destiny. They were in 1779, when nineteen of the local citizens of Bayou Castein took the oath of allegiance to the United States, just before becoming Spanish citizens. They were also opposed to the West Florida Rebellion, but found themselves part of the Republic of West Florida.

One of the most difficult administrative problems the United States encountered was the confirmation of foreign land titles. The various treaties of the United States with Great Britain, France, Spain, and Mexico by which were set its continental limits provided clauses that the inhabitants were to be protected in the free enjoyment of their property. No principle of international law is better recognized than the "inviolability of private property in exchange of sovereigns." People change their allegiance, the relation to an ancient sovereign is dissolved, but their relations to each other and their rights of property remain undisturbed.

In 1803, when the United States acquired Louisiana little was known about the territory. In setting up the temporary government and in order to legislate concerning the adjustment of foreign land titles, Congress had to proceed on meager intelligence. Shortly after the treaty was signed, President Jefferson made considerable efforts to get all the information he could by addressing letters of inquiry to men in the territory he considered reliably knowledgeable.[5]

Jefferson's research benefited Congress when it met in December 1803. He reported that lands in Louisiana were held in some instances by grants from the crown, but mostly from the colonial government. Probably not one quarter of the lands granted were held by complete titles, and a large number depended upon a written permission of a commandant. Not a small proportion was held by occupancy, but with a simple verbal permission of the commandant. The practice had always been followed by the Spanish government in order that the poor might, when financially able, apply to obtain a complete title.[6]

According to President Jefferson, it was impossible to ascertain the quantity of lands granted without calling on the claimants to produce their titles. Land ownership in Spanish West Florida in the early 1800s was a very complicated mixture of French measures, British grants, Spanish claims and United States aspirations. Consequently, the surveying business was of critical importance to the wealth and well-being of the inhabitants. To complicate the existing problem, the registry of titles was incomplete and maps made by different surveyors were burned in the fires of New Orleans of 1788 and 1794.[7]

With the transfer to the United States, American speculators were interested in driving up the value of their West Florida lands to reap future profits. The officials who were charged with issuing the rights to survey as well as the certificates and the patents that allowed formal recording of land ownership were often cajoled and entreated, or threatened. Others found willing cohorts in former Spanish officials who, for a few cents an acre, would provide them with a warrant of survey, a surveyor's certificate, and the final grant bearing dates prior to the cession of Louisiana from Spain to France. As a result, Congress spent an inordinate amount of time, built up an intricate maze of laws and procedures, while the courts piled up a mass of precedents. Many land lawyers profited from the proceeds of tedious and endless litigations.

The lands that surveyors were employed to survey were still mostly wild and uninhabited, often covered in canes, crossed by rivers, bayous and swamps, afflicted by snakes, mosquitoes, unfriendly animals and settlers.

During the Civil War and the Reconstruction periods, the violence that consumed St. Tammany was aggravated by disputes over conflicting land claims that had long been dormant. The long enduring Jolly-Cousin feud originated in a dispute over a piece of land that an ineffective legal system never properly adjudicated. The feud that lasted more than thirteen years climaxed in 1897 with "a pitched battle involving pistols, shotguns and clubs, that left four dead and two wounded."[8] It had taken many years before the final chapter on the land disputes would be closed.

The right to own land has always been an incentive for people to relocate from one country to another or from one part of a country to another. When the first colonists came to this country, they were anxious to own their own land, often a privilege they had not been afforded in their native countries. Some arrived for a variety of reasons including an escape from famine or war, the right to own land, the prospect of owning a farm, adventure or a new start in life. On the other hand, some came by force. Whatever the reason, immigration in this country has made it the culturally and ethnically diverse society it is today.

Large forces of laborers were needed in Colonial America. An important source was the indentured servant. Europeans who wanted to improve their economic condition and were unable to pay their passage to the colonies were transported at the expense of colonial entrepreneurs. In return, they had to sign a contract for their employer for periods ranging generally from five to seven years (usually three years in New France). At the end of the period of indenture the employer usually gave the servant some clothes and tools, and the colonial government frequently gave him land, abundant and relatively easy to obtain. Thus, the ex-servant was able to become an independent farmer while a few ascended to the higher echelons of society.[9]

Ownership of land has been a matter of public record from early colonial days in America, dating back to the early 1600s. In Louisiana, the French during the first half of the eighteenth century gave large grants to the wealthy and politically high-placed individuals. They, in turn, reminiscent of the manorial system in Europe, parceled relatively small tracts of land from their concession to the ordinary settler.

The French entrepreneurs shortly after the settling of New Orleans were eager to promote trade with the Indians who lived on the north shore wilderness, referred to as "as the other side of the lake" (*l'autre côté du lac*). The French in Louisiana were reluctant to give large grants across Lake Pontchartrain. The landscape abounded with mature pine trees stretching out on generally level topography. Two bayous, where Natives and animals lived, helped define the terrain and swamps appeared through the area. The lumber potential of the area amazed the early *voyageurs* but inadequate transportation retarded the advance of the industry. Hanno Dieler wrote that in 1724-1727 only five families (14 persons) were living on the north shore of the lake.[10] The hopeful beginnings were nullified in 1729 by the Natchez massacre. By 1734 there were three or four tar works on the north shore, and more works were planned.

After the French were defeated in the Seven Years War, St. Tammany and the surrounded regions of the Florida Parishes became part of English West Florida. This is when the real tempo of expansion and development quickened when a second wave of settlers arrived in the area. By a treaty with the Choctaw in 1765, the British won the right to settle in West Florida without Indian interference.[11]

The British policy toward inhabitants included recognizing formal land grants, not possessory rights. The inhabitants had to take an oath of allegiance to the new sovereign, George III. Many French habitants left West Florida, forcing the British to seek new settlers.

During the American Revolution, British loyalists who wanted to escape persecution in the Thirteen Colonies were attracted to the area of West Florida. Bayou Castein and Chinchuba saw its first wave of settlers.

When Spain gained control of Louisiana in 1762, its policies with regard to land grants were markedly differently from those of the French regime, they were far more liberal and diffuse. Grants of land were made directly from the Crown, and put in possession of the colonists who were small owners, the common men. It was usually the head of the family who initiated the process of land acquisition; first presented to the local commandant then he would annotate the petition with a scrawl, usually placed at the bottom of the page, so as to indicate whether or not the desired property was available or unencumbered. The petition was then sent to the governor at New Orleans for his approval or refusal. If the land title was clear, the governor's approval most often followed. His confirmation was added to the petition itself.

The first Spanish administration began with the arrival of Don Alexander O'Reilly on July 24, 1769, although Spain had received the Province of Louisiana seven years before. At first it was decided to continue the French system in regard to the laws relating to land grants but after an inspection of parts of the Territory, Governor O'Reilly decided otherwise. He attempted to improve the recording of land grants because French grants were not well documented or clearly recorded, causing internal instability in the colony. O'Reilly, with the Crown's approval, in a proclamation dated February 18, 1770, initiated the first official land policy in Louisiana. His proclamation read in part:

> All grants shall be made in the name of the king, by the Governor General of the province, who will, at the same time appoint a surveyor to fix the bounds thereof, both in front and in depth, in the presence of the ordinary judge of the district and of two adjoining settlers, who shall be present at the survey. The above mentioned four persons shall sign the process-verbal which shall be made thereof, and the surveyor shall make three copies of the same; one of which shall be deposited in the office of the Escribano of the government and Cabildo (scrivener); another shall be delivered to the Governor General, and the third to the proprietor, to be annexed to the title of his grant.[12]

O'Reilly came to Louisiana as the delegate of royalty itself, and was invested as such with unbounded powers of legislation, prescribed the manner in which all future concessions of land should be made. At a later period, it became a question debated in the courts on how far the French laws had been repealed by O'Reilly by his proclamation of November 25, 1769.

A royal decree in October 1798 overturned the 1770 proclamation, and the power to grant lands was given back to the authority of the Intendant, not the governor. In 1802, Intendant Don Juan Morales closed the land office in New Orleans because of the death of the assessor of the intendancy.[13] According to O'Reilly's decree, he and succeeding Governors General, would appoint surveyors to fix the bounds of the land grants most often through the drawing of detailed land plats. Surveyor Charles (Carlos) Trudeau was first appointed to the post in the early 1780s, until 1805, when he resigned his post. After his resignation as Spanish Survey General, he decided to remain in Louisiana as an American citizen. Vicente S. Pintado, the first assistant, became surveyor general of West Florida.

Another Spanish official who is known to have issued regulations governing the granting of lands is Governor Manuel Gayoso de Lemos who, on September 9, 1797, issued a set of instructions to be observed by the commandants of the post of the province for the admission of new settlers. There were eighteen articles in his instructions. Among one of the regulations was one that provided if the stranger was not a farmer, nor married, nor possessed of property, he had to be a settler for four years before being allowed to obtain land. The same rule applied to the immigrant who was unmarried and had no trade or profession. Should he have lived in the country for two years and found another farmer who was willing to give him a daughter in marriage, then the grant could be applied for.

The privilege of enjoying liberty of conscience was not to extend beyond the first generation, and the children of those who enjoyed such privilege must positively be Catholics. The commandants were ordered to take particular care that no protestant preacher or one of any sect other than Catholic should be allowed into the province, and the least neglect on the part of the commandant in this respect was to be subject of great reprehension. Most settlers did not give up their religion. There were a few traveling ministers, under cover, for marriages and baptisms. When a Protestant minister was unavailable, they would wait until later when one would travel to their area.

Every new settler who filled the requirements, and married, was to receive 200 arpents of land plus 50 additional for each child brought with him. Immediately upon arrival every new settler under oath was required to prove that the wife whom he brought with him was his lawful wife.

A new settler was required within the first year to establish himself upon his land, and by the end of the third year to have in cultivation at least ten arpents in every hundred. A land claimant was expected to work his claims by clearing the land, planting crops, and building some sort of dwelling place, along with repairing and maintaining his claim's roads and ditches. These efforts by the claimant were called "improvements". After three years of working the land, the claimant could then petition the Spanish Crown and be officially given title to the property.

Grants were to be made in such manner as not to leave vacant land between one another, in order to reduce the risk of exposure to raids by the Indians.[14]

Connected with the history of Spanish land grants in Louisiana are records of bitter quarrels between Governor Gayoso and Intendant *ad interim*, Juan Morales. By a royal ordinance dated at San Lorenzo on October 22, 1798, the power to make land grants was restored to the

Intendant, but it appeared that the Spanish Governor continued to exercise the power, going so far as to establish a protestant settlement on the Bastrop concession in what is today the northern part of the State of Louisiana. It was Morales who emerged triumphant in the controversy.

The area of Bayou Castein became Spanish territory after the Treaty of peace of 1783. Under Spanish law, Thomas Spell applied for recertification by having his land surveyed. Below is the English translation of the verification of his claim shown on the opposite page: "Don Carlos Trudeau, Royal and Official Surveyor of the province of Louisiana, certifies that the above plat is in agreement with the original survey of Lt. Colonel Don Gilberto Guillemard, Aid major to the city according to the plan remitted in our office on the 20th day of January in the year 1798."

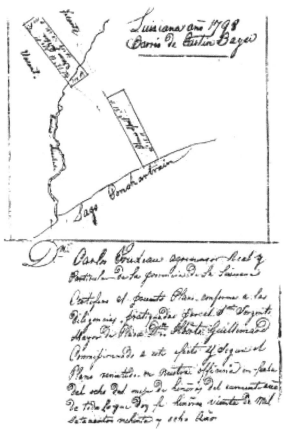

Confirmation of the Thomas Spell land grant of 1798

By the terms of a secret treaty dated October 1, 1800, the province of Louisiana was returned by Spain to France. In consideration was the fact that the French Republic engaged itself to procure for the infant Duke of Parma an augmentation of his territory by the annexation of the Duchy of Tuscany.[15] Evidently, the French had completed part of the secret bargain and, on October 15, 1802, the royal order was issued by the Spanish monarch to retrocede to France the colony and province of Louisiana, November 30th, 1803.[16]

From October 1, 1800, to November 30, 1803, the Spanish officials governed the territory, and even after the latter date remained in control of the territory east of the Iberville River as far as the Perdido. Realizing they would soon be out, land grants were made with a lavish hand to speculators for profit.

The fifty U. S. States are divided into two distinct types of land organization: state-land states and public-land states. The distinction between the two types is important because of the way they are measured and recorded.[17]

Metes and bounds was the method used by surveyors for measuring the earliest land grants in the English Colonies. Compasses were used for direction. Land term units of measurements varied from rods, perches and poles depending on the time period involved. Twenty states used this system of measurements and markers for recording land surveys. They include: Connecticut, Delaware, Georgia, Hawaii, Kentucky, Maine, Maryland, Massachusetts, New Hampshire, New Jersey, New York, North Carolina, Pennsylvania, Rhode Island, South Carolina, Texas, Vermont, Virginia and West Virginia. Land segments were measured using three main parts: direction, degrees and distance.[18] A land description might state, "Beginning at the large oak tree, and continuing..., then north so many degrees and so many chains to the corner of John Doe's land, then so many degrees south and so many chains or furlongs to another tree or Creek..." Surveyors in British West Florida used the method introduced in the Thirteen Colonies, that of "bounds and metes".

Federal or public land-states include Alabama, Alaska, Arizona, Arkansas, California, Colorado, Florida, Idaho, Illinois, Indiana, Iowa, Kansas, Louisiana, Michigan, Minnesota, Mississippi, Missouri, Montana, Nebraska, Nevada, New Mexico, North Dakota, Ohio, Oklahoma, Oregon, South Dakota, Utah, Washington, Wisconsin, and Wyoming. In Federal land states the attempt was made to place an imaginary grid upon the Earth. Federal land surveys are delineated according to large divisions by meridians, resulting in a township consisting of a square six miles on each side, then smaller blocks resulting in thirty-six squares, each with one mile on a side called a section, then a particular parcel of land. The breakdown is usually as follows: a section contains 640 acres; a half-section contains 320 acres; and a quarter-section contains 160 acres.[19]

The Act of Congress on March 26, 1804 nullified any Spanish grant subsequent to December 20, 1803, but particularly nullified any grant which exceeded one square mile, or 640 acres.[20] Although the requirements for the confirmation of foreign land titles were to be made more lenient by later enactments, the Act of March 2, 1805, established a strict and legalistic system designed to protect the government from fraud and speculation. It would appear that there was intent in the act to reject an old and amorphous system of land disposal and to substitute the up-to-date American system.

In the Act of Congress on March 2, 1805, surveyors were sent to the territory of Orleans to establish a system of dividing the vacant public lands. The Act gave important provisions on land claims: First it allowed individuals to obtain legal possession of their land or to acquire land. Congress appointed district land registers and opened the United States District Land Office in New Orleans for the eastern division of the territory of Orleans and a land office at Opelousas for the western division of the territory of Orleans. Later, other land offices were opened for the convenience of the inhabitants.

Second, inhabitants with French, British or Spanish land grants were required to appear before a board of commissioners with their proof of ownership. If approved by the board, evidence was then forwarded to Washington.

Third, surveyors established a meridian and base line. Measurements for surveyors changed from bounds and metes to township and range. By 1807 the United States had established "a meridian and a base-line." What it means is that Louisiana is a federal-land state acquired from the foreign sovereigns of France, Britain, Spain, and from the United States government.

The United States officially claimed West Florida under the Louisiana Purchase therefore it refused to recognize any grants made by the Spanish after 1803. However, it did recognize the claims of actual settlers between 1803 and 1810, regardless of their Spanish titles or lack thereof. By the Act of Congress dated March 3, 1807, Congress confirmed the title of any settler to land who had been in possession for ten years prior to December 20, 1803, and which did not exceed 2000 acres.[21]

When one looks at the extended history of St. Tammany Parish, it is difficult to visualize the troubled historical background that has characterized development in the territory located on the north shore of Lake Pontchartrain. Conflicts that consumed St. Tammany were often aggravated by disputes over conflicting land claims. France, Britain, Spain, and finally the Americans had offered land grants that often conflicted and overlapped. Some of the feuds that emerged centered on strictly personal disputes while other cases related directly to these conflicting claims. After the Spanish take over, many English grants were found abandoned at Bayou Castein. As a result, many of the grantees were legally dispossessed by officials who reassigned such lands to valid settlers.

The Loofbarrows had abandoned their land for more than fifteen years, thus making it open land under Spanish law. George Richardson had squatted on land with his family, cleared a ten-acre field to grow crops (in the same location as the Ambrose family) and enclosed some pens for his livestock. In 1801, this American frontier man left the area to "follow the lakes." Renez Baham of the Tchefuncte testified in an 1825 court case that it was legal in those days: "It was common practice and this is how settlers did things in those days."

Later, after the newly formed United States took control in 1810, Acts of Congress upheld this method of obtaining land. In 1813 after West Florida became under the jurisdiction of the United States, Zachariah Faircloth of Bayou Castein applied to James O. Cosby, Commissioner of Land Claims, District West of the Pearl River, to claim the land he was living on under a law passed by Congress. In his statement, he claimed "improvement was made in the year 1796 by George Richardson (his father-in-law) and by him in the year 1801 transferred to myself, on the waters of Chinchuba in the parish of St. Tammany, adjoining Thomas Spell and inhabited twelve years last past." It was witnessed by Lawrence Sticker. Faircloth qualified for 640 acres under the Congressional law of March 3, 1819 and was issued a Certificate of Ownership by Commissioner Cosby. He was now the owner of 640 acres under United States laws.

Jacob Bartle, who made his living as a boat Captain hauling freight around the lakes, was at Bayou Castein in 1811 when he purchased land from Dorothy O'Brien-Sanders. He received his land title in accordance with the Act of Congress passed the 3rd March 1819: Entitled an "Act for adjusting the claims to land, and establishing Land-offices in the District east of the island of New Orleans." We certify

100

that Claim No. 273 in the report of the Commissioners marked, claimed by Jacob Bartles—original claimant Wm Bryan is recognized by the said Act as VALID against any claim on the part of the United States, or right derived from the United States: the said Claim being Four Hundred Acres ~~arpens~~, situated in the parish of St. Tamany and claimed under a ~~SPANISH~~ PATENT (Spanish substituted with the British) dated 10th April 1777.

Given under our hands this 8th day of April ~~1819~~ 1820.

Signed by Charles S. Cosby, Registrar and Fulwar Skipwith, Recorder

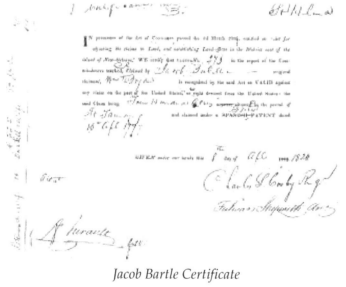

Jacob Bartle Certificate

Samuel Lloyd arrived at Bayou Castein in the year 1798 and settled on the abandoned Spanish tract of Joseph Rabassa who had abandoned the land between Jacques Lorreins/Lorance and James Goodby in 1790 for a tract of abandoned land on the East side of Bayou Castein near its mouth. This is where he and his wife Mary C. Davis raised their children. In 1806, Lloyd purchased the western half of the Edward Ross grant of 600 acres. The statement of the Rabassa heirs confirmed that Samuel Lloyd had legally purchased the western part of the Ross tract before he died. The Tobin map of that year shows that his wife, Mary C. Lloyd was the owner of the 600 acre tract.

In the 1813 claim of Mary C. Lloyd to James O. Cosby, Commissioner of Land Claims, District West of the Pearl River: "Take notice that I claim as much land as the Government may think proper to grant in virtue of a settlement and improvement made in the year 1806 on the waters of Chinchuba in the Parish of St. Tammany joining Thomas Spell, which improvement I have cultivated seven years last past and inhabited five months last past."[22] Mary C. Lloyd is believed to be the daughter of Lewis Davis who had a British grant on the East side of Bayou Castein at its mouth. A Braxton Lloyd was claimant to one half of the original Samuel Lloyd grant of 1798. He may have been a brother of Samuel, or even his oldest son.

Jacques Lorreins/Lorance whose land was to the West of Braxton and Samuel Lloyd acquired the two thousand one hundred and fifty seven arpents under the laws of the United States because he had occupied the land before 1800. Jacques Lorreins was heir to a large plantation on Bayou St. John but sold it in 1798 to be divided into a subdivision. He then relocated and settled on land opposite Baham village (Madisonville) before 1800. Charles Parent, Commandant of the Tchefuncte under the Spanish, claimed the land by right of a grant from Baron Carondelet, in 1796, dated the twentieth of May 1804 by Spanish Intendant Juan Morales. The United States Land Commission under James O. Cosby rejected this claim and awarded the land to Jacques Lorreins. Lorreins died in 1819, and the son of Charles Parent, Charles Junior, bought the land from the Lorreins heirs.

Starting in 1790, Spain had offered land grants to encourage settlement to the sparsely populated and vulnerable Florida colonies. When the United States assumed control of Florida, it agreed to honor any valid land grants. Yet, residents had to prove that validity through documentation and testimonials. Those records were the dossiers filed by grantees to the U.S. government. They were either confirmed as valid or unconfirmed as invalid by the United States government through land commissions, federal courts, or by the U.S. Congress.

At the time of Surveyor Trudeau's resignation there was an understanding for the division of documents then forming the archives of the surveyor's office. Trudeau retained the papers that related to lands in what was then recognized as the Louisiana actually sold to the U.S., while Pintado held the documents that related to lands in the West Florida territory – the section along the gulf which was not recognized by Spain as forming a part of the Louisiana Purchase.[23] There was misunderstanding as to the nature of that division. Some papers taken by Pintado to Pensacola included vitally important papers relating to lands in Louisiana that the United States had purchased from France. This transitional period and the removal of documents from the territory constituted serious problems for American officials.

On February 22, 1817, the legislature of Louisiana passed "An Act, that provided for the purchase of certain papers" which empowered the government to buy from the widow and heirs of Charles Trudeau.

102

These were to include books, papers, records, drawing, plates, warrants and certificates of survey. And on March 18, 1818, the state legislature passed "An Act to create a Surveyor General and parish surveyors in the State of Louisiana."

Unfortunately, most of the records of West Florida are missing. The Spanish land grants have been a continuous problem for surveyors, from the very first attempts until the final disposition of the grants by their private owners. The land commissioners were handicapped, so were the courts for "there was no Spanish comprehensive code of land laws which could be used to determine the ultimate validity of the grants."

James O. Cosby, U.S. Land Commissioner West of the Pearl River, died in 1814; however his report was submitted to Congress on January 5, 1816.[24] It consisted of Register "A" of 432 claims founded on complete grants derived from the British and Spanish governments, recommended for confirmation; Register "B" containing 320 claims founded on orders of survey or other written evidence, also recommended for confirmation; and Registers "C" and "D" containing some 270 claims recommended for rejection mainly because the grants postdated the treaty of purchase.[25] A glance at Cosby's report reveals the widespread speculation that had gone on in private land claims.

For the United States Deputy Surveyors, it would be their job to locate and accurately map the grants that had been so loosely defined or questionably conveyed by officials. The land grants have been a source of disagreement, court battles and attempts to defraud. It is impossible to cover each and every problem created by the Spanish land grants, but an attempt was made to give an adequate overview of the major problems that caused confusion and acrimony in settling land disputes.

NOTES

1. Dunbar, Rowland, ed., *Official Letter Books of W.C.C. Claiborne, 1801-1816,* Jackson, State Department of Archives and History, 1917, Volume 5, 64.

2. Morgan, H.G., Jr., "Tammany, Origin of name," *Publications of the Louisiana Historical Society*, Volume 5, 54.

3. Casey, Powell A., "Military Roads and Camps in or near Covington and Madisonville, Louisiana," *St. Tammany Historical Society Gazette*, Volume 2, 59.

4. Dunbar, Rowland, ed., *Official Letter Books of W.C.C. Claiborne*, Volume 5, 62.

5. Thomas Jefferson to W.C.C. Claiborne, July 17, 1803, in Clarence E. Carter, *The Territorial Papers of the United States*, IX (Orleans, 3-4.)

6. Coles, Harry L. Jr., "The Confirmation of Foreign Land Titles in Louisiana, *The Louisiana Historical Quarterly*, No. 38, October 1955, 2. His study is based to a considerable extent on Joseph M. White, *A New Collection of Laws, Charters, and Local Ordinances of the Governments of Great Britain, France and Spain etc.*, Philadelphia, 1839 and the documents in *American States Papers, Public Lands*, V, 631-774.

7. President Thomas Jefferson, "Description of Louisiana," November 4, 1803, *American State Papers, Miscellaneous*, 1, 344-356. Refer to Coles, 3.

8. Hyde, Samuel Jr., *Pistols and Politics: The Dilemma of Democracy*, Louisiana State University Press, 2006, 242. *New Orleans Daily Picayune*, January 26, 1883; August 10, 1898.

9. Campeau, Anita R., & Sharp, Donald J., "Land Records Helpful in Research," *New Orleans Genesis*, Volume XLVII, January 2009, No. 185, 1.

10. Dieler, Hanno J., *The Settlement of the German Coast and Creoles of German Descent*, (Philadelphia: German American Historical Society, 1909.

11. Hamilton, Peter J., *Colonial Mobile*, 1897; reprint, Mobile, Alabama: First National Bank, 1952.

12. Burns, Francis P., "The Spanish Land Laws of Louisiana," *The Louisiana Historical Quarterly*, Volume 11, 1928, 561. Refer to end note, no. 6.

13. State Papers, Volume 5, 735.

14. State Papers, Volume 5, 730.

15. White, Joseph M., *A New Collection of Laws, Charters, and Local Ordinances of the Governments of Great Britain, France and Spain*, 516.

16. Burns, Francis P., "The Spanish Land Laws of Louisiana," *The Louisiana Historical Quarterly*, Volume 11, 1928, 579.

17. A standard reference book on this subject is E. Wade Hone, *Land and Property Research in the United States*, Salt Lake City: Ancestry, 1997.

18. Ibid.,

19. Ibid.,

20. United States Land Laws, Ch. 70, Volume1, 112. Refer also to article by Burns, Francis P., "Spanish Land Laws," *Louisiana Historical Quarterly*, 580.

21. Burns, Francis P., "The Spanish Land Laws of Louisiana," *The Louisiana Historical Quarterly*, Volume 11, 1928, 581.

22. Greensberg Land Claims, Book 1, Part 1.

23. Arthur, Clisby Stanley, "*A History of the Pintado Papers*, v-vi; Walker, "The Pintado Papers," 161.

24. American State Papers, Public Lands, 111, 6-76. See Coles, "Confirmation of Foreign Land Titles," 11.

25. Ibid., 11.

CHAPTER 8

STATEHOOD, THE EARLY YEARS: 1810-1820

The north shore of Lake Pontchartrain and Maurepas had been an important part of the foreign policy of both Spain and the United States since the Louisiana Purchase on December 20, 1803. The American purchase had meant little to the people living near Bayou Castein as West Florida was not a part of the territory the United States occupied. To cross the lake was to cross and international boundary separating Spanish West Florida to the north from the American Isle of Orleans to the south. With the takeover of the Florida Parishes by the United States, in December 1810, the last international boundary was eradicated. As a result, traffic down the Mississippi River increased, and the people on the north shore of Lake Pontchartrain had easier access to New Orleans.

There was great need for roads to connect the interior with New Orleans. In 1811, United States troops began to cut a series of roads that terminated at Madisonville, from which place boats crossed Lake Pontchartrain to Bayou St. John and New Orleans. Colonel Leonard Covington was in charge of building a road known as General Wilkinson's from Baton Rouge to Fort Stoddert on the Mobile River. This road passed through Springfield and Madisonville, along the south side of the Bogue Falaya, and crossed the Pearl River at the confluence with the Bogue Chitto. Part of this road may have been the old King's Road, which led from Baton Rouge to Bay St. Louis, crossing the Tchefuncte at Madisonville.[1] Transportation improvements brought more settlers to the shores of Lake Pontchartrain. The quickest route to New Orleans was across Lake Pontchartrain to Madisonville and Covington and, from thence, north by road.[2]

There was a road that led from the "Mount" of Bayou Castein to Bayou Lacombe. In 1792, George Sharp had obtained a Spanish grant on Bayou Castein where the road leads to Bayou Lacombe. He held the land for about four years, and then sold it to his friend Zachariah Faircloth prior to returning to Kentucky. This road also led west to the settlements along the lakefront. Today it follows the general path of Highway 190.

The direct route to Nashville was the Military road which was constructed by U.S. Army troops in the years 1817-1820. Between Covington and the Mississippi state line, the Military road probably followed the road which General Andrew Jackson and Major H. Tatum used, in 1814, when they marched south to defend New Orleans cutting a new trail through the region that would later emerge as the Jackson Military road. It is fortunate that General Jackson's Topographical Engineer, Major H. Tatum, kept a diary in which he details the route followed, and offered comments on the country through which he passed.[3]

The overland route which led northwest from Mobile to the Pearl River, just above the Louisiana state line, was used by General Jackson and his party. The night of November 28, 1814, was spent at Alston's place at Strawberry Bluff on the Bogue Chitto River. The next day, they proceeded, in all 16½ miles, to the town of Wharton on the Bogue Feliah, "the seat of justice for the county." The lands between Alston and from Rose's plantation were described as poor, with the growth of pine. About five miles between Rose's residence and the Cantonment, the land was nearly bare of timber due to a severe hurricane. The lands from Wharton to the town of Madisonville are a mixture of pine and oak and contain several tolerable farms and plantations. From Wharton, proceeded to Madisonville and halted for the night. According to legend, General Jackson en route to New Orleans stopped here at the home of General David B. Morgan.

The town of Madisonville, Tatum described as "small and improved" situated on the west bank of the Chefuncta River about two miles from its junction with Lake Pontchartrain. It lies about two miles from the navy yard.

By the time of the purchase, *Chiconcte* (Madisonville today) and Barrio of Buck Falia (Wharton, then Covington from 1816) had begun to develop as trade and transportation centers. Madisonville, originally called Cokie (from the French *coquille*) because of the abundance of shells in the area, was renamed for President James Madison. The town was the site of the Spanish grant made to Juan Baham on the west side of the Tchefuncte River, about two miles above its mouth. The grant included the site of Chifoncte. Madisonville was incorporated by legislative act, approved February 18, 1817. It was the site of a Navy Yard in the early 1800s.

Soon after the purchase, the United States made its presence felt. The Jefferson Administration realized that a United States naval presence was necessary in New Orleans. The Secretary of the Navy alerted a detachment of Marines under the command of Captain Daniel Carmick to prepare for the Gulf Coast. During the Quasi-War with France, Captain Carmick commanded the marine detachment in *Constitution*, and served with distinction in the Mediterranean.

The Marines were the first element of the United States Navy to arrive at New Orleans in March of 1804. Two years later, in 1806, a United States naval facility was to be established when the newly

Commandant Captain John Shaw was appointed to the mission. He arrived in New Orleans on the brig *Franklin* on March 16, 1806, with Purser Keith Spence and some senior lieutenants. Captain Shaw was ordered to construct gunboats for coastal defense.[4]

Gun Vessels Nos. 11 and *12*, recently arrived, at the mouth of the Mississippi River from the East Coast, had been ordered from Boston in September by the Secretary of the Navy to New Orleans Station with the brigs *Aetna* and *Vesuvius*. On arriving at the Belize (mouth of the Mississippi) Captain Shaw, concerned about the report of two Spanish cruisers on the "lakes" sent them to Lake Pontchartrain. Their orders were to show the American flag to the Spanish and explore the lakes and find suitable watering and repair places for the future gunboats to arrive. The vessels were given numbers instead of names like larger vessels of the Navy. Gun vessels were the current choice of the Jefferson administration because they were more economical and the opposition of a large navy. These vessels or gunboats were to play an important part in the military diplomacy and defense on the lakes during the next nine years.[5]

Lt. Joseph Bainbridge, who had distinguished himself with honors during the Barbary Wars, was in command of *Gunboat No. 11.* Some time between late October and December 1, 1806, he entered the mouth of the Tchefuncte River and sailed up the three miles and anchored on the west bank opposite a little settlement which consisted of a few log cabins and huts built by Juan Baham and his sons. This incident would change the "status quo" and have repercussions for years to come. *No. 12* followed with Sailing Master John Rush in command. He was the eldest son of the well-known Dr. Benjamin Rush of Philadelphia, a signer of the Declaration of Independence, as was his father-in-law. After five weeks of exploring Lake Maurepas and Pontchartrain the Gun Vessels returned to the Mississippi and ascended the river and anchored at New Orleans. The *Aetna* and *Vesuvius* had already ascended and were waiting in the river. From 1808 until 1814, the Tchefuncte River, along with the base at New Orleans, was used a major repair facility.[6] The site had been chosen by the agents of the Navy Department for repairing and building small vessels of war for the southern station. It was an ideal site for the bosky landscape abounded with oak, pine and cypress. Tar could be made in abundance, plus the spun hemp or rope yarn of Kentucky could be bought cheaply, and the rigging could be laid at the navy yard with the greatest of economy, to the advantage of the public service.

The Port of Bayou St. John, in New Orleans, began trade excursions across Pontchartrain to the settlements, and vessels began to be built on the north shore.

When W.C.C. Claiborne became governor of the Louisiana Territory in 1804, he appointed David B. Morgan as surveyor general of Louisiana and Mississippi. Born in West Springfield, Massachusetts, on August 21, 1772, Morgan was issued from a prominent family that pre-dated the Mayflower landing.[7] Morgan, a civil engineer by profession, worked around Boston and Plymouth prior to removing to the Natchez area about 1800. In 1801, he received a 760-acre land grant on the Mississippi below the Post of Concordia where he cultivated this land, and where he held many public posts. He married Elizabeth Middleton, a rich widow, on May 25, 1805, in Natchez. Elizabeth was said to be a descendant of Arthur Middleton, of South Carolina, a signer of the Declaration of Independence. Her brother Hatton died in the Creek massacre at Fort Mims in 1813; her brother William lived at the Post of Concordia.[8] Five children were issued from this marriage: David Jr., Adeline, Charles H. Morgan, and twins born January 20, 1816, who died the same day. Morgan's wife, Elizabeth, died two days later in Madisonville on January 22.[9]

As early as 1804, David B. Morgan visited St. Tammany Parish as a surveyor. He claimed Spanish land by 1807. Governor Claiborne later appointed Morgan commander of the Louisiana Militia with the rank of brigadier general. David B. Morgan held the office of Representative in the territorial Legislature, was a member of the convention for the formation of the State Constitution, and was elected first state senator from Concordia Parish in 1812.

In the early years of statehood, Governor Claiborne faced many problems in the new state of Louisiana, but he quickly reacted to solve the problems, and make the American presence known. The strategic location of the territory was highlighted to protect New Orleans from capture during the War of 1812. A few miles from Natchitoches, a boundary dispute existed between Spanish and Americans, until a neutral ground was established between the Sabine River and the Rio Honda. With that matter once settled, the next concern in St. Tammany was Indian trouble that broke out in the latter part of 1812, which persisted for some time.

The eastern states had been invaded by the British in the War of 1812, and in 1813 the Creek uprising began in Alabama and Georgia. On July 9, 1812, Captain John Shaw received word by express that war had been declared with Great Britain. Even though the New Orleans station was a long way from the Atlantic Coast, the farthest from the nation's capital, it began preparation for war. Captain Shaw had at his command some four hundred officers and men, distributed among two brigs of war and eleven gun boats. A mobilization was called and the citizens of Pontchartrain Post were called to defend their land.

On August 19 and 20, 1812, a hurricane ferociously hit the Gulf Coast area and New Orleans. The Navy-hospital had half of its roof carried away, and the kitchen and other "appendant buildings" were blown away. The hospital contained upwards of one-hundred patients, and had to be repaired immediately. The Military also sustained much injury. The French Market-house, in point of spaciousness and elegance (perhaps equaled by scarcely any in the United States) across the street from the Navy Yard was completely leveled, and under the ruins many people who had sought shelter from the storm were buried.

Several Gun Vessels *Nos. 27, 66*, and *163* under the command of Lt. Daniel S. Dexter were caught in open water from the Balize, and had a very difficult time as the gale raged with unabated fury. Some tried to anchor near shore but several had their lines broken and were driven up on shore. Some threw their cannons overboard to stay afloat! Lt. Dexter feared the loss of *No. 66*.[10]

In January of 1813, the bodies of five sailors were washed ashore at Bayou Castein. They were badly decomposed having been in the water for such a long time. The local inhabitants reported the bodies to Parish authorities of St. Tammany and the bodies were buried along the lake shore. The presence of the Navy which was close by on the Tchefuncte River never acknowledged the death of these sailors. No records were found in which the US Navy claimed them.[11]

The hurricane set back military preparations for many months with great material damage and some loss of lives. It also demonstrated the weakness of the naval forces on the New Orleans station and their vulnerability to natural catastrophes.

In a letter to General Wilkinson dated December 12, 1812, Captain Shaw mentioned that he was returning to the Tchefuncte to inspect gun vessels *No. 24* and *No. 5* that were being repaired and that he had some contracts for timber to be made, and that it would occasion his absence from six to eight days.[12] It was on this trip that he made his decision to build the Block Ship across the Lake instead of Bay St. Louis.

Captain Shaw was shown a bend of the river located on the property of Jacques Lorreins, the owner of 2,700 acres of land. Today it is the Beau Chêne Subdivision. Captain Shaw agreed to terms with Jacques Lorreins for twenty acres and a ten year lease at twenty dollars a year. In a letter to Paul Hamilton, Secretary of the Navy, Captain

Shaw pointed out that "the bend" was the ideal location for building the ship and others, if necessary. It had a good view of the river, plenty of excellent oak, pine and cedar, and a slight incline for launching. On the Gulf it would be vulnerable to a British invasion, but on the Tchefuncte it would be better protected. By January 14, 1813, Captain Shaw was back in New Orleans after a one month absence.

Once an agreement was reached, Lt. Michael B. Carroll and Sailing Master Jonathan Ferris were put in charge of navy crews that started clearing the land in order to build the flat bottom boat frigate a few miles away.[13] Permission had been granted to Shaw by Paul Hamilton, the Secretary of the Navy, and he could proceed with the construction.

Captain Shaw hired Master carpenter François Pichon of New Orleans to be in charge of building the block ship *Tchifonta*, a flat-bottomed frigate to measure 152'9" on deck and 43' molded beam with an 8'6" draw. The *Tchifonta* was to carry 42 pieces of cannon, 26 of which were 32 pounders. It was to be used on the lakes and the Louisiana coast. The two men hired what carpenters that could be had in New Orleans and the rest of the civilian labor force were hired from residents of the North Shore. Thomas Spell and Joseph Sharp were among those who were hired. As early as 1813, Thomas Spell's slaves were seen cutting wood on the O'Brien tract.

Captain Shaw reported his activities in the preparation for building the ship to Paul Hamilton, Secretary of the Navy, and received his approval. In January, Lt. Michael B. Carroll and Sailing Master Jonathan Ferris had crews cleaning off the land and preparing the stocks on which the boat would be built. Construction began in March, 1813. It was an economic stimulus for the north shore. Workers were paid as much as $28.00 a month, plus rations. There were as many as 150 civilians who worked on the ship during the peak months, many from the surrounding parishes.

Aug., site of U.S. Navy Yard.
Courtesy St. Tammany Parish Archives

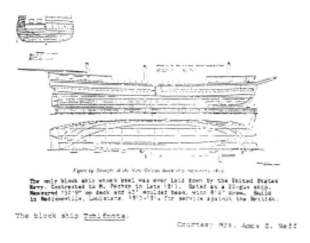

The only block ship whose keel was ever laid down by the United States Navy. Constructed to M. Pechen in Late 1813. Rated as a 51-gun ship. Measured 733'9" on deck and 43' molded beam, with 8'4" draw. Built in Madisonville, Louisiana, 1813-1814, for service against the British.

The block ship Tchifonta.

Courtesy Mrs. Anna K. Neff

Map site of the U.S. Navy Yard and picture of block ship,
Courtesy St. Tammany Parish Archives

Thomas Spell, Robert Badon, Benjamin Havard, Joseph Hertraise, Benjamin Beakham (Bickham), the first police jurors of St. Tammany Parish, were appointed commissioners by legislative act of March 25, 1813.[14] Their first task was "to fix on the most convenient place not exceeding what they may perceive to be within three miles from the centre of said parish for the purpose of erecting a court house and jail." The court house was constructed on the property of Judge Thomas Cargill Warner, near Enon on the Bogue Chitto River.[15] In the 1817 election called to fix the seat of justice for the parish, the people must have voted to move the site of the court house because in a legislative act of March 16, 1818, commissioners were named "to select the most proper site for a permanent seat of justice in or near the town of Covington." The town of Claiborne was the selected site. The town did not expand, as was expected, even with the presence of a court house. The court house was moved to Covington, where it has since remained.

Concerned about the Indian menace, Governor Claiborne, wrote from New Orleans in the spring of 1813 to the Secretary of War: "About the same time (9th ult) I received sundry letters from respectable Citizens of the parishes of St. Helena and St. Tammany within this State, informing me of the frequent menaces of the Choctaws and requesting that measures might be taken for the safety of the settlements." The inhabitants were in a state of panic, so much so that several farms were abandoned, and the frontier settlers fled to the interior for surety.[16] He requested a vessel to

111

take him to Madisonville; plus he ordered to be taken one hundred muskets, powder, lead, and flint from the arsenal in New Orleans.[17]

Before leaving New Orleans, he ordered several detachments of militia held in readiness for service. He and Captain Shaw crossed the lake to Madisonville in early September to meet with the Parish leaders. One of his aims in visiting the North Shore was to unite the militia of the state and to take some measures for the safety of the inhabitants. Governor Claiborne came up with a plan: he would use the string of forts already in place and build another fort, this one a stockade, with the help of the workers at the yard. It would be located across the Tchefuncte River from Madisonville and adjacent the main trail leading to the navy yard.

Captain Shaw told the Parish leaders that he would have the fort manned with an Officer and a Detachment of Marines, along with a few heavy cannons. This would give protection for the workers of the navy yard and the residents of Madisonville. The other forts in Claiborne's plan would be Ford's Fort on the Pearl River, the fort at Springfield, and the fort at Baton Rouge.[18]

While in St. Tammany Parish, Claiborne received details of the Creek massacre. It was on August 30, 1813, Creek Indian warriors surprised Fort Mims, a blockhouse and palisade fort on the east side of the Alabama River north of Mobile. Five hundred civilians and members of the garrison were massacred. Fear of further Indian attacks swept through the area north of Lakes Maurepas and Pontchartrain. Defense of the state became an urgent matter since it was feared in Louisiana of both British and Indian attacks. If the Creeks were to unite with the Choctaws, there could be an attack, but it was presumed unlikely. Captain Shaw wrote to the Secretary of the Navy that he thought the Creeks were too far away, and even if they attacked, he was sure that he could defeat them. (Several old fortifications of logs were found in the northern part of some of the West Florida Parishes, possibly the result of the Creek threat).

Governor Claiborne's visit to St. Tammany was successful. The Indian troubles seemed to have been solved. The presence of troops at the cantonment and at the navy yard may have succeeded in bringing back calm to the area. Plus, the 13th Regiment of the state militia was formed in that parish.

William Jones who replaced Paul Hamilton, the Secretary of the Navy, put little value on the gunboats at New Orleans or the building of flat bottom stationary frigates. He thought they were useless and a waste of money. The new Commander, Daniel Patterson, at New

Orleans tried to defend the "block ship". He wrote to the new secretary that the block ship "Tchefuncte" was more than 80% complete and would be useful for the defense of New Orleans, but his comments fell on deaf ears. In April of 1814, the Secretary wrote to Commander Patterson to stop construction, lay off the workers, and close in the block ship on its stocks. Unfortunately, from the very beginning General Thomas Flourny had underestimated the dangers of war in Louisiana. The War Department agreed with him, despite the urgings by Claiborne and Patterson. General Andrew Jackson on December 16, 1814, wrote the secretary of war urging the finishing of the *Tchifonta*.[19]

Construction was halted in March 1814 because the administration had decided that there was no danger of an attack on New Orleans. *The Tchifonta* had been designed specifically to operate in the shallow waters of the approaches to New Orleans, but was still in the stocks when the Battle of New Orleans took place.

The War of 1812 had first been confined to the east coast, but by 1814 the British strategy was to attack New Orleans. Major General Andrew Jackson, who had triumphed with victories over the Creek Indians and the capture of Pensacola, was appointed to command the defense of New Orleans.

The British Armada showed up on the Gulf Coast and anchored off Ship Island in early December. Led by Vice Admiral Sir Alexander Cochran, in his 74 gun flagship *Tonnant*, the over fifty ships was the largest foreign armada ever to approach American shores. Lt. Commander Michael B. Carroll, before the battle, sailed the *Bomb ketch Aetna* up the Tchefuncte and blocked any traffic going up or down the River in an effort to protect the yard and block ship from being attacked and burned.[20]

A general mobilization order was issued for the Louisiana Militia on December 16, 1814. The 13th Regiment was composed of men from St. Tammany Parish with Colonel Thomas C. Warner, the parish judge, as commanding officer.

Renez Baham was commissioned a major in the 1st Battalion, 13th Regiment of the Louisiana Militia in the Battle of New Orleans.[21] Thomas Spell was drafted at the Tchefuncte Navy Yard in the 13th Regiment on December 23, 1814, and discharged on March 7, 1815. He died there eight days later.

Joseph Sharp, born September 3, 1794, the son of Joseph Sharp and Elizabeth Richardson, was a veteran of the War of 1812. Family members say that Joseph was a bugler for his company. With him were his soldier buddies Abner Jenkins and Braxton Lloyd, son of Samuel and Mary Davis of Bayou Castein. They were in the 12th Regiment of St. Helena under Major Lawrence H. Moore of St. Helena Parish who owned a store, was on the Police Jury, and bought Shepherd Brown's last property at Port Vincent, Louisiana, in 1815.[22]

Listed as privates for St. Tammany, in the 13th Regiment under Captain William Bickham's Company, at the Battle of New Orleans in 1815 were: Joseph Sharp, Abner Jenkins, Mark Lloyd, John Spell, Thomas Spell Sr., Jacob Barth (Bartles), Thomas Spell Jr., and Aaron Spell.[23] Later, the two Regiments were combined and, at times, caused confusion. This is why sometimes you will read that Joseph Sharp was under the command of Major Lawrence Moore; and by his discharge document, he was in Captain Abner Bickham's Company.

Fighting erupted in the waters off St. Tammany as Thomas *ap* Catesby Jones tiny naval flotilla engaged the British in Lake Borgne near the Rigolets as they advanced against New Orleans.[24]

The Battle of Lake Borgne occurred when British Admiral Cochran gave the order "to clear the Lakes." Forty barges loaded with soldiers and sailors attacked the five gunboats which were led by Lt. Thomas *ap* Catesby Jones in *Gunboat No. 5*. The gunboats were overwhelmed after a desperate fight.[25] Lt. Jones, an important player in the formative period in U.S. naval history, was wounded in the shoulder and all of the gunboat crews were captured. The Battle of Lake Borgne had given General Jackson three precious days to establish his defense.

Born in Philadelphia, in 1772, Marine Major Daniel Carmick was appointed lieutenant of Marines in May 1798, and entered the new Marine Corps as captain July 11, 1798. During the Quasi-War with France he commanded the marine detachment in *Constitution*, and served with distinction in the Mediterranean.

A night battle occurred on December 28, 1814, at Villere's Plantation on the river below New Orleans. Major Carmick commanded the Marines in the Battle of New Orleans. He was wounded in this engagement. He died of his injury in St. Tammany Parish on November 6, 1816, and was buried in the New Orleans St. Louis Cemetery.

John D. Henley, a Barbary War veteran, commanded schooner *Carolina* during the Battle of New Orleans. After the delaying action by Lt. Thomas *ap* Catesby Jones at Lake Borgne, *Carolina* and other ships harassed the British with naval gunfire while protecting General Andrew Jackson's flank on the Mississippi River. Henley's ship was destroyed, but he made a major contribution in the last great victory of the war.[26]

John D. Henley rose to the rank of Captain on March 5, 1817, and continued to serve with distinction until May 23, 1835, when he died on board *Vandalia* at Havana, Cuba.

General David B. Morgan of Madisonville who commanded the forces on the west bank of the Mississippi was charged with the primary task of defending a battery of guns commanded by Commodore Daniel T. Patterson which had been engaged in bombarding the British troops attacking General Jackson's forces on the other side of the river. Patterson requested help for Morgan.

On January 8, 1815, some 250 poorly armed Kentuckians arrived, men who had marched all night, on empty stomachs. At once, Morgan sent them to the line; then sent word to Major Paul Arnaud, at the outpost three miles below the line, to retreat to the line. The British had landed on the west bank of the river. Arnaud and his men retreated completely, and the Kentuckians, seeing the retreat, joined in. Order was maintained, until one Kentuckian called, "Every man for himself," and they fled in disarray. Morgan gained control of the few remaining troops much below the line. Morgan's soldiers were routed by British troops commanded by Lt. Colonel William B. Thornton and the battery was lost. The British claimed victory on the West bank.

Later, a court of inquiry was held to investigate the defeat on the west bank. General Morgan was cleared; the blame was placed on the Kentuckians and Major Arnaud.

A picture of a plaque in New Orleans states the role that General Morgan played during the "Battle of New Orleans". From the script at the Cabildo in New Orleans, Louisiana:

> Simultaneous with the main battle on the east bank of the Mississippi, U.S. and British forces engaged in combat on the west bank. British Colonel William Thornton led 300 soldiers, 200 marines, 200 sailors and part of the 5th West India Regiment against about 1000 Louisiana and Kentucky militiamen commanded by Brigadier General David B. Morgan. Thornton's mission was to silence U.S. Commander Patterson's batteries and use them against Jackson's flank.

On January 9, 1815, Captain Sam Dale of Mississippi was sent on horseback by General Jackson to deliver word of the victory at New Orleans to the government in Washington. He traveled by boat to Madisonville and continued the journey overland.

The war ended, General William B. Carroll and his Tennesseans headed home. They crossed Lake Pontchartrain to Madisonville, then using public wagons from the navy yard at Madisonville to transport the troops, they headed northwest on the Madison-Liberty-Mississippi road to a point on the east side of the Tangipahoa River. From there, they cut a new road, straight north, to the Choctaw agency on the Natchez Trace, above the present city of Jackson, Mississippi.[27]

Lt. Merrill's movements during the Battle of New Orleans are obscure. It is likely that he was at the facility on the Tchefuncte River protecting the Block Ship with Lt. Michael B. Carroll. The Navy Yard on the Tchefuncte had been used during the War of 1812 to induct men on the north shore into the Louisiana Militia. A month after the Battle of New Orleans, the order was given to discharge the 12th and 13th Regiments at the Navy Yard immediately.

Three of Morgan Edwards and Margaret Smith's children fought in the Battle of New Orleans. Daniel Edwards, born 1787, died July 5, 1877 at the age of 90. He built a home near the boundary between present-day Washington and St. Tammany parishes where he was a planter and raised livestock. In his young adult life, Daniel operated schooners on Lake Pontchartrain. In 1810, he represented the St. Ferdinand District in the convention that called for an end to Spanish rule in the West Florida Rebellion. He served in the War of 1812 as a private in the 10th Regiment of the Louisiana Militia, and fought in the Battle of New Orleans. After the end of the hostilities, he was elected to the rank of general in the Louisiana Militia by a joint committee of the state legislature. He served in the Louisiana Legislature from 1828 to 1832, representing St. Tammany Parish. In 1845, he was elected to the state senate. On April 7, 1814, Daniel married Mary "Polly" Cooper, daughter of Henry and Elizabeth Cooper. They had five children. His second marriage was to Elizabeth Ann Bankston, daughter of Elizabeth Brewer and Lesley Bankston with whom he had ten children.

Robert Thomas Edwards born 1794, died *circa* 1835. He married Easter Gill and they had three children. Robert served as a private in Thomas Bickham's Company, 12th and 13th Consolidated Regiments, Louisiana Militia, in the War of 1812. He represented Washington Parish in the state legislature in 1832 and 1833.

Charles Morgan Edwards, born December 8, 1797, died February 1866. He married Elizabeth Roach, daughter of Mary Cobb and Jordan Roach. They had seven children. Charles was baptized in the St. Louis Cathedral in New Orleans on April 17, 1798, at four months of age, one week after the death of his father. He was two years old when his mother married Hugh Samuel Sheridan. He served in the War of 1812 as a private in Captain Sprigg's Company of Boatmen (Louisiana Volunteers). After his marriage in 1818, he was living in Jackson, Mississippi, where he operated a tavern.

A month after the Battle of New Orleans, Major John Wright who had command of the navy yard was ordered to muster out the men and retain all arms. A U.S. Navy census of ships at New Orleans, in 1816, shows that the *"Tchefuncta"* was still on its stocks and still on the Navy rolls. Lt. Michael B. Carroll had resigned his commission and returned to Maryland, where he married and became a "gentleman farmer."

In the latter part of 1816 Lt. Merrill commanded the Navy Yard in St. Tammany. He was in charge of the *Tchifonta* when, in 1818, a fire broke out one night at the yard. A few Marines, on guard, had lit a fire to keep warm and it got out of control catching a shed on fire which burned down. He had a run in with Captain Daniel Patterson, in 1818, over that fire and went on half pay retirement.[28] In 1821, the new Navy Secretary ordered Captain Patterson to recall Lt. Merrill to full time duty. His re-entering the service did not last long. He died at Madisonville on July 17, 1822.

The early years of statehood were eventful for the area north of Lake Pontchartrain, but American control did not herald the emergence of prosperity in the region. Pioneers had become enthusiastic citizens by latter 1814 and had rallied behind General Jackson, in 1814, when he marched his mountaineer soldiers across the Pearl River and improvised a road through the forest.

With the War of 1812 and the Battle of New Orleans in 1815, changes had come rapidly to the North shore. New roads had been built, providing easier access to New Orleans. A cantonment was constructed on the banks of the Little Bogue Falaya River, a few miles north of Covington, and was occupied by the 3rd Regiment of Infantry of the United States Army during 1812. By 1813, it was said to be vacant.

On June 26, 1814, the headquarters of the Seventh Military District were established at the navy yard near Madisonville under the command of Brigadier General Thomas Flournoy. The Seventh Infantry Regiment had been transferred earlier that month with Major John Nicks in command. The men stationed there did not appreciate the area.[29]

Fort Oak was still standing at Madisonville as was indicated on a map of Louisiana of 1819.[30] It disappeared from the map shortly after 1820.

Washington Parish was created out of the northern section of St. Tammany in 1819. The new parish line was described as "beginning at David Robertson's on the Tanchipaho, thence a direct line to Daniel Edwards' on the Tchifoncta, thence a direct line to the Strawberry Bluffs on the Bogue Chitto, and from thence a line on east until it strikes Pearl River.[31]

John Spell Jr. was fifty years old in 1817 when his children Aaron, John and Thomas left the Bayou Castein area to relocate to the northern part of St. Tammany that became Washington Parish. Sanders Spell married Ann Vardeman in 1816 in St. Tammany parish and Aaron Spell married Jemina Vardeman. The Spells settled on vacant land near the Vernardo settlement on the Bogue Chitto River. The Vardeman or Vernardo were early settlers in Washington Parish, but no settlers of a permanent nature appeared earlier than 1810. The settlements were founded mostly on "headrights" granted by the Spanish colonial power in the first years of the nineteenth century shortly and prior to the Louisiana Transfer.

Congress passed a law in 1818 giving the President the power to sell military facilities that were no longer needed. In 1822, the decision was made to break up the Block ship *Tchefuncta* on its stocks and send the useful parts, the finest live oak that could be used, to the navy yards on the East Coast.[32] The government was interested in using trees for boat construction.[33] By 1823, the navy yard was reported abandoned.

James Cathcart was assigned by the War Department to survey the coastal area for oak trees, especially those on public lands, while J.D. Ferris was requested to report on oaks in the Tchefuncte area, relaying the reports through Commodore Patterson to Cathcart. There was an available market for trees! In 1821, at Bayou Castein, Elizabeth Goodby, widow of Thomas Spell, started her slaves cutting trees on disputed land.

NOTES

1. Boagni, Ethel, *Mandeville, Louisiana*, The St. Tammany Historical Society, Inc., 1980, 18.
2. Ellis, Frederick S., *St. Tammany Parish, L'Autre Côté du Lac*, Pelican Publishing Company, Gretna, 1998, 101.
3. Ellis, Frederick S., *St. Tammany Parish*, 95.
4. Campeau, Anita R. & Sharp, Donald J., "The United States Navy and the Naval Station at New Orleans, 1804-1826, "*New Orleans Genesis*, Volume XLIX, July 2011, 258.
5. Ibid., 259.
6. Ibid., 259-260.
7. Appleton's Encyclopedia of American Biographies and Company, 1900.
8. Calhoun, Robert Dabney, History of Concord: *Historical Quarterly*, XV, 1932.
9. Probate #38, Elizabeth Middleton, Probate B. Morgan, 1848, 8th Judicial District Court.
10. Lt. Daniel S. Dexter to Captain John Shaw, U.S. Gun Vessel *No. 162*, August 23, 1812.
11. Campeau, Anita R. & Sharp, Donald J., "The United States Navy and the Naval Station at New Orleans, 1804-1826," *New Orleans Genesis*, Volume XLIX, July 2011, No. 195, 270.

12. Captain John Shaw's Letter Book: December 18, 1810, to December 31, 1813, Library of Congress, 560 pages. Reference made to the letter of Captain Shaw to General Wilkinson, New Orleans, dated December 12, 1812, 500.

13. Inquests March 8, 1813, Probate 122½, Advertisement. Twelve copies distributed to Judge Tate, Covington Court House).

14. Act of Louisiana Legislature, March 25, 1813.

15. Parish Judge for St. Tammany Parish from October 1811 to March 1813.

16. Letter, Claiborne to Armstrong, April 14, 1813. Rowland, *Official Letter Books*, Volume VI, 267.

17. Dunbar, Rowland, ed., *Official Letter Books of W.C.C. Claiborne, 1801-1816*, Volume 6, Jackson: Mississippi State Department of Archives and History, 1917.

18. Campeau, Anita R. & Sharp, Donald J., "The United States Navy and the Naval Station at New Orleans, 1804-1826," *New Orleans Genesis*, Volume XLIX, 272.

19. Boagni, Ethel, *Mandeville, Louisiana*, 21. Her reference: A. Cacarriere Latour, *Historical Memoir of the War in West Florida and Louisiana in 1814-1815*, Gainesville, University of Florida Press, 1964.

20. Casey, Powell A., *Louisiana in the War of 1812*, 1963, 10.

21. Boagni, Ethel, *Mandeville, Louisiana*, 9.

22. Campeau, Anita R. & Sharp, Donald J., "The Tom Spell Memorial Cemetery, Part 4," *The New Orleans Genesis*, Volume XLVIII, October 2010, No. 192, 373.

23. Crane, John, *Annotated Genealogical Listings of the Southern Bickhams*, Second Edition, 1992, 75.

24. Campeau, Anita R., & Sharp, Donald J., "The United States Navy and the Naval Station at New Orleans, 1804-1826," *New Orleans Genesis*, Volume XLIX, July 2011, No. 195, 268.

25. Gun Boat No. 5, built in 1804, in Baltimore, Maryland, was captured by the British on December 14, 1814.

26. Text is from the public domain *Dictionary of American Naval Fighting Ships*.

27. Boagni, Ethel, *Madisonville, Louisiana*, 23.

28. Campeau, Anita R. & Sharp, Donald J., "The U.S. Navy and the Naval Station at New Orleans, 1804-1826," *New Orleans Genesis*, July 2011, 274.

29. Letter of Captain William McClellan to General Andrew Jackson dated July 10, 1814.

30. Tanner's map of Philadelphia.

31. Act of Louisiana Legislature, March 6, 1819, 89.

32. Letter from Smith Thompson of the Navy Department to John Rogers, President of the Naval Board dated June 7, 1822.

33. Prichard, Walter, Kniffen, Fred, and Brown, Clair A. (eds.), "The Journal of James Leander Cathcart," *Louisiana Historical Quarterly*, XXVIII, 1945.

CHAPTER 9

THE GOODBY & SPELL FAMILY CONNECTIONS AT
BAYOU CASTEIN

The Amite River begins in what is the present state of Mississippi and courses down through the parishes of East Feliciana, St. Helena, East Baton Rouge, Livingston, and Ascension forming boundary lines between the same. On a Louisiana map, note that in Livingston Parish the Amite turns eastward to finally empty into Lake Maurepas. Its deep waters were ideal for commerce and transportation. The Comite River is a tributary to the Amite River with a confluence near today's city of Denham Springs, located east of Baton Rouge.

According to early surveys, the land along the Amite River was divided into long narrow strips with so many arpents of river frontage allotted to each owner, thus creating a line-type village similar to the pattern that existed on the St. Lawrence River in Quebec. The ribbon farms on the St. Lawrence were 40 by 80 arpents in depth (1½ by 3 miles). The pattern of long lots is a feature of North American geography that may be seen from Quebec, to the Illinois, to Texas. The cultural geographer, Terry G. Jordan, loosely defined a long lot as any rectangular parcel of land whose depth was at least three times in width.[1]

Orders from Governor Peter Chester, in British West Florida, directed that each grant should contain a proportional number of profitable and unprofitable acres so that the choicest locations might not be monopolized by the few. The breadth of each grant was to be one-third of the length, and the length of any tract did not extend along the banks of any river, "but into the mainland, that thereby the said grantees may each have a convenient share of what accommodation the said river may afford to navigation of otherwise."[2] There were several environmental reasons that favored location and shape of lots since it gave access to the settlers to the main artery for transportation, the river. This type of survey gave access to the river for fishing, an important source of food. The width gave convenient proximity to one's neighbors on either side for protection and companionship.

An important document that helped us in our research was the William Wilton Map of 1774. Wilton was Deputy Surveyor General of the Province of West Florida during the early 1770s. His map, upon the request of Governor Chester, is entitled "Part of the River Mississippi from Manchac to the River Yazous." It appears that this map remained in the lower Mississippi Valley when the British departed in 1781. It became the property of an East Baton Rouge Parish surveyor; then a private collector purchased the map in 1848 from that official. Eventually the map came into the possession of the Mississippi River Commission. It came to light in the 1930s when historian Stanley C. Arthur found the original manuscript in the files of the Mississippi River Commission at Vicksburg. Copies were made and placed in various Louisiana repositories, one of which is the Center for Southeast Louisiana Studies, in Hammond, Louisiana. The Goodbee lot on this map is site number 306.

The Goodbee (also Goodby, Godeby, Goteby, and Goadby) family tree has been traced all the way back to the *Domesday Book*, in 1086.[3] For our purpose, we begin with the Goodby family history with Thomas Goteby, born December 27, 1626, in the village of Earl Shilton, Leicestershire, England. He died February 16, 1668 in Hinckley, England.

Beginning in the year 1629, Englishmen lived through perilous times, a period in history that can be described as the struggle between the English Parliament and a king who claimed to be an absolute monarch that led to the establishment, first of a republic, and then a monarchy more powerful than that, which the Civil Wars had destroyed. In 1649, after the trial and execution of King Charles I, a Commonwealth was proclaimed and this fragment of a Parliament was maintained for four years after his death.[4]

In 1662, Thomas Goteby who had sided with the Royalists prudently decided to hide out in the market town of Hinckley some 13 miles of Leicester. His son John was born there on March 2, 1654. The history of the patriarch of the clan in America begins with John and his wife, Elizabeth Dallison, daughter of Robert Dallison and Sarah Goodman. They brought the Goodby blood line to Berkely County, South Carolina.

On May 12, 1682, John Goteby "was brought to the province by Mr. James Weetch, his master, in the ship called *Billbow* (Balboa), commanded by the merchant James Pullman who arrived on the coast of South Carolina and entered Charleston harbor."[5]

On the 6th day of February 1692, by arrival rights, the Governor of the province gave instructions to surveyor Thomas Smith "of which survey to make a certificate for a land grant in the community of Goose Creek, Berkely, South Carolina."[6] John Goteby was recorded as living there in 1690, and it is where he died on October 18, 1720. The National Society of Colonial Dames list John Goodby (1654-1720) as a landowner and that he had military service in South Carolina.

Six children were issued from this marriage, of which James Goodbee, born about 1686, died March 29, 1736, at 50 years of age, in Berkely County, South Carolina.

James Goodbee/Goodby has the title of Captain which was probably a militia rank in South Carolina. He could have had a first marriage to Anna Gordon prior to 1725, exact date and parents unknown. He is said to have been 43 years of age when he married Hannah Warnock, *circa* 1729. They were the parents of Thomas Goodby, probably the eldest child, since he was listed as the executor of his father's estate. Sarah Goodby married there to John Middleton in 1746. James, born June 21, 1730, married Sarah Miller in 1760.[7] We have no information on siblings Anna and Robert Goodby. Elizabeth Goodby married William Guy. Joseph Goodby, probably the second eldest child, married Anna Atkins, date of her birth, marriage and parents unknown.

Hannah Warnock has a second marriage to John Mimmack, a school teacher, on February 23, 1737. She died in 1740.

Captain James Goodby's Last Will and Testament is recorded in the South Carolina Will Book, 1732-1737. Whereas "Son Joseph's bequest was for two hundred acres in St. Thomas' Parish, ...bounded on the east by Mr. Welswysen, on the west by Mr. Joseph Singleterry's, and two hundred acres more on Four Hole Branch known by the name of Joseph Bryan's Spring; a negro boy named Billy and a negro girl named Lena, to take possession at twenty years of age." Obviously this was a date still in the future.

There is no record of the disposition of the land in South Carolina inherited by Joseph from his father. Still, it is recorded in the Council Journal (advisory council to the Royal Governor of the colony) for 1751 that "Joseph Goodby, who has six Negroes in his family for whom he has no land asks 300 acres on the south side of the Saluda River." This request was granted. Thus according to the above facts, the wealth amassed by John Goodby Senior and passed along for two generations had, by the 1750s, disappeared.

Joseph Goodby left South Carolina and removed to the Colony of Georgia in 1756, as evidenced when he received, on September 8 of that year, a land grant from the British Crown on the south side of the Newport River in St. John's Parish, District of Midway (present-day Liberty County).[8] In Colonial Georgia, the earliest political subdivisions conformed to the Church of England parishes. Counties, as we know them, did not come into existence until 1777.

On November 25, 1756, two months after he had received a land grant, Joseph Goodbee sold his tract of land to Thomas Carter.[9] It appears that Mr. Carter did not take immediate possession of the property. Joseph Goodby is then listed as a resident of Satilla, Georgia. His presence in Georgia is once more confirmed on March 17, 1761, by the fact that he witnessed a land sale by Robert Lucas to Jacob Lockerman in St. John's Parish, Georgia.[10]

James Goodby and Anna Isabel Atkins had James, born in Georgia, but the exact date of birth is not known. He arrived in Louisiana with his parents who first settled at Manchac. Their daughter Elizabeth because of the number of children she had, 13 over her lifetime, and the year she died in 1844 strongly indicates that she was born between the years 1772-1775 on the Amite River. In that case, she could very well be one of the first white children born on the Amite in the limits of what is now the city of Denham Springs.[11] There is a possible John of whom nothing is known.

The land grant that Joseph Goodby and Anna Atkins received on July 24, 1772, in British West Florida, consisted of 300 acres on family right above the junction of Amite and Comite rivers which would be located today in the heart of Denham Springs, a few miles east of today's bustling Baton Rouge, Louisiana. According to their location, early residents could have depended on the springs for drinking water. The Goodbee tract was adjacent to that of Landon Davis, (No. 305) and Elias Durnford (No. 307).

Landon Davis, also of Georgia, on July 28, 1772, was given a tract of 300 acres, (No. 305). He received on December 31, 1775, 100 acres on family right and 100 acres by purchase at the junction of Amite and Comite rivers.

The Goodby family lived on their plantation on the Amite River to 1778, until forced out by Captain James Willing and his raiders when they plundered the area, burning houses and destroying crops and livestock that they could not take with them. Everyone fled the River! Families crossed the Iberville River as did the Goodby, Davis, Westcott and Canty, while others fled to Natchez or Pensacola.

In the spring of 1778, merchant John Fitzpatrick asked Thomas Westcott: "Have you been to the forks of the Amite River lately?" Thomas Westcott's answer to Fitzpatrick: "No, there is no one left on the river. All have gone and all homes have been destroyed. It is too dangerous to go there!"

"What Willing's men did not burn and destroy, the Indians finished the job," said Governor Chester in London before the Claims Committee in 1785.

It was in November 1778 that, Bernardo de Galvez, on a reconnaissance mission to explore his new territory in order to ascertain where to strengthen Spanish defense against the British in West Florida arrived at the northeast corner of the Isle of Orleans where Bayou Manchac converges with the Amite River. In his report dated January 15, 1779, he stated that he had "inspected a site of high lands near the junction of the rivers Amite and Iberville not known until now by the people of the country, and discovered by chance by the English and Americans who had fled to the possessions of the King of Spain." It is known that the Goodby, Davis, Westcott and Canty families fled there from across the river after raids by the American Captain James Willing and a raid by Indians.

The squatters were welcomed by the Spanish governor who extended to them the colony's hospitality and protection. They formed a village and named it Galveztown as a mark of gratitude to the Governor under whom they had found refuge.

The capture of West Florida by Galvez spelled the ruin for Galveztown for with the passing of British rule went the major reason for its existence. Deprived of government support, the settlement began to disintegrate and within a few years it was deserted.

After 1783, the land on the north shore of Lake Pontchartrain was under Spanish authority and land grants could now be officially granted. James Goodby and his sister relocated to the area in 1790 after having received a Spanish land grant.

The Goodby family did not return to the Amite, even after the Treaty of Peace was signed in 1783. It would take another ten years before a few settlers applied for the Spanish grants at "the fork of the Rivers". This was the start of the American settlers coming in from the east. The history of the patriarchs of these clans is blurred by the tragic and catastrophic events of their time, but it is these families that are credited with colonizing the area. Life on the Amite had been tragic and difficult!

In the eighteenth century Bayou Manchac was called the Iberville River. The Iberville or Manchac River mentioned in the various treaties and laws is no longer in existence. It connected with the Mississippi River a short distance from Baton Rouge, and entered into Lake Maurepas at its extreme western end. The river was closed by order of General Jackson shortly before the Battle of New Orleans. Today there are no vestiges of a town or a fort at Galveztown.

About 1788, James Goodby married Diana Ross, daughter of John Ross and Maria Morrison. On November 6, 1776, John Ross obtained 350 acres on family right on the south side of Bayou Pierre. He arrived in the province, in May 1773, with his wife and four children.[12]

James and his wife, Diana Ross, and his sister Elizabeth Goodby, came down about 1790 to the lake front at Bayou Castein, then called Pontchartrain Post, and settled on the land that Hugh Davis had previously occupied on the banks of Bayou Chinchuba. In those days the area was known as "Hugh's Bank." They had signed their allegiance to the Spanish Crown. Edward Ross, Diana's brother, moved to the Bayou Castein area that same year and settled on a 1,200 arpents Spanish land grant on abandoned land between James Goodby and Morgan Edwards.

In 1804, there was trouble at Baton Rouge when the Kemper Brothers attempted to ferment a rebellion against the Spanish. Edward Ross, a Lieutenant in the Spanish militia, was called into active service. He was an interpreter and guide for a Spanish expedition from Pensacola to Baton Rouge. For his services, he was entitled to apply for a land grant: 1,000 acres of land on the lower Amite River where "the King's Road crosses the river on the way to Baton Rouge." After selling half of his land to John Knight and the other half to Samuel Lloyd, he moved with his family to his new grant in 1806. The 1200 arpents Spanish grant he sold plays a key role in Court Case No. 225.

John Goodby, son of James and Diana Ross, was baptized in the Catholic Church, St. Louis Cathedral, New Orleans, on May 22, 1791. Old Joseph Goodby, the child's grandfather and now a widower, appears in the baptismal records of St. Louis Cathedral.[13] Joseph Goodby, the widower, has a second marriage to widow Marguerite Morrison (sister of Marie). Joseph Goodby died about 1800, in Louisiana.

James Goodby and his family lived on their Spanish grant on Bayou Chinchuba for fifteen years in the family home he had built. Diana died shortly after the birth of her fifth child in 1799. Where was she buried? Perhaps Chinchuba! If not, there may be a reason why she was not buried on their property since there was no catholic cemetery on the north shore. She was Catholic. John Ross and Margarita Morrison, her parents, lived at Galveztown along with her brother Stephen Ross. Edward Ross, Diana's brother, had moved in next to the Goodby place from the Tchefuncte River in 1798. He and James Goodby could have taken the body across the lake to Galveztown and buried her in hallowed ground.

James Goodby, the widower, left Bayou Chinchuba with his family and brother-in-law, Edward Ross and family. They relocated to the new 1,000 arpents Spanish grant at the road crossing on the Amite River, about sixteen miles from Galveztown.

James Goodby's second marriage was recorded at the St. Gabriel church, in Galveztown, on June 11, 1801. His bride, Nancy Bush, was the widow of Ignace Hamilton who had a plantation in Pointe Coupee Parish. Nancy Bush, born August 16, 1768, was the daughter of Daniel and Diana Louis (Lewis). Witnesses were Maurice Dousse and Daniel Landry.

Daniel Bush was born about 1730 in Virginia, and Diana Lewis born about 1752, died at age 32. She was originally from Booneville, Owsley, Virginia. On October 13, 1775, Daniel Bush was granted 1,000 acres near the Amite River, about two and a half miles back. He had petitioned for 2,000 acres on the Mississippi River between Point Coupee and Manchac on August 6, 1768. He said that there were 24 persons in the family. He was granted 1,000 acres if the grant was taken up in seven months.[14]

James Goodby moved to Iberville Parish where he claimed a tract of land, on the right bank of the Mississippi that was inhabited and cultivated on December 20, 1803, and for more than ten years prior thereto." At the time of his death James Goodby left three children, to wit: John Lawrence Goodby, Anna Cecilia Goodby, deceased, wife of Webb, and Mathilda Goodby.

John Lawrence Goodby, son of James and Diana Ross, was born November 3, 1794, on Bayou Castein, and died March 8, 1869, in Covington, Louisiana. He was first married to Sarah Wilson on September 9, 1822, daughter of George Wilson and Hannah Doughty. His second marriage, in 1829, was to Nancy Ann Lloyd, daughter of Samuel Lloyd and Mary Catherine Davis.

John Lawrence Goodby served as a private in Captain Charles R. Hick's Company of Colonel Alexandre DeCluet's Regiment of drafted Louisiana Militia during the War of 1812.[15] He was in the siege of New Orleans in December 1814 and January 1815 and was honorably discharged at the termination of the war.

Governor Claiborne had ordered Captain Hick's Company stationed at Lafourche to New Orleans. They were equipped with one twelve-pound cannon. In the battle of December 23, 1814, the company was still there. The regiment fought in the battles on the West bank of the Mississippi River on January 7 and 8, 1815, but it is not known if Captain Hicks' Company took part.

After his discharge, Private John Goodby returned to his home in Iberville Parish. He later moved to the Covington area of St. Tammany Parish. On April 5, 1830, he purchased a lot in Claiborne Hills, Covington, for $30.00. He built a small house and his wife named it Spring Hill Cottage. In 1840, he purchased a 240 acre tract from Judge Jesse Jones on the Bogue Falaya River.

John Lawrence Goodby died on March 8, 1869, and was buried in St. Tammany Parish. On October 12, 1869, in the J.J. Mortee Papers (St.

Tammany Probate Judge), Nancy Lloyd stated that the following nine children, all of whom are full age, were born of their marriage:
1. David Goodby, no other information.
2. Harriet Goodby was first married to James Hornby in 1853, and has a second marriage to Freeman Burns.
3. Duncan Goodby married Sarah E. Eudley in 1865.
4. Francis (Frank) Goodby was first married to Cynthia Ann Ewing, and second to Rosetta Camelia Spell.
5. Roseria Goodby never married.
6. Thomas Goodby never married.
7. John Goodby never married.
8. Eliza Ann Goodby married William T. Sondman.
9. Serenia Goodby married Thomas M. Gill.

Frank Goodby, the fourth child of John Lawrence Goodby and Nancy Ann Lloyd, married Rosetta Camelia Spell, daughter of Thomas Spell and Sarah Peters, on January 7, 1873; she died January 1, 1937. Their daughter Sarah Goodby, born in 1876 may have died at a young age. Rosetta's grandparents were Thomas T. Spell and Mary Sodon, and her great-grandparents were Thomas Spell and Elizabeth Goodby. Rosetta Spell has a second marriage to John Dash who was born in 1859; he died in March 1898, and was buried in the Mandeville Cemetery.

After the Civil War, Frank Goodby joined Morgan's Raiders. On his return, he brought some loot home and buried it on the Goodby property along the Bogue Falaya River, north of Covington. On October 8, 1878, he rode his horse to Covington and on this fatal day got into a fight and died without ever revealing where he had buried his loot. His treasure was never found, so the story goes.[16]

Nancy Ann Lloyd is listed as a widow of the War of 1812, List of Pensioners, and was awarded a monthly pension of $8.00 in 1874 when she was living in Covington.

Shortly after her arrival in Bayou Castein, Elizabeth Goodbee married Thomas Spell, born about 1769, in South Carolina, the son of John Spell and Cecilia MacLemore. We now credit him among the early British settlers on the north shore of Lake Pontchartrain.

The name Spell first appears in America in the early 1700s. The named John Spell was brought to Charles City, Virginia, as an indentured servant by Thomas Thrower and George Passmore, colonial planters. In 1745, John and Thomas Spell were listed as early settlers from Brunswick County, Virginia, to Edgecombe County, North Carolina. In 1747, John and Thomas Spell of Brunswick County, Virginia, bought land on the Tar River in Edgecombe County, North Carolina. Several land transactions show that the Spell brothers owned a quantity of mother earth and had a very good start in life.

John Spell Sr. married Cecilia "Seely" MacLemore, daughter of Wright MacLemore, of Tarboro, Edgecombe County, but the date of their marriage and the name of her mother are not known. John Spell and his wife Cecilia sold land on January 25, 1774, in Edgecombe County to Davis Coker for 40 pounds, current money, a tract of 118 acres on the north bank of White Oak Swamp at the mouth of the Tantrough Branch; it being the land that was granted to Wright MacLemore from the Right Honorable John Earl Granville, Viscount Carteret, by deed bearing date 28 June 1760.[17] This recorded transaction could suggest that Wright Macklemoor (*sic*) had given this land for the purpose of helping his daughter and son-in-law get their start in life.

Originally from Tarboro, North Carolina, John and Cecilia MacLemore relocated to Charleston, South Carolina, when the hostilities broke out in the Thirteen Colonies. From there they went to Florida, possibly St. Augustine, for a short period of time. They followed the trail through the panhandle of Florida and Pensacola, arriving around 1775. Mager Spell and John Spell petitioned the government requesting land on Bayou Castein and Lake Pontchartrain on November 11, 1775. Since Mager Spell reported to the officials along with John Spell, in 1775, when John Spell made his application for land left by the deceased Joseph Spell, we presume that this Joseph Spell could have been John's father or his brother.

The children of John Spell and Cecilia MacLemore later made their homes on property that is now Mandeville, Louisiana. Joseph Spell was identified as an uncle of the Thomas Spell children and was appointed guardian of the minor children in June 1815.[18]

On December 4, 1786, John Spell Jr. married Sarah "Rosalie" Westcott, at Galveztown. It was stated on the marriage record that John's parents were deceased. Sarah Rosalie's father, Thomas Westcott Sr., was a pioneer from Virginia who brought in a load of settlers in 1770. From the *Letter book* of John Fitzpatrick, a merchant at Manchac, we learn that William Canty and his wife Elizabeth Westcott died in 1778, and that Thomas Wescott, whose wife was a Canty, was appointed administrator for the deceased on June 8, 1778.[19] He and his wife died less than a year later at Galveztown.[20]

The minor children were taken in by relatives or close friends. Sarah (Rosalie) Westcott who was raised by her uncle Michael Jones and her aunt Amy Canty stated that she was twenty years of age when she married. That would make her about 13 years of age when her parents died. She gave the name of her uncle and aunt as her maternal parents.

John Spell Sr. and Cecilia MacLemore died prior to December 1786 at Pontchartrain Post. We do not know exactly where they were buried, possibly on the Spell property as was the custom of the day to be buried on your improvement. In the year 1795, from a Spanish document, we learn that at the time of his death John Spell Sr. "left two legitimate sons by his wife Cecilia McLemore of Lake Pontchartrain," and that he had "lived with a certain Ana Davis, unmarried, and upon his death she took over his estate." Not satisfied with the outcome, John Spell Junior gave power of attorney to José Piernas to institute action against the said Ana Davis to recover his share of the estate of his father.[21]

John Spell and Rosalie Westcott were the parents of five children: John A, Joseph, Sarah "Sally", Aaron and Thomas Spell. Rosalie Westcott does not appear in records after 1795 and there were apparently no more children. When she died is not known. In 1816, John Spell sold his share of his father's land to Sanders Spell, who in turn sold it to Elizabeth Goodby, widow of Thomas Spell. Through a witness heard in Court Case No. 225, it appears that John Spell Jr., was living by himself in the woods of his 640 acres, purchased for ten dollars from John Knight in 1810. A declaration by John Spell Jr. dated July 5, 1817, attests the latest date of his presence on the North Shore. There is no certainty, but he could be buried next to his brother Thomas Spell.

John, Aaron, and Thomas Spell and Sarah, wife of Joseph Sharp, of St. Tammany, were the only legal heirs of the deceased John Spell Junior.

In 1790, James Goodby, brother of Elizabeth, made an assignment of his land to Thomas Spell. The record reads: I, James Goodbee, of the District of Casten Bayou do assign all my right and title of a certain tract of land situated on a certain branch in said district known by the name of Chinchuba or Hugh's Banks's Branch, unto Thomas Spell of the above district for values received.

The document dated February 20, 1791, was signed by James Goodby. The section was originally granted to James Goodby by the Spanish Crown as was confirmed by Carlos Trudeau, surveyor general, on January 8, 1798. The David Bannister Morgan map indicates for the first time the original "Road to Covington" cutting through the land tract and crossing Chinchuba Creek where it intersected with an East-West "road to Bayou Lacombe." West of the Covington road is located the house of Delisle de la Barthe, an early settler of the area. On the eastern side of the Goodby tract, close to where the Covington road crosses Chinchuba Creek was the house of Thomas Spell.[22]

It was stated in a document dated 1813, by order from James Goodby to Thomas Spell: "I do authorize and empower Thomas Spell of Lake Pontchartrain district of Castin Bayou to receive the Plot of a Certain tract of Land situated on Chinchuba or Hugh's Banks's Branch surveyed by Major Gilmore for me in the year 1798."[23]

Elizabeth Goodby and Thomas Spell raised a family of twelve children. The children above the age of maturity in 1815 were Helen, Thomas T., Amelia, and Cecilia Spell.[24] Since the family is now quite numerous and widespread in several States, it is important to write down the names of the first generation born at Bayou Castein.

1. According to her Certificate of Baptism, Helena Isabel Spell was born on the 20th of May 1793, place not indicated, and was baptized on the 24th of November 1795 at St. Louis Cathedral, New Orleans, by the Reverend Father Luis de Quintanella. The sponsors were Ursine Bouligne and Isabel Labatte. A note says that the parents were natives of Carolina in North America and residents of this parish.[25] She married Freeman George about 1808. They lived on the Goodby/Spell tract (320 acres) until 1812.[26] They then moved to the Tangipahoa River to be next to his father and brothers.

In 1821, Freeman George, his wife, and his large family of seven sons removed to Texas to join Stephen F. Austin in his settlement of Texas. They were among the original 300 settlers.[27] On July 7, 1824, Freeman George, one of Austin "Old Three Hundred," received title to one league and a labor of land in present Matagorda and Waller counties. Freeman George and his sons appear if the First Census of Texas, where he is listed between forty and fifty years of age, and his occupation listed as a farmer and stock raiser. He died in Matagorda. As he died intestate, his brother David was appointed administrator of his estate on November 26, 1834. His widow and her son Nicholas are found in the 1850 Wharton County Census living in the home of David George, his wife and children.[28] Only two of the eight sons lived to adulthood, married and had children. There is no record of the location of the burial sites for this couple. Permission was granted for their descendants to place a cenotaph in the Old City Cemetery of San Marcos, Texas. It is located on the plot where their son David George and grandson Jefferson are buried. On this monument is a bronze medallion that says "Stephen F. Austin's Old Three Hundred."

2. Thomas T. Spell born October 26, 1797, died December 20, 1858. He married Mary Sodon, the daughter of Henry Sodon, and the widow of Amos Richardson who died in 1823. It was on February 10, 1816, in St.

Tammany, that Mary Sodon married Amos Richardson, son of George and Mary Shepherd McFadden. The Richardson had settled on the abandoned land of Widow Rebecca Ambrose. Mary died in 1858 and was buried Chinchuba Cemetery. The Spell couple stipulated in their succession that "two acres should be retrieved as a family graveyard."[29]

Henry Sodon testified in court Case No. 225 that he settled at Bayou Chinchuba in the year 1808 by permission of William McDermott. His land was located a mile to the edge of the Labyteau tract. William McDermott was living at Bayou Chinchuba as early as 1791, and after having been evicted from the former Labyteau tracts, he obtained permission from Widow Mary C. Lloyd to settle on the Edward Ross tract that her husband had purchased in 1806.

3. Amelia Spell, born 1802, married John Morton on January 31, 1818. No children were issued from this marriage. She was buried in Chinchuba Cemetery. Judged as insane was noted in probate records for mother Elizabeth who died in 1844, death written in January 28, 1852.

4. Celia (Cecilia) Emelita Spell was born July 1795; baptized November 24, 1795 [30] She brought into her marriage a herd of 32 cattle and a slave as a dowry when she married Edmund Morse, on November 21, 1820, St. Tammany.[31] Edmund was born July 24, 1790, possibly a brother of William Morse who owned property in and around Covington. Edmund was involved in a retail establishment in Covington in partnership with Love Green and Eliza Watson. The business did not prosper and he was sued by creditors in 1823. Two years later, his partners sued him over business losses, including store merchandise that had not been paid for. In 1825, his own wife sued him because he sold her cattle and her slave and did not remit her the money. These suits are indexed under "Moss". The couple separated, and Edmund went back to Biloxi where he died August 31, 1837, aged 47 years. Celia remained at Bayou Castein.

Listed in the succession was an improved lot in the town of Biloxi and slaves, and his five daughters with Celia Spell:
a) Martha Morse, aged 17, married John G. Pujol on April 14, 1842.
b) Frances Morse, aged 14, married Henry McVey.
c) Adeline Morse, aged 13, married Joseph Duke (sometimes written as LaDuc).
d). Jane Morse.
e) Virginia, aged 5, married Marshall (known as Marsh) Sharp in 1855 and had a large family. Marshall Sharp was one of the original

purchasers of land in the town of Mandeville, bought directly from Bernard de Marigny.

Celia Spell has a second marriage to Jean J. Pujol, on July 12, 1841. The witnesses were Lemuel Durham, Benedict Myers and Hugh Spell. Pujol bought two lots of ground in Mandeville in 1841 from the succession of Louis Jouet (or Jonett). The lots are described as Square 82, lots 1 and 2. A man named Thomas Spell also bought property from this succession.

Martha Morse, Celia's daughter, married John G. Pujol, (Celia's stepson) originally from France, born 1820. He divorced Martha on October 28, 1845, stating that she was an alcoholic and had chased him around swinging an axe at him. In the divorce proceedings, John Pujol stated that he lived in Lewisburg until his home was destroyed by fire.[32] John G. Pujol remarried after his frightening experience with Martha Rose. He is buried in the Lewisburg Cemetery with his second wife, Ellen Lurin, born County West, Heath, Ireland.

Jean Joseph Pujol died in 1850. He left his house and land in Mandeville to his wife Celia Spell. The matriarch of the family, Celia Spell Morse-Pujol, died February 5, 1858. At a family meeting following her death, her son-in-law, Marshall Sharp applied to be named as administrator for her estate. Celia was still living in Mandeville, on the corner of Lake and Coffee Streets, the same property purchased in 1841. Celia's estate listed 18 slaves, various livestock, home furnishings, and cash.

5. Joseph Jacob Spell was born December 20, 1799. He married Elizabeth Wheeler, born 1814. Joseph left Bayou Castein with his cousins, sons of John Spell Jr., and settled in Washington Parish, then moved on to Mississippi territory when Indian lands opened up through treaties. He died in Simpson County, Mississippi territory. Joseph gave his share of his father's succession to his mother Elizabeth Goodby. In the 1850 census, Elizabeth Wheeler was listed as a 36 year old widow.

6. Nancy Josephina Spell was born December 15, 1800, place not indicated, and was baptized St. Louis Cathedral, New Orleans, on May 7, 1805, by the Reverend Father Antonio de Sedella. Paternal grandparents: Juan Spell and Francisca MacMoor. The sponsors being Juan Sainet and Josephina Utran. Since the record was written in Spanish it could be Josephina Strain. The mother was listed as "Isavel Godeen". The parents said to be natives and residents of the other side of Lake Pontchartrain.[33]

Nancy married William T. Sharp on July 18, 1821, in the presence of Judge R. Jones for the Parish of St. Tammany. The marriage license law in Louisiana required the prospective union to post a marriage bond and procure a license. Nancy, being under the age of accountability, needed the written permission from her parents to unite in wedlock. The necessity to procure a bond was dropped as a prerequisite to marriage prior to the Civil War, and only in isolated cases will there be a consent slip.

After his marriage, William Sharp built a house on what was said to be the Goodby tract. He settled on the land by permission of his mother-in-law. He was the chain carrier when Mr. Whitney, U.S. Surveyor, ran the lines of the tract and found that his house fell upon the Faircloth tract "agreeable to that survey and that his house was 70 or 80 yards from the line."

After having found out that he was living on Zachariah Faircloth's land, William Sharp and his wife Nancy decided to relocate to the Bogue Chitto River. Their new homestead was located right on the St. Tammany and Washington Parish line, about 10 to 12 miles north of Covington. The couple had ten children. William Sharp donated land for a cemetery located 3½ miles off Highway 40, Howze Creek road. Sharp's Chapel, north of Covington, was started by his descendants.

Inscription reads: "William Sharp/October 1796-1882
"This is old Grandfather Sharp,
He gave this cemetery to his grand-children for
burying ground.
May he rest in glory, Remember me."

7. Elizabeth (Eliza) Spell married François Beaujeaux, born about 1800, in Alsace, France. Leaving from the port of Le Havre, he was on the passenger list that arrived in New York on August 13, 1832.

François died accidentally. He fell from the second story of his sawmill and "died Wednesday night, 13 March 1850," noted in the Coroner's inquest.[34] His 160 acres of land was situated in the Parish of St. Tammany being the corner of sections Nos. 24, 23 and 26, township No. 7, Range No.11 east with buildings and improvements consisting of a dwelling house, steam sawmill running, one running saw with running gear and fixtures. This property was put up for sale at public auction in the town of Mandeville on the twenty-first day of October 1850 by advertisement in the English and French languages, published in the *Louisiana Advocate*. The said property was adjudicated to the highest bidders, Matthew Dicks and Marshall Sharp, for the price of one thousand and fifteen dollars, (Dicks to have an interest of two thirds and M. Sharp an interest of one third).[35]

Elizabeth Spell has a second marriage to Steve Berlier whose mother was Marie Louise Strain, the daughter of Uriah and Victoria Pizetta. Steve Berlier bought at a Sheriff's sale the 320 acres of the James Goodby place for $650.00. February 3, 1859 (probate 156½). Steve later purchased 94 acres of the estate of Hugh Spell at a Sheriff's sale in 1882.

8. Evaline Adeline Spell married Robert Weston Smith in 1827; he died prior to 1837. She has a second marriage to Charles Hatto Morgan, son of David Bannister Morgan and Elizabeth Middleton. He was born September 24, 1813, in Natchez, Mississippi territory. In a DVD dated March 21, 1993, Edgar Sharp, of Mandeville, stated that Robert S. Weston Smith was the original ancestor of the Smiths in Lewisburg.[36]
Charles Morgan has a second marriage to Sarah Peters, widow of Thomas Spell 3rd. During the Civil War he commanded the Mandeville Rifles which represented the little village on the lake shore in the Confederate forces. He was an early Justice of the Peace in Mandeville.

9. Hugh Spell born about 1808, died in 1849. He married Julia Waters. He was executor of his mother's estate in 1844.

10. Louise Spell, about 1824, married Raymond Felix Delisle de la Barthe, a native of Auche, in the department of Gers, France. He was first married to Pouponne Ozenne on January 3, 1803, at Opelousas. The couple lived on the 320 acres of the Spell/Goodby tract with the permission of the matriarch, Elizabeth Goodby. She died in 1831 and was buried in Chinchuba Cemetery. After Louise's death La Barthe disappears.

11. Matilda Spell was born September 18, 1811; died July 18, 1855, and was probably buried in Chinchuba. She married Samuel C. Thompson in September 1832. He was born March 22, 1808, son of Carter Thompson and Nancy Morton, Prince Edward County, Virginia. She died October 17, 1873, in Louisiana. The couple may have settled in St. Helena parish after their marriage. Matilda was buried in the Darlington Community of St. Helena Parish. Darlington Creek is located in the northern part of the parish and runs into the Amite River.

12. Hannah "Anna" Spell born about 1812, died February 1, 1845. She was married to Thomas Taylor, born in Ireland.

Thomas Spell, husband of Elizabeth Goodby, died at the Naval Barracks, on the Tchefuncte River, on March 15, 1815, eight days after the Louisiana Militia had been ordered mustered out. This was slightly more than two months after the Battle of New Orleans. He had a stroke and his family was summoned from Covington where they had gone for safety from the British. According to family lore, Thomas (alias Tom) Spell had chosen his burial site at no cost to his family, but he had to be transported there. He is said to be the first person to have been buried in the cemetery that now bears his name. The Spell family story that has been passed down from one generation to the other is that one day as Thomas was out riding, in the company of his Negro slave, he stopped to rest on the east side of Bayou Chinchuba. While sitting under the shade of a tree and contemplating the scenery, he reminded his slave that it was such a pretty spot that when he died he would like to be buried there, and so he was.

This story has become part of the family lore, but in actual case, old John Spell died *circa* 1795 and may have picked this spot for a cemetery because of its elevation and its distance from the lake shore where he possibly buried his wife, Cecilia McLemore. We believe that on this special day, Tom Spell could have brought his slave to clean and weed the grave site of his parents. As he sat there, amidst the beauty of nature, Tom could have been reflecting on the life of the loved ones who had died, and thus he expressed his desire to be buried near his parents.

Travel was difficult in the early part of the nineteenth century. Land transportation was the horse and the ox wagon. The family transported Tom's body from the Tchefuncte to his home at Bayou Castein.

Thomas Spell died intestate and there was an inventory made of his possessions by Antoine (Anthony) Bonnabel and François Cousin, the biggest taxpayer in the 1811-1812 tax roll, followed by Thomas Spell and Juan Baham.[37] More than half of Tom's wealth came from the ownership of Negro slaves, 16 acquired over the years to be exact.

After the death and burial of Thomas Spell it was decided at a meeting of the family and others "deemed friends of the minor children" that it was in everyone's best interest if Elizabeth Goodby were permitted to purchase the property at the appraised value of $7,696.25. The inventory of the estate did not include the Goodby tract, which leads us to believe that although James Goodby had assigned it to Thomas Spell at the time of his marriage to Elizabeth, it was actually her dowry which could not be included in the estate of the deceased. The purchase of the property consisted of Elizabeth signing a mortgage to each child for their portion of the estate, which consisted of 300 acres of prime real estate, 15 slaves, 300 head of cattle, and a generous assortment of other livestock. Arrangements were formally approved by Judge Jesse R. Jones.[38]

Elizabeth Goodby hired an overseer to help her manage her property and the work of the slaves. She was left in an excellent financial position, the combined family wealth accumulated through hard work and the use of natural resources on the north shore. Tom had put his slaves to work in the forests producing tar, pitch, rails and bark to be sold in New Orleans. He had cattle and horses that roamed the sprawling woods.

After a mourning period, Elizabeth Goodby married, on August 11, 1818, Jacob Bartle (Bertell). He was listed as living in Natchez in 1786. He was a small boat captain and delivered cargo to various landings on Lakes Maurepas and Pontchartrain. In 1803, "a Jacob Bartle" was registered in New Orleans as a ship owner. The name of his first wife is not known, but three children were issued from their union: daughter Maria was born in 1804, in New Orleans, and later married McLin Lloyd, son of Samuel Lloyd and Mary Davis. Son, Marshall Bartles, married Elizabeth Letchworth, born May 9, 1848, daughter of Stokeley Letchworth and Nancy Morris, daughter of Wettenhall Morris and Sarah Richardson. We have no available records for the third child, Sophie Bartle.

In 1811, Jacob Bartle purchased the William O'Brien British land grant from Dorothy O'Brien, wife of the New Orleans merchant John Travis Sanderson. She passed on the original British land grant deed with its survey and attached with the Great Seal of West Florida. The land that Jacob Bartle purchased in 1811 was later destined to play an important part in the history of Mandeville.

Bartle operated a business from Bayou Castein in his boat named "The Madison". It was he who transported the wood from the Spell place on the lake-front for sale in New Orleans.

Elizabeth Bartle may have been Jacob's and Elizabeth Goodby's only child, born in 1819, but she was issued from a long line of children, the Spell siblings. Elizabeth Bartle was first married, on April 8, 1835, at the age of sixteen, to Peter Ochsenreiter, about whom nothing is known except that he died young and left her a widow with two children, Louisa and Elizabeth.

Elizabeth then had a second marriage to Henry Birch, son of Charles and Catherine Trump, on July 8, 1844. She brought into this said marriage the sum of five hundred dollars, two slaves, to wit a Negro woman named Susan, aged about thirty years; also a Negro boy named Battiste, aged seven years; cattle consisting of about forty head, and about 30 hogs.[39]

136

On April 1, 1848, Elizabeth Bartle, wife of Henry Birch, gave birth to a daughter named Catherine. The following year she sued her husband because he was liable for several debts and she feared that she could lose her valuable property. She petitioned the court to be authorized to bring suit against her husband, to be authorized to acquire property without the interference of her husband, and that she recover the sums of money he owed her.

The Court granted Elizabeth a Separation of Property and also ordered Henry to repay the 500 hundred dollars he had "expended," plus the fifty dollars he had received for the sale of her hogs. Years later, Henry had still not repaid Elizabeth her money. Creditors were snapping at him from all sides! On March 16 1856, a meeting of the Creditors of Henry Birch was held at the offices of Angus Bowie, Notary, at Covington. It was ordered that the sheriff be directed to make sale at public auction after due and legal advertisement, of the effects ceded by Henry Birch.

On August 2, 1856, to be sold at the residence of Henry Birch were the following property for cash, to wit: "a tract of land containing one hundred fifty-five and seventy-five one hundredths acres situated where the said Henry resided, a glass factory, three horses, two carts, and two wheelbarrows." Incredible as it may seem, no one showed up to bid on the property and so Elizabeth stole it under the noses of the creditors. For the sum of $25.00 she became owner of Henry's land, residence and glass factory, and for the sum of $10.00 she purchased the rest of the items that had been put up for sale. Because the court had awarded Elizabeth a judgment for Separation of Property, she was entitled by law to bid on her husband's ceded property at the public auction. The twenty-two creditors wound up sharing a grand total of $35.75.[40]

Soon after Elizabeth rescued Henry's property, the glassworks opened for business and it was a successful enterprise for several years, probably due in part that Henry was competent as a glassmaker and that Elizabeth held the purse strings since Henry had demonstrated that he had no head for business. The Civil War put an end to all civilian enterprises in St. Tammany Parish. When the war was over, Catherine and Henry Birch paid the civil War Tax on their property and the factory went back into operation temporarily, for with the death of Henry the glassworks closed down for good.

It has been over two hundred years that the descendants of the Spell, Goodby and Sharp families settled at Bayou Castein. These early settlers left indelible marks upon the land. The fundamental problems they faced involved the day to day struggle with clearing the land, and their struggle with the elements. The land that was for so many years more wilderness than anything else needed much optimism to make the going possible on a day to day basis. They were a part of a long and complicated history of America in which Indians, French, English and Spanish confronted each other, but also worked with each other, intermarried, and influenced each other. Just as important is the old Tom Spell Memorial Cemetery, with its first confirmed burial in 1815. Rich in the history of the town, it should be considered as an important historical site in Mandeville.

It is all the ingredients that we have described which contributed to a slow and steady pace of development in the parish of St. Tammany. By about 1820, the early American Colonial pioneer period came to an end, and a new phase of growth and development began.

NOTES

1. Jordan, Terry G., "Antecedents of the Long-Lot in Texas," *Annals of the Association of American Geographers*, March 1974, 70-86.
2. Johnson, Cecil, "The Distribution of Land in British West Florida," *Louisiana Historical Quarterly*, Volume 16, No. 4, October 1933, 545.
3. The *Domesday Book* contains the records of a survey of English lands and landholdings made by order of William the Conqueror about 1086.
4. Campeau, Anita R., and Sharp, Donald J., "The Tom Spell Memorial Cemetery, Part 1, *New Orleans Genesis*, Volume XLVIII, No. 189, January 2010, 22.
5. *Warrants for Lands in South Carolina: 1680-1692*, Clearfield, Volume 2.
6. Ibid.,
7. Register of St. Andrews Parish: Berkely County: 1719-1774, copied and edited by Mabel L. Webber.
8. Grant Book A, as extracted in An Index to English Crown Grants, 1755-1775.
9. Land grants, Conveyance Book S, 171-172.
10. Conveyance Book C-2, 563.
11. Campeau, Anita R., and Sharp, Donald J., "The Tom Spell Memorial Cemetery," *New Orleans Genesis*, January 2010, 23.
12. Petersen, Mary A., "British West Florida: Abstracts of Land Petitions," *Louisiana Genealogical Register*, Volume X1X, No. 3, September 1972, September 1772, 247.
13. Sacramental Records of St. Louis Cathedral, 1791-1795, Volume 5, 1901.
14. Peterson, Mary A., "British West Florida: Abstracts of Land Petitions," *Louisiana Genealogical Register*, December 1971, 329.
15. *Regiments of the Louisiana Militia*, Louisiana Genealogical and Historical Society, Clearfield Co., Baton Rouge, 1963, 53.
16. Holden, Doris E. Martin, *Descendants of John Spell and Cecilia McLemore*, Dogwood Printing Company, MO., 1992, 35A. Donald Sharp worked on the Sharp and Spell line for this book.

17. Watson, Joseph W., *Abstracts of Early Deeds of Edgecombe County*, North Carolina, 1772-1788, Volume 2, 1967, 27.

18. No. 24, Estate of the Late Thomas Spell: Petition for appointment of an under Tutor to the minor children of the deceased dated June 2, 1815.

19. Dalrymple, Margaret Fisher, Editor, *Merchant of Manchac: The Letter books of John Fitzpatrick, 1768-1790*, Louisiana State University press, 325.

20. Ibid., 329.

21. File No. 32, for the year 1795. This folio has 7 sheets numbered from #1 to #7 which equals to seven pages. The document is written in Spanish.

22. Campeau, Anita R., and Sharp, Donald J., "British and Spanish Land Grants: From Bayou Castin to the Tchefuncte," *New Orleans Genesis*, Volume XLVII, April 2009, No. 186, 135.

23. The document was dated 22 February 1813, from Guillemard's plan of 1798.

24. Petition of Amelia Morton and her husband John Morton to the Honorable Jesse R. Jones, Judge of the Parish of St. Tammany, dated October 15, 1819.

25. *Sacramental Records of St. Louis Cathedral*, Volume 2, 1786-1796, 340, Act No. 547.

26. St. Tammany Census taken in the year of 1812.

27. Wolfram M. Von-Maszewski, Editor, *Austin's Old Three Hundred: Histories of the First Anglo Colonists*, Eakin Press, First edition, 1999, 45.

28. U.S. Federal Census, 1850, Wharton County, Texas.

29. Succession of Thomas and Mary Spell, Eighth District Court, Parish of St. Tammany, December 20, 1858.

30. *St. Louis Catholic Church Sacramental Records*, Volume 2, Act 1548.

31. Genealogy Trails, St. Tammany Parish, Louisiana Marriages 1811-1820, 14.

32. Suit No. 519-B of the 8th District Court, St. Tammany, Louisiana.

33. *Sacramental Records of St. Louis Cathedral*, Volume 4, 1802-1806, 96, Act No. 601.

34. This information was copied by Donald J. Sharp from Mrs. Amos Neff's Card files, Covington Court House, Covington, Louisiana.

35. Eighth Judicial District Court of St. Tammany Parish in the matter of the succession of François Beaujeux deceased numbered on the docket of said Court 36, 354.

36. DVD titled Old Mandeville, Part 1, March 26, 1993; Part 2 dated May 23, 1993.

37. Superior Council, *Louisiana Historical Quarterly*, July 12, 1929, 482.

38. Ibid., 482.

39. Campeau, Anita R., and Sharp, Donald J., The Tom Spell Memorial Cemetery, part 2, *New Orleans Genesis*, Volume XLVIII, April 2010, No. 190, 138.

40. Ibid., 140.

CHAPTER 10

ZACHARIAH FAIRCLOTH AND MARTHA RICHARDSON

The Fayerclough/Faircloth surname is of English origin with roots that go as far back as the 1300s. Leaving behind several generations, we begin with William Faircloth, born 1601, in Warrington, Lancashire, England. He and Elizabeth Mather begot William, born about 1640, in Chorly, Lancashire. The British Loyalist, Zachariah Faircloth, a resident at Bayou Castein, during the Spanish period, is a direct descendant.

From Lancashire, England, to Virginia and North Carolina, the Faircloth family has become vast in 300 years of history. They have spread throughout the United States and beyond leaving a legacy of achievements and adventures through war and death on the battlefields from the Revolutionary War to the Civil War, and beyond.

William Faircloth I came to America as a "headright" with Colonel John Carter, *circa* 1665. Colonel Carter, the son of the Honorable William Carter, of "Casstown," Hereford County, and the Middle Temple, England, had been granted 4000 acres "being a neck of land on the north side of the Rappahanock River in Virginia. The land tract was bounded on the westward side by the Cassatta Woman Creek which runs north and east towards the head of Wiccomico River."

The tract of land claimed by Colonel Carter had originally been granted to Captain Samuel Matthews on August 1, 1643, but had been abandoned by him. Captain Matthews came to the Virginia Colony in 1622 [1] and was chosen as governor by the House of Burgesses in 1656.[2] In April 1658 mainly to signal their displeasure with Oliver Cromwell who had taken the title of Lord Protector of England, with all the powers of a king, the Burgesses ceremoniously dismissed Matthews and reelected him in a single Act.[3] Because of his loyalty, as governor to Cromwell, he was often assumed to be a Puritan himself, although in fact he had been known as a persecutor of the Puritan sect in Virginia in the days before Cromwell.

In 1659, shortly before the English Restoration, Captain Matthews died in office, and the Burgesses at that point simply reinstated the former Royalist Governor, William Berkeley by unanimous vote. Thus in the view of historian, Robert Beverley Jr., writing in 1705, "Virginia colony was the last of the King's Dominions that submitted to the Usurpation, and afterwards the first to cast it off."[4]

By May 1660, Charles II returned to the kingdom which he had left nine years before as a hunted fugitive. The country seemed as if it had awakened from a long nightmare, and were wild with enthusiasm with his return. The glories of Cromwell's reign were forgotten; men remembered only the intolerable taxation and the vexatious laws that had forbidden both drunken carousals and the innocent festivities of Twelfth Night or May Day, and had visited theatres and beer gardens with the same condemnation. The age of feudalism had long passed, but it was dissolved at the end of 1660; however many estates in England were still held by feudal tenure. The troubles of the previous eighteen years had thrown the already outworn system in such hopeless confusion that Parliament had been forced to abolish it altogether. Such were the conditions in England in the latter part of the seventeenth century when William Faircloth journeyed to America.

Upon petition by Colonel Carter, by order of the General Court, dated October 12, 1665, the land abandoned by Captain Matthews was granted to him, and was to further the transportation from England of 80 persons among who was William Faircloth who settled in the area near the County of Isle of Wight, Virginia.

William Fairclough I owned 277 acres of land in 1704.[5] He died about 1710, aged 70, in Northumberland County, Virginia. Married to Jane Thomas, who died after 1704, in James County, Virginia, we know of three children: William II, Thomas, and Edward who died between the years, 1724-1726, in Pasquotank County, North Carolina.

William Faircloth Jr. II, born about 1663, in Lancashire, Shevington Township, England, married Mary Morland, about 1690, since Moses, their first child, was born in 1692. William obtained a land patent for 175 acres in Isle of Wight County, Virginia, on November 13, 1713.[6] This is where he settled with his family. He died there, in 1727, leaving a Will naming his sons Moses, Benjamin, Samuel and William Jr. III, and daughters Elizabeth Faircloth Mercer, Sarah Faircloth, born about 1700, Isle of Wight, County, VA., married there, about 1731, to John R. Revels, and Hannah Faircloth.[7]

Sarah Faircloth by deed of gift in 1727, was given 75 acres near Nottaway Swamp by her father, William Farecloth.

William Faircloth III, born about 1710 in Isle of Wight, married Mary Ann Johnson. He and some of his descendants later removed to Tarboro, Edgecombe County, North Carolina, formed in 1741 from Bertie County. It was named after Richard Edgcumbe, a Member of Parliament from 1701 to 1742, and a lord of the treasury, who became 1st baron Edgcumbe in 1742. In 1746, part of Edgcombe County became Granville County; in 1758, another part became Halifax County; in 1777, yet another part became Nash County.

On or about 1745, William Faircloth III moved to Edgecombe County where he patented a tract of land on the Tar River, and where he resided until 1755. He sold this land and removed to Dobbs County where he settled and was still living in 1790. He died about 1791, aged 81 years. Issued from this union was William 1V, and Benjamin who married Letitia Garner. Benjamin died about 1782, and Letitia died about 1793, in Edgecombe County, North Carolina.

William Faircloth IV, born about 1730, is associated with Sarah, of unknown origins. They are listed with three children: Zachariah Faircloth, born there about 1751, died St. Tammany Parish, Louisiana; Hardwick (Hardy) Faircloth, born about 1754, Samson County, North Carolina, died there in 1810; John D. Faircloth, born 1759, Sampson, died in 1779.

William Faircloth IV, husband of Sarah, died fairly young, of unknown causes, leaving three orphan sons, in Edgecombe County, in 1765. The Edgecombe County, North Carolina Records, from April 1746 to August 1772 are the ones where the Faircloth siblings were recorded and there was no mention of their father in both entries of 9 July 1765 and 11 July 1765. Having no records for the birth of the three "baseborn" children mentioned in the Judicial Record, we would have to speculate about their origins, but suffice to say that they are listed as orphans under William Faircloth and Sarah.

Repetitive naming of Williams brings frustration and bewilderment when individual records can't be unraveled in the local records. Bless Zachariah's father and mother who had some verve and imagination to bestow their progeny names of uncommon distinction.

Zachariah Faircloth, whose birth is shrouded in mystery, aged 14 years, "baseborn child" as the court record states, was "bound out" to Noah Sugg by his mother.

Noah Sugg (1742-1800) helped establish American Independence while acting in the capacity of Sheriff of Edgecombe County, from 1774 to 1776. He was the Justice of the Peace in 1776. He also rendered some kind of services in the Revolutionary War, as his name appears twice in the North Carolina Army Records. On record, two warrants issued about 1782: Nos. 75 and 182 in the amounts of sterling 11.12.6 and sterling 10.7 respectively.[8]

It was common practice in those days for parents to "bind out" their elder children to someone to learn a trade. Upon entering the house of the master, the young apprentice would begin training for a specific occupation or trade such as carpenter, blacksmith, stonemason, wheelwright, or baker. The master, by law, was obligated to provide what the child might lack, according to his circumstance, plus they had to house, feed and clothe the child, usually for a specific time, which

142

could be until the child reached the age of 18 or 21 years of age, after which he would be on his own.

Hardwich (Hardy) Faircloth, 11 years of age, and John Faircloth, 5 years of age, "baseborn children" of William and Sarah were bound to Benjamin Faircloth, the children's uncle. However, in a published book written by Marvin K. Dorman Jr., entitled *Edgecombe County, North Carolina Abstracts and Court Minutes 1774-1776, 1757-1794*, it does not include the full details of the original text and leaves out the word "baseborn". The North Carolina Courts often eased the transition to orphanage by apprenticing siblings to the same master where possible.[9] This was particularly true in the case of illegitimate offspring – the Quinn brothers, Faircloth brothers, Johnson sisters, and Revel sisters – and belied a sympathetic understanding on the part of the justices of the more difficult adjustments to be made by those children.[10]

When the American Revolution broke out in 1776, many white households who were loyal to the Crown fled "behind British lines," to East and West Florida bringing with them the few possessions they could.

Hardwich (Hardy) Faircloth served as private in the Duplin Militia. He drew 1 RW pay voucher. He bought land from the state of North Carolina on November 10, 1784, and was listed in Samson County in the 1785 tax list. He married Sarah Sugg, daughter of Noah Sugg and Murphree Howell. All of his 15 children were born before 1800. The family was living in Sampson County in 1790. He died about 1810. His soldier brothers were John and Zachariah.

John Faircloth's military records say that he was the son of William and Sarah Faircloth. Sergeant John Faircloth was killed on April 5, 1779, serving in Company F, 10th Regiment of Cumberland County Militia. He apparently never married.

In the late 1760s, Zachariah Faircloth's uncles and their families moved from Edgecombe County to what was then part of Duplin County and which later became part of the new Sampson County. In 1771, Zachariah witnessed a deed between Jacob Surginor and Benjamin Faircloth, his uncle, who bought land in Duplin. On July 9, 1773, Zachariah bought 100 acres of land in Duplin (Sampson County) from Benjamin Faircloth, his uncle. On January 9, 1777, Zachariah sold the above 100 acres to Solomon Sessoms. This transaction was witnessed by his brother Hardy. Zachariah appears on the 1779 tax list of Montgomery County, located west of Cumberland and Sampson counties where the Faircloth family was concentrated.

Zachariah Faircloth joined the Tories late in the American Revolution. On December 22, 1781, he enlisted in Colonel Samuel Campbell's Regiment of His Majesty's Militia until April 1, 1782.[11] He reenlisted from April 2 until May 1782, then from May 6 to August 5, 1782, serving as a Lieutenant on James Island during this period. No evidence has been found to support a marriage, although he was said to have married a Mary Armstrong and had children.

After the War, each man had to make his own decision about his future loyalty. The Revolution had broken the unity of the British Empire, but by clarifying obscurities surrounding loyalty to the Empire, it had reinforced the ties between Canada and England. About 35,000 loyalists settled in the Maritimes, giving birth to New Brunswick and Upper Canada. Those who chose the St. Lawrence Valley did not exceed four or five thousand. Others went to Louisiana or other western areas which were then not part of the new United States. The British government came to the relief of these Loyalists, arranging transportation for those who wished to leave and giving assistance in the form of free land, rations, and farm stock. Lands were even granted to the sons and daughters of Loyalists.

At the end of the War, Zachariah Faircloth because of his Loyalist convictions, probably left with a wave of settlers, crossed the mountains into Kentucky and settled near Boonesborough where he met and became friends with George Sharp. The two men participated in the "river system" of marketing tobacco to New Orleans. It was first initiated by General James Wilkinson during the spring of 1787, through a trial shipment which he sold direct to the Spanish officials at New Orleans. Captain John Halley was the first to bring tobacco and farm produce down to New Orleans after General James Wilkinson made an agreement with the Spanish in 1787.

John Halley, the Boonesborough pioneer tobacco planter and trader, made two trips to the New Orleans market. The journal of the first voyage in 1789 begins on May 2 at the mouth of the Ohio and ends in New Orleans on June 2. Halley provides more detail about the 1791 trip. They left Boonesborough on April 27 and arrived in New Orleans on June 8. Captain Halley started with two boats, stopping at warehouses on the Kentucky River to pick up 80,000 pounds of tobacco; then he caught up with two of his other boats at Louisville. He reported that the four boats carried 159,000 pounds of tobacco, plus other goods.

144

The flat boats were piloted by Captain Halley, Mr. Sharp, Mr. Wilkerson and Captain Blinco or (Briscoe). There were five hired men on each vessel, making it a crew of 24.

On each trip, a fleet of four flat-bottomed "Kentucky boats" were used to transport the valuable cargo. These flatboats or flats, built in various sizes, were rectangular, flat-bottomed boats without keels. They were relatively easy to build, but this simple and affordable design also destined them to be awkward one-way craft.

Captain Halley kept a detailed journal, in which he described his "journeys down the rivers to sell tobacco at the Crescent City." Each strenuous trip down the swollen rivers required approximately 43 days.[12] Ten weeks, more or less, were required to complete a round trip, depending upon the weather. On each trip Captain Halley met with the Spanish Governor at Natchez and the Governor in New Orleans who required a bill of lading, the number of men aboard, and their names. Somewhere in the Archives of Spain, one could possibly find the record of the men listed by Captain Halley. We believe that Zachariah Faircloth, because of his friendship and dealings with George Sharp, and a later testimony, was part of the Halley venture to Louisiana.

To move all the Kentucky freight, there evolved "a new type of humanity"- the river man - who replaced the French on the Mississippi. When the French voyageurs got to New Orleans they mixed well with the crowd, and many of them never thought of leaving. It was different with all those new freighters who ventured out to Louisiana to sell their farm produce! The "Kaintucks" as they were called were men with muscles of steel who toiled long and valiantly poling, rowing, or holding onto bucking steering oars, in all sorts of weather. They took those long arduous trips because they liked the life of the river. It was a young man's game, anyone of them over thirty-five was inevitably called "Pappy." The men were a close-knit group while afloat, for they were kept busy.

These trips were usually made by professionals. The leader of the crew, or a captain called the patroon, was hired directly by the owner and, sometimes he himself was a part owner of the vessel or cargo. The patroon's word was absolute and final for the laws had to be obeyed. But when the vessel was tied up at a town, the overseer kept out of the way for, off duty, the men could be rough and rambunctious.

In the Crescent City, the Kaintucks did not care what nation owned Journey's end.[13] To them it was a place where they got paid and took a break. That France really owned Louisiana and was letting Spain administer it temporarily was by this time common knowledge, but few cared as long as business was booming and kept on booming.

There were many attractions from prostitutes to gambling and the pubs for these men who had been penned and reined in for weeks when they descended on Bourbon or Giraud Street – a district known as "The Swamp". Tavern proprietors greeted them with a grin, and the police never entered unless in squad strength. Nobody else liked them! It went all the way back to James Willing and his ruffians. "Anybody who came out of the north was hateful, for that was a land of evil. A Kaintuck was a man to avoid."[14]

The highlight of the 1791 voyage to New Orleans was an encounter which the crew had with a large alligator. Captain Halley reported that the action-packed battle lasted for 30 minutes, and that the conquered gator weighed 300 pounds and was 10 feet and 9 inches in length. Another incident was when the flat boat that Sharp commanded became stuck on a sandbar half way down the Mississippi River. Halley's other boats being a considerable distance behind attempted to land above a bluff and the two of them got stuck on a sandbar. Sharp got off some time after dark and fell down below the bluff and landed safely. Two young men from Halley's boat who assisted him broke their oars in the landing.

On September 15, 1791, in early morning, Captain Halley met with the Governor, made out a bill which the Governor signed, and the latter accepted a present of bacon and ham. After conversing for some time, Captain Halley took his leave to return to his boats in order to move on. He was detained by his men scattered through the town, finally collected them together with much difficulty, and several hours later was able to move on. Captain Halley does not say how he came out financially on the venture, but at the time tobacco was selling at New Orleans for $10.00 a hundredweight.

From June 8 to September 15, while the crew was in New Orleans, George Sharp, and his companion Zachariah Faircloth, decided to stay instead of returning to Kentucky. They applied to Governor Estevan Miro for a Spanish grant. Possibly because of the friendship and influence of Captain Halley, the request was granted and 640 acres were granted high up on the West side of Bayou Castin in late 1791. In 1792, George Sharp filed suit against John Spell for back wages.[15]

Zachariah Faircloth was listed in the 1812 Tax List for St. Tammany with: 1 man, 1 woman, 1 child, and 5 slaves.[16]

In an affidavit dated July 21, 1820, Zachariah Faircloth in the presence of David B. Morgan, Justice of the Peace, St. Tammany Parish, testified that "George Sharp settled at a place on Castein Bayou about the old crossing place to Bayou Lacombe previous to the year 1800, and lived on the old place several years thereafter, and that previous

146

to the year 1803, the precise time this deponent does not recollect, the said George Sharp sold the said improvement to him."[17] Zachariah was now close to 70 years of age.

It is known that Zachariah Faircloth purchased George Sharp's Spanish grant for $40.00 in 1795, prior to returning to Kentucky. Zachariah was driven out of his cabin by a storm in 1798. He lived for some time with Thomas Spell on the Goodby tract and with the Paul Labyteau family on the lake-front. It was about this time that Zachariah met Martha Richardson, and they began to live together as man and wife.

Zachariah Faircloth sold his improvement to John Castonquat in 1807 for $40.00. George Sharp and Zachariah's land had not increase in value in eleven years.

John Castonquat lived on the said place until September 1818, on or about, at which time, he sold to Richard Rico who resided at the said place and had continued to do since his purchase.[18] The said grant had been cultivated every year since its first settlement, except for one year, to the present time, attested Faircloth. He further said that he was well acquainted with George Sharp, "and lived a neighbor to him" and is positive in declaring that the said George Sharp never made or claimed any settlement right in this State except the above mentioned one.

Richard Rico sold the original Spanish land grant of George Sharp to Christopher Greenlick/Greulich, of Germany, on February 18, 1820. It was described as "a certain tract of land, one section of 640 acres, situated on Bayou Castein on the northeast side of the road leading from Lorreins, being the same which was located by John Castonquat, who sold his settler's rights to Richard Rico by act, under private signature, dated September 18, 1818." Rico obtained Certificate No. 583 dated February 23, 1820, of his settler's right from the Commissioners of the Land Office for the District East of the Island of New Orleans. He afterward sold the same to Christopher Greenlick by act signed before William Marbury, Notary Public for the parish of St. Tammany, on February 20, 1820.

From Christopher Greenlick/Greulich, formerly of Germany, the land went to his only daughter, Wilhelmina Greulich, who appointed her husband Christian Lehmann to act as her attorney-in-fact to settle the estate of her deceased father. There is no death date for Christopher Greulich anywhere on any document.

When Christopher Lehmann presented his power-of-attorney from his wife Wilhelmina Greulich, Judge Jones placed Lehmann in curatorship. On March 20, 1823, Jesse R. Jones proceeded to make an inventory of the property at his residence on Bayou Castein, having appointed and sworn Thomas Spell and Edmond R. Morse (Moss) as appraisers.

Charles Korner acquired the property on February 14, 1824; then sold it to Louis Biller of New Orleans.

Zachariah Faircloth legally married Martha Richardson, born about 1777, daughter of George Richardson and Mary Shepherd McFadden, in St. Tammany Parish. The marriage document reads: "I hereby certify that it appears from the documents on file in my office that Zachariah Faircloth and Martha Richardson were legally married on the 20th of August 1821. In testimony of which I here unto set my hand and affix the Seal of my office this 18th day of October 1825. Signed Jesse R. Jones, Parish Judge."

Attestation by Jesse R. Jones of marriage

Although it was likely somewhat unorthodox at the time, the decision of Zachariah and Martha to get married, after so many years of living together as man and wife, was most propitious for later family historians.

On August 6, 1823, in the year of our Lord, and the 48th year of American Independence, Zachariah Faircloth, in preparation for his eternal journey, in a Donation Deed, in the presence of William B. Ligon, Notary Public duly commissioned, who did the writing, gave and granted his wife Martha "for her services to me as a lawful wife" his land (431 acres) and property and one hundred head of cattle, more or less, branded and marked with a crop and a half crop in the left ear; plus a Negro man named London. To his nephew, Joseph Sharp, he made the gift of two hundred acres that bordered the O'Brien tract. It was primarily the land that was being trespassed and later contended in Court Case No. 225.

Jacob Bartle and Edmund B. Moss, duly sworn, witnessed the deed of the gift which was recorded in the notary's office notebook Book A, page 40. The document was dated on the 11th day of August 1823.

Martha's father, George Richardson, and her uncle Henry, signed an oath of Allegiance to the Spanish at Natchez as early as January 4, 1787.[19] The two brothers were at Bayou Castein in 1796. Commandant Charles Parent was called to settle a land dispute between Henry and Morgan Edwards. Having lost his battle, he and family removed to Manchac where he died a few years later. The inventory and estimation of his estate was near nine or ten thousand pesos in land, slaves, horses, cattle, etc.[20]

Henry's widow, Mary Sarah Aldrich, married John Pippen, but the marriage did not last, and they separated after two years. John Pippen sued his wife for an annulment of a partition made between her and her children by the former husband, Henry Richardson, and claimed a share of the estate. The children were Theophilas, Zachariah, Amos, and Dorcas, by marriage Dorcas Lyon.

In the document dated September 16, 1809, Pippen requested that the testimony of Henry Richardson having been annulled by a decree from Governor de Grand Pré because it was made contrary to the law, and the widow having proved that all the property which her deceased husband possessed upon his death was acquired since his marriage. The same Governor decreed that half of the property should belong to the said widow.[21] The widow, since that time, had been legally married to him, for two years, and had been advised to make a contract with her children which was executed before the alcalde of the District of New Feliciana in which document she agreed to accept in place of half of the succession, two hundred and forty arpents of land, some cattle and some furniture, all of which would revert to the children after her death, as it appeared in the certified copy of the contract submitted. Pippen's request was to annul the contract since his former wife did not have the authorization to make a contract without the consent of her husband.

Pippen also complained that her children and other relatives took, by force, the Negroes, furniture, hogs …although he claimed it was the product of his own hard work.

The result was that the children agreed to give up to their mother Sarah Pippen in lieu of claim that she has or might have on the Estate of their late father Henry Richardson to have and to hold during her lifetime for her sole use the benefit of the following property to revert to them at the death of their Mother: six negroes, five hundred and fifty acres of land off the lower end of the Tract on which they now live, six cows and calves, one yoke of oxen, one trunk, one large iron pot, one Dutch oven, etc. It was understood by the parties in case of decease in the Negroes property it would be the loss of the children, and any increase in the Negro property it would be for the benefit of the children. This was done in the presence of the *Alcalde* John Rae and the two assistant witnesses Adwell Adkin and Llewellyn C. Griffith.

What happened to Joseph and William Sharp's mother Elizabeth Richardson and their sister Patsey after they came down to live with their uncle Zachariah and Aunt Martha on the lakefront at Bayou Chinchuba? On July 30, 1818, Elizabeth Sharp, their mother, married Asa Rogers. They bought a lot in Covington. Mother and sons lived close by for a few years. She was around when Joseph Sharp married Sally Spell, in 1816, witnessed by General David B. Morgan, Justice of the Peace. A few years later they moved to the newly created Washington Parish to the north. Elizabeth's daughter, Patsey Sharp, married David Mayfield on September 25, 1816, St. Tammany.[22] They bought a lot in the new town of Madisonville. Two years later the property was sold to merchant Joshua Aydelotte of Madisonville, and the Mayfield couple moved to new land on the Pearl River.

Nancy Richardson, sister of Martha, was born between the years 1780-1789. She married Joseph Lawrence Martin Sticker, son of Joseph James Sticker, of German origins, and Anna Maraugh Crowley. Lawrence Sticker's name was first documented on a list of passengers aboard the ship *Lydia* which docked at the port of New Orleans on June 13, 1788. He was listed as 12 years of age. The family settled at Bayou Sara, a thriving port town nestled on the bank of the Mississippi river between Natchez and Baton Rouge. It was through Catherine Sticker, who married Edward Ross, the brother of Diana Ross-Goodbee, who had settled at Bayou Castein, that Lawrence met Nancy Richardson, whom he married about 1798/1799.

Amos Richardson, Martha's brother, married Mary Sodon. Widowed, she married Thomas Spell Jr., son of Thomas Spell and

Elizabeth Goodby. Of importance with this couple for the local history of Bayou Castein is that the word "cemetery property" first appeared in their succession. Their will stated that two acres had been set aside for the family graveyard and was not to be sold with the rest of the 320 acres. They were deceased by 1859. The problem was that the land had not been surveyed and the location of the cemetery could not be legally identified.

It was Alma Armstrong's father, a surveyor in the Parish, who in 1895 purchased the two acres for one hundred dollars from Mrs. Ana Marchan (sic), wife of John Caillot. He had the land surveyed and the sale was recorded in the Parish Court House. Mrs. Armstrong's grandfather was Zachariah Sharp, born January 26, 1823, in the little log cabin where his father Joseph Sharp was living with his wife Sarah Spell.[23] The modest lodging was located next to the Jacob Bartle tract on the lake front at Bayou Castein.

Joseph and Sarah Sharp named their new son Zachariah in honor of Joseph's uncle, Zachariah Faircloth. Zachariah died intestate on August 14, 1823, aged 72 years. He was buried on his property. The following year, his widow married Joseph Letchworth and, as Jacob Bartle put it, he was "a contentious man."

This completes the story of a man's journey to Bayou Castein, that of an individual who left North Carolina after the end of the war in 1783, in a movement that became an exodus, partly because of people who were afraid to stay, but mainly of those who no longer wanted·to.

Zachariah Faircloth, in giving his allegiance to the monarch of Spain, obtained a land grant, farmed, raised cattle, and became financially independent. He found security for himself and his wife Martha, and his two nephews, by leading a sober and industrious life, and making judicious business arrangements. He was known as a man who did not want to talk about events that happened a long time ago. But, one of the pleasures of history is being able to uncover some of those links that help us explain the meaning of one's past and how each person added to his community.

While Zachariah, and his neighbors, witnessed the unfolding of the new nation, the colonial character of American life was slowly altered as a national feeling and outlook took place.

NOTES
1. Bruce, Philip Alexander, *The Virginia Magazine of History and Biography*, Virginia Historical Society, 1893, 91.

2. Cooke, John Esten, *Virginia: A History of the People*, Houghton, Mifflin and Company, 1883, 205.

3. Ibid., 207.

4. Robert Beverley, *The History and Present State of Virginia*.

5. Rent Rolls of James City County for the year 1704.

6. English Duplicates of Lost Virginia Records by Louis des Cognets, Junior. A list of patents granted for land in this colony by the Honorable Alexander Spotswood, His Majesty's Lieutenant Governor and Commander-in-Chief of this Dominion.

7. Will of William Faircloth, Will Book 3, dated 1 September 1727, 95-96. Refer also to Virginia Wills and Administration, 1632-1800 by Clayton, Torrence, Gen. Publication Co, 1965.

8. Certified copy of Pay Voucher #5500, Raleigh, North Carolina from Chief Archives and Records Section.

9. Watson, Alan D., "Orphanage in Colonial North Carolina," *North Carolina Historical Review*, Volume 52, No. 2, April 1975, 105-119.

10. Ibid., 105-119.

11. *Loyalists in the Southern Campaign*, The Genealogical Publishing Company, 1981.

12. Our information is taken from Judge Samuel's Wilson's photo static copy collection number 49W31 copied from the original copy of Captain Halley's Journal to New Orleans performed in the years 1789 & 1791. The copy is in the Special Collection & Archives of the Margaret I. King Library, Lexington, Kentucky.

13. Chidsey, Donald Barr, *Louisiana Purchase*, Crown Publishers Inc., New York, 1972, 124.

14. Ibid., 124.

15. Ellis, Frederick S., *St. Tammany Parish: L'Autre Côté du Lac*, Pelican Publishing Co., Gretna, 1998, 62.

16. "An Index to the 1820 Census of Louisiana's Florida Parishes, and 1812 St. Tammany Parish Tax List," compiles by Mary Elizabeth Sanders, 1972.

17. Affidavit No. 583 by Zachariah Faircloth dated 21 July 1820.

18.[1] Certificate #583, Covington Archives.

19. The copies of their signatures appear in a book entitled Fearless, Faithful and Forgotten by Jack Curtis. The book is self published. Mr. Jack Curtis wanted to learn more about his ancestor, Richard Curtis Jr., who founded the Old Salem (Cole's Creek) Baptist Church in a time when Spain did not allow religious freedom in Natchez. Mr. Curtis travelled to Seville, Spain to the Spanish Archives and found copies of the Oath of Allegiance taken in Natchez. E-mail from Angela Reid to Don Sharp, Friday, January 6, 2012.

20. Possibly the Spanish West Florida Records, Volume XV1, 231.

21. Ibid., 618.

22. Genealogy Trails, *St. Tammany Parish, Louisiana, Marriages 1811-1820*, 3.

23. Campeau, Anita R., & Sharp, Donald J., "The Tom Spell Memorial Cemetery, Part 1," *New Orleans Genesis*, Volume XLVIII, No. 189, January 2010, 29.

CHAPTER 11

MARTHA LETCHWORTH AND ELIZABETH BARTLE

Martha Letchworth and Elizabeth Bartle, daughters of English pioneer settlers, were residents at Bayou Castein during the Spanish period. Martha's father, George Richardson, had not recognized the need to adapt or perhaps was reluctant to do so. He gave up the land he had squatted on, and moved on to Manchac. Martha remained to confront the wilderness, and found a companion, Zachariah Faircloth, in whom she had much to gain. Elizabeth who married Thomas Spell, the son of an original settler, had reasonable accommodations in which to stay. And, in later years, both of these women had Negro slaves to help with the daily labors of life. They enjoyed a luxury that many of their nameless pioneer sisters did not have.

By 1823, forty-five years had elapsed since the first British immigrants set foot on the shores of Lake Pontchartrain. Though it had been scarcely more than a decade from the time of annexation to the United States, there could be felt a new awareness of the impact of change and the passage of time on the landscape. The year 1810 had become not only an important date, but a founding date.

With the changes taking place on the north shore, the early pioneer period in St. Tammany Parish was coming to an end, and a new phase of development was taking place. Covington and Madisonville, recently founded, were developing as important trading centers, and transient traffic which resulted from roads into St. Tammany from the north stimulated the growth of shipbuilding and the across-the-lake trade.

In seeking to explore the important contributions to the development of the north shore of Lake Pontchartrain by the countless number of pioneer women, we find that there are very few texts documenting those first heroines who worked hand-in-hand with their male counterparts. The Merriam-Webster Dictionary defines pioneer as "an early settler in a territory." We should not overlook the fact that women as well as men were pioneers. Concrete historical documentation on the first women at Bayou Castein is scarce to say the least, but we cannot negate the enormous contributions they made to the development of the north shore. Countless historical texts document the endless tales of male heroes with axe in hand clearing the land, erecting temporary shelters, and tilling the soil. It is fair to say that the pioneer wife immediately became her husband's right hand man.

In retrospect, when we analyze the early years of settlement, we know that when a husband and wife obtained land it was often difficult to get to. The region of the land entitlement and the exact land boundaries were often difficult to identify. We should not forget to mention that once the pioneer husband and wife found their land, the acreage would often be completely covered with a variety of hardwood trees. A couple likely endured a decade or more of isolation and backbreaking conditions. But they did endure. Usually a temporary shelter was built, later to be used as a shed. The land was a challenge not only physically but psychologically. Part of their dilemma would be rooted in the first settlement process in which the pioneer faced two obstacles, the new land and their old culture.

The presence of medical doctors was non-existent in the early days of a settlement. Regardless of the heroic efforts put forth by pioneer women, sanitary conditions were often poor. Diseases such as dysentery, cholera, burns, fractures, and wild animals plagued the settlers.

Women would come to the rescue with their herbal medicines and homemade cures. Many met their deaths due to childbirth complications. Women had to rely on one another, in the presence of midwives, to ease the birthing process. Seldom did they charge for their services, unlike their later male counterparts who stayed clear of delivering babies until they could see a monetary profit in it; then suddenly midwives were unwanted competition.

The one institution which enabled women to fulfill their natural, god-given vocation was marriage, and devoted children at their feet. A married woman was defined as being one with her husband, gave up her name, and virtually all her property came under her husband's control. The popular image of an unmarried woman (old maid) was an object of pity, unnatural and outside the bounds of accepted social and community practice.

When we look at the historical documentation with regard to women, female status was almost non-existent. The wording most often used in legal documents was "authorized and assisted by her husband" or "has not the authorization to make a contract without the consent of her husband" or "by his marital powers." Until the middle of the nineteenth century, married women were considered possessions of their husbands and had virtually no control over their money and property.

The early society which had taken form had very little time for arts and letters as it was concerned with its own growth and its own urgent future. Elizabeth Bartle, who could not read or write, now seized the opportunity to educate her daughters, by hiring a tutor, so they could at least learn the basics and be able to sign their name. Times were beginning to change!

Martha Richardson, widow of Zachariah Faircloth, married Joseph Letchworth, on May 12, 1824, St. Tammany Parish, Louisiana. Joseph Letchworth was in Louisiana by 1812 and operated the ferry across the Bogue Chitto River near Strawberry Bluff.

If you lived across a lake or a river in those days, one had to have access to a boat. Zachariah Faircloth bought from Jacob Bartle the schooner called the "Sea Horse of the Chefuncte". Zachariah, who was not a mariner, had hired Joseph Letchworth to be the Captain. This possibly explains how his wife, Martha, first met him.

Letchworth was the successful ship's master in New Orleans, in 1823, of the ship named Sea Horse, sized at 17 and 33/45 tons. It was registered out of the Custom's House in New Orleans. It was licensed for the Coasting (also written as Costing) and was registered as a "Vessel under 20 tons to carry on the Coasting trade for one year, no. 108, District of Mississippi Port of New Orleans…employed in Coasting and Fisheries. Joseph Letchworth of the Parish of St. Tammany and John Gillmore of New Orleans had given the Bond. Her license was authorized (or renewed) at the Customs House in New Orleans November 10, 1825.[1]

Joseph Letchworth later sold the Sea Horse, all her tackle, etc. and a one years license to Guillaume Parent, a free man of color of St. Tammany Parish for $500.00.

From a previous marriage, Joseph Letchworth, born in North Carolina, had a son named Stokeley, born about 1818, who married Nancy S. Morris, born about 1819, daughter of Wettenhall Morris and Sarah Richardson. Nancy's father was born about 1794, in South Carolina, and died May 22, 1849, in St. Tammany Parish. Her mother, Nancy Richardson, was born about 1800 in Bulloch County, Georgia. They were married on January 24, 1818, by her Uncle Benjamin Richardson, the magistrate.[2] Wettenhall was a veteran of the War of 1812 and the Battle of New Orleans.

The historian has neither the time nor the methodological means to deal with all the particular persons, during a covered period, but knowing and valuing a few out of a hundred or more adds an important dimension to historical understanding. Martha and Elizabeth are two women important to Mandeville's history, not because of their status of women, but because they were persons. The most important historical content was what they thought and felt, and how each reacted. After Zachariah Faircloth had received his land Certificate from the Commissioners, he had amicably told Elizabeth that he considered the land as his, and that she should stop her slaves from cutting timber on his land. Elizabeth would not listen! She understood that this was her land!

Elizabeth and Martha inherited the successions of their deceased husbands. Scholars interested in the economic history of the period will find the Inventories of the Estates useful. In the Succession of Thomas Spell, land was valued at $1.00 an acre and the 12 slaves listed were valued at $5,025.00. The Negro man named Abram, 35 years old, was worth $500.00 and Joseph, age 25, and Philip, 18 years of age, were valued at $550.00 each. There certainly were economic reasons for the sharp increase in the number of slaves.

The 300 head of stock cattle @ 6.50 per head was worth $1,950.00; 7 horses @ 16.00 a head, valued at $112.00; 21 goats @1.00 per head, valued at $21.00; 11 heads of stock hogs @ 2.00 a head, valued at $22.00; 33 sheep @2.00 a head, valued at $66.00.

There were 3 spinning wheels in the home, which explains the number of sheep to produce your own wool; kitchen equipment; table and chairs; a variety of farming utensils and cooper tools, plus a fair amount of tar in the pit.

Edmund R. Moss, son-in-law of Elizabeth Spell, "as an agent for the heirs of Thomas Spell, deceased" claimed five acres front on Lake Pontchartrain in St. Tammany Parish and forty acres in depth bounded east by O'Brien and West by Labyteau/Labatut. This land had been surveyed by Ira Kneeland during the jurisdiction of the Spanish Government, improved and cultivated in 1805.[3] It had to be a forged letter since the O'Brien's always owned the property.

The inventory was returned to Elizabeth on the 15th day of June 1815; her oath taken before the subscriber James R. Tate, Parish Judge for St. Tammany. A true copy of the original on file was affixed with the Seal of Office by Judge Jones, on the 13th of October 1825. It was deposited as evidence on the first day of the trial Letchworth & Wife *vs* Bartell and Wife that had was scheduled for the second week of October 1825.

The heirs of Zachariah Faircloth claimed a section of land situated in the Parish of St. Tammany by virtue of a certificate No. 480, dated 11 March 1825, by Charles S. Cosby, Registrar, and Fulwar Skipwith, Receiver. And, there appearing to be no complication in this claim to be located and surveyed as follows: "to begin on the borders of Lake

Pontchartrain at the line of Jacob Bartles and run through with the Lake shore to the line of Paul Labatut and from those two points on the Lake to run back with the lines of Bartles and Labatut for the compliment of six hundred and forty acres and no more." Given under our hands this 11th day of March 1825.
Signed: James Runnells, Registrar & William Kinchen, Receiver

Elizabeth Bartle needed help in managing her plantation. The following is a letter probably written by the teacher Love B. Green at the request of Elizabeth Bartle to the Commissioners of the Land Office:

"Know all men by there present and Elizabeth Bartles...do hereby implore and authorize my son Thomas Spell of the state and parish aforesaid to do and transact business for me my lawful agent at the land office of St. Helena with the commissioners of said land office, to adjust all claims and do any and every business with said commissioners of said land office of St. Helena to all intent and purpose the same that I would do myself if present, given under my hand and seal this twenty second day of April 1825."

Elizabeth Bartle signed with her usual mark, an X. The letter was witnessed by L.B. Greene and Delisle DeLabarthe, her son-in-law.

On June 18, 1825, Jesse R. Jones, Parish Judge, authorized by an order of the Court of Probates, proceeded with the inventory of the property belonging to the succession of Zachariah Faircloth who had departed this life on the fourteenth of August 1823. It was in the presence and at the request of Martha Letchworth, the late widow of the said deceased, "authorized and assisted by her Husband Joseph Letchworth" and in the presence of Branch W. Miller, Attorney at Law, "duly appointed to represent the absent heirs" of the said deceased. Lawrence Sticker and Joseph Sharp were duly appointed and sworn as appraisers, in the presence of John Edwards and William Sharp as witnesses.

First, commencing at the late residence of the deceased near the Lake Pontchartrain with the plantation as tract of land containing six hundred and forty acres with the improvements valued at one dollar per acre making $640.00; one hundred heads of horned cattle running in the range valued together for the sum of $400.00, four heads of horses valued together at $100.00; ten heads of sheep valued at $15.00.

One Negro man named Louis, aged forty seven years, a cooper, valued at $400.00 and London, very old Negro man- slave, was valued at $50.00.

Of importance was one schooner called the "Sea Horse of the Tchefuncta" with her tackle and apparel, valued at $250.00 Zachariah's succession amounted to one thousand eight hundred and eighty dollars ($1,880.00).

This completed, followed the inventory of the papers belonging to the Succession: Bundle A contained a land certificate signed by Charles S. Cosby, Registrar and Fulwar Skipwith, Receiver, certifying that Zachariah Faircloth was entitled to 640 acres of land in the Parish of St. Tammany. Item 2 was a Bill of Sale from James Goodbee to Zachariah Faircloth for a Negro man named Lucy. Item 3 was a bill of sale from John George to Zachariah Faircloth for a Negro man named Shigal.

Bundle B contained receipts and received accounts and other papers. The official document was signed by Jesse R. Jones, Parish Judge, dated the twentieth day of June 1825.[4]

On October 5, 1823, Martha and Joseph Letchworth became the legal owners of Zachariah Faircloth's land, minus the 200 acres deeded to the nephew, Joseph Sharp.

After being reminded to stop cutting wood by Letchworth, Elizabeth retorted that the disputed land was hers, and that she would continue to do what she wanted with her land. In turn, the Letchworths "forewarn" Elizabeth that unless she stops trespassing and cutting wood on her land they will sue. William Sharp was living on Zachariah Faircloth's land, about 70 yards over the disputed line on the south side of Bayou Chinchuba. The land in dispute was further down towards the lake between the Bartle line and the Labatut. Joseph Sharp had his cabin there and was donated 200 acres by deed of gift from his uncle Zachariah Faircloth.

In the suit brought forward by Letchworth and Wife, the original petition showed that Martha Faircloth had inherited the property of her deceased husband and that the said Joseph Letchworth intermarried with the said Martha, and "by his marital power became the administrator of her property and possessed with her the said lands."

A Certificate of the appointment of Branch W. Miller to "represent the absent heirs" of Zachariah Faircloth, deceased, was given on June 8, 1825. Jesse R. Jones certified the appointment and affixed the seal of his Office on October 13, 1825. Who were the absent heirs? We do not know, but it was reported by a witness that Zachariah had told a friend that he had an uncle living in North Carolina. However, the clause of "absent heirs" was not allowed as evidence in court.

The plaintiffs, Letchworth and Wife claimed that during the last five years and at diverse times the Bartles forcibly entered and trespassed upon a tract of land they owned. The land in question was "bounded on one side by the lands of Bartles and Wife, and on the other side by lands belonging to one Labatut," and had cut down, destroyed, barked and otherwise injured their timber...particularly oak, cypress, and pine, although frequently warned and forbidden by Petitioners, and by the person from whom they derived the title.[5]

The Bartles having refused to make compensation, the petitioners brought suit against them through their Attorney Branch W. Miller who requested that Bartle and wife be cited according to law and to appear at the next District Court to be held for the Parish of St. Tammany on the second Monday in October next to answer the complaint of the Petitioners, "and after due proceedings that they be sentenced and condemned to pay petitioners fifteen hundred dollars with interest and costs of Suit, and that such other and further relief be extended to the Petitioners as the Justice and nature of their case may be required."[6] The Sheriff served the citation to the defendants on May 28, 1825. It was filed with the court by clerk, Sam Mallory, on June 11, 1825.

Elizabeth Bartle denied all the allegations in the suit. Unfortunately for Elizabeth, Jacob Bartle died on October 1, 1825, about two weeks before the opening of the trial. This left her as the sole defendant! A woman in mourning! Elizabeth "accepted the community under the benefit of an inventory."

Branch W. Miller, Attorney for the petitioners, at the request of Labarthe DeLisle, wrote to the Honorable Jesse R. Jones with regard to the estate of "Jacob Bartells"who died intestate, leaving a considerable property, and the following heirs: Maria Bartells, wife of McLin Lloyd, and Sophia, Marshall and Elizabeth Bartells, minor children of the said deceased and under the age of puberty. The petitioner, Labarthe DeLisle, further showed that he was a creditor of the said succession and that he wished to enforce his rights..."to which end he prays that the said heirs may be cited to appear before your Honorable Court, there to declare whether they accept or refuse the Succession of their said Ancestor." Signed B. W. Miller, Attorney for petitioner.[7]

On December 28, 1826, in conformity to an order of the Court of Probates for the Parish of St. Tammany, for the purpose of making a partition of Jacob Bartle, deceased, among his heirs and according to their respective rights, Judge Jesse R. Jones proceeded to the sale of his property at the last residence of the deceased. Terms of the sale were to be paid in cash.

The former O'Brien tract was to be sold to satisfy the claims of the Bartle heirs. The tract of land of ten arpents frontage, on Lake Pontchartrain with forty arpents in depth, was sold to William Bowman, a Prussian, who came to Madisonville in 1827,[8] for the sum of three hundred dollars ($300.00). Bowman also purchased four horses running on the range for seventy-two dollars ($72.00).

Joseph Sharp purchased an old Negro woman named Nancy for ten dollars and fifty cents ($10.50), plus one yoke of work oxen for thirty dollars ($30.00), and a pair of cart wheels for six dollars and fifty cents ($6.50).

The schooner called "Madison" with her tackle and apparel went to Elizabeth Bartle for seventy-five dollars ($75.00).

One stock of cattle, thirty heads were sold to Macklin Lloyd for one hundred and eighty dollars ($180.).

Amount of the sale came to $674.00, from which were deducted charges for the Parish Judge, his fees $83.87 and $15.00 for the sheriff's fees, for a total of $98.97.

The proceeds of the schooner, being community property, one half of which after deducting proportion of charges was to be paid to the widow, amounted to $32.00. Net receipts of the sale came to $543.12. The schooner Madison had been purchased by Jacob Bartle and Elizabeth a few years earlier from Henry Cooper Junior, the son of Henry Cooper Senior.

Monies received from the estate sale were disbursed as follows:

To Macklin Lloyd and wife	$155.18
To Marshall Bartle	$155.18 (Joseph Sharp was tutor to Marshall Bartle).
To Sophia Bartle	$155.18
To Elizabeth Bartle	$77.59
Total disbursed:	$543.12.
(Signed by Jesse R. Jones, Parish Judge.)	

William McDermott, of unknown origins, was in Bayou Chinchuba as early as 1791. That year, James Goodbee came down from Galveztown with his sister Elizabeth to settle. An educated man, who had no problems using a pen, McDermott wrote and witnessed the document of the "Goodbee assignment" of his land to his brother-in-law, Thomas Spell: "To James Goodbee of the district of Casten Bayou do assign my right and title of a certain tract of Land situated on a Certain Branch in Said District known by the name of Chinchuba, or Hugh's Banks unto Thomas Spell of the above tract for Value Received."[9] In 1798, when surveyor Gilberto Guillemard surveyed the land, it was still owned by James Goodbee.

Why McDermott did not apply for a Spanish land grant when he had the opportunity remains a mystery. In 1798, when Lt. Colonel Gilberto Guillemard came to survey the Goodbee and Thomas Spell property, William McDermott was living on the abandoned British grants of Ambrose and Ferguson.

In 1814, William McDermott wrote his Will, which reads as follows:

To all those people to whom these present shall concern, I W.W. McDermott do send greetings. Know ye that the said W.W. McDermott of the Parish of Saint Tammany and district of Castin Bayou North Side of Lake Pontchartrain, farmer for and in consideration of the Love, good will and affection which I have and do bear towards my Loving wife, Mary McDermott and our Children William McDermott and Elenora Elizabeth McDermott of the same Parish or District have given and Granted, and by these presents do freely give and Grant unto Said Mary McDermott, William McDermott and Elenora McDermott one tract of Land in the above parish or district containing four hundred acres land bound on the East by the Land of Thomas Spell and on the West by the Lands of William Dewees known by land of Paul Labateau, and on tract to the North of said tract joining the Lands of Samuel Lloyd Containing two hundred acres, One Negro Woman named Prince or Pony with her four Children a Mullatto Boy named Theodore born June the 10th 1807 and Negro Child named Charity born March the 15th 1811, and Negro Child named London born September 20th 1812, and Mulatto son named Charles Born January the 7th 1814, and all my horned cattle be they moved or left branded thus MD, the number or sex uncertain which by these presents I have delivered them the aforesaid, Mary McDermott, William McDermott and Elenora Eliza McDermott their heirs and assigns from hence forth as their property absolutely without any manner of Condition.

The document was Signed, Sealed and delivered in the presence of Brackston Lloyd who made his mark, and Thomas White who signed. "In Witness Where of I have hereunto put my hand and Seal this 20th day of February, in the Year of our Lord one thousand eight hundred and fourteen and the 39th year of American Independence."
Signed W. W. McDermott, to which was attached a wax seal.
Written below: State of Louisiana, Parish of Louisiana

On April 12, 1814, before James Tate, Judge of the aforesaid Parish, personally appeared Brackston Lloyd, one of the subscribing witnesses to McDermott's Will, who testified that "he saw the party Grantor to said Instrument sign and acknowledge the same of the purpose therein specified." Then, on the 17th of April appeared Joseph White who before James Tate, Judge, acknowledged same as the above-named Braxton. Followed by the certification of James Tate who certified the foregoing instrument to be truly recorded. Dated the 20th day of April 1814.[10]

In May of the year 1825, Joseph Letchworth made an inquiry to David B. Morgan, Surveyor, about the claim of the heirs of William McDermott to land adjoining the settlement of Zachariah Faircloth.

In answer to the inquiry, on May 21, 1825, Surveyor Morgan replied that he felt authorized to say, "...that the donation to his Heirs have no just claim to any land in the neighborhood under any land law now in existence."

According to Morgan, McDermott was employed by William Dewees to live and work on a piece of land which Dewees had purchased from the representatives of the heirs of Labatut and, in 1813, McDermott pretended to claim the land for himself from his settlement. "And I know that Dewees brought suit against him in 1813, and obtained possession from McDermott and has remained in possession."

"The lands now pretended to be claimed by the heirs of McDermott were lands granted by the former English government to Paul Labatut and, by the Spanish Crown, went another grant to his sons. Possession has always been had by the Representatives of the Labatut,"...and continued Morgan: "I have never heard any one but old William McDermott pretend there was any other claimant, and I have never heard anyone but himself, say that he had any claim to the lands. My own opinion is that the man who has originated the claim anew has done it from a natural 'malination' to be in the law & benefit by the ignorance of others."[11]

Signed: David B. Morgan.

Evicted from Dewees's property, McDermott and his family removed to Mary Lloyd's land, and it was with her permission. McDermott died in 1814, and his family tried to claim the land in the 1820s.

In the case McDermott *vs* Letchworth, the Land Office of St. Helena proceeded to hear the evidence offered and rendered the following decision: "It appears that Farrecloth (Faircloth) settled at an early date, twenty years elapsed between the surveyed lines of Labatut, Spell, Bartell and Lloyd, and in those bounds only 550 acres were contained.

In 1813 McDermott was employed as an agent in the claim of Labatut which was a British grant that when Labatut lines were resurveyed the improvement of McDermott was not taken in and this part of the improvement was not taken as a settlement claim.

The board are therefore of opinion that they are not at liberty to alter the old lines but if a resurveying of all the adjoining claims around the claims of McDermott that then an order of survey would be granted but if there should be no vacant land discovered no further proceedings will be had in this office in the claim of McDermott."

Signed: James Runnell, Registrar, & William Kinchen, Receiver.

Martha Richardson legally obtained possession of Zachariah's acreage on August 6, 1825.[12] On that day, she gave bond and security agreeable to law, attested Jesse R. Jones, the Parish Judge: "therefore due faith and credit is due to all her acts as surviving wife inheriting in default of Heirs of said Zachariah Faircloth.[13]

Martha had the land she legally owned surveyed on August 27, 1825, shortly before the start of the trial. Surveyor David B. Morgan certified that the plat he drew was a fair representation of the Settlement the deceased Zachariah Faircloth owned. On three sides, the lines had long been established and the other two were natural boundaries being the Lake and Bayou Chinchuba. The last of which was the conditional line between Lloyd and Faircloth. The contents included between these boundaries 550 acres as near as could be calculated without a traverse of the Bayou. Surveyor Morgan certified that he had appertained by actual survey the front on the Lake, and two sides line, that of Paul Labatut, the other of Jacob Bartle, and found it as divided in the plat. The back line and Bayou were not measured by him.

Surveyor Morgan left out the two hundred acres that Zachariah Faircloth gave to his nephew Joseph Sharp. The land was located on the western boundary of the Jacob Bartle property, the land where the encroachment had taken place.

From St. Tammany, on September 3, 1825, a letter written on behalf of Mary C. Lloyd was addressed to the Honorable Commissioners of the Land Office in St. Helena. It stated there had been an order of survey fraudulently obtained by the Heirs of Thomas Spell, deceased. Her request was for the Commissioners to revoke survey until further investigation could be had, and "that your petitioner can have an opportunity of showing to the land Commissioners aforesaid that the said order of survey was fraudulently obtained and was of material damage to her."

Valuable information on Louisiana surveys can be found in the litigation between the two prominent women, Martha and Elizabeth, during the second decade of the American Regime. In the survey made by David B. Morgan, in March 1825, he sketched a rough map locating the houses of Elizabeth Goodby's two sons-in-law, that of Edmund Moss and the DeLisle house, and the house of Thomas Spell, and the old improvement house.

Attestation that Martha owns Zachariah's property in default of heirs

Morgan's survey map of 1825

Louisiana did not inherit the English common law, thus followed rules developed in continental Europe. Under their community property systems each spouse is considered owner of half of the earnings of the other, and all property acquired during marriage (other than gifts and inheritances) is jointly owned by both spouses, regardless of who paid for it or whose name it is in. The result was the same because the husband was considered to be the head of the household and as such could manage and dispose of the community property as he wished.

We feel as we begin to chronicle *Court Case No. 225* that Elizabeth Bartle, regardless of the laws in those days concerning women, chose not to be overlooked, deleted, or shunned by later historians. She definitely provided a source of welcomed escape from the drudgery and the boredom of a small community with a trial that went on and on.

NOTES

1. Recorded July 29, 1826, B-1, 113-114. Courtesy of Robin Leckbee Perkins, Covington Court House Archives.
2. Genealogy Trails, St. Tammany Parish, *Louisiana Marriages: 1811-1820,* 9.
3. Notice No. 17, Edmund B. Moss to the Commissioners Office of the Land Office at St. Helena Court House
4. Recorded on the Notarial Record Book B, page 50, Parish of St. Tammany, and State of Louisiana.
5. Suit of Letchworth and Wife vs Jacob Bartles and Wife, Parish of St. Tammany, in a supplemental petition by Ripley and Miller, Attorney's for the Letchworth.
6. *Court Case No. 225,* 8ᵗʰ District Court of St. Tammany, Letchworth and Wife vs Bartles and Wife, Citation filed on June 11, 1825
7. State of Louisiana, Parish of St. Tammany, letter by B. W. Miller for the petitioner Labarthe DeLisle, to the Honorable Jesse R. Jones, Judge of the Court of Probates in and for the parish aforesaid.
8. Boagni, Ethel, *Mandeville, Louisiana,* The St. Tammany Historical Society, 1980, 46.
9. A certified copy of the assignment by James Goodbee to Thomas Spell was filed on the October 17, 1825, with regard to the trial Letchworth & Wife *vs* Bartle & Wife.
10. State of Louisiana, Parish of St. Tammany, recorded on page 65 of the Notarial Record Book A for the Parish aforesaid.
11. Reply to Joseph Letchworth by Surveyor David B. Morgan dated May 21, 1825.
12. Letchworth & Wife *vs* Bartells & Wife, Court Case No. 225, put in the Succession of Zachariah Faircloth.
13. Seal of Office affixed to testimony on August 6, 1825, by Jesse R. Jones, Parish Judge.

CHAPTER 12

THE JUDICIAL SYSTEM, ST. TAMMANY PARISH

The Legislative Act of 1804 established a territorial government dividing Louisiana in two sections. Dissatisfied, the people of New Orleans complained that Governor William Charles Coles Claiborne was unacquainted with the language, their laws, and mainly their interests, and that he favored only his countrymen. The Governor continued with the organization of the judiciary with the establishment of a Court of Pleas consisting of justices. The next task was to organize a judicial system for the Parishes.

The necessity for a court house in St. Tammany Parish originated December 22, 1810, when the land west of the Pearl River became a part of Orleans territory. The area referred to as the West Florida Parishes was made part of the state when President James Madison approved the bill passed by Congress. With the creation of the new parishes, came the need for seats of justice.

Governor Claiborne issued a commission as Judge for St. Tammany Parish to Thomas Cargill Warner, on July 18, 1811, an office which combined executive and the usual judicial functions, with the added duty to act as president of the police jury. He was the first territorial judge of present day St. Tammany. The site chosen by the police jurors to build a court house and a jail was near Enon on the Bogue Chitto River on the property of Judge Warner.

Thomas C. Warner, son of Wettenhall Warner and Elizabeth Cargill, was born April 8, 1772, in Laurens District, South Carolina. His family was of the Anglican or Episcopal faith. He married there Tabitha F. Cargill on October 23, 1794. The family moved to Louisiana between 1802 and 1806.[1] That year, Warner acted as surveyor in establishing the boundary between two Spanish grants.[2] He was the commanding officer of the 13th Regiment of the Louisiana Militia which participated in the Battle of New Orleans. Little is known about his life, but he was well educated for his time, and served well.

On March 2, 1813, the Louisiana Supreme Court met for the first time in order to continue with the organization of the judicial system. Seven distinguished men stood before the bench and each swore that "I will demean myself honestly in the practice as a counselor or attorney, and will discharge my duty, in every respect to the best of my knowledge and ability."[3] James Tate was named Judge of the parish court on June 5, 1813 to March 1819.

Louisiana's legal profession passed through two distinct periods of growth. The pioneer period lasted until 1839. Opportunities were endless regardless of an attorney's background or preparation. Some ambitious men used the law as a springboard into other areas of Louisiana Society.[4] There were few rules to control admission to the bar, and the question of what constituted proper training was left open. By 1840, there was concern and changes were made over applicants' qualifications to be appointed judge, and this led to the adoption of stricter rules.

Ahead of the waves of emigration had been the lure of cheap lands and the fact that the Indian menace had been removed. Some were squatters on the public domain who had no intentions of obtaining a title. They lived there for a few years, readily sold the improvements they had made to a more substantial newcomer, and journeyed further westward. To a certain extent they had helped to break the dominance of the forest and to drive in the wedge of civilization. The newcomers became involved in a process of social-economic evolution that marked the course of human development from primitive to a more modern time which made possible the local store, the doctor, the lawyer, the church, school and mills. The need for surveyors, land commissioners to register titles, and lawyers to settle land disputes between neighbors was felt as never before.

The credit system ruined some over anxious settlers and had failed to impede speculation, plus the hard times of 1819 brought demands for new legislation. The changes in land laws were in part the result of pressure brought by the "Great Migration" which lured men westward. In 1820 the minimum price for public land was about $1.25 an acre, to be paid in one cash payment, and the smallest unit of purchase was reduced to 80 acres. Thus a settler could secure immediate ownership of a farm.

James Tate succeeded Judge Warner in 1813. Upon the death of Judge Ebenezer Ford in 1821, Thomas Warner filled the vacancy for Washington Parish. Shortly after, the Washington parish court was moved from the site of Enon to a spot up the river, later known as Franklintown. It was made the parish seat by an act of the legislature approved February 10, 1821.[5] Thomas Warner sold his section of land and moved up the Bogue Chitto to the Louisiana-Mississippi line to a place known as Warnerton. He served there until his death on March 25, 1833. Judge Warner had a large family of thirteen children, six sons and seven daughters who in turn had large progenies.

The origin of the next courthouse began by an act of the Legislature, February 18, 1817. An election was called to fix the seat of justice for the parish, and with the electorate voting in favor, James Villere, the governor of Louisiana, approved of the decision.[6] A proper site for the permanent seat had to be chosen in or near the town of Covington. A team of commissioners was needed to make the appropriate decision. By another legislative act, on March 16, 1818, a group of prominent men, David B. Morgan (appointed by Governor Claiborne as brigadier general with the Louisiana militia), William Ligon, J. Tillery, John Littlejohn, Thomas Tate, William Bagley, John Wright, William McFarlan, Joseph Lawn, Joseph J.B. Ligon, Griffin Rinsine, James Morgan, Samuel Thomas, Jesse R. Jones, James Tate, and Daniel Edwards were named as commissioners to make this decision.[7]

Knowing a courthouse would generate business opportunities to the surrounding areas, the members of the commission selected a site in the newly dedicated Town of Claiborne located across the Bogue Falaya River. The town had been laid out by a syndicate known as the Claiborne Company and was run by Robert Layton. Considering the success of the previous lumber yard, they offered to build a courthouse and jail at their expense.[8] The commissioners could not refuse this enticing offer, and an agreement was reached on July 10, 1818.

On October 12, 1818, a suitable lot of 1,765 acres of so-called "superficial land" located on the east bank of the Bogue Falaya was purchased for the price of $5,000. The site, located opposite Covington, had been purchased from John Henry Ludling through a sheriff's sale for a mere $350.00, and both parties were probably satisfied with their deal.

Once the arrangements were completed, the northern portion of St. Tammany Parish was split and Washington Parish was created on March 6, 1819. Colonel Thomas C. Warner's barn housed the first court for Washington Parish, with Colonel Warmer himself acting as the first Parish Judge.[9]

The original seat of justice, located in Enon on the Bogue Chitto River was then moved to Claiborne Hill and the construction of the new courthouse soon began. Specific instructions were given by the commissioners to three New Orleans architect for the design of the building.

According to the records there would be two buildings, each two stories high. The courthouse was to measure 40 by 30, and the jail 21 square feet. The brick walls were to be 18 inches thick and were probably fired on site. The Claiborne Company supplied the lumber that came from the original mill. The roof with its cupola produced a semblance of a ship's tower.[10] With the river as a background, and standing on a hill flanked by lofty pines, it was a beautiful stately building with each room having access to the towering fireplaces. The ornate trims were crafted from pine. The courthouse had a porch stretching across the front on both floors.

Despite the presence of the regal courthouse, the town of Claiborne did not develop and prosper as expected. By a legislative act, the seat of justice was moved to Covington in 1838, and this is where it has remained ever since.

After the seat of justice was moved, the old courthouse served as a private residence and a Catholic seminary before being renovated and restored in 1880 by the Jaufroid family for use as a hotel. It soon became a popular resort for people from New Orleans.[11]

James Tate, the son of Joseph Tate and Elizabeth Pattison, was born in eastern Pennsylvania, on March 28, 1773, and his brother Thomas was born in Maryland in 1775. The Tate family was in Augusta County, Virginia, in 1778, settling three miles east of Fairfield. When Rockbridge County was formed in 1779, Joseph Tate was in the area buying land in 1781 and 1793; selling that land in 1796 and September, 1810. He remained in Rockbridge County until 1811; then removed to 1,000 acres of land he had purchased in April 1810, on Caesar's Creek in Massie Township, Warren County, Ohio.

James Tate, who succeeded Judge Warner, moved to Madisonville, Louisiana, before February 28, 1812, evidenced by a land sale on Bayou Feliah. His brother Thomas joined him in business, and they were known as "James Tate and Brother."

James Tates' marriage contract to Anne Corran was dated March 17, 1817. They were married on the 17th in St. Tammany. Anne, born about 1780 in England, was first married to William Wharton Collins, the son of Thomas Wharton Collins and Mary Hinton, of Philadelphia. William followed the life of a sailor, became Mate and subsequently was made Captain of a ship plying between New Orleans and Liverpool. He married there to Anne Corran in, 1802. He settled in Madisonville about 1810. He lost his life on Lake Pontchartrain in January 1816, leaving only one child George Thomas Wharton Collins, born at sea in 1811.[12]

William was the brother of John Wharton Collins who purchased the Jacques Dreux tract, a Spanish land grant, who on July 4, 1813, dedicated the town of Wharton.[13] The town was formally incorporated, and its name changed to Covington by a legislative act adopted March 11, 1816.[14] The town was named in honor of General Leonard Covington, a soldier of distinction who was with Governor Claiborne in Baton

Rouge at the demise of the West Florida Republic and who, dying in battle, distinguished himself during the War of 1812.

James Tate was replaced as judge by Jesse R. Jones on March 1, 1819. Anne Corran died September 20, 1821, in the area that is now Sabine County, Texas. She left behind her son, George Thomas Wharton Collins (1812-1892). A daughter with James named Anne had already died "at the age of ten months in the Province of Texas."

On January 28, 1823, James and his brother Thomas mortgaged considerable lands in St. Tammany and Washington Parishes and in Pike County, Mississippi to satisfy creditors. The mortgaged property was transferred February 12, 1823, on which date, James was listed "of Iberville parish."[15]

For a former judge, James Tate was a disreputable person. One day while camping near St. Augustine, James told his stepson George that he was going to get some fresh meat, but never returned. Abandoned, the young boy walked into St. Augustine, and was taken in by a lawyer as his apprentice. Having reached the age of sixteen, George ventured to New Orleans where he passed the bar exam. While in the Crescent City, George discovered that his stepfather had been appointed his guardian in 1821 and had sold his inheritance to satisfy his own creditors in 1823. It followed that George sued James in St. Tammany Parish and won a judgment in 1830. George never received his inheritance because James Tate was in Texas.

George Wharton Collins returned to Texas and became the first sheriff of Angelina County, Texas. He married Martha Anne Bridges on October 30, 1837, in Angelina County, Texas, and raised a large family. He is found in the 1880 census in Precinct 3, Angelina County, Texas, age 68, born in Louisiana to parents born in New York and England, with wife Martha, age 60, born in Louisiana.

James Tate received 4,428 acres of land, surveyed February 17, 1826, in Leftwich's Grant Robertson's Colony, Province of Texas, on the west side of the Brazos River above the San Antonio Nacogdoches Road. He wrote to Stephen F. Austin on February 27, 1827, stating that his land was partly on Leftwich's Grant and partly in Austin's Colony, but because of Indian activity he had been unable to occupy his land. He proposed a scheme for selling that land to purchase slaves to work in Austin's Colony to raise sugar cane and manufacture sugar.[16] There is no record of Austin's reply! He did receive another tract of land in Leftwich's Grant west of the Brazos on February 19, 1830. His name can be found on the tax list of Washington County, Republic of Texas in 1839. Tate might have been talented, but he does not figure among the virtuous men who served among the judges of St. Tammany.

Jesse Ruble Jones, who replaced Judge James Tate, served as the third parish judge of St. Tammany, his term beginning in 1819. He was on the first town council elected in Covington. In addition to his judicial responsibilities he served as ex-officio president of the police jury. The law changed in 1830, and he was relieved of his duties.

The son of David Jones and Jane Ruble, he was born October 9, 1787, at Charlottesville, Virginia. His parents were married at the ages of 16 and 18 years, and lived together within a few months of sixty years. His great, great grandfather, of Welsh descent, came to America as a boy to Montgomery County, Virginia, about the year 1700. Jesse remembered his great grandfather and grandmother, who were more than ninety years old, and who used to tell him stories about their childhood in Wales.[17]

Jesse's mother was the daughter of Owen Ruble, of German extraction, who commanded a Company of Militia at the taking of York Town during the Revolutionary War. Jesse's father was a subaltern in his Company.[18] Major Turly (*sic*), son of his sister Elizabeth, once wrote to her brother that her husband was wearing the sword which had belonged to their father at York Town.[19]

Jesse Jones was with his parents when they removed to Kentucky. There, he studied law and after graduation he went to Natchez, in 1808, for health reasons. We find him in St. Tammany parish in 1811. This is what his daughter Susan wrote to her cousin Clara in 1902. His parents removed to Missouri. His mother and father, David Jones (1761-1838), a Revolutionary soldier, was buried in the Walter Reid Cemetery, Blackwater, Cooper County, Missouri.

There were opportunities in the forested hills of St. Tammany parish. In no time, Jesse Jones became a successful merchant, manufacturer, planter, jurist and statesman. His public career began as foreman of the first grand jury to be impaneled in St. Tammany parish in 1813. He married Lemandee Kirkland, daughter of Obed Kirkland, a well-to-do merchant, and an early settler there. She died on April 11, 1822, aged 21 years 4months and 17 days. The widower has a second marriage to Rebecca Ragan.[20] Her father lived on a farm and had a flour mill located near Milledgeville, Georgia. Jesse Jones moved his family about 1814 to Covington, Louisiana.[21]

Jesse R. Jones served as a volunteer in the battle of New Orleans in 1815. He was a second lieutenant in Captain William Bickham's Company, 13th Regiment of Louisiana Militia, commanded by Colonel

Thomas C. Warner. He filed for his state pension in 1874 as a resident of St. Tammany. A statement signed by Abner Jenkins and McLin Lloyd attested to the fact that Jones had served in the 13th Regiment as claimed. These men affirmed that they served in the same Company. Lloyd drew a state pension for his service. In the file submitted by Jones was a record from the St. Tammany district court dated December 1814 showing that he was the foreman of a grand jury at that time. The other was a document by Governor Villere showing that Jesse R. Jones was appointed judge of the Parish of St. Tammany on February 4, 1819.

The home of Judge Jesse Rubel Jones located at the corner of Portsmouth and New Hampshire ca. 1823-1830

Picture of his house in Covington

The microfilmed index to the federal pension records identifies Jones' wife as Rebecca Jones. Her maiden name is not given.

The Bogue Falaya River was once the site of the Jones Brickyard, an industry he started immediately after his arrival. The clay reached his plant on wooden rails mounted with mule carts, an industrial innovation of the day. During his career on the bench or in business, he accumulated a large fortune in the practice of law, owned 56 slaves, had a beautiful home in Covington located at the corner of Portsmouth and New Hampshire, and he had acquired considerable property in New Orleans.

Judge Jesse R. Jones also served from April 1835, until November 1846, and as judge of the 6th Judicial District from May 1865, until May

1866. Like other citizens of Louisiana, during the Civil War, he suffered much in his pecuniary affairs.

He represented St. Tammany Parish in several Legislatures and State Conventions. His public career was one of leadership beginning as foreman of the first grand jury to be impaneled in St. Tammany Parish in 1813. He was elected State Representative first in 1816 and remained in office either in the Legislature or on the bench throughout the active period of his life.[22]

He died in New Orleans on Tuesday, March 23, 1880, aged 92 years and 8 months. He had the esteem of all who knew him.

The Eighth Judicial District Court was created February 15, 1822, with Judge Henry H. Pattillo serving from April 8, 1822, to 1827. Thomas B. Robertson was elected governor of Louisiana in 1820. In March 1823, his house in Madisonville was rented to Judge Henry H. Pattillo who was to pay $10 a month rent, half of which could be used for repairs. Pattillo died prior to December 15, 1827, having paid no rent for the use of the house.[23] Shortly before his term as governor expired, Robertson resigned to become U.S. District Judge, appointed by James Monroe. For reasons of health, he resigned that post in 1828 and returned to White Sulphur Springs, West Virginia, where he died and was buried. .

Judge Pattillo's estate was filed as a vacant succession, no heir identified or coming forward.[24] There is no mention of a death date, nor any information on possible family members, names or places of origin in the documents. It is not known when he arrived in St. Tammany, or even when he arrived in Louisiana.

Jesse R. Jones, Jonathan Gilmore (an attorney), and Lazarus B. Ragan examined paperwork, probably the contents of Judge Pattillo's office, on December 15, 1827, looking for titles, notes, books of accounts, or credits of any kind. They stated that they did not discover any. What they found were several letters and receipts dating from 1820 to 1827.

James B. McCay applied to act as a curator because he claimed to be one of the principal creditors of Pattillo. He made this application on November 15, 1827. Jesse R. Jones appointed James McCay as a curator on December 15, 1827. He declared that there was due from the State of Louisiana to the Succession the sum of $210.00 for services as District Judge. The amount of property inventoried totaled $1,243.50.

A library of various law books and several sets of clothes were inventoried by McCay, Jonathan Gilmore, and Henry Tyson on January 20, 1818. The value was set at $72.06. John A. Ragan was appointed as attorney to represent the absent heirs of the deceased.

174

A sale was held of household furnishings, clothes, and a large private library on April 12, 1828. The sale netted $1,109.75. Pattillo was certainly a well-dressed and literary man. Debts were presented from firms in Baltimore and Washington, D.C. The court then instructed James B. McCay to use the proceeds to settle the debts owed by Pattillo.

Proceedings against the estate of Judge Pattillo yielded $485.00 at 5 per cent interest. Witnesses on behalf of Judge Pattillo testified that he had made many repairs to the house. He had also built outbuildings at his own expense.[25]

After the death of her husband, Leila Skipwith Robertson, daughter of Fulwar Skipwith, began probate proceedings in St. Tammany. The house and lots in Madisonville were sold to Clark Woodruff for $550.00. Leila spent her final days at her home in Virginia.

Clark W. Woodruff succeeded Judge Pattillo to the 8th District. His term of office was from April 14, 1828 to April 1835. Born August 23, 1791, in Litchfield, New Haven, Connecticut, he was the son of James and Lucy Morris. He was in St. Francisville, Louisiana, in the summer of 1811, as noted in an advertisement which appeared in *The Time Piece* informing the public that "his academy would open on the first Monday in September next for the reception of students." He proposed to teach a variety of subjects: English Grammar, Geography, Astronomy, Elocution, Composition, Penmanship, Latin and Greek.

He may have studied law with General David Bradford as historical tours convey, but this would conflict with the article just mentioned, unless he arrived before Bradford's death in 1808, studied law, then returned to Connecticut, and came back to St. Francisville in 1810. Then, it is possible that Woodruff may have not known his future father-in-law.

Clark W. Woodruff (26) married Sarah Matilda Bradford (19) in 1817. He appears in the 1820 and 1830 census. He listed his occupation as teacher, lawyer, judge and friend of Andrew Jackson. He purchased the plantation from his mother-in-law, Mrs. Bradford, for a mere $2.50 an acre, to which he added crops of cotton and indigo.

Legend has it that Judge Woodruff had a reputation for integrity with men and the law in his district, but in his personal life he was known for being promiscuous.

In 1834, he sold his plantation to Ruffin Gray Sterling for $46,853.00. Woodruff later moved to New Orleans where he served as judge until his death on November 25, 1851, at Oakland Plantation, near Carrolton, Louisiana. He was buried at Girod Cemetery in New Orleans. During the first half of the 20th century, the cemetery fell into disrepair with an overgrowth of vegetation. In 1957, the Cemetery was deconsecrated;

bodies were exhumed and removed to other locations. Judge Woodruff's current resting place is not known.

Branch W. Miller, born about 1795, possibly New Orleans, was the son of Jeremiah Miller. Branch's father operated a water operated saw mill on the Bogue Falaya River in 1821. In that year, he was authorized to clear logs and trees from this river to give free navigation from Covington to Miller's Mills.[26]

He bought 636 acres on Chappapeela Creek from Moses Moore. The property was bounded above and below by property of lawyer Alfred Hennen, described as "20 miles from Madisonville." Moses Moore also sold property to lawyer Joseph H. Hawkins (a co-founder of Texas) on Chappapeela Creek around 1821.

Jeremiah Miller died intestate on November 28, 1822, in Covington. He had severe pulmonary problems and ran up medical bills consisting of liquor, opium, and plasters for his chest. His sole heirs were his sons Thomas C. Miller and Branch W. Miller. Thomas renounced his claim to his father's estate, and Branch became the sole heir of the saw mill and the 640 acres. He sold the property on October 9, 1824, to Jonathan Gilmore.

Branch W. Miller married Eliza Anne Delaybach Kurk, born in South Carolina. They were living in New Orleans in 1820. He acquired property in Covington: Lot #11, Square 7, in the Division of St. John. It had a 54 foot front on Florida Street, and was 129 feet deep. It was purchased with all buildings from Henry T. Tyson on August 17, 1820.[27]

He was around Madisonville and Covington as early as 1820-1823. In 1825, he represented the defendants Joseph Letchworth and Martha Richardson in a trespass case known as Court Case No. 225. He was District Attorney from 1823 to 1831 in New Orleans, and was personally involved in many local lawsuits. In 1828, Branch W. was on the board of men interested in establishing a school in Covington.[28]

He was a reporter of the Louisiana Supreme Court from 1831-1834, in which year he died, at the age of 39 years.[29] He was buried in Metairie Cemetery, Section 14, plots 34-35.

Miller's succession was filed primarily in Orleans Parish. The document was held in St. Tammany in the inventory of his St. Tammany property provided by local Judge Lymann Briggs, July 3, 1834. His wife sold the Chappapeela Creek property to Mrs. Charlotte Prince of New Orleans, the wife of Hugh Faurie.[30] The sale was recorded by Lyman Briggs, August 12, 1835.

Eliza Anne Miller died in New Orleans on March 21, 1877, aged 78 years, and was buried with her husband.[31]

176

James Henning, a surgeon in the British Navy, came from Ireland to Elk Ridge Landing, Maryland, in 1782. He married Ann Waters, daughter of Thomas Waters and Sara, in 1784, in Prince George County, Maryland. Their son, Alfred Hennen, was born October 17, 1786, at Elk Ridge. The grandparents were John Hennen, born 1744, a surgeon in Castlebar, Ireland, and Catherine Sharpe, a granddaughter of Archbishop Sharpe of England.

Grave of B. W. Miller, Metairie Cemetery

Alfred Hennen worked as a merchant's clerk in Philadelphia, but soon realized he had no interest in mercantile pursuits. He graduated from Yale College with honor, winning the Berkely prize. Alfred's father, James Hennen and his mother moved to Virginia, then Tennessee in 1796. Son Alfred studied law at New Haven and Nashville, Tennessee.

Photo of Alfred Hennen from a portrait by Jules Lion

Alfred came to New Orleans in 1808 to practice law. He came down the Mississippi on a flat boat, a voyage that took three months. He brought with him a large selection of books from his college days. Adding to his collection, until the week of his death, he had accumulated one of the largest private libraries in the southwest. He mastered six languages, could plead a case in English or French, and was well versed with the Greek and Roman classics, law texts, and literature.

In the second war with England, on the advance of General Packenham, Alfred Hennen helped defend his country by serving on General Jackson's staff at the Battle of New Orleans. He married twice and had thirteen children. His first wife was Anna Maria Nicholson. His second marriage, in 1820, was to Anna Davison, born April 2, 1783, New Jersey. She died in New Orleans on June 19, 1871, aged 89 years. One of their daughters married Confederate General John B. Hood.

In 1828, shortly after his involvement with Court Case No. 225, Alfred Hennen purchased 1,280 acres in what is now Tangipahoa Parish, land that was originally settled by Thomas Joiner in the 1790s. He built a luxurious summer home the following year which he named "The Retreat". He became one of the wealthy men in the parish. By 1850, he owned 117 slaves who were engaged in maintaining his "Retreat."[32] Later in life, he became a director of the old Bank of Louisiana. By 1860 he was the third largest rice producer in Louisiana. After his death on January 19, 1870, his daughter Cora, wife of John A. Morris, the financial backer of the Louisiana lottery, purchased the property. They fenced the entire tract and brought in exotic animals and game birds. The property is now known as the Zemurray Gardens.

Alfred Hennen was the founder and an elder of the First Presbyterian Church in New Orleans. He was a man who never tasted distilled alcoholic liquor, nor smoked, and never used spectacles. He taught the Bible and Catechism to his Negro slaves when in his rural retreat. When in the city of New Orleans, a favorite activity was to visit orphan asylums on Sabbath afternoons to teach them the gospel.[33]

He became known as a distinguished civil lawyer, and was for a time a professor of Constitutional Law at the University of Louisiana, later known as Tulane. A learned man, he attained a most brilliant and enviable reputation in his manner of pleading. Described in a portrait by Jules Lion, Alfred Hennen was "tall, handsome, self-possessed, and he stuck to the facts."

Alfred Hennen was engaged in several celebrated causes in his time. In 1825, he represented the defendant Elizabeth Bartle, of Bayou Castein, in a boundary dispute that resulted from the conflicting grants of the preceding governing powers. The problems that ensued with

178

the case could have been with Elizabeth Bartle since she was not willing to accept a vague property line, and would not compromise.

The families involved in the trial would certainly have preferred events to have unfolded otherwise but the matriarch, Elizabeth Bartle, was a hard-headed and determined woman who did it her way. The legacy she bequeathed, a good fortune for we, the recipients, will continue to pay dividends for subsequent generations for the wealth of genealogical facts and clues that it provides to her descendants and even local historians. Not only does she shed light on a family tree but she also provides a link with the times and the circumstances in which she lived. By contrast to twentieth century women, Elizabeth Bartle chose to manage her financial affairs as an independent woman.

NOTES

1. Family Tree Maker's Genealogy site.
2. Ellis, Frederick S., *St. Tammany Parish, L'Autre Côté du Lac*, Pelican Publishing Company, Gretna, 1998, 126.
3. Acts Passed at the First Session of the Second Legislature of the Territory of Orleans.
4. Gaspard, Elizabeth, *The Rise of the Louisiana Bar: The Early Period, 1813-1839*, published by the Louisiana Historical Society, 183.
5. Ibid., 79.
6. Act of Louisiana Legislature, February 18, 1817.
7. Mangiapane, Erin, "The Forgotten Courthouse, Parish's first courthouse unearthed," *News Banner*, Sunday, October 18, 1998, 1.
8. Ellis, Frederick S., *St. Tammany Parish*, 91.
9. The History of Bogalusa, the "Magic City," *Louisiana Historical Quarterly*, Volume 29, 1946, 79.
10. Mangiapane, Erin, "The Forgotten Courthouse," *News Banner* 9-A.
11. Ellis, Frederick S., *St. Tamany Parish*, 201.
12. Copy of a Document lent by Adrian D. Schwartz, *History of St. Tammany Parish, Louisiana*.
13. Ellis, Frederick S., *St. Tammany Parish*, 88.
14. Act of the Louisiana Legislature, March 11, 1816.
15. Web site: http://jliptrap.us.gen/ismith.htm
16. Stephen F. Austin's Papers #1608.
17. From a letter written to a cousin Clara Jones in Crystal Springs, Mississippi, on November 25, 1902, by Susan B. Jones, an unmarried daughter of Jesse R. Jones.

18. Excerpt from a letter written by Jesse R. Jones to his nephew R.E. Jones, M.D., on May 6, 1877, from New Orleans. The envelope was postmarked from Covington, Louisiana. David Jones-View Media-Ancestry.com

19. Letter of Jesse R. Jones, May 6, 1877.

20. Schwartz, Adrian D., *Sesquicentennial in St. Tammany: The Early Years of Covington, Madisonville, Mandeville and Abita Springs*, published under the auspices of Covington City Council, 1963, 23.

21. Susan B. Jones writing to her cousin Clara Jones, November 25, 1902, from Covington, Louisiana.

22. Obituary Notice for Judge Jesse R. Jones, *St. Tammany Farmer*, March 27, 1880, 2 C: 1.

23. Boagni, Ethel, *Madisonville, Louisiana*, 30.

24. Probate Court Succession #136 ½ (1828) in Covington Court Archives. Information from Ms. Robin Leckbee Perkins, Archivist for the Covington Court House.

25. Probate #39, Thomas B. Robertson, 22nd Judicial Court, 1829, Covington, Louisiana.

26. Ellis, Frederick S., *St. Tammany Parish*, 107.

27. Information provided by Robin Perkins, Archivist, Covington, Louisiana.

28. Ellis, Frederick, S., *St. Tammany Parish*, 113.

29. Fortier, A.L.C., *Louisiana comprising sketches of parishes, towns, events, institutions, and persons arranged in encyclopedic form*, Volume 3, 1799-1800,

30. COB E-1, 150-151. Information provided by Robin Leckbee Perkins, Covington.

31. Metairie Cemetery, Louisiana, Section 14, lots 34-35.

32. Ellis, Frederick S., *St. Tammany Parish*, 130.

33. Biographies of Early American Presbyterians.

CHAPTER 13

AN INTRODUCTION TO COURT CASE NO. 225

Beginning January 1824, events foreshadowed trouble for Elizabeth Goodby/Spell and her husband Jacob Bartle. It appears that Jacob, in his malaise, had confided to a friend that "the cankerous old man, Joseph Letchworth, was planning to marry Martha, widow Faircloth, and had threatened to cause them trouble and would sue." With a marriage license obtained in May 1824, Letchworth could legally control Martha's money and property. He was in his right to tell Elizabeth and Jacob Bartle to stop their slaves from cutting wood on the disputed land and that he would no longer allow them to trespass on their property. The eventual confrontation was inevitable!

Elizabeth, who was calling the shots, began to gather her forces around her. Her first venture was to send her son Thomas Spell with a letter, dated April 22, 1825, to the land office of St. Helena, requesting the Land Commissioners to name him "her lawful agent". She then convinced her son-in-law Raymond de Delisle de La Barthe to write letters on her behalf. Next, she bribed Love B. Green, the man hired to tutor her children. With the use of a quill, ink and paper, Elizabeth expected to forge her way to victory.

The 1807 copy of the letter shown below, signed by Ira C. Kneeland, the Deputy Spanish Surveyor, was to be used as evidence when needed. Written at Bayou Sarah, where Kneeland resided on December 12, 1807, the missive was addressed to Mr. Thomas Spell, Elizabeth's husband:

I have orders from the Spanish Government to cause every one for whom I have made surveys to make immediate payment. I have your Plats ready & would send them by Mr. Alston but tis [it is] necessary where I give the Plats to the People that they should either send an order or give me a receipt for them. I will send them to you on your giving an order or coming yourself. I have given Capt Alston an order to receive the money from you and also from Miller and McDermott, the amounts are as follows:

for yours	30. Dolls
McDermott	30. do
Millers four tracts	40. do
	$100.

If the money is not paid to Mr. Alston I shall be obliged to commence suits immediately which I should be very sorry to do.

The letter was signed Ira C. Kneeland. Elizabeth was aware that in 1806, Kneeland was called upon by Mary O'Brien Sanders to survey, next to her land, the 500 arpents tract of land located at Bayou Castein, a donation received from her mother, Mary Knowles.[1] The "William Bryan" British land grant dated April 16, 1777, consisted of 400 acres on Lake Pontchartrain.[2]

In 1805, Ira Cook Kneeland was the Deputy Surveyor of the Jurisdiction of Baton Rouge, reporting to Surveyor General Vicente Sebastian Pintado, originally from the Canary Islands, Surveyor General of Spain, operating out of Pensacola. Kneeland's areas of concern included the Feliciana districts, Bayou Sarah and Thompson's Creek. Surveyor Kneeland lived and died during very turbulent times. He was a special breed of man who braved the wilderness and the near anarchy of Spanish West Florida to survey parcels of land in a climate of political uncertainty, in a world where people were discontent and insecure about their land holdings. Newcomers were hungry for land, and so were speculators who wanted to reap substantial profits. Kneeland had to please landowners who were fearful of having their own claims reduced in dimension. Not surprisingly, he was a much hated man!

In a book entitled *The Nation's Crucible*, Peter Kastor asserts that the American settlers were frustrated by the difficulty of establishing land claims, and that it was a force behind the revolt of 1804. The Kemper brothers were expelled from Feliciana over land titles, but returned that year with a vengeance to declare West Florida independent. It was a traumatic experience for them, and they felt the sting of their failure. The brothers fled "Across the Border" into the United States.   At a later date, on the night of September 3, 1805, Ira Kneeland led a posse from the Spanish side and crossed into Mississippi territory at Pinckneyville and captured the three brothers in their bed. They were taken across the line and turned over to the Spanish militia. Subsequently, they were freed, but it did not take long for them to take their revenge. Even though many other men had participated in the violent kidnapping, two Kemper brothers focused on Ira Kneeland. He was severely lashed by Reuben and Samuel. Legend has it that one or both of his ears were lopped off. To make it more painful, it was reported that the knife used was a dull one. According to the story, the ear or ears were displayed in a jar of alcohol at the Kemper tavern in Pinckneyville.

On September 22, 1810, when the Anglo-American rebels attacked and captured the Spanish Fort in Baton Rouge, Mr. Kneeland gathered up all the surveys and documents in his possession and fled to Pensacola, not only because he was so widely hated, but because he had to protect the land documents in his possession. By June 1811, there were legal notices of his death posted in St. Francisville, Louisiana. It was said that he died of yellow fever. Rather unusual, but possible, even in the month of December. Some claimed that he was murdered. Among his personal effects on October 3, 1811, were found several clues that he had led a life filled of stress, danger, sprinkled with the intrigues of political and colonial America in the early 1800s.

Definitely, surveyor Kneeland could not be called as a witness. Was the letter authentic? If not, then could it be proven that the letter was not really written by Kneeland? Three names stand out: Thomas Spell, McDermott and Miller. Thomas Spell, deceased. The land was in favor of Elizabeth, his widow. The tract of land had been surveyed eight years before. Why would a second survey be necessary? As for William McDermott, it was shown that he was deceitful, could not be trusted, and he was dead. Convenient for Elizabeth! The third person, Jacob Miller, was living in Opelousas.

It is a known fact that early surveys were often inaccurate. Elizabeth used the measurements of the old British grant of John Spell, the tract of land she purchased from Sanders Spell in 1816. Lt. Colonel Gilberto Guillemard had made a survey map of this grant in 1798. It would be used as evidence in the forthcoming trial.

Edmund B. Moss, under the influence of his mother-in-law, made a claim to the Land Commissioners. He requested five acres by forty on Lake Pontchartrain for the heirs of Thomas Spell. The measurements added up to 200 acres, and that was the extent of the British grant to John Spell. Elizabeth felt confident that she had a leg to stand on!

Prior to the trial, several documents "Bills of Exceptions" were filed with the Court by Letchworths, the plaintiffs, and Bartle, the defendants. What follows is an itemized list with the recorded dates.

Dates and documents filed on behalf of the Plaintiffs, the Letchworths:

- February 21, 1820: Zachariah Faircloth's affidavit.[3]
- August 6, 1823: Deed of gift by Zachariah Faircloth to wife Martha Richardson and nephew Joseph Sharp.[4]
- September 18, 1823: Martha Letchworth is legally placed in possession of the tract of land left to her by her husband Zachariah Faircloth.[5]
- May 12, 1824: Marthe Richardson, widow Faircloth, marries Joseph Letchworth.[6]

- March 11, 1825: Land Commissioners issue Certificate (No. 480) of ownership of claim of Zachariah Faircloth's heirs, dated June 19, 1820.[7]
- April 20, 1825: Deed of gift. William McDermott deeds land to family, April 20, 1814.
- April 25, 1825: Original Certificate (No. 52) of Thomas Spell calling for 360 arpents found in a survey executed under the Spanish authority in 1798.
- May 21, 1825: General David B. Morgan's response to the claim of ownership of land by the heirs of William McDermott to Joseph Letchworth.
- May 25, 1825: Petition Letchworth and Wife *vs* Bartles & Wife No. 225.[8]
- August 6, 1825: Seal of Office on August 6, 1825, by Parish Judge Jesse R. Jones, confirms that Martha inherits in default of heirs of Z. Faircloth.
- August 27, 1825: Martha has the land she inherited surveyed by David B. Morgan. Lawrence Sticker, in the presence of David B. Morgan, Justice of the Peace, affirms that there was a conditional line made by the land of James Goodby and Edward Ross, and that he was present at the surveying of the said land. He attests that the claim of Edward Ross was legally transferred to Samuel Lloyd, now deceased, is now owned by the representatives of Samuel Lloyd.
- September 3, 1825: Petition to Land Commissioners by Mary C. Lloyd stating that the heirs of Thomas Spell fraudulently ordered a survey of land.
- September 5, 1825: Copy of Land Commissioners' decision on ownership of the disputed land.
- October 11, 1825: Heirs of Zachariah Faircloth order of survey.
- October 12, 1825: Act of sale. Joseph Sharp sells "land gift" from Zachariah Faircloth to Joseph Letchworth.
- October 13, 1825: Certificate of appointment of Branch W. Miller to represent the absent heirs of Zachariah Faircloth, June 8, 1825. Seal of his Office on October 13, 1825.[9]
- October 18, 1825: Jesse R. Jones affixes the Seal of his Office in regard to the marriage of Zachariah Faircloth and Martha Richardson.
- October 13, 1825: Plaintiffs put in possession of Zachariah Faircloth's estate.[10]
- October 20, 1825: Order of Survey by Runnels, dated March 11, 1825, filed by Samuel Mallory.
- Dates and documents filed on behalf of the Defendants (Bartles):
- April 22, 1825: Note to Land Office by Elizabeth Bartles.[11]
- April 25, 1825: Original Certificate (No. 52) of Thomas Spell calling for 360 arpents of land found in a survey executed under the Spanish authority in 1798.

184

- August 27, 1825: Affidavit of Lawrence Sticker on settlement of James Goodby and David Ross.
- September 29, 1825: Jacob Bartle order of survey for 400 acres in St. Tammany Parish to Land Commissioners' Office. Document was filed October 17, 1825.
- October 1, 1825: Notice of the death of Jacob Bartle.
- October 14, 1825: Power of Attorney from Elizabeth Bartle to Thomas Spell, Junior.[12]
- October 17, 1825: Assignment of land from Thomas Goodbee to Thomas Spell, February 20, 1791.[13]
- October 17, 1825: Land titles and survey of Dorothy O'Brien Sanders who sold tract of land to Jacob Bartles, August 10, 1811.
- October 17, 1825: Certificate of ownership from Land Commissioner Charles S. Cosby to Jacob Bartle, April 8, 1820.[14]
- October 17, 1825: Map marked "J".
- October 18, 1825: Certificate of marriage between the defendants.[15]

The most valuable document brought in as evidence at the trial was the William O'Brien tract purchased, in 1811, by Jacob Bartle, from Mary O'Brien Sanders, daughter of William O'Brien and Mary Knowles. The sale was made for and in the consideration of the sum of five hundred dollars of the United States. The land had been surveyed by Ira C. Kneeland, Deputy Surveyor, during the Spanish Regime. Description of the location of the tract was certified to having been accurately resurveyed for Mrs. Mary O'Brien being five hundred arpents of land situated on the North side of Lake Pontchartrain, agreeable to an ancient Patent from the Government of Great Britain and registered into the Surveyor Generals' Office in the Spanish Government.

The British title with the attached West Florida Seal and the Spanish survey that Mary O'Brien gave to Jacob Bartle were documents requested by an order of the Court.

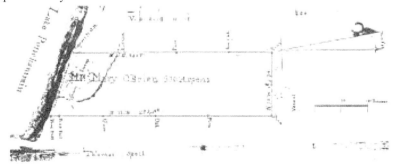

Survey map made by Ira C. Kneeland in 1806

The O'Brien tract was bounded to the East by the land of Thomas Spell and South by Lake Pontchartrain. West and North by vacant land agreeable to the figuration plat in which are seen all the boundaries both natural and artificial.[16]

There was talk during the month of August 1825 that Zachariah Faircloth had heirs back in North Carolina. It was reported that Zachariah had told a friend at one time that he did have an uncle back there. Alfred Hennen, Attorney for Elizabeth, brought up the possibility of Zachariah having heirs. Martha Richardson and William Cason Cooper signed a $900.00 bond in case that some qualified heirs did appear.

In his sworn testimony, Henry Sodon who had lived on the lake front testified on the 28th of July 1825 that he knew Zachariah Faircloth since 1807. He believed that he left no children or other relations. He had never heard of any heirs of said Faircloth.

On the same day, Obed Kirkland, under oath, says he knew Zachariah Faircloth since 1817 until his death, but never knew of his having any relations and never heard of his having any heirs.

186

There were many important persons summoned as witnesses in the Letchworth & Wife vs Bartles & Wife Court Case No. 225. Of vital importance was surveyor David B. Morgan who testified on the boundaries of the land in question. David B. Morgan and partner Thomas Fenton were on the lower Tchefuncte River as early as March 1804. Fenton died in August in New Orleans, and Morgan returned to Natchez. Morgan started down from Natchez by horseback overland in September to return to the Tchefuncte River to finish the surveying contract. When he arrived in the vicinity of Baton Rouge, he was taken prisoner by Spanish troops under the command of West Florida Governor Vincent Folch and held on board a Spanish gunboat for almost two months until he was able to escape at Bayou St. John in November.He escaped some time later and sued the Spanish in December to get his personal items back: slave, horse, and surveying equipment. He was not successful.[17]

General David Bannister Morgan, during the War of 1812 was in charge of the Louisiana and Kentucky militias. He was an influential early settler in Madisonville, moving there in 1812, as he stated in the October 1825 trial. He kept active in parish affairs, holding office as justice of the peace and as police juror.

After his second marriage to Mary Constance Baham, daughter of Major Renez Baham and Isabel Milon, June 13, 1819, St. Louis Cathedral, New Orleans, he continued his work as a surveyor and remained active in civic affairs. Constance Baham brought money and property into their marriage. She was a shrewd business woman often at odds with her husband's money matters, and on occasions she bought her husband's mortgages.

Subpoenas were given to other designated persons, namely: Daniel Edwards (29 January 1787 and 5 July 1877), the son of Morgan Edwards and Margaret Smith. In his young adult life, Daniel operated schooners on Lake Pontchartrain. He served in the War of 1812 as a private in the 10th Regiment of Louisiana Militia, and fought in the Battle of New Orleans. It was reported that he was presented a sword by Andrew Jackson which hung in his house until the 1850s. He married Mary "Polly" Cooper, daughter of the Loyalist Henry Cason Cooper on April 7, 1814. He settled in St. Tammany on the west bank of the Tchefuncte River in 1811 where he was a planter and raised livestock.

In 1819, the surveyor set up his instrument in the center hallway of Colonel Edwards' house to set the boundary between Washington and St. Tammany Parishes, leaving the south part of the house in St. Tammany, but placing the north part in the new Washington Parish. When Tangipahoa Parish was formed in 1869, the house was reunited again.

Daniel Edwards was a Representative of the St. Ferdinand District of West Florida to the 1810 Convention; area representative to the legislature of the short-lived Republic of West Florida; represented St. Tammany Parish in the Louisiana State Legislature from 1828-1832; elected a State Senator in 1845, and was made a Brigadier General late in life. He is buried in the Edwards Cemetery on Snow Creek, a well-kept cemetery located on a nice hilltop on private property.[18]

Renez Baham, born in Mobile, December 6, 1766, was the son of Jean Baptiste Baham *dit* Gentil and Françoise Guillory.[19] A date of reference to Jean Baptiste Baham was October 1764 when he took an oath of allegiance to British King George III of England, along with other French inhabitants of Mobile.[20] During British rule, Baham cultivated land on the Tensaw River near Mobile. Jean Baptiste's wife, Françoise Guillory, died in Mobile in 1782. Following her death, Jean Baptiste and his five sons moved to New Orleans. He was granted a 1000-arpent Spanish land grant on the left side of the Tchefuncte River in 1782.[21] The land grant was located on the abandoned Thomas Berwick and James Oliphant British land grants on the west bank of the Tchefuncte River, two miles up. Pierre Baham received a grant of land below his father's. Spanish surveyor Carlos Laveau Trudeau stated that the Bahams were living on their grant as early as April 24, 1783. This was before the Treaty of Paris was signed on September 4, 1783. After that date the land legally belonged to Spain. Baham's grant covered most of present day Madisonville, including the strategic river bank. The town of Madisonville was laid out by the Bahams, according to a plan surveyed by Ellis McCarty in 1814.[22]

After the War of 1812, Renez Baham was given the rank of Major in the Louisiana Militia, a title he used for the rest of his life. He ran brick making and cutting operations along the Tchefuncte River. He married Elizabeth Antoinette Milon, daughter of Jean and Marie Lafond, at St. Louis Cathedral on December 31, 1795. They had 10 children. Renez died in Madisonville on January 23, 1842.

Lawrence Martin Sticker, born 1778, son of Joseph and Anne Marie Crowley, was first documented on a list of passengers aboard the ship, *Lydia*, which had sailed from Philadelphia, by way of Cuba, before her arrival at the port of New Orleans on June 13, 1788. Lawrence Joseph Sticker was granted 400 acres on Bayou Sara, near Baton Rouge, on January 27, 1790.[23]

Lawrence married Nancy Richardson, sister of Martha Faircloth. On May 20, 1813, Lawrence claimed 640 acres lying in St. Tammany Parish on the west side of Bedico Creek. In his claim, he stated that he first settled on the land in 1809, and that he had cultivated and inhabited the improvement for the past four years.[24] This is where he stayed for the rest of his life.

Lawrence Sticker served in the 2nd Division 13th Consolidated Regiment, Louisiana Militia and fought in the Battle of New Orleans. His name appears, along with other St. Tammany Parish veterans of the War of 1812, on a marker that was placed in the Madisonville Cemetery, Louisiana, to recognize their service.[25]

He died prior to September 1838, leaving his widow Nancy and four children. Nancy, Lawrence's widow died about 1844. The Sticker estate was sold to John Wilkes Edwards, son of Daniel Edwards and Mary Cooper, daughter of Henry Cason.[26]

John Wilkes "Jack" Edwards (July 26, 1784 to September 20, 1847) was the son of Morgan Edwards and Margaret Smith. He married Mary Jane Weathersby, but had two children by Nancy Ann Lloyd. The Census of 1840, Washington Parish, shows him aged 50-60.

Henry Cason Cooper was born to Henry Couper, Sr. and Unknown Wife, about 1759 in Pitt County, North Carolina. His birth year is verified by Henry's statement which he gave when he witnessed the marriage of his cousin, John Lanier, before a priest in Baton Rouge. Henry further stated that he was born in "Carolina". When the American Revolution began, the Coopers sided with the Loyalists. When the Revolution ended, the Coopers refused to surrender. During this period Henry Cason was partially blinded by bird-shot. Ultimately the Coopers were driven out of Georgia. The family fled to East Florida, near present-day St. Augustine.

The Cooper family then pinned their hopes on Spain and the Natchez area. When Spain turned over Natchez to the United States around 1798, the Coopers made plans to sell their land grants and leave Natchez for West Florida, where Spain still ruled. In 1801, Henry Cason was granted 640 acres directly from the Spanish Crown, by settlement, on Black River, now called Black Creek, just outside Madisonville. He moved his family to this grant and made it his permanent home. His wife died before 1825, but Henry Cason Cooper lived to a ripe old age. He died in 1842, and it is believed that he was buried in the old Edwards Cemetery. His funeral was attended by a host of local citizens, according to the minutes from the Old Sharon Church. He was a respected citizen of St. Tammany Parish.

Henry Cason's second son, known as Henry Cooper Jr., born around 1800, in Natchez, married Martha Sticker, daughter of Lawrence and Nancy Richardson. Henry Jr. was a successful farmer who owned substantial property and at least 21 slaves.[27] He was also asked to testify in Court Case No. 225.

Uriah Smith, baptized January 16, 1774, Christ Church, (Church of England) in Poughkeepsie, Duchess County, New York, was the son of Morris Smith and Mary, born Smith. In 1819, he testified that the 200-acre British land grant in West Florida was granted by the British to his father on September 21, 1777, and surveyed January 15, 1798, by Spanish surveyor Gilberto Guillemard. About 1807, Uriah married Frances George, eldest child of John George and Frances, unknown.

Abraham G. Penn owned a saw mill on the Tchefuncte above Covington.[28] Abraham served as Sheriff from 1843 through 1848. The Penn family was a prominent one in the early days of St. Tammany Parish. Penn's Water Mill, located on the Tchefuncte River, west of Covington, was owned by Abraham Penn. He sold the property to Alexander Penn who built a lovely home on the property. It later burned to the ground while trying to get rid of an infestation of fleas.

Henry Sodon settled at Bayou Chinchuba in the year 1808 by permission of William McDermott. His land was located a mile to the edge of the Labatut tract. His daughter Mary married Amos Richardson, brother of Martha, in 1816. Widowed, Mary Sodon married Thomas T. Spell, son of Elizabeth Goodby.

A most interesting and cautious witness was Love B. Greene, the teacher that was hired by Elizabeth Bartle to teach the Spell and Sharp children.

In a promissory note, written in Covington, dated February 7, 1825, Mr. Green promised "to pay Edmund R. Moss or his heirs twenty five dollars from the first day of this month (for the use of his farm on Chinchuba Creek of the St. Tammany State Louisiana) until the first day of February 1826 and to suffer no infringement on either Garden of fences to keep them in good order and to pay the above named and sum of twenty five dollars quarterly if required by said Moss. Given under my hand this day and date above written. Signed L. B. Greene."

Most of the interaction between Greene and Mrs. Bartle began in the spring of 1825. Shortly after being used by Elizabeth, they quarreled. He sued Mrs. Bartle for the money she owed him.

Other witnesses were John Lanier, a cousin of Henry Cason Cooper; Macklin Lloyd, John Powell, and Mr. Raymond, a resident of Madisonville.

William Sharp married Nancy Spell, Elizabeth's daughter, and Joseph Sharp married Sarah "Sally" Spell, daughter of John Spell and Sarah "Rosalie" Westcott of Galveztown. Nancy and Sarah Spell were first cousins. William and Joseph Sharp were key witnesses at the trial. These were trying times for the two brothers who were the nephews of Martha Richardson, their mother's sister.

On October 12, 1824, Joseph Sharp sold and conveyed to Joseph Letchworth his tract of land containing two hundred acres, the land on which he lived and acquired from Zachariah Faircloth by his deed of gift. The purchase price was two hundred dollars, and Joseph agreed "to warrant and defend the tract of land from himself, his heirs, executors, administrators and from all lawful claims." The sale was witnessed and signed by Hezekiah Thompson and Lawrence Sticker.

William B. Ligon, Notary Public, in and for the town of Covington, certified that the deed of conveyance was truly recorded in the notarial records on the 12th day of October 1825, and in the fiftieth year of the Independence of the United States.[29]

Further to this document, Joseph Letchworth released Joseph Sharp "from all claims rights or demands of every nature in consequence of his having executed to me a quit claim deed bearing date October 12, 1825 of two hundred acres of land being part of parcel of the Faircloth tract, the said land being situated in the Parish of St. Tammany adjoining the tract called the O'Brien tract and reference to said Sharp deed executed on the aforesaid being had for a further description." Signed by Joseph Letchworth and witnessed on October 24, 1824, by B.W. Miller.

The trial to settle the dispute between the two feuding families was set to begin on Friday, October 14, 1825. This was two days after Joseph Sharp had sold his tract of land to Joseph Letchworth and his aunt Martha Richardson, and two weeks after the death of Jacob Bartle, Elizabeth's husband.

The suit is a historical gem and it is fortunate that it has survived all those years. The sub thrust of the case centers around the original settlers on the lake-front and who were the rightful owners at the time of the 1825 trial.

Known as Court Case No. 225, Letchworth & Wife *vs* Bartles & Wife taken from the Judicial Records for the 8th District Court, in the State of Louisiana, we are given an insight into the judicial system of the early nineteenth century. Neighbors who quarreled would often appeal to the courts to settle their differences.

Testimonies were received from every old-timer who lived in the area between Castein Bayou and Chinchuba, either called up by the defendants or the plaintiffs to testify. Some reminisced about times and people long gone by – about when James Goodby really did live on the Goodby tract, in a log cabin that he had built for himself. Who really owned the property? On whose surveys you wanted to go by? The Faircloth (Letchworth property) was originally a British grant, and according to the old British survey, Rebecca Ambrose first owned the parcel of land. But, the Goodby tract had been a Spanish grant, and according to the survey, Elizabeth Bartle owned it.

The case rested in the hands of the two prominent lawyers Alfred Hennen and Branch W. Miller. The jurors, after being charged, would render their verdict.

NOTES

1. The arpent was a unit of measurement commonly found in the records of New France. One hundred arpents equals 84.63 acres = 34.25 hectares.
2. Peterson, Mary A., "Abstract of Land Petitions: British West Florida," *Genealogical Register*, December, 1971, 328.
3. Zachariah Faircloth Affidavit, in presence of David B. Morgan, Justice of the Peace, St. Tammany Parish, 583, page 1, ; No. 20 Abs B, Richard Rico.
4. William Ligon , Notary Public, witnesses signatures of Bartles and Edmond Moss. Notarial Records Book A, page 40.
5. Supplemental Petition, in the Suit of Letchworth & Wife vs Jacob Bartles & Wife, by Ripley and Miller, their attorney, State of Louisiana, Eighth District Court, September 18, 1823.
6. *Marriage Index*, Book 1, 65.
7. James Runnells and William Kinchen.
8. Eighth District Court, Parish of St. Tammany, Petition filed by Samuel Mallory, May 21, 1825.
9. State of Louisiana, parish of St. Tammany, Seal of Office affixed by Parish Judge Jesse R. Jones.
10. Folio 13, October 1825, E 225, Letchworth & Wife vs Bartles & Wife. Plaintiffs put in possession of Z. Faircloth, Samuel Mallory, Public Notary.
11. Letter witnessed by L. B. Greene and Delisle de LaBarthe.
12. Filed by Samuel Mallory, No. 5, Court Case No. 225
13. Assignment of James Goodbee to Thomas Spell, filed October 17, 1825, James B. McCay, Clerk.
14. Court Case No. 225, Commissioner's Report letter A, Certificate No. 102, Land Office, St. Helena.
15. Jesse R. Jones, Parish Judge, affixes the seal of his Office stating that Elizabeth Spell was legally married to Jacob Bartles on August 11, 1818.

16. Survey of the O'Brien tract registered in Baton Rouge by Surveyor Ira Cook Kneeland, June 25, 1806.

17. *The Historic New Orleans Collection,* Spring Issue, 2012.

18. E-mail from Angela Reid to Don Sharp January 21, 2012.

19. Baptismal Records Book 4, Mobile, Alabama, Cathedral, 229.

20. Tate, Albert Jr., "The French in Mobile, British West Florida, 1763-1780," *New Orleans Genesis*, Volume 22, No. 87, July 1983, 265-268.

21. Boagni, Ethel, *Madisonville, Louisiana*, 9.

22. Madisonville Museum Brochure.

23. *American State Papers*, 569.

24. Lawrence Martin Sticker Claim No. 72 C759.

25. E-mail from Donald Sharp to Anita Campeau, May 13, 2011.

26. St. Tammany COB A-2, 259.

27. E-mail from Angela Reid to Donald Sharp dated January 6, 2012.

28. Boagni, Ethel, *Madisonville, Louisiana*, 69.

29. Notarial Records of William B. Ligon, Office Book A, page 46.

CHAPTER 14

COURT CASE NO. 225: LETCHWORTH & WIFE *vs* BARTLE & WIFE

On May 21, 1825, the Letchworths filed a petition through their lawyer Branch W. Miller, against Jacob Bartle and his Wife, neighbors living east of them. The trial date was set to begin in the second week of October. The feud went on as each side prepared for the eventual confrontation. Tensions were high in the community as family members and neighbors began to take sides.

Jacob Bartle died on Saturday, October 1, 1825, two weeks before the trial. In her bereavement, Elizabeth Bartle, remained her own person – intense and vigorous.

On Friday, October 14, 1825, the two *grandes dames* of Bayou Castein faced each other in the St. Tammany Parish Court House, in the town of Claiborne, the parish seat for the Eighth District, St. Tammany Parish.

The first step before the beginning of the trial was the selection of the Jurors, to be selected for a courtroom from the pool of available persons. However, we were unable to find the list of names of those who were picked for jury duty.

In the opening statements, each side had the opportunity to outline the proof to be presented to the jury during the trial. Jacob Bartle and his wife were accused of trespassing and damaging the Letchworth property to the extent of $1,500.00. The suit involved a piece of land on the north end of the Letchworth and the south end of the Goodby tract located in the vicinity of Covington road. The defendant, Mrs. Bartle, denied all charges, claimed the land was hers and that she had every right to cut wood on her property. As is known, trials are often messy, inconvenient and divisive. This one was no exception!

The plaintiffs (Letchworths) or the prosecution's case was presented first. As each witness testified, the side that called the witness asked the questions in direct examination. Then the side that did not call the witness had the opportunity to ask questions in cross examination. Physical evidence such as documents and maps were admitted into evidence and numbered for identification.

General David B. Morgan, surveyor, a most important witness, introduced by Attorney Miller for the plaintiffs, duly sworn, said that he was acquainted with Z. Faircloth in his life and that he lived on the place where the present plaintiff now lives. Mrs. Letchworth was considered the wife of Mr. Faircloth, and that when he (witness) arrived here in 1804, Faircloth and Martha Richardson were living on the same tract of land. He (witness) was absent until the year 1812. From that time until the death of Faircloth, upwards of two years since, Faircloth and Martha Richardson lived together on the same tract. She continued to live on the tract as the said widow Faircloth until her marriage with Letchworth and to the present time. Witness Morgan lived in the neighborhood and never knew Mrs. Faircloth to live anywhere else.

Morgan stated that he always understood that Mr. Faircloth was in possession of the lands between Jacob Bartle on the east and Labyteau/Labatut on the west fronting Lake Pontchartrain. He knew the posts to the rear corner of the western boundary of Bartle's tract. He considered the order marked C as his authority for surveying the land contained in the place that the house in which the Letchworths now live, a distance he considered from Bartle's line to be fifty or sixty perches.[1] The front of the tract on the lake from Bartle's corner to Labatut was 208 perches. When he made the survey, he received a note from Jacob Bartle stating that he could not attend because he was indisposed. Mrs. Bartle was present.

To Morgan's knowledge, Mr. Faircloth left no children when he died. Morgan married the present plaintiffs. Defendants admitted that the plaintiffs were legally married.

In cross-examination by attorney Hennen, General David B. Morgan ascertained the east boundary line of the plot to be 101 chains, 25 links.[2] He had made the survey in the following manner: "beginning at the E. corner of the plan at a post that Mrs. Bartle's neighbors said were the boundary of Bartle's land and then ran south 10 degrees west about 220 perches which he supposed to be the course. Found it so badly marked that he off set and ran a right line from that to intersect Letchworth's line, thence on that line to the lake, thence along the lake to Jacob Bartle's corner, the south east corner of the plan. Witness knew Letchworth's line to be a well marked line and therefore went across to it."

When the survey was made, Morgan had the copy of Letchworth's plan which he made from the original himself; he did not the have the original of either Labatut or Bartle's plan, nor their titles. At the S. E. corner of the plan, he found a post which was pointed out to him by some of the neighbors among which were Mr. Morton, Lawrence Sticker and Mr. Moss. When Madam Bartle went away, Moss went with her and observed that Morton would go with Morgan and that would do as well. General Morgan never ascertained from actual measurements the eastern line plat filed and marked C.

General Morgan was acquainted with Thomas Spell, the former husband of Mrs. Bartle. In 1804 and in 1813, he was at his house where the defendant Mrs. Bartle now lives. It was apparently an old settled place, about a quarter of a mile from Lake Pontchartrain and about a mile from the tract of land he surveyed, above alluded to.

The defendant's counsel here dismissed witness with a right to recall him and cross-examine him later.

Daniel Edwards, introduced by Miller for the plaintiffs, duly sworn, said he was acquainted with Z. Faircloth in his life time, as early as he knew everybody. He first recollected him as living in three different places. Two of which were on the tract of land where he died, and in sight of each other. When he left the neighborhood in the year 1813, Faircloth was then living on this tract and he thinks he lived there several years before. He never knew of any boundaries between Faircloth and the Bartle land and was unable to say the distance from Faircloth's house to Bartle's line.

In cross-examination for the defense by Hennen, Edwards said he knew nothing of Faircloth of having an order of survey neither did he hear of his having an order of survey or grant or of its having been surveyed. There might have been instances of persons settling down at that time without order of survey but he does not know of any. When he first knew Faircloth, he was living with Labatut on the tract adjoining the place now called "Paradise" - Labatut's tract. He knew that Faircloth lived at Castein Bayou, had a house, and that he lived at another place to make a settlement out in the pine woods when he was driven out by a storm from the lake. He knew of no boundaries to any tract of land on which Faircloth lived, and he saw him cultivating a place called Ambrose's old field located south of where Faircloth lived, between him and the lake. He supposed that the old field lay west of Bartle's claim though he knew nothing of the lines since he never traced them. There were from 7 to 20 acres cleared in the Ambrose old field, and added that there were other old fields in the neighborhood, one of which was on Bayou Chinchuba.

Edwards did not know William and Mary O'Bryan. They had left the country before and he had no knowledge of them. The place where Bartle lately resided was the place where Meeks formerly resided. He knew Thomas Spell, the former husband of Mrs. Bartle. Said Spell, in 1813, was in the habit of making rails on the tract to the west of Bartle's land but, he was not positive of the fact. Witness recollects Spell had shipped some bark that was hauled to the margin of the lake but where it was cut, he could not say positively. The bark was shipped by Sanders

Spell, a member of the family, in 1811 or 1812. Edwards mentioned the big swamp in front of Mr. Labatut's tract through which it was impossible to pass with a team and that Mr. Faircloth could not have gone directly from his residence to the lake down to this landing without seeing the bark. There was a schooner load of bark. He never heard Faircloth make any complaint about this, nor had he any knowledge of any other of the family of Spell cutting bark on this land, nor had he any knowledge of Faircloth cutting bark on this land. He had seen rails and other things cut and lying about Mr. Faircloth's plantation, but he made fencing as many ordinarily do who live on a place.

To Edwards' knowledge, Thomas Spell had no residence either permanent or temporary between Labatut's land and where Bartle lately resided. Meeks left the place he occupied about the year of 1806, 1807 or 1808. He never knew that there were any differences or difficulty between Spell and Faircloth about lands while he resided in the neighborhood. Thomas Spell was residing at the place where Mrs. Bartle lately resided, ever since he recollects, until 1813. Cross-examination closed by Hennen, with leave to return.

Examination in chief returned. Daniel Edwards says that the residence of Faircloth which he spoke in his testimony at Labatut's place at Castein Bayou and in the Piney lands were all previous to Faircloth settling on the land between the Bartle line and Labatut line. He knew the time that Faircloth settled on the land where he died, and where he had lived for several years previous to the year 1813 and, afterwards, until his death. When he speaks of the O'Bryan and Bartle line, he intends to convey the same idea.

Edwards says he will be thirty nine on 20th January next. Record of his age was given to him by his parents correctly.

In cross-examination by Hennen, Daniel Edwards stated that Faircloth's cultivation was near his house and Ambrose's Old Field, the only two places that he knew of. Faircloth's residence was about three quarters of a mile from the lake.

Renez Baham introduced by Miller for the plaintiffs, duly sworn, says that he had been a long time acquainted with Mr. Faircloth and that he lived on the same tract of land that Mrs. Letchworth now lives on. When he first knew Faircloth, he was living with Thomas Spell, the father of the Spells. After that, Faircloth lived with Labatut - but whether as a partner or not, he does not know. Says he knew Faircloth for about 12 years, perhaps more or less, and he resided on the spot where the Letchworths now reside. That after Richardson's death, Faircloth lived upon the land. George Richardson was the father of Mrs. Letchworth, and had resided on that land for several years, perhaps three or four.

Baham stated that Thomas Spell resided on different tracts of land. Mrs. Letchworth lived there, up to the present time, and since the death of Faircloth. As far as he knew, while Faircloth resided on the place, he was in peaceable possession.

In cross-examination by Hennen, Baham says he has never known of Faircloth having had the land surveyed nor knew of any boundaries fixed to the land. He only knew him to settle down on the spot, the same place. The place was cultivated, five or six acres more or less. The field was enclosed, and some with pastures. He can't say what the extent of the enclosure was, he never observed. In addition to the places witness has known Faircloth had lived to the one named. He then he removed from Labatut to Castein Bayou where he lived several years. The exact time, he doesn't know. After the death of Richardson, he removed to the place where he died and where Mrs. Letchworth now lives. In those times, he believes it was usual for people to settle down without any authority for many persons did that on tracts of land. When people settled down in this way, he knows of no rule, method or manner by which they settled their boundaries. He has known some to settle pretty close together and some a good ways off.

Baham stated he was fifty seven years of age and had lived here thirty five or forty years, and has never known or heard of Faircloth having any boundaries to this land, either for Faircloth or any one else. He had frequent occasion to go through that part of the parish.

When Faircloth settled down on his land, Baham knew nothing of his having an order of survey; neither did he even hear of his having an order of survey or grant or of its having been surveyed. There might have been instances of persons settling down at that time without order of survey but he does not know of any. When he first knew Faircloth he, Faircloth, lived north of Labatut on the place adjoining now called "Paradise" - the Labatut tract. He was aware that Faircloth lived on Castein Bayou, resided there and had a house. Also knew that Faircloth lived on another place and made a settlement out in the Pine Woods where he was once driven out by a storm from the lake. Baham knew of no boundaries to any tract of land on which he lived. He has seen Faircloth cultivating a place called Ambrose's Old Field, that lay south of where Faircloth lived between him and the lake. Witness supposes Ambrose's old field lies west of the Bartle claim, though he knew nothing of Bartle's lines, he never traced them. There were other old fields in the neighborhood one of which was on Bayou Chinchuba. There were from 7 to 10 acres cleared on Ambrose's old field.

William Bryan left the country and Baham had no knowledge of him, nor did he know the Mary O'Bryan property lines. Witness Baham had once seen the line of Labatut run by Mr. Lorreins. The line started from the west between Labatut and west pointing and running east towards Mr. McDermott's house but witness quit them before they got to the house. He does not know how far they went. He does not know whether the old line is marked or not, and knows nothing of the lines of Spell. He never had any conversation with Mr. Faircloth about the land he claimed or the extent of it. He never knew the defendants had cut any wood near where Faircloth lived; neither did he know of Faircloth cutting any wood there.

The cross-examination of this witness by Hennen here closed.

Lawrence Sticker was introduced by Miller for the plaintiffs and being sworn said that he has never seen defendant's hands cutting wood but had seen them hauling wood from Letchworth's place. Witness saw eight or ten cords of wood that was hauled four or five months ago. He doesn't know whether this was before or after this suit was instituted. He has heard Mrs. Bartle say that when General Morgan came in to survey she told him that she had land in there and not to interfere with it. He has known Faircloth for 25 years and has known him to live on the place for 20 years. He always had peaceable possession and, knew nothing to the contrary.

Sticker never knew Bartle or his wife to make any claim to the land where Faircloth lived previous to his telling him that she had told General Morgan not to interfere with his lines. That on the day of the survey Mrs. Bartle said she told General Morgan not to interfere with her lines and he said he would not. He was present when General Morgan made the survey. Mrs. Bartle was there, but not all the time. He did not hear Mrs. Bartle point out any of the posts but said if her Negro man was there he could.

John Richardson and the two Mr. Sharps showed General Morgan the posts where he started from. It appeared to be an old post. Sticker doesn't recollect whether Mrs. Bartle made any other remarks when General Morgan started the survey, more than not to interfere with her lines – he heard her make no objections to that post being the true boundary. She stayed there while General Morgan commenced running the line from that boundary and went some distance with her till they came to a road – she then said the woods were very thick and that it was useless for her to go any further, and left them. She requested Mr. Morton [Amelia's husband] and Mr. Moss to go with General Morgan – they were her sons-in-law. Sticker said he had been through the tract of land several times within two or three years and had observed the appearance of a good deal of hard timber being cut off.

Cross-examination by Hennen, Sticker says that he knew Richardson, the father of Mrs. Faircloth. He was married in 1799, and knew him a few years before. At the time, Mr. Richardson lived in the place where Mrs. Letchworth now lives.

Sticker said he had never seen either of the defendants cutting wood on the place, that he had seen wood cutters on the place cutting wood hired by Mr. Letchworth. This was about one quarter or half mile from the lake. This was last spring, but he doesn't know what was cut. This was about a half mile to the eastward of Labatut's landing where the wood was cut and about a mile to the westward of Jacob Bartle's landing. Sticker said he saw the Negroes of Mrs. Bartle taking wood from the place where Letchworth's men had been cutting and carrying it out on board Bartle's schooner. This was either in April or May but didn't know whether it was in the beginning of May or end of May. He can't recollect the precise time of the two months but rather thinks it was in April. He cannot explain why he thinks it was in April. He saw the Negroes loading wood, but doesn't know where it was cut, and for all that he knows to the contrary it might have been cut on the land of Jacob Bartle. He never saw the Negroes of the defendants cutting wood any where to his recollection, not there but has known them a long time and has seen them at work in other places on their master's plantation and in the pine woods and other places.

Asked by Hennen if he heard Mrs. Bartle say to General Morgan not to interfere with her lines or land claimed by her, Sticker answered that remark was not made in that way. What he heard her say to General Morgan was that he must not interfere with any of her lines. Interrogation by Hennen continued.

Q. Did Faircloth ever show to you any lines as the boundaries of the tract of land which he claimed nor do you know of any lines that were marked as surveyed for such land, or have you ever heard of any previously to the 21st of May 1825?

A. He never showed me any but he would wish to abide by the lines of Mr. Labatut and Mr. Bartle.

Q. You know of no lines?

A. No.

Q. Did any surveyor to your knowledge ever run off any land for Mr. Faircloth?

A. No, not as I know of.

Q. Did you ever hear Mr. Faircloth say that any surveyor had ever run off any land for him?

A. No.

Q. Did you ever know or hear that Mr. Faircloth had any title from the Spanish Government.

A. No.

Q. To any tract of land in this Parish?

A. No.

Q. Do you know by whose permission, by what right or by what title Mr. Faircloth settled down at this spot you have just spoken of?

A. He bought it from Richardson, his father in law.

Q. How do you know this?

A. I saw it. I heard it.

Q. Was the sale verbal or written?

A. It was verbal.

Q. What was the price given?

A. A cow and a calf.

Q. What was the quantity of land sold?

A. There was no quantity mentioned. He sold him his improvement, his right.

Q. What was his right?

A. A settlement right in which people settled on in these times.

Q. When did Richardson make this sale to Faircloth?

A. I can't recollect exactly, it is as far back as 1804 or 1805.

Q. By whose permission did Richardson settle there?

A. I don't know.

Q. Were there any boundaries fixed to the land that Richardson sold to Faircloth?

A. None that I heard of.

Q. Who was then living at the place where Jacob Bartle lately lived? Had he cut any timber on land now claimed? Made any claims to the land?

A. A man by the name of Meeks. He left the place about 14 years since. Said he was not aware if Meeks had cut timber on the land now claimed by Mrs. Letchworth and he had never heard of Meeks claiming any portion of that land. Meeks had not made many improvements to the place.

Q. What was the extent of ground cultivated or enclosed by a fence at any time by either Faircloth or Richardson?

A. Not more than five or six acres. He had a pasture enclosed for cattle of 20 acres, not more than 20. There might be more.

Q. Where was this land cultivated?

A. Some around the house and some in the Ambrose's old field. The Ambrose old field was at a distance from the house.

Q. What is the distance of Ambrose's old field from the house?

A. I suppose it to be very near half a mile, not more.

Q. What is the distance from Jacob Bartle's house?

A. Not quite a mile, but very near it.

Q. Was Ambrose's old field included in Richardson's improvement?

A. It was. Richardson improved it.

Q. By what right did Richardson improve it?

A. I never heard.

Q. What is the distance of Ambrose's old field from the lake?

A. I suppose it to be half a mile.

Q. Had Richardson built a house and fenced in land when he sold to Faircloth?

A. He had a house built and land fenced in.

Q. Did you know where Faircloth lived previously to this?

A. He lived on Castein Bayou.

Q. How long have you known Jacob Bartle?

A. Twenty five years.

Q. How long has he been living on the place where he lately died?

A. Fifteen years of more.

Q. Do you know of the Spells or Mrs. Bartle having any claim to this land?

A. I have heard she claims it.

Q. Have you any knowledge of the defendant or any of the Spells forbid the plaintiffs to cut wood on this land?

A. I have none.

Q. What were the words used by Mr. Faircloth when he forbid Mrs. Bartle to cut wood on the place?

A. He told her he did not wish her to cut any more on the land, for he considered the land his and did not wish the timber destroyed.

Q. Did not Mrs. Bartle say that she considered the land hers?

A. She did say she considered the land hers and that she had as much right to cut wood as he had and that she could cut wood there as long as there were any to cut.

Q. Did not Mr. Faircloth say to Mrs. Bartle you have forewarned me from cutting on the land and now I forewarn you?

A. No. I don't think there was any such thing said in my presence.

Q. Who was present at this conversation?

A. Some of the children of Spell, and were in her house.

Q. Were you present at the time of this conversation?

A. I was not present during all the conversation. After the conversation above stated by me I left the room and they were still talking.

Q. When did Faircloth die?

A. Two years ago on the 15th, last August, as well as I recollect.

Q. Have you any knowledge of Mr. Letchworth's wife and wife having cut wood on this land at what part of the land, and when?

A. Yes, about sixty or seventy cords - some last winter and some last summer, and about the same place where Mrs. Bartle's Negroes cut.

Q. Did they carry the wood off to town?

A. Yes, they carried some of it a way and some is still there I believe.

Q. Are you interested in the event of this suit?

A. I do not consider myself interested.

Q. Have you ever heard or understood if Mr. Faircloth left any relatives?

A. I have heard him speak of an uncle to be somewhere in America. This conversation was some five or six years before his death. That he had but very few relations. Spoke of an uncle but did not say whether he was dead or alive. The way the conversation commenced he said that he had no relations and that he wished to leave his property to only his wife. The cross-examination of Sticker is hereby closed.

Love B. Green introduced by Miller for the plaintiffs, duly sworn, said that Mrs. Bartle had conversed frequently with him on the subject of this case. She first came to his residence to get him to do some writing for her. She mentioned that Mr. Letchworth was to sue her about a tract of land and that unless she could get some person to do some writing for her it would break her up. From that observation, he thought it was some writing he was not authorized to do, and told her so. She made several offers to get him to do the writing, all of which he refused. Between the middle of June and the middle of August Mrs. Bartle mentioned it to him several times. After the middle of August she offered $200.00, never to tell it to any person or to tell it in court. She also asked his opinion and advice about a suit that Letchworth was to sue her about cutting a quantity of cypress and pine. She said she had cut five hundred cords or upward of oak wood but she had not cut any pine or cypress. She did not think that they could hurt her for it was not mentioned in the petition. To her question, he said he had not seen the petition. She insisted that he do the writing saying that she sent her children to school to him, and was as good a neighbor as he had. Mrs. Bartle observed that she had always caused people to believe that it was their land, but that it was not theirs, since they had not the least shadow of right or title to it. As to giving his advice, he was no attorney.

Asked by Miller if he had heard Mr. Letchworth propose to Mrs. Bartle to leave it to an arbitrator, he replied: "I did, and Mrs. Bartle said no. The law should decide it."

In cross-examination by Hennen as to when this proposal was made, Mr. Green stated that it was during the life of Mr. Bartle, before any proposals were made to him to forge papers; it was in the month of March or April.

Asked if Mrs. Bartle could read or write, he had no knowledge, but he heard say she could not.

Q. Did you ever draw up any act or piece of paper for Mrs. Bartle and what was it?

A. I did at one time, when I was very much confused in mind. The intention of which was to authorize Mr. Delisle or Thomas Spell to transact business for her in the land office. One or both of them, I can't recollect which.

Q. Did Mrs. Bartle sign the writing?

A. I believe she did but don't recollect positively.

Asked if it were possible for him to declare under oath whether any man or woman of his acquaintance can neither read nor write? He replied that when he was acquainted with a man or a woman and saw them read or write, he knew they could, but if he neither saw nor heard, he could not say whether they could or not.

Q. What is your profession?

A. I am teaching school at present.

Q. Has this always been your profession?

A. I have followed different businesses in my life, the farming business.

Q. Is this all the businesses you ever followed?

A. This is the principal business that I have pursued to procure a livelihood.

Asked if he had ever practiced medicine and receive pay for his services, he replied that he had sold medicine and received pay, but he had never been paid for his services. He had visited his neighbors when sick but he did not consider himself a practitioner of medicine under the laws of this State and some other States. Never received any pay for his services in any State, but had sold medicine in several of the States.

Q. Did not LaBarthe Delisle of this Parish pay you nine dollars once or twice by written orders in your favor on Mr. Whelock of Covington for medical services rendered to him or some part of his family within the last year?

A. I received a part of this sum for medicine and a part for other things.

Q. For what other things?

A. One of the articles was for a stone jug; some more of the things particularly in the last case were things I could order under the class of garden vegetables. I do not recollect all the articles of vegetables nor how many.

Q. What was the medicine you sold to Mr. Delisle?

A. I sold him calomel[3] and jalap,[4] laudanum[5] and salts.

As to what amounts of medicine he had sold to Mr. Delisle, he could not recall the particular amount of medicine or vegetables sold as they were both included in the orders. He could not recollect anything else in the orders at this time, and he did not like to say under oath what was included in any order that Mr. Delisle requested.

Q. Did you not act as a man midwife to someone of Mr. Delisle's family either black or white and charge for the services as practical services?

A. About five months ago after Mr. Delisle was married as I understood from Mr. Delisle I was sent for by one of Mr. Delisle's servants and understood from the servant that Mrs. Delisle was in travail. Agreeable to the request I went to visit Mr. Delisle and found her in labor and delivered her. I charged Mr. Delisle for medicines furnished him different time but did not charge him for delivering his wife.[6]

Q. Did you furnish Mrs. Delisle with any medicines at the time she was delivered and to what amount and what sort?

A. I did furnish her with medicines previous to the delivery. I gave her hartshorn[7] for which I did not charge after her delivery. I gave her cream of tartar, a part which she took and a part I left with her. I also left with her the sugar of lead.

Q. Did you charge for any of these things?

A. The sugar of lead I charged for with the other mentioned.

Questioned whether or not he had a quarrel, a dispute difficulty or lawsuit with Mrs. Bartle, Mr. Green answered that he sued Mrs.

Bartle after having asked her money that she justly owed him to pay his just debts. He had no other motives.

Q. Were you not obliged to pay the costs in this case and did you not lose by the suit?
A. I did not consider that I lost by the suit with Mrs. Bartle

Mrs. Bartle settled Green's demand or the principal part with Justice Briggs and it did not come to trial. It was his impression that Mrs. Bartle came forward and settled without a trial. The laws of the State condemned her to pay the costs. However, when asked he could not state positively if he had been condemned by judgment to pay the costs.

Mr. Green was then asked if he had ever followed the profession of preacher. He replied that agreeable to the understanding that he had of the definition of preacher, he never had.

Q. What do you understand by the definition of the word preacher?
A. I understand the meaning of the word preacher to be the delivering moral and Gospel Lectures or a person who stands up before a public assembly and commenting on some particular passage of Holy Writ.
Q. To what denomination of Christians do you belong?
A. I have or have been a Baptist.
Q. Were you never expelled or excommunicated from that Society?
A. I never was unfellowshiped by any Gospel Church. I was legally dismissed from the Baptist Church when I left the state of Pennsylvania and never have resided within the bounds of one since.
Q. When did you leave Pennsylvania and when were you dismissed as you have stated, and how long since?
A. I was dismissed from the Big White Lick Church in Green County, Pennsylvania, bordering on the Monongahela River in the month of September 1822.[8]

Mr. Green, questioned by Hennen as to whether he rendered any services to Negro women of Mr. Delisle, he answered in the negative. He never charged nor did alter any order that Mr. Delisle gave him.
Q. Did you present the two orders given you by Mr. Delisle to Mr. Whelock?
A. I did to Mr. Whelock or some one in attendance in his store, and in one of the orders Mr. Delisle had stated for services rendered a Negro woman. I told him I did not charge for my services to the Negro woman, and would not have the order. He then crossed the word

services or some part of it and said he supposed that would do and I take it and presented it as above stated. I believe all my neighbors know very well that I do not charge for my services; but am willing to visit any one that is in distress that I can relieve.

It appears that Mrs. Bartle had tried to bribe Mr. Green. The topic of questioning by Hennen then focused on the exact proposals that were made to him by Mrs. Bartle and how often the proposals were renewed.

Q. Did you believe from the tenor of her conversation that you were the person that she wished to forge a letter for her?

A. She offered me $200.00 to forge Governor Grand Pre's signature to some instrument of writing, the form of which I do not know. But the object of which seemed to be put up a claim to the land in controversy.

Q. When or to whom did you first disclose this offer made by her to you?

A. I do not remember that I have ever disclosed it to any person as I fully as I now have. I have hinted it to several persons and it was blazoned thro' the neighborhood but I never did intend to mention it to any person had I not been called into court to explain my answer when I said I did not intend to mention it. I was summoned to attend as a witness in this case before her offer to me was made and for that reason I determined not to mention it until I was called into court. My impressions were that I was summoned to attend court to prove proposed compromise and that this was Letchworth's principal motive for having me summoned, and after I was sworn I considered it my duty to tell the whole truth between the parties, that my judgment dictated to me had any bearing in the case.

Q. By whom was this story blazoned about in the neighborhood and when?

A. I heard it much mentioned by Joseph Sharp, Mr. Letchworth, and Mr. Sticker that I had reason to believe that Mrs. Bartle did not keep her own secrets.

Q. What was the story you heard?

A. The substance of what I heard was that Mrs. Bartle wanted me to forge writing.

Q. Did you not receive an anonymous letter offering you $200.00 to run off from the neighborhood?

A. I did find a paper in my yard where I lived offering me a reward to leave the neighborhood.

Q. Did you not show this paper to John Edward?

A. I think it very likely that I did.

Q. Are you not sure you did?

A. My impressions are that I did, but I am not sure that I did.

Q. About what time did you find that paper?

A. It was in the month of August or September.

Q. Was it money, land, Negroes or any other kind of property that Mrs. Bartle offered to you for services if you would forge papers for her?

A. It had the appearance to me of money. I did not take hold of it.

Q. Was each of the offers you have mentioned of the same kind?

A. She has at various times made me offers by offering she would reward me very handsomely if I would do her writing but never offered me money but at one particular time - she never offered me any particular sum, nor showed me any thing that had the appearance of money but one time.

Q. How many times were these offers made to you? Were they made more than twice or thrice?

A. They were made more than twice or thrice.

Q. Were they made more than five times?

A. I do not know that they were.

Q. Were they made more than four times?

A. To the best of my recollection they were made to me between three to six times but do not recollect the exact number of times.

Q. When was the first offer made to you?

A. I believe the first offer was made in the month of June.

Q. When was the last one made?

A. Towards the latter part of August.

Q. Was any one present at either time when the offers were made?

A. There were others present at one of the times and took an active part in the business.

Q. How many persons were present beside Mrs. Bartle?

A. There were two.

Q. Were there ever any persons present but at the one time?

A. I do not recollect that there were.

Q. Were there never three persons present at any time when an offer was made you or a proposal made to you?

A. I do not recollect that there were more persons present than two beside Mrs. Bartle within my view.

Q. Where were the proposals made to you when there were more than two persons present with Mrs. Bartle?

A. At my own residence.

Q. Was your wife present when any of these conversations took place?

A. There were two when Mrs. Bartle took my wife into the garden. In their absence the two persons alluded to make me some proposals apparently in behalf of Mrs. Bartle. After Mrs. Bartle and my wife returned from the garden Mrs. Bartle made me same propositions herself during which time my wife was posing about doing house work as she does her own house work herself.

Q. Where were you born?

A. I have understood I was born in the State of Virginia.

Q. Where do you now live? On whose plantation?

A. Mr. Letchworth has the place in possession I believe.

Q. How far from Mr. Letchworth?

A. I do not know. I have not measured the distance.

Q. Was it a mile?

A. No.

Q. Was it a quarter of a mile?

A. I do not know, but believe it is not a quarter.

Q. Was there any enclosure between you?

A. There were fences between the two houses I believe.

Q. Look at the paper now handed you and say is it all in your handwriting and if not state what part is in your hand writing?

A. I believe a part of it is in my handwriting. There is a part that I believe not to be in my hand writing. The last signature of Delabarthe Delisle as a witness is not in my handwriting.

Q. Do you see anything else on that paper that is not in your handwriting?

A. My impressions are that all the rest are in my handwriting except what is on the back.

Q. Look at the signature directly under the signature of L.B. Green and say if you did not write it?

A. My impressions are at this time that if I did not write that name by the directions as request of Mr. Delisle on his stating to me that he could not see. He did state to me and many times previously that at that time he could not see to write as well as he had done.

Q. Are the two persons now living who accompanied Mrs. Bartle to your house when she made the proposals to you to forge papers for her?

A. The word papers rather embarrass me in making an answer. The reason why that I do not know or recollect at this time that there was but one forged paper mentioned or alluded to as such. This is all my answer to the question not knowing what the court may require of me. If it applies to that part that mentions are the persons now living, it is not all. The persons are now living that I alluded to in my observation yesterday.

Q. What was the cause of the confusion in your mind at the time you wrote the power of attorney alluded to?

A. In the first place I was a poor man in this country. It mortified my feelings that people tried to take advantage of my poverty to induce me to commit unlawful acts which from the opportunities that had been in the case my impression at that time that the real intentions of certain persons were to take advantage of me or to tempt me from my then present necessities to commit unlawful and unjust acts as such it mortified my feelings to such a degree that I might well call it confusion of mind – that any of my neighbors should be so mistaken in me that I could be hired because I was poor to violate the laws of God and man, under these impressions and consideration it amounted to what I call confusion of mind.

Q. How long after the institution of the suit by the plaintiffs against the defendants was it when Mrs. Bartle came to you and asked your opinion whether she could be hurt for cutting down oak timber on the land claimed by Letchworth if only pine and cypress timber were mentioned in the petition?

A. I do not know or remember at what time the suit was instituted.

Q. Was it before or after the institution of the suit that she asked this advice from you?

A. It was after. I understood that there was a suit instituted against her.

Q. When was the subpoena served on you as a witness in this suit?

A. I believed it was served in the month of May.

Q. You knew that suit was instituted against Mr. Bartle and wife when the subpoena was served on you. Did you not?

A. I did not. Doubt the Parish seals when viewing its impressions.

Q. Was it before or after that the subpoena was served on you in this case that the first proposals were made to you which you have stated in the forging part of your examination to write or to forge any paper?

A. Some of the connections hinted such things to me. I believe before the suit was instituted, apparently to me to try to ascertain whether it was best to stand a suit. I do believe that owing to the nature of their minds, they could not believe that a man under my then present necessities could reject their proposals.

Q. Was it before or after you received the subpoena that Mrs. Bartle came with two persons to your house for the purpose of getting you to forge a paper for her?

A. At this juncture of time I am not positive in mind but believe it was after the service of the subpoena.

Q. Did Mrs. Bartle ever make any proposition to you such as you have hereto before stated before she came to you with two persons as you have already stated?

A. She had hinted such things to me, the words in which it was done I do not precisely recollect.

Q. Do you mean to convey by your answer that it was before or after the two persons came to you?

A. When I am relating under oath my intentions are to tell the truth to the best of my knowledge and recollection without any idea to conveyances.

Q. When did Mrs. Bartle first propose anything improper to you?

A. I do not recollect at this juncture of times or the precise time.

Q. Was it longer ago than January last?

A. No.

Q. Was it longer than April last?

A. I believe not, such are my impressions.

Q. When did you first come into this Parish?

A. The latter part of January or beginning of February 1825.

Q. How long after you had been in the parish did you first became acquainted with the defendant Mrs. Bartle?

A. But a few days after I had been in the parish the acquaintance commence.

Q. Did the defendant Jacob Bartle ever make any improper proposal to you?

A. Jacob Bartle never did hint to me in any shape or form that he wished me to commit a criminal act.

Q. Who were the two persons? Please name them who came to you with Mrs. Bartle as you have heretofore stated and requested you or wished you or hinted to you that you would forge some papers or title as you have mentioned in a proceeding part of your examination for the purpose of aiding Mrs. Bartle in the defense of this suit?

A. They were Thomas Spell and Labarthe Delisle.

Q. Did ever any other of the connections of the defendant in this case make besides the two you have mentioned make similar propositions or hints to you?

A. I do not recollect at this time that any other ever did.

Q. What month and day did this take place?

A. In May or June, the day I do not recollect.

Q. Where were you then living?

A. At a house hired from E. R. Moss.

Q. Was it hired by a written or verbal lease?

A. Written.

Q. Look at the writing now handed you and say if the signature is yours?

A. It is not. I cannot judge so well of my signature owing to my eye sight but there are things stated in the paper that makes me positive that it is not my signature except to prove by 5 witnesses that I was not in Covington on the day it is dated.

Q. What was the appearance of the money offered to you as a bribe for forging a paper requested of you? Was it a roll of bank notes or a bag of coins?

A. It appeared to be in silver and in bank notes but it was neither in a bag nor in a roll.

Q. Who had the money or held it or who offered it, the money above spoken of?

A. Mrs. Bartle.

Q. At what time was this offer of money made to you by Mrs. Bartle? In what month and on what day of the month was the money offered?

A. In the month of August, the day not recollected.

Q. Was this the first time that money was ever offered to you by Mrs. Bartle or any one for her?

A. It is the only time that I recollect at this time of the money being presented into my actual view. There had previous to this several times and hints been made purporting to be offers or rewards but nothing presented to my view.

Q. Who was the first person that ever made these propositions to you?

A. In answering the question agreeable to my understanding of the word propositions to the best of my recollection at this time, Mrs. Bartle was the first person.

The cross-examination of witness Love B. Green by Hennen is now closed.

Macklin Lloyd was introduced by Miller for the plaintiffs and being sworn stated that he was acquainted with the tract of land where Letchworth, the plaintiff, now resided. He had known this land for about eighteen years, and when he first knew it, it was in the possession of Mr. Faircloth. He believed that Mr. Faircloth continued to be in possession to the time of his death. After Mr. Faircloth's death, his widow had possession and Mr. Letchworth since their marriage.

He had seen once the Negroes of Mrs. Bartle cutting wood on the disputed land about a year ago. He was present when Mr. Letchworth demanded damages from Mrs. Bartle. As well as he could recollect, it was sometime in May, in the forepart of May.

In cross-examination by Hennen, Mr. Lloyd said he understood that Mrs. Bartle and family claimed the land and as long ago as six or seven years, perhaps more, perhaps less. He did not know of any agreement between Mrs. Bartle and Letchworth about any part of this tract of land.

William Sharp was introduced as a witness by Miller for the plaintiffs and sworn and in answer to the questions provided answers as follows:

Q. Are you acquainted with the tract of land where Letchworths now reside?

A. Yes, I have seen it and been on it.

Q. Who did you first know in the possession of this land?

A. Zachariah Faircloth.

Q. How long have you known Mr. Faircloth to have been in possession of that land and how many years?

A. Ten or eleven years, I am not certain which.

Q. During that time has he not been always been in peaceable possession of that land?

A. Yes, I believe he has.

Q. Did you ever hear of anyone else having a claim to that land?

A. Yes, I have heard that Spells say they had a claim to it.

Q. Did you ever know of Bartle or his wife or their Negroes to cut wood timber or rails on that land?

A. I never knew of Bartle, but I have known of Mrs. Bartle's Negroes cutting and splitting rails.

Q. On what part of the land was the wood cut and the rails split?

A. The rails were split near Bartle's line but on the tract claimed by Letchworth from Bartle's line across to the Labatut line, the wood was cut.

Q. How much wood was cut?

A. I don't know.

Q. About what time was this wood cut?

A. About two years ago. Some sooner, some later.

Q. Did you ever hear either Mrs. Bartle or Mr. Bartle say how much wood their Negroes had cut on this land?

A. I never did.

Q. Mr. Sharp, are you not confident that there has been two hundred cords or more cut on this land?

A. I suppose there were nearly 200 cords cut.

Q. How many rails do you think there were split, were there 5000?

A. I suppose they split 3 or 4 thousand.

Q. Did not Mrs. Bartle's Negroes cut a considerable quantity of wood on this land?

A. They were cutting the most of the last winter.

Q. Do you know where this wood was sold?

A. I don't know, I suppose it would be in New Orleans.

Q. Do you not know that it was shipped to New Orleans?

A. Yes, I have seen them loading for New Orleans.

Q. What was wood selling for in New Orleans during the last winter?

A. It was selling for $4 or $5.

Q. What was rails worth on a plantation?

A. A dollar a hundred.

Q. Were you present when Mr. Morgan ran the line of the land claimed?

A. I was present and I saw the post at which they started.

Q. Do you know who put that post down?

A. I do not know.

Q. Did you ever hear Mr. or Mrs. Bartle say who put it down?

A. I never did.

Q. Was Mrs. Bartle present when the survey was made?

A. She was present a part of the way.

Q. Did you know Mrs. Bartle make any objections to that corner being the boundary?

A. I did not hear her make any.

Q. Did you hear her say she thought that post had long been cut down?

A. I did not.

In cross-examination by Hennen, William Sharp answers:

Q. Did you not ask of Mrs. Bartle permission to cut wood on this land?

A. She gave me permission and I did cut wood under that permission. I can't state exactly the time but it was over a year a half ago.

Q. How often have you cut wood under that permission?

A. I cut at one time about a week and never but once.

Q. Was any of the wood or rails cut on any other land by the defendants than that which you have heretofore stated was claimed by the Spells?

A. The wood and the rails were cut on the land which they claimed.

Q. When did you hear the Spells make the claim which you have stated in your examination in chief?

A. It has been about 4 or 5 years ago when I first married into the family.[9]

Q. In whose possession was the land of which you cut wood by permission of Mrs. Bartle?

A. By her giving me permission I supposed it was in her possession.

Q. ~~Did you believe that you were committing a trespass when cut down that wood or did you intend to do so?~~

Q. Have you any knowledge of Faircloth cutting wood along there, as near the same place?

A. I never saw or knew of his having cut any.

Q. How long have you been acquainted with Faircloths and the Spells?

A. Ten or eleven years.

214

Q. Did Faircloth ever point out or show to you lines of any tract of land claimed by him in that neighborhood?

A. No.

Q. Did you ever hear of any lines to any tract of land claimed by him?

A. No.

Q. Have you any knowledge from the declaration of Faircloth himself that he had any relatives?

A. I have not.

Examination in chief resumed by Hennen.

Q. Whether were not some of these places where timber was cut outside of Spell's pretended claim?

A. I don't know what they pretended to claim nor how far.

The examination of this witness here closed.

Joseph Sharp introduced by Miller for the plaintiffs, being sworn, answers as follows:

Q. Were you acquainted with the tract of land wherever Letchworth now resides, formerly the land of Faircloth?

A. I was.

Q. How long have you known the tract of land?

A. A great while. Faircloth was in the possession when I first knew it.

Q. Have you seen either Bartle's or Mrs. Bartle's Negroes cutting wood on it?

A. I have seen Mrs. Bartle's Negroes cutting wood on it.

Q. At what time have you seen them cutting?

A. At different times.

Q. Did you know them to have cut wood there during the last winter?

A. I saw them cutting wood there during the last winter.

Q. On what part of the tract was it you saw them cutting?

A. About half way between Bartle's line and the Labatut line and near the tract in controversy.

Q. About how many cords of wood do you think there was cut?

A. There was a great deal, they were cutting there for several years.

Q. Do you not know that Faircloth during his life often forbid them cutting wood on this tract?

A. I have known Mr. Faircloth during his life to forbid Mrs. Bartle once.

Q. Did you ever hear Bartle tell his wife not to cut wood on this land?

215

A. I never did.

Q. Were you present when the survey was made by General Morgan?

A. I was present.

Q. Did you observe the corner's post from which he started?

A. I did.

Q. How long have you known this corner post?

A. I have known it seven years. Mrs. Bartle put it there. The old one appeared to be rotten down, and he Mr. Bartle renewed it. This was the post from which General Morgan started.

Q. Do you not believe or know that there were 4 or 5 hundred cords of wood cut on this land?

A. I suppose there were 3 or 4 hundred cords cut.

Q. Was there not also a quantity of rails cut by Mrs. Bartle's Negroes?

A. Yes there were some cut, how many I do not known.

Q. Did you ever hear Mrs. Bartle give order to her Negroes to cut wood on this land?

A. I never did.

Q. Did you ever see Mrs. Bartle present when her Negroes were cutting wood on this land?

A. I never did. I have seen her present when they were hauling wood from off the land.

Q. Did Mr. Faircloth in his life ever give you permission to cut wood on this land?

A. He did give me permission about four years ago.

In cross-examination by Hennen for the defense, Joseph Sharp answers:

Q. Where about did you cut wood on this land?

A. I did cut wood on the land, about half a mile from the lake below Ambrose's old field.

Q. Do you know of your brother cutting wood on this land?

A. I do not know.

Q. Have you ever seen the British grant for the place on which your brother lives when you came to the lake in 1810?

A. I never saw it. I saw one or two seals but there were no papers to them.

Q. Such as the one on file?

A. Yes.

Q. Have you any knowledge of your brother cutting wood on the land to the westward of Bartle?

A. I have not. There was very little wood cut on it when I first saw it.

Q. Were you on the tract of land to the west of Jacob Bartle with your brother?

A. Yes, two or three times.

Q. For what purpose did you go there?

A. I went merely to look at the land once or twice and one time I went after some horses.

In cross-examination by Miller, Joseph Sharp answered:

Q. In speaking of the tract of land that your brother lived on, which tract did you mean, the one which Faircloth lived on or the one to the eastward of Bartle?

A. Eastward of Bartle.

Attorney Hennen, for the defendants, produced the witness B. Delisle who was sworn and examined. In the course of his examination it appeared that he was a curator of one of the minor heirs of Thomas Spell, the former husband of Elizabeth Bartle. Attorney Miller, for the Plaintiffs, produced certain proceedings of the probate court showing that Elizabeth Bartle held the mortgage on the land that witness Delisle was living on. Therefore, Miller claimed that Delisle's testimony was tainted in favor of his mother-in-law, and he was directly interested in the cause. The court over ruled the said motion, wherefore much of the same allegations do not appear on record. Plaintiffs tendered this, his "Bill of Exceptions" and prayed it could be allowed in the Court.

Signed by Charles Bushnell, Judge for the 3rd District, holding session in the 8th District.

Judge Bushnell, a native of Boston, came to Louisiana within the first decade after the purchase of Louisiana had been accomplished. He was Judge of the 3rd District Judicial Court having taken the oath on September 6, 1822 (recorded the same day) and February 1823 (recorded the same day).[10] He was a gentleman of great legal erudition, devoted to his profession, but he found the time to enjoy the arts. His daughter Mary Bushnell, whose mother descended from an old Creole family, was known as a southern writer.

John Lanier on the part of Bartle, defendant, after being sworn, said he knew the place where Thomas Spell lived and died. He had known the place for about 25 or 26 years. Asked by Hennen when he first saw the place, he replied that it appeared to be an old inhabited place with very old fields.

Q. Did Faircloth ever state to you anything about the tract of land to the south of Ambrose's old field lying on the lake?

A. I asked Mr. Faircloth, why do you not improve the place? He answered the reason I do not is that I believe there is an English title for it but I do not know whether this conversation had reference to the north or the south part of it.

Q. Did you know that old field of Ambrose?

A. I saw what was called Ambrose's old field about sixteen or seventeen years ago, it was then grown up with bushes, it may even be longer. Mr. Spell told me it was Ambrose's old field. This field of Ambrose was between Jacob Bartle and the place where Faircloth lives.

Q. Did you know James Goodby and how long?

A. Yes, very well. It is about twenty five years since I became acquainted with him.

Q. Did you know of Richardson's cultivating any part of the tract of land and when?

A. He lived there a few years prior to Mr. Faircloth going there. I can't say how long.

Q. Do you know what became of Richardson?

A. He died I believe on Bayou Manchaque.

Q. Who did Freeman George marry?

A. Helen Spell, the daughter of Thomas Spell was understood to be his wife. And, the examination of this witness here closed.

In cross-examination by attorney Miller, John Lanier answers:

Q. Whether the tract above alluded to where Thomas Spell lived was not to the eastward of the Bartle tract?

A. It was.

Q. What distance do you think it was from Thomas Spell's house to the west line of the Bartle tract?

A. I do not think it was more than a mile when I rode through it. I made no computation.

The examination of this witness by Miller was here closed. It was admitted by the plaintiffs in this cause that Jacob Bartle died on the 1st of the present month (meaning October 1825.)

John Edwards on the part of the defendants was sworn in and answered that he was raised in the neighborhood of Bayou Castein, and that he was nearly forty-one.[11] He had known the defendants in this case and where they resided ever since his recollection, that is Mrs. Bartle.

Q. Where did Mrs. Bartle and her family reside?

A. Ever since her first and second marriage she has resided on the place which she now resides on.

Q. Have you ever seen any of her family residing on the improvement of James Goodby?

A. Freeman George and his wife lived there. William Sharp now resides there. Both of them are sons-in-law of Mrs. Bartle.

Q. At what time did Freeman George begin to live there and how long have he and Sharp lived there?

A. George must have lived there prior to 1812, I think.

Q. Who lived there after George?

A. William Thompson lived there after Freeman George.

Q. When did Sharp begin to live there?

A. Sharp has been living there one or two years.

Q. What is the earliest time that you have known any of the Spells to have resided on this tract of land?

A. I do not recollect any of them having permanently resided on it since Thomas Spell cultivated it.

Q. How long did Thomas Spell cultivate it?

A. Nearly twenty years more or less.

Q. Was Faircloth living on the land when Spell first went there to cultivate it?

A. I do not think Faircloth ever lived on that tract of land which Spell cultivated.

Q. Do you have any knowledge of Guillemard having surveyed that tract of land and when?

A. I believe that Guillemard had surveyed it. I did not see him do it and do not know at what date.

Q. When Guillemard made your father's survey did he collect the neighbors to ascertain the boundary lines or did he run the lines by your father's direction?

A. There were no boundary lines existing at that time but those made by the English surveyors. He made them according to directions from Government.

Q. How did you know that he had directions from Government?

A. My father had papers to show him.

Q. Do you not mean by those papers the title and survey which your father had in his possession under the British government?

A. He had but one. It was not included in the survey made by Guillemard.

Q. Did you see any commission or authority that Guillemard had from the Spanish government authorizing him to come over here and make these surveys?

A. I did not see him exhibit any.

Q. How long did he stay here making these surveys?

A. Two or three weeks.

Q. Were any of the neighbors present when he made your father's survey?

A. They were.

Q. Do you not know that Guillemard was a Spanish officer and surveyed land in this neighborhood and a tract for yourself?

A. Yes.

Q. Where about, what year was this?

A. It was sometime before 1800.

Q. Are there any acknowledged lines between Faircloth and Spell to this tract of land to your knowledge?

A. I do not know of any other than those that were made by that surveyor if they were made.

Q. How does the house of Faircloth bear in respect to the house of Sharp where he now lives?

A. I expect it would be about a southeast course from that of Sharps.

Q. What distance are they apart?

A. I expect the houses are about four hundred yards apart.

Q. Do Sharp's fields extend across the Bayou Chinchuba embracing both sides of it?

A. Know they do not.

Q. Are not the fences of the Plaintiffs (Letchworth) and those of Sharp adjoining and does not one fence serve for to divide their field pasture?

A. The fences join.

Q. Did you not see the announcement piece of paper offering a reward to L. B. Green to leave the parish and state what declaration did you make at the time as to the person who had written it or a part of it and in whose hand writing do you believe that it is in whole or in part written?

A. It was offering a reward, I do not think it stated to whom. I thought at that time that the letters bore a resemblance to those made by Mr. Green himself.

Q. Have you had any reason to change your opinion since?

A. No, I have not made a thought about it since.

Q. Have you seen L. B. Green write or any of his acknowledged hand writing?

A. I have seen of his writing. I don't recollect of having seen him write.

Examination in chief resumed by Hennen.

Q. Where was this land of your father which was surveyed by Guillemard?

A. It is fronting on the Lake and Castein Bayou to the eastward of Uriah Smith and Major Spell.

Q. Was this vacant land at the time?

A. My father lived on it. It had never been surveyed until that time.

Q. Have you ever been disquieted in the possession of that land?

A. Not materially yet.

Cross-examination resumed by Miller.

Q. Has not that land been confirmed to you by the commissioners and how many acres?

A. It has been confirmed by the commissioners, 1800 or 1900 hundred acres including the English survey. (What is meant is that Morgan Edward, his father, had two Spanish land grants, one in 1783 and the other in 1787 and that he purchased the Mager Spell British land grant of 100 acres to be next to his mother-in-law.)

Q. Is there any claim set up to any part of that land now?

A. Mr. Delisle has a kind of claim and he sets up his claim to that very part which was surveyed by Guillemard at the time above stated.

John Four on the part of the defendant being sworn answers that he had knowledge of the defendants having cut wood on the tract of land to the west of the O'Brien tract of land. In the month of November 1823, he saw the Negro man named Abraham cut ash trees. He believes Abraham belonged to Mrs. Bartle. This was four or five arpents west of Jacob Bartle's land. He knew of the defendants taking wood from this part of land because he had lent to Mr. Bartle, at different times, his pirogue skiff and flat for the purpose of loading wood from this tract on board of the vessel the *Sea Horse*.

Q. State how long before you saw the Negro Abraham cutting wood that it was of Jacob Bartle loaded the wood which you have just mentioned?

A. Since the year 1812, during ten or eleven years.

In cross-examination by Miller was asked: Will you state whether you have lent your pirogue continually during the ten or eleven years or not?

Four replied, I mean to say that I have lent it from time to time during the ten or eleven years and between. I have lent it at least twenty five times and that sometimes for landing at this place and sometimes at Bartle's place and other places.

Joseph Sharp was questioned by Hennen on the part of the defendants having been sworn.

Q. How long did Goodby live on that tract of land?
A. He must have lived there 10 or 12 years, perhaps longer.
Q. Was it always under cultivation during the time he lived there?
A. I believe it was.
Q. Who went on it after Goodby left it?
A. Thomas Spell used to cultivate the field and make tar barrels in a shop close by.
Q. How long did Thomas Spell continue to cultivate that field?
A. I think it has been cultivated by him or his people off and on ever since. What I mean by on and off is that they would let it remain uncultivated for two or three years and then renew the cultivation.
Q. How long did Freeman George live on this place?
A. He lived there one or two or three years I believe.
Q. Do you have actually seen him there?
A. Yes, I have seen him there and been at his house frequently.
Q. He married one of the Spells did he not?
A. Yes.
Q. In what direction is this tract of land from the west corner of Jacob Bartle's land on the lake?
A. North. Something west, I speak initially of the field.
Q. How far is Thomas Spell's field from the lake?
A. Something better than a mile.

In cross-examination by Miller, Joseph Sharp answers:

Q. How long did you know that dividing fence between Sharp and Faircloth's improvement?
A. The fields are near each other, that I suppose the fences have existed for some time.
Q. Has not Faircloth been always in peaceable possession for the land below the dividing fences?
A. I have never known or heard of any difficulty between them.
Q. Is the house which Sharp lived in immediately on the Bayou?[12]
A. No, it is not.

222

Q. Were there any settlers living to the northward of Mr. Sharp?

A. Across the creek, Mr. Delisle and Mr. Thomas Spell live.

Q. Do not Thomas Spell, Delisle, Moss and Mr. Sharp all live on the same tract and is not that the Goodby tract?

A. They all live together. I understand on one tract and that is the Goodby tract.

Q. Have you not seen L.B. Green living on the same tract of land on which Moss lived?

A. I have seen him living there.

Q. Does not this tract of land form a part of that claimed by Thomas Spell?

A. It does, I believe.

Q. Where does L.B. Green now live? And in whose employ is he as a schoolmaster?

A. He lives in Mrs. Letchworth's pasture and within her enclosure. He is employed by Letchworth, Bartle and Sharp as a schoolmaster, but I believe Mrs. Bartle may have withdrawn her children. I do not know.

Q. How long have you known the Spells to have been in possession of the tract of land between that of Uriah Smith and that of Mary O'Brien lately in the possession of the defendants?

A. Spell has had possession of it ever since I have known him which has been as long as I can remember.

Q. Will you state whether you have knowledge of the Spells or the Negros of Mrs. Bartle cutting wood and rails on the tract of land to the westward of Jacob Bartle? To what extent and how long? State all your knowledge herein?

A. Spell claimed it under some pretext or other which I do not know. Whether he has any title or not, he said he intended to live there one of these days.

Q. When did Spell die?

A. He died in 1815.

Q. What use did Spell make of the land?

A. He never lived on it, but he cut rails on it and tar barks.

Q. For how many times and how long have you seen or known Spell to cut wood or bark there?

A. I don't recollect to have seen rails but once. I cannot say how long since it was before the bark was got.

Q. Have you any knowledge of any other acts of use made by Spell of that land and state what they are?

A. Mrs. Bartle has cut wood on the place I believe, but what amount I don't know.

Q. During the last year or 18 months past?

A. I believe she had some cut last season.

Q. Do you know who went and settled on Chinchuba down where Spells now lived?

A. Goodby was the first who settled on Chinchuba where William Sharp now lives.

Q. Who settled first on Chinchuba Bayou, Richardson or Goodby?

A. I declare I don not recollect which of them settled first. I was quite young when either of them came.

Q. Have you known of many surveys in this parish?

A. Not many.

The testimony of Joseph Sharp, witness, here closed.

Uriah Smith on the part of the defendants being sworn answers questions by Hennen.

Q. Did you know James Goodby and William McDermott?

A. I knew James Goodby and William McDermott to the year 1804.

Q. Will you state where James Goodby lived?

A. I knew James Goodby living on Chinchuba high up and low down on the creek.

Q. About what position on the creek did he live?

A. Not far from Mr. Faircloth, if little bushes had been cut down you might see the house.

Q. How long did he live there?

A. I don't know how long, he did live there but I do not think I was grown when he lived there.

Q. What age are you?

A. I was fifty two on the 29th September last.[13]

Q. Where were you brought up and raised?

A. On the Lake near Castein Bayou.

Q. Where did your plantation join?

A. I lived on a tract of land on the lake claimed under a British grant adjoining John Spell on the west, the same post served as a boundary for us.

Q. Where about the position of this tract of land of Spells?

A. It lies between mine and Mrs. O'Brien. I never knew of any other land being there.

Q. Is your British Title in existence or is it destroyed?

A. It is totally destroyed. I gave the remains of it to Mr. Cosby. I never could get them.

Q. Whose tract of land did yours call for on the West?

A. I believe it was John Spell.

Q. How long had the Spells been living on the tract of land adjoining you on the west?

A. I believe Thomas Spell had been raised there.

Q. Who was the eldest, you or Thomas Spell?

A. I do not know. I believe there was not much difference.

Q. Who was the father of Thomas Spell?

A. I do not know but I have a slight recollection of one John Spell who was said to be his father.

Q. Were the family connections of Thomas Spell living in the neighborhood?

A. He had a brother by the name of John Spell.

Q. Was the tract of land to the west of you on which the Spells lived cultivated?

A. Thomas Spell lived on it and cultivated it.

Q. Can you remember any period at which it was not cultivated?

A. Not that I recollect of since Thomas Spell was married.

Q. Who settled first on Bayou Chinchuba near where the plaintiffs now live Goodby or Faircloth?

A. They both lived high up on the Bayou Chinchuba at the same time. I believe Goodby settled first, low down near where the plaintiffs now live.

Q. How long had Goodby been living there to the best of your recollection before Faircloth came to settle there?

A. It was a considerable time before Mr. Faircloth came to settle on that place.

Q. Do you know Goodby's hand writing?

A. I have seen him write and of his writing but it is so long ago that I should not know his writing.

Q. Do you know William McDermott's writing?

A. I think I should as I have seen a great deal of his writing. He has done some for me in his life time. He is now dead.

Witness shown a paper by Hennen answered that he thought it was written in McDermott's hand writing.

Q. Have you any knowledge of Guillemard having surveyed the land in this neighborhood at any time before or after the year 1800?

A. He must have surveyed before 1800 from a plot I found at my house after coming home from New York to which place I set off in the year 1798.

Q. Did you know Guillemard?

A. I have seen him in New Orleans.

Q. Was he a Spanish Officer?

A. He was said to be.

Q. Did he wear the Spanish uniform?

A. I do not recollect.

Q. After Goodby left the place on Chinchuba did any one reside on it and cultivate at the lower tract of land, the tract of land which you have already described as Goodby's.

A. I have known Thomas Spell to cultivate it.

Q. For a short or for a long time?

A. He may have made two or three crops on it.

Cross-examination of Uriah Smith by Miller for the plaintiffs

Q. Did you live there when you were grown (*sic*)?

A. I am not able to say.

Q. Did Goodby ever live there five years to the best of your recollection?

A. He might or might not.

Q. Did you ever recollect of Mr. Thomas Spell ever having made one crop?

A. I do not recollect of more than one crop but he might have made more for all that I know.

Q. What did that crop consist of?

A. I believe corn.

Q. What point of compass did Goodby's improvement bear from Faircloth's house?

A. It bears northerly what I mean by northerly is when it lies north westward or north eastwardly or north itself.

Q. Whether does it not bear north westward?

A. It might for all I know.

Q. After Goodby went away did you know of any other occupation made of that land except the crop already spoken of?

A. I moved away in 1807 and do not know of any other to my own knowledge.

Q. How many years before you moved away from Castein Bayou? Was it to the best of your recollection that Goodby went off?

A. A good while before I moved away.

Q. On which side of the Chinchuba was this crop of corn made by Mr. Spell?

A. I should call it eastwardly.

Q. How far was it from the house of Faircloth?

A. I do not think it was half a mile, it might be a quarter.

Q. Do you not think it was more than a quarter of a mile?

A. I think it not more or a very little more.

Q. Recollect as well as you can how far off you have known the division fence between the Goodby tract and the tract on which Faircloth lived?

A. In Spells time I was not particularly acquainted and did not know whether their fences joined or not but since Mr. Sharp has lived there they have always had a division fence.

Q. On what part of this tract was the bark cut?

A. It was about half way between the line of Bartle and that of Labatut and about half a mile from the lake.

Examination in chief resumed.

Q. How far do the enclosures of Faircloth's improvement extend to the southward of his house?

A. About 200 yards.

Q. Has not the whole of this tract of land from the lake upwards to within a few yards of Faircloth's house always remained without any fences or has it not remained so far from ten years back?

A. I have seen Ambrose's old field in cultivation by Richardson and Faircloth but not within the ten years past.

Q. How long has Faircloth been living on the land?

A. He was there in 1803 when the Government took possession of New Orleans and had been there some time previous but I cannot say how long.

Q. Was it not some time before you moved away from Castein Bayou that Thomas Spell made this crop?

A. I cannot say for certain it runs in my head that it was.

Q. Did you or did you not know any conditional line having been run between Faircloth and Goodby?

A. I understood one being run by the Government but I did not know it to be a conditional line nor do I know anything of it myself.

Q. Whether for the last twenty years you have known of any act of habitation, or cultivation occupation, or improvement on the tract of land on which Faircloth lived either on the part of Thomas Spell or any other person under him?

A. I do not.

Q. Whether do you know of any act of habitation, cultivation, or improvement on the tract of land which Goodby lived for the last twenty years by Thomas Spell or any other person claiming under him?

A. I do not think there was.

William Sharp, on the part of the plaintiffs, questioned by Hennen:

Q. Have you never heard Mrs. Bartle say since the commencement of this suit that she had no title to the land and that all she wanted was to get rid of damages in present suit?
A. I did.

Witness further states that he is the son-in-law of Mrs. Bartle. The parole testimony here closed.

The defendant Elizabeth Bartle now comes into court and says for supplemental answer that she sets up no title to the land situated to the west of the tract of land purchased by Jacob Bartle on July 25, 1811, from Dorothy O'Brien wife of J. P. Sanderson.

Each side having presented all their evidence, it was now the time to "rest" their case. The attorneys summarized the evidence in order to persuade the jury to find in favor of their respective clients.

Charge to the Jury submitted by plaintiffs (Letchworth) was filed on Thursday, October 19, 1825, by James B. W. Coy, Deputy Clerk.

1. That the action is an action for disturbance to the plaintiff's possession. (Charged)
2. That if the Jury believe that the plaintiff has proved the habitation and cultivation of   Zachariah Faircloth – of the tract of land Bounded by Bartelles' and Labatuts' lines, on or before the fifteenth day of April 1813, that by the Act of Congress of 1819 he became entitled to the said tract as a donation provided it does not exceed 640 acres on making application therefore to the Commissioners. (Charged)
3. That the Certificate of the Commissioner issued in pursuance of said law *prima facia*[14] as evidence of his title – and that an occupation of part of a tract of land having title to the whole is a legal possession of the whole tract sufficient to maintain an action for disturbance. (Charged)
4. That the Jury believes that Mrs. Bartle set her slaves to work on the plaintiff's land she was a trespasser to the plaintiff's possession and for such an act can be sued by the person injured, although she was a married woman. (Charged)
5. That whatever Mrs. Bartle slaves did by her command she is responsible for.

6. That in the certificate for 300 acres given to the heirs of Spell, there is no legal evidence before the Jury, where it is to be located, and that in the absence of all proof, the Jury cannot legally locate certificate on the tract in controversies. (Refused)

7. That this being an action for disturbance done to an immovable is not barred by the prescription of one year. (Charged)

8. That the measure of damages to be assessed is the full damages which plaintiff has sustained. (Charged)

Filed by James B. W. Coy, on Thursday, October 19, 1825, the Counsel for Defense, Alfred Hennen, requested the Court to Charge to the Jury as follows:

1. To charge the Jury that the present action is not for the purpose of being maintained in possession of the land in controversy. (Charged)

2. If the Jury believes that the defendants have given in evidence from the land commissioners for 360 arpents of land to the west of O'Bryan's British grant under a Spanish survey in 1798 – Then their title is better than that of the plaintiffs. (Refused)

3. That the plaintiffs had no legal possession of the land that they claim until the 6th day of August 1825, when the wife of Letchworth was put in possession by the Parish Judge. (Refused)

4. That the plaintiffs can maintain no action for damages on account of any trespass committed by the defendants on any land in their possession; of the trespass complained of was committed more than one year prior to the filing of the suit. (Refused)

5. That if the Jury believe that the plaintiffs and defendants have each of them taken a certificate for the same land, then they will pay no attention to them, and decide the cause by the rights of the parties before they obtained their certificates. (Charged)

6. If the Jury believes that a trespass has been committed by only one of the defendants, then they will find a verdict against such defendant only. (Charged)

7. The wife of the Defendant is not responsible for any of her actions committed jointly with him. (Charged)

8. That ~~without possession of the land by the~~ if the Jury believes that the plaintiffs are not in possession of the tract of land on which they complain that the plaintiffs were committed they must find a verdict for the defendants. (Charged)

The jury retired to the deliberation room to consider the case they had just heard and to reach a verdict. William B. Bogert was the foreperson who was to see that the discussions were conducted in orderly fashion and that the issues pertaining to the case were fairly and fully discussed.

On Friday, October 20, 1825, the jurors had reached a verdict: "The matter of law and evidence addressed on the part of this court bring in favor of the plaintiffs, and the verdict of the Jury brings also in his favor. It is also judged and decreed that the defendants owe the plaintiffs the sum of $82.50 plus $207. 62 ½ cents costs."

Judge William H. Pattillo

William H. Bogert, foreman of Jury

The court had delivered their opinion in this case of trespass relating to land in which the respective titles of the parties had been brought into view. It was now up to Mrs. Elizabeth Bartle to accept or refuse the verdict.

NOTES

1. The perche is a unit of land measurement equal to 19.888feet or 5.85 meters or 5 ½ yards.
2. A measure of 100 links, or 66 feet, used in land surveying.
3. Calomel was occasionally used in medicine as a purgative.
4. Jalap was used as purgative drug.
5. Formerly used in the preparation of opium; a tincture of opium.
6. Louise Spell, daughter of Thomas Spell and Elizabeth Bartle, married about 1824 to Raymond Felix Delisle de la Barthe.
7. Hartshorn, a chief source of ammonia, was used in the preparation of smelling salts.
8. A river N.W. Virginia and S.W. Pennsylvania flowing north to unite with the Allegheny River at Pittsburgh forming the Ohio River.
9. William Sharp married Nancy Spell on July 18, 1821.
10. Cornell University, English Collection, Southland Writers. File prepared by Pam J. Rice and Joyce A. Rogers: http://usgarchives.net/a/files.htm
11. John Edwards was born July 26, 1784.
12. Reference is made to the location of William Sharp's house.
13. According to this information he would have been born on September 29, 1773. He was baptized on January 16, 1774.
14. From the Latin expression *prima facie,* meaning *on its first encounter.* It is used in the modern legal English to signify that on first examination, a matter appears to be self-evident from the facts.

CHAPTER 15

IN BETWEEN TRIALS

The State of Louisiana commanded James Daniels, the sheriff of the Parish of St. Tammany, to demand from the representatives of the estate of Jacob Bartle, deceased, the sum of eighty-two dollars and fifty cents debt with two hundred and seven dollars sixty-two and a half cents costs which Joseph Letchworth and wife recovered by a judgment of the District Court held at the Parish Court House on October 19, 1825.

If the monies were not paid then he, as sheriff, had cause for the said sum owed to be made of the personal estate of the succession of Jacob Bartle. First, it was to be taken from the personal estate of the said succession, exclusive of slaves. If these were not found in sufficient personal estate of the succession exclusive of slaves then he, as sheriff, had cause for the sum owed to be made of the real estate and slaves of the said succession he, the deceased, was the owner on the 19th day of October last. Sheriff James Daniels was to have the monies before the Court at Claiborne, to render to Letchworth and wife on the 20th day of January 1826.

The letter was witnessed by the Honorable William H. Pattillo, Judge of the 8th District Court on the 19th of November 1825, and the 50th year of the Independence of the United States, and it was signed by Samuel Mallory, Clerk.

Elizabeth Bartle could have paid the damages and court costs incurred, and the case would have been closed, and her story would end here. Instead, she ordered her attorney Alfred Hennen to make an appeal to the Louisiana Supreme Court.

The Supreme Court of Louisiana met on Monday, January 2, 1826. Present were the Honorable George Matthews, the Honorable Francis Xavier Martin, and the Honorable Alexander Porter. The court on this day delivered their opinion in writing. The case No. 1221, Joseph Letchworth & Wife, Appellees, *vs* Jacob Bartles & Wife, Appellants, "is an action of trespass relating to land in which the respective titles of the parties are brought into view; these claims appear to have been severely contested in the court below if we may judge from the number of points made and supported pro and con and the many bills of exceptions which appear on the record, and on which the case is principally brought before this court." (Supreme Court of Louisiana,

January 2, 1826 - Case No. 1221, Letchworth & Wife, Appellees vs Jacob Bartle & Wife, Appellants).

Of these exceptions the judges deemed necessary to examine only two. They were clearly of opinion "that the judge *a quo* error in rejecting the evidence, which gave rise to one of them taken by the defendants who are here appellants." The evidence offered was a survey of part of the disputed premises alleged to have been made by and under the authority of the Spanish government as exercised in the province of Louisiana. The plat or plan certified by Carlos Trudeau, the Surveyor General of said province as having been executed by one of his deputies.[1]

Since the change of government and opening of the land office under the authority of the United States "this plan of survey was regularly registered and a certificate obtained from the commissioners in favor of the person claiming under it. They have therefore, for and on the part of the U.S. organized to as evidence of title and we believe in strict conformity with the act of Congress of the 3rd March 1819, cited and relied on both parties to this suit. The legal effect which it may have in opposition to the plaintiff's evidence of title will be fully considered after its introduction.

In relation to the other exception which the judges thought proper to notice, i.e. to the permission given to the plaintiff to amend his petition by supplement, they were of opinion that the judge below did not err. It does not appear to us radically to change the demand. Actual possession when legal and peaceable is sufficient to maintain an action of trespass. In the present case the supplemental petition sets forth the manner of possession and title under which the plaintiffs hold; this cannot fairly be considered as a change in the substance of the demand."

The judges therefore ordered, adjudged and decreed that the judgment of the district court be avoided, reversed and annulled, and it was further ordered adjudged and decreed that the cause be sent back to the court below for a new trial, with instructions to the judge *a quo* to admit in evidence the plat or plan of survey, offered by the defendants. The Appellees were to pay the costs of the appeal. The true copy of the judgment was signed by B. LeBreton, Clerk.

The Supreme Court of Louisiana certified that the costs of this appeal amounted to twenty-one dollars and seventy-five cents. Dated: January 11, 1826, by Clerk LeBreton.

It wasn't over for Elizabeth Bartle. The Probate Court still had to settle the estate of Jacob Bartle, her deceased husband, who died intestate.

In Elizabeth Bartle's petition to the Honorable Lyman Briggs, Judge of the Parish of St. Tammany, State of Louisiana, and *ex officio* Judge of the Court of Probates for the Parish, Mrs. Bartle stated that she was first the widow of Thomas Spell, deceased, and now widow of Jacob Bartle, deceased, residing in the Parish of St. Tammany, in the State of Louisiana.

She represents that she is the natural tutrix to her minor daughter Elizabeth Bartle, legitimate daughter of said Jacob Bartle, deceased, and as such has been duly confirmed. Secondly, that a tract of land containing four hundred acres belonging to the heirs of her deceased husband, situated in the parish, contains ten acres front with forty arpents, or acres, in depth on Lake Pontchartrain, was sold in order to affect a partition amongst the said heirs in the year one thousand and eight hundred and twenty-six, the purchase of the same by William Bowman who has since sold said land to Bernard Marigny.

The said Bowman and Marigny fearing that some irregularity could exist in the proceedings relative to the sale of the said land, now prepare "to pay to your petitioner as tutrix of minor daughter the sum of two hundred dollars for the full and complete ratification of the said sale." The intent for this sum of money was to remove all rights and claims to the said land and all pretentions and actions arising from any nullity or want of formality in the sale of said land to Bowman or in any of the proceedings relative thereto particularly the want of an order of the Court of Probates authorizing said sale, and also the nullity arising from the circumstance of the sale having been made for less than the appreciated value of the land in question.

As petitioner, Mrs. Bartle requests that a meeting of the friends of the said minor may be ordered to deliberate upon the propriety of accepting the monies offered in order to ratify the sale in the name of the said minor and "that your honor with the advice and consent of said family meeting will authorize your petitioner to compromise or that they will account for the same."[2]

The petition was signed by Jean Favre Senior. Witnesses who signed were L.B. Greene, Albert Lorreins, and Thomas Spell. Witnesses who made their mark were James Stump and Macklin Lloyd. Elizabeth Bartle made her usual mark.

Jesse R. Jones, Parish Judge, certifies that the foregoing petition was duly recorded and affixed with the Seal of his office on January 12, 1826.

Macklin Lloyd was married to Maria Bartle, one of the children and heirs of Jacob Bartle. Through Branch W. Miller, the attorney for his wife, Macklin Lloyd petitioned the Honorable Judge Jesse R. Jones for a Judicial partition of the estate of his father-in-law, on behalf of his wife and the minor children Marshall and Sophia; Elizabeth Bartle being of a different mother of the other heirs, still living.

In the succession of Jacob Bartle, Joseph Sharp and Macklin Lloyd were held and firmly bound unto Jesse R. Jones, Judge of the Parish of St. Tammany, "in the just and full sum of four hundred thirty one dollars well and truly to be paid to him or to his successors in office for which payment they hereby bind themselves, their heirs, executors, and administrators firmly by these present dated this twenty third of September 1826."

The above condition of the above obligation is such "that when us, the above, bound Joseph Sharp has been appointed Curator *ad bona* to Marshall Bartle, a minor, now if he shall well and faithfully do and perform all the duties incumbent upon him as such and shall render an account of his acting and doings as such and the same shall be examined and approved by the Judge aforesaid and shall pay over to the said Marshall Bartle or whomsoever shall be entitled to receive the same whatever sum of money or property may remain in his hands belonging to said Marshall Bartle then the above obligation to void and of none effect else to remain in full force and virtue in law."

Witnesses were David L. W. Coy and William Clayton. Joseph Sharp and Macklin Lloyd made their marks. The document was executed before Jesse R. Jones, Parish Judge, and registered on the 23rd day of September 1826.[3]

Dated January 29, 1827, at Covington, was received of Jesse R. Jones the sum of three hundred and nine dollars, it being the share of the proceeds of the sale of the Estate of Jacob Bartle, deceased, belonging to Maria Bartle, wife of Macklin Lloyd, and Sophia Bartle. Macklin Lloyd made his mark. Witness was David L. W. Coy.

The following month, on February 3, 1827, Joseph Sharp received one hundred and fifty four dollars and fifty cents, being the amount of the share due Marshall Bartle from his father's estate. Joseph Sharp, curator, made his mark.

In an Act passed before Judge Jesse R. Jones bearing the date December 20, 1826, William Bowman of the Parish of St. Tammany became the purchaser of a tract of land belonging to the succession of Jacob Bartle, deceased. This was the original tract of land granted to William O'Brien by the British government and sold to Jacob Bartle by Dorothy O'Brien Sanderson in 1811.

William Bowman, on November 17, 1829, by an Act passed before Hugh R. Gordon, Notary Public in and for the city of New Orleans sold and delivered unto Bernard Marigny this tract of land of 10 arpents front on Lake Pontchartrain and forty arpents in depth. The outcome of the sale would not be completed until May 1834.

The Letchworths began preparations for the eventual trial not yet scheduled, but to be held in early March of 1826. Branch W. Miller, Attorney for the plaintiffs Letchworth and Wife, petitioned Judge Pattillo of the District Court to petition for a commission to take testimony from William Kinchen and Samuel J. Runnels residing in the parish of St. Helena as material witnesses for them in the retrial of their case.

They requested that his Honor order a commission issue directed to Jacob Smith to take the testimony of the two witnesses to be read as evidence in the trial of the above cause upon filing interrogations and giving the defendants the notice of the time and place of taking said testimony. The Petition was filed on March 10, 1826, by James B. Coy, Deputy Clerk.

It would be a long wait for the litigants! The second trial, Court Case No. 225, Letchworth & Wife *vs* Bartle & Wife, was scheduled for the April 1827 term, to be held in the Court House located in Claiborne, in the State of Louisiana.

NOTES

1. Reference made to Gilberto Guillemard, the French surveyor in the employ of Spain.
2. Elizabeth Bartle, Family meeting copy, No. 2420, COB-Book "B"/90, Parish Judge Jesse R. Jones, filed and Seal affixed on January 12, 1826.
3. COB Book A/12. Registered by Parish Judge Jesse R. Jones, September 23, 1826.

CHAPTER 16

SECOND TRIAL: LETCHWORTH vs BARTLE

Elizabeth Bartle won her appeal from the Louisiana Supreme Court on January 2, 1826. Her case came up before the open courts of the 8th Judicial District in April 1827.

Regular procedures completed, Daniel Edwards, first introduced by the plaintiffs and sworn, answered the questions proposed to him by Attorney Branch W. Miller. Asked if he had any conversations with regard to his lines between him and Faircloth, he replied in the affirmative. He related that one day when he and Mr. Spell were riding together, he turned out of the yard and rode a short distance to a tree which he called a corner tree. Spell said, "This is the corner that divides the Goodby tract and Faircloths." Spell then pointed westward to a Negro fellow's house or shop and said the line went there, and that this was the line that divided him and Faircloth, line which ran east or west or nearly so.

That tree was considered as one of the boundaries. At the time, Mr. Spell pointed out a tar kiln at a place near where the line runs and asked me if I remembered that old tar kiln. I did. Mr. Spell answered and said that Mr. Faircloth could come but very little further on account of Madam O'Bryan's line and then said that the tar kiln was on or at the line of Madam O'Bryan and Faircloth. Spell then said that the Goodby and O'Bryan tracts cornered on the same tree.

Daniel Edwards said he was on the line with General Morgan and he showed him that corner tree from which they began the survey. General Morgan went near the tar kiln to run the line to the lake shore. He, the witness, went with him and they followed the old British blazes. The chain went near or over that old tar kiln.

Questioned by Attorney Miller if he had a conversation with Mr. Spell after the latter had gone to Baton Rouge to obtain orders of survey from Governor Grand Pré, Daniel Edwards replied that Mr. Spell had told him he had obtained three orders of survey of five hundred arpents each.

Q. Did Mr. Spell state to you where those tracts lay?

A. He did. He told me that one was on Lake Maurepas, and opposite of the Cypress Swamp, that one lay over the Bogue Chitto on account of his cattle, and the other at the Ponchitolawa.

Q. Were you intimate with Mr. Spell and did you ever hear him say that he had an order of survey for the tract of land claimed by Faircloth?

A. He never told me that he had or had not. I never heard him make any claims to this tract of land.

In cross-examination by Attorney Alfred Hennen for the defendants, Mr. Edwards was asked: "When did this conversation take place?" He replied that he did not recollect, it was a good many years ago. It was after Natchez was taken by the United States or after New Orleans was taken by the United States.

Daniel Edwards reintroduced by Miller for the plaintiffs now says that he corrects the evidence taken at the former trial of this cause. The swamp spoken of in his former testimony was incorrectly taken down. "The swamp lines are in front of the land now in controversy and not in front of Labatut's plantation."

With regard to surveys made on the lake by Guillemard, Edwards knew of several. He recollected the survey of ten or twelve arpents on the place that Mrs. Spell now lives on. He was there when the posts were planted.

Q. Do you not know that Guillemard made a survey of the front of the O'Bryan tract for Meeks?

A. I know that he did, but he run no further to the westward that I know of.

Q. Did not Guillemard survey the front of the Goodby tract?

A. He surveyed the Goodby tract which lay north of Faircloth.

Q. Did you carry the chain at the time?

A. I was too small at the time. I was about eleven years old.

Q. What became of the plats that Guillemard made of this tract?

A. I have seen the plats in Trudeau's office. I do not recollect of seeing but the one plat with the plans that Guillemard made on front of the lake.

Henry Cooper Junior, the son of Henry, the former British loyalist, was introduced by Miller for the plaintiffs and sworn.

Q. Did you have a conversation with Mr. Bartle at the time you sold a schooner to him?

A. I did. Jacob Bartle came up to take the schooner down and I went with him to the mouth of the Castein Bayou. We came in near the shore and near a pile of wood which he observed to me was the wood his wife wished to take to New Orleans. I told him there was a good deal of wood and that perhaps it would be cheaper to buy a schooner to carry it.

He said that Letchworth was about to marry into the family of Faircloth and as this wood was cut on the claim of Faircloth and as Letchworth was a contentious man he was afraid he would commence a law suit and that it would cost more trouble than the wood was worth.

Mr. John Woods was introduced by Attorney Hennen for the defendants and sworn. He stated that he was the chain carrier when Mr. Kneeland surveyed land on Lake Pontchartrain. The land surveyed was on the west line of Jacob Bartle on Lake Pontchartrain. It was for Thomas Spell about the year 1807.

Judge Jesse R. Jones was sworn on the part of the defendants. He was questioned by Attorney Hennen on the general character of Love B. Green with regard to truth and veracity. The judge answered he had heard the subject mentioned by a great many person and he thought a majority is unfavorable, but the opinion could be nearly equal.

Q. Have you ever heard any remarks for truth and veracity unfavorable previous to the former trial of this case?
A. The first observation that I have heard as to the truth and veracity was on a trial before Justice Briggs where Love B. Green denied a signature alleged to be his – the majority of persons with myself then thought it was his. I have since changed my opinion and believe it was a forgery.

Mr. John Wood was again introduced on the part of the defendants. Attorney Hennen proceeded with the cross-examination of Mr. Wood.

Q. State whether you have any knowledge of Mr. Ambrose having cultivated the old field called Ambrose's old field.
A. I have none.
Q. Did you ever hear Mr. Faircloth say anything about his claim south of Ambrose's old field?
A. I never did hear Faircloth claim it. I have always heard Spell claim it.
Q. How long have you lived in this country?
A. I have lived in this country thirty one years upon the lake.
Q. Where did you come from?
A. Pennsylvania.
Q. Were you ever in the army?
A. I was. I was discharged.

A woman named Margaret Woods, married to a John Woods in 1773, petitioned the Court at Natchez on January 16, 1784, to have her children and her slave Rebecca returned to her. She had set off on a business trip from Natchez with her passport to go to New Orleans on November 12, 1783, but was prevented. She stated that her husband, John Woods, a simple man and addicted to liquor, bought a plantation while intoxicated for $1,500.00 far beyond its value. When payment became due the plantation, plows, animals and slaves were sold. In above testimony, Woods stated that he had been on the lake for 31 years. This corresponds to the same time John Woods of Natchez was absconded in 1784.[1]

A. Haroldson was introduced and sworn by the defendants. Asked by Attorney Hennen if he had traced out the British lines of the tract belonging to Jacob Bartle, he replied that about twelve months ago, while attending court in St. Tammany, he was employed by Mrs. Bartle in the absence of Mr. Hennen, the original counsel to attend to the defense of a suit brought against her by Letchworth and Wife. On the Friday or Saturday preceding the Monday of court, in the company of Abraham Penn and John Whitten, United States Deputy Surveyors, they went down to the disputed premises for the purpose of attending to the survey of what he conceived to be the land in dispute.

Said, they first ascertained the corner of the old Jacob Bartle line to the O'Bryan tract by going north or northwest, five degrees from the lake point where they were standing. Mr. Letchworth was present. He had come at the invitation of Mr. Delisle or someone sent by him undertook to point out the southeastern corner of the Goodby tract. This was deemed necessary in order to ascertain the location of the Thomas Spell tract under the survey of ninety eight.[2]

Mr. Letchworth stated that he knew where the southeast corner of the Goodby tract was and he went with the surveyor, Mr. Whitten, about a hundred and eighty or two hundred yards from the place where we were standing. It was thought by us to be the northwest corner of the Bartle or O'Bryan tract. This was done to ascertain, if possible, the identity of the spot where the corner stood and whether it stood in the same direction with the south east line of the Tom Spell tract. Finding it to be so, we started from the spot where we had been standing which we considered to be the corner of the O'Bryan tract and pursued a chopped line, which we supposed to be Kneeland's at that time from the date, to the lake. At the lake, or close by, it perhaps not in a straight direction with the line we found a chopped cypress marked MB. This chopped line did not run in the direction of south

The History of Mandeville

fifteen degrees west. At the cypress, I requested to Mr. Whitten to make a calculation founded on a variation of a line as described in the Thomas Spell tract with the line we had just run.

The calculation was made; then we run up the lake west. What distance, I forget. We stopped at the limit of this calculation within thirty or forty feet of a large live oak just on the bank of the lake which had every mark of a corner on the east and on the north. We run six hundred yards up the lake.

Mr. Letchworth, at this point, appeared confused and did not consent to anything that was done during the day.

Abraham Penn, introduced by the defendants, said that he had gone to the disputed premises and attended there with Mr. Whitten. They found a marked line from the place where they commenced operations in a south direction to the lake. They saw some trees marked which they supposed to be a line.

Q. Did you find a cypress marked MB at the point of termination on the lake?

A. We found a cypress marked as such on the margin of the lake, at the termination of the line.

Q. Did you make a calculation with Mr. Whitten of the distance you should run up the lake from the cypress on a variation of the line he had traced?

A. Mr. Whitten made the calculation in my presence.

The next question and answer excepted (objected to) by Counsel, Branch W. Miller, for the plaintiffs Letchworth and Wife.

Q. Do you recollect the distance that you went up the lake from the cypress pursuant to that calculation and whether was found a tree marked as a corner at or near the point of computation?

A. We run as well as I recollect nine arpents on the lake, and we fall short one chain and thirteen links of being the nine arpents. We saw a live oak directly on the margin of the lake marked with a cross and I think three chops. I think on the east, we fell to the north of the oak. From the course, we run from the cypress up about thirty feet. This oak stood at or near the point of computation from the cypress within about forty feet. I should think the chops, from their appearance, had been made about twenty years. It might have been longer or not so long a time.

240

Cross examined by Branch W. Miller, for the plaintiffs, Abraham Penn said he made a plot of the survey and it was given to Mr. Haroldson or Mr. Delisle.

Q. Was there any sign of a post or corner on the bank line that you run?
A. I saw none. I made the survey at the instance of Mr. Delisle.
Q. Did you run all the line of the O'Bryan tract of land?
A. We only run one line, the west line to the lake. I cannot say positively what the course was. I think it was ten or eleven degrees west of the south. I have the field notes at home. I think I run the west line of the Guillemard plans. I think we run from the south east corner of the Goodby tract down the west line of the Guillemard survey. We run near or about an old tar kiln.

John Woods introduced by the defendants was asked, by Mr. Hennen, if he had ever seen Mr. Spell in possession of the tract of land to the west of the Bartle tract which had been surveyed with him by Kneeland. He answered that he had seen Mr. Spell make rails both before and after the survey of Kneeland on that tract of land.

Q. Do you know of Mr. Spell being in the possession in any other way or manner or forbidding any one from cutting wood on it?
A. No further than what I have stated.
Q. Do you know of his having sold wood of this land?
A. I do not.

Mr. Woods was then questioned by Attorney Branch W. Miller for the plaintiffs:

Q. Did you ever know Mr. Spell to build a house on this land?
A. I never knew him to build a house on it or to cultivate it or to fence it.

David B. Morgan introduced by the plaintiffs says that he surveyed the land agreeably to the plan now exhibited. He began at a corner post, the northwest corner of the O'Bryan tract, which was pointed out to him as the old corner. When he first commenced with this corner, Mrs. Bartle was present. Thence he ran that line, the course marked in the plat. The posts appeared to be very old and the many marks seen in the line also appeared to be very old. Morgan ran out the whole survey. He did not have the O'Bryan survey with him at the time, but had the minutes of the survey which he had taken some time anterior.

He run his compass south 15 degrees west and found the course south fourteen degrees west from the upper post to the corner on the lake. On the lake shore, he found a cypress post covered with green moss shown to him as the ancient and southwest corner of the Bartle tract.

In cross-examination by Counsel Hennen, he was asked:

Q. How do you know that you and Mr. Whiting started from the same post?
A. I only know from his having told me where he started from. He was not present when I started nor was I present when he started.
Q. On running the west line of the Bartle tract, did you find any oak trees marked?
A. I found no trees that I considered station trees, though I found some trees marked.

After hearing the above testimonies, we now leave the court room. Mr. Morgan was asked to resurvey the lands in dispute. The survey was made on September 27 and 28, 1827, of the lands in controversy between Letchworth and Wife and Bartles and wife. It was filed in open court on April 15, 1828, for the opening of the spring term.

NOTES

1. McBee, May W., *Natchez Court Records*, 164-167.
2. Reference made to Lt. Colonel Gilberto Guillemard, Aide Major, for New Orleans, Spanish officer who made survey for Samuel Smith, Thomas Spell, James Goodby, and Morgan Edwards, in the year 1798. He spent about three weeks to complete the survey. He notes that the first concession to Edwards was made June 2, 1783, and the second on December 18, 1787.

CHAPTER 17

THE EVIDENCE STANDS: THE SURVEYORS OF COURT CASE NO. 225

English, French, Spanish, and United Sates surveyors and the instruments they used played an important part in the development of America. Dividing up the land, determining passages and routes across the vast American continent was an important factor related to the growth of specific areas and country.

Encouraged by land grants, emigrants from the English colonies or from Britain poured into West Florida during the period of 1772-1779. British Loyalists who fled the east coast to escape the ravages of the Revolutionary War also caused an influx of people. Temporarily, these Anglos found a safe haven in the sanctuaries established by the British in East and West Florida. The north shore of Lake Pontchartrain attracted about twenty families during the peak of settlement between 1776 and 1779. At the close of the War, when it was brought to West Florida by Captain James Willing, and his marauders, many settlers abandoned their land.

Don Bernardo de Galvez, the Spanish governor, was successful in driving out the British from the Floridas. With the surrender of the two British provinces in April 1781, British loyalists were forced to make a decision: submit to the new rules or leave. Many chose to become subjects of the King of Spain. Spain inherited several large plantations that the British had worked hard to cultivate. Grants that were unoccupied or unimproved were reassigned to valid settlers.

The West Florida period ended with the West Florida Revolt which preceded West Florida's annexation with the United States.

From the testimonies of witnesses in Court Case 225, the name of Gilberto Guillemard stands out. This man, in the service of His Majesty, the King of Spain, would prove through his long and distinguished career that a Frenchman could make a very good Spaniard. Born in Longuay, in the Diocese of Trèves, France, on September 27, 1746, Gilberto, as he was called by the Spaniards, was the son of Arnoult and Elizabeth Marechal Guillemard. He entered the service of Spain in January 1770, as a cadet, and served for a few years before being sent to Louisiana where he distinguished himself in the campaigns of the Spanish Governor Don Bernardo de Galvez against the British at Manchac, Baton Rouge, Mobile and Pensacola in 1779-1780.[1]

Guillemard was the nephew of Don Isabel de la Roche, his mother's sister, wife of the noted Gilbert Antoine de St. Maxent, one of whose daughters was the wife of Governor Unzaga and another, the wife of Governor Bernardo de Galvez, later Viceroy of Mexico.

In 1786, Gilberto Guillemard held the rank of Captain of Infantry and town aid-major of New Orleans, "charged by commission of the government with the functions of engineer and surveyor in this Spanish province."[2] In 1787, Gilberto Guillemard married Marie Félicité Barbeau-Boisdoré.

His engineering abilities were employed in 1787 when he designed fortifications for the harbor and the San Carlos Battery at Pensacola. In 1790, he drew plans for a church at Natchez as well as for several buildings in that area for Governor Miro. Being the most qualified architect in New Orleans at the time, and with his distinguished military career and family connections, it is not surprising the Almonaster selected him to design the new parish church and rectory that he offered to rebuild at his own expense. In 1792, he drew up beautiful plans for the proposed fortifications at New Orleans and the most beautiful colonial buildings: the Cabildo, *the Presbytère*, Saint Louis Cathedral, *the Petit Théatre du Vieux Carré* and the Charity Hospital of St. Charles.

In 1796, while acting as adjutant-major of the New Orleans garrison, Guillemard was named cartographer and surveyor of the Spanish boundary commission destined to meet with the American Commissioner Andrew Ellicott to draw the thirty-first parallel separating Americans from Spanish territory in accordance with the Treaty of San Lorenzo. News of an impending attack on Spanish Louisiana from Canada *via* the Great Lakes in 1797 frightened the Spanish governors, and Guillemard did not join Ellicott. He and another engineer, Juan Maria Perchet, were sent to the Spanish military post of Nogales, located at the Walnut Hills near the confluence of the Yazoo and Mississippi rivers where Vicksburg stands today.

Guillemard was ordered to inspect the works and make necessary improvements so that Nogales could repel any attack directed against it from above. Difficult a task, for carelessness and lack of funds had caused the fort's stockade to crumble in the constant rains. By the end of the summer, Nogales was in a reasonable state of defense.

Morgan Edwards was one of the first to come and settle on the north shore after hostilities began in August 1779, and after many British settlers had abandoned their land. In 1781, he settled east of Samuel Smith. He was given a concession of land by the Spanish on June 2, 1783.[3] The war was still on, but he had the oral and written permission from the Spanish Governor. He like the remaining few, who chose to remain, did not have their land surveyed until later.

244

Edwards later encountered land problems caused by Jacob Miller, the German bricklayer, interested in a brick making operation. Governor Carondelet had granted the land before checking it out. Commandant Charles Parent was ordered by Carondelet to investigate.[4] Almonester y Roxas, an influential man in the Spanish government, requested Gilberto Guillemard to survey the tracts. Edwards went to New Orleans to get him. Guillemard's survey map, with notations written in French, is a key reference for the surveyors who followed.[5] The information provided is important because it not only relates to the pre-history of present-day Mandeville, but for its connection with original British grants in which the old British lines drawn by Elias Durnford were used. On the tracts of land that belonged to Thomas Spell, Samuel Smith and Morgan Edwards, Guillemard indicates the depths of the former English boundaries, and notes that most of the other habitations had been abandoned. He therefore judged it appropriate to divide the land in depth, in order to give less land to Durio, since he had the distinctive advantage of bordering on the Bayou.

Guillemard also established in 1798 the lines of James Goodby, which became the downfall of Elizabeth Bartle, as the boundary lines did not extend all the way down to the lake as she claimed as her land.

John and Daniel Edwards, sons of Morgan Edwards and Marguerite Smith, recalled surveyor Guillemard who came to survey their father's land. They were young at the time, but they still remembered. Questioned at length about the Guillemard survey, John Edwards in his testimony in 1827, said about his father: "He went over and got Guillemard." Asked if Guillemard had used an old survey when he came over, Edwards said, "no the land was never surveyed." Guillemard went by what the Spanish government, Estevan Miro, put down in the book: "the land was never surveyed." Guillemard followed oral instructions from the Spanish government.

Ira C. Kneeland, of which little is known before he came to Spanish West Florida was from Massachusetts. In 1801, he was employed by George Cochran and John Rhea, partners in a general store at Natchez. We do not know where Kneeland trained as surveyor, but he was an educated man.[6] Kneeland surveyed the William O'Brian tract at Bayou Castein in 1806. It was registered in the Surveyor's Office of Charles (Carlos) Trudeau, the Royal and Particular Surveyor of the Province of Louisiana, in New Orleans. The important point that the Kneeland map makes is that the western boundary of the O'Brian tract was bordered by vacant land, plus it confirmed the original British survey and boundary lines that established the disputed land.

George Richardson, Martha Faircloth's father, was settled on this land for about ten years prior to the tract being surveyed by Kneeland. Zachariah Faircloth stated in his petition to the Land Commissioners that Richardson had settled in the year 1796, and sold him the land in 1801.

From a map of the old British land grants, it appears that this part of the lake front was part of the Thomas Loofbarrow grant. It was abandoned by him when hostilities broke out between the British and Spanish in 1779, and never occupied again until George Richardson settle on it in 1796.

Surveyor Whitten for the American government brought to light that William Sharp was living on land that was granted to Zachariah Faircloth by Congress in 1819.

General David B. Morgan, in later years, testified that he had been in Louisiana at the post of Concordia in 1801.[7] He received and cultivated a 760-acre land grant on the Mississippi River below the post.

David Morgan was authorized by a Spanish official and Carlos Trudeau to do survey work north of Lake Pontchartrain along the Tchefuncte River. It was Carlos Trudeau who put his name on the finished plats. David Morgan certified on July 23, 1804, that he surveyed a tract of land for Basile Krebs, lying on the west bank at the mouth of the said river and containing thirty-two arpents. It later became the site of the Lighthouse in 1837. Basile Krebs, born March 8, 1763, New Orleans, was the son of Ernest Hugo Krebs and Marie-Anne Chauvin *dite* Joyeuse, of Pascagoula, Mississippi.[8] Basile married Felicité Marchand on June 18, 1799, and died in New Orleans in 1815.

Soon after the Louisiana Purchase, in 1803, Morales doing a "brisk" business of selling land to speculators in West Florida needed qualified surveyors. This is why Mr. Morgan and Mr. Thomas Fenton were employed for a one-year term to survey land in the part of West Florida bounded by the Mississippi River between the Island of New Orleans and the Mississippi Territory.[9] This is where Morgan was taken prisoner and confined on board of a King's schooner called the "Favorite" and belonging to his Catholic Majesty, a vessel mounting 12 guns and about 40 men. For what crime, he was not told. The order issued was for taking Mr. Fenton and Morgan, but the Spanish were not aware of Mr. Fenton's death.

A letter dated December 4, 1804, penned by David Morgan to Adam Comstock of New York, fills in the early gap of his surveying activities. It compliments David B. Morgan's survey of land on the north shore of Lake Pontchartrain at the "mouth of the Tchefuncte River on the west bank."

The Morgan letter is a recent acquisition for the fourth quarter of the year 2011 (October to December) for the Historic New Orleans Collection.[10] It complements an earlier Collection acquisition. David B. Morgan's survey of land along the north shore of Lake Pontchartrain at the junction of the Tchefuncte River (1977.128) was prepared on July 23, 1804, less than two months prior to the surveyor's abduction by Captain Garcia in September 1804 (2011.0313).

This letter also complements about eight exchange letters of Governor Claiborne and Casa Calvo in New Orleans in November, 1804, of what happened before and after Morgan's dramatic escape from a Spanish naval schooner where he was held in captivity over two months and upwards.[11]

Anchored for 12 days in Lake Pontchartrain about 1½ mile from the mouth of Bayou St. John where a fort was located with American troops, Morgan meditated an escape at the risk of his own life. A few days after making up his mind, a pirogue - another name for a canoe - came along side the Spanish vessel. Morgan wrote: "As soon as the people came on board, I made a leap into and paddled for the shore with all my might." The wind that had been in his favor, had swung. The Spanish vessel was placed in such a manner that they could not bring her guns to bear on Morgan for some time. They hoisted out a boat, and with four oars pursued him to the shore. Fortunately, Morgan arrived first and made his way for the fort. They overtook him, and a scuffle ensued between him and five Spaniards. He called for protection to the sentinel who informed the corporal of that command. They came to his rescue and he was taken into the fort.

Three days later, Morgan in an attempt to regain possession of his surveying instruments, caused a warrant to be issued for the arrest of Captain Garcia. The warrant was served where Captain Garcia and the Spanish troops often were garrisoned during their stay in New Orleans, at the home of Vincente Folch y Juan, Spanish governor of West Florida. Garcia refused to surrender when the warrant was served.[12]

The incident created quite a stir in the town of New Orleans, and almost caused an international incident when it first appeared that it might result in an open clash of military arms between the Spanish guards at Folch's house and the U.S. army soldiers called in to assist in Garcia's arrest.[13] In response to the arrest, Casa Calvo sent his representative to Governor Claiborne with a formal protest.

The reasons for Morgan's abduction were never explained, nor why he was seized and his survey equipment was confiscated, and why he was held prisoner in one of the Spanish ships for several months.

Morgan's letter to Comstock of Greenfield in the County of Saratoga, State of New York, explains his long silence and his adventure as a prisoner among the Spanish since the 26th of September. This was about six days after he wrote from Natchez to inform his friend not only of the death of Mr. Fenton but about two performance bonds put up with the Spanish, one for $6,000 and one for $1,000. The six thousand dollar bond was given for and in consideration of deeds for then thousand acres of land, being double the amount of debt owed them. However, wrote Morgan to his colleague: "I expect we shall be able to make it appear an amount of damage of the non performance of the contract. That we shall be entitled to the greatest part if not all, the consideration, having two days since commenced a suit on the bond, and as soon as the money can be recovered, I shall forward it by the first safe conveyance. That is Mr. Fenton's share. The one thousand is for cash, and payable the first day of January next, and good security for both. That is all we have left except the land I mentioned in my other letter. I shall no longer entrust the Spaniards. You must not blame me for this misfortune, for I did not remove this property myself, it was done by Mr. Fenton and by our joint consent...but it will take months to oblige."[14] It appears that Mr. Comstock was in on a deal to obtain West Florida land and David Banister Morgan was telling him that they could lose some of the bond money.

Morgan complained to Governor W.C.C. Claiborne, the new governor of the Louisiana Territory, and requested from him satisfaction from Governor Folch who was then in New Orleans. He was told he had to apply to Congress for redress, but he felt it was too much trouble for him to undertake and it would be too expensive.

This incident leaves no question as to Morgan's personal courage and his determination in a stressful situation. It also demonstrates that the history of land grants and surveys are almost continuous with the history of Mandeville and the State. Who owned what has always been of vital concern to people.

The way that Morgan handled himself as a Spanish captive, his escape, and the actions that he took must have impressed Governor Claiborne. In 1804, he appointed David Morgan as surveyor general of Louisiana and Mississippi, and at a later date appointed him commander of the Louisiana Militia with the rank of brigadier general.

The land on the north shore and the people must have left an impression on Morgan, for in 1812 after West Florida became American territory, he returned and permanently settled. He held the office as justice of the peace and as police juror in St. Tammany Parish. By Act 10 of 1820, the Covington Academy was incorporated and he was one

248

of the members.[15] While living in Madisonville, Morgan remained active in his profession as surveyor and took part in civic affairs.

The need for surveyors was never greater after the Louisiana Purchase of 1803. In 1815, James Monroe, President of the United States, ordered an 1815 survey of the Louisiana Purchase lands in order to prepare for westward settlement.

Known as a surveyor, statesman, and soldier who played a prominent role in the Battle of New Orleans, Surveyor Morgan is an important witness in Court Case No. 225. He states on the stand that "when he, the witness arrived here, in 1804, Zachariah and Martha Faircloth were living on the same tract of land," and "witness was absent till the year 1812," suggesting that he came to live in Madisonville in1812.[16] This influential settler first worked in St. Tammany Parish in the capacity of surveyor.[17]

Surveyor Morgan provided three surveys for Court Case No. 225 (1820, 1825, and 1827). At the 1825 trial, it appears that his survey was wrong in size and he was requested by the court to do another after Mrs. Bartle won her appeal from the Louisiana Supreme Court for a new trial.

It is known that early surveys were often inaccurate. We can't assume dishonesty on Morgan's part to account for this mistake. There were many reasons for errors to occur. It is known that the iron chains often stretched with use, and an error of one link (about 8 inches) in 3 to 5 chains would be considered normal. Equipment had to be re-calibrated, and the magnetic compass could be a major source of error for it was subject to lunar variations in the earth's magnetic field, plus solar magnetic storms and static electricity.

On the 1827 Morgan survey map, measured in acres: Reference A shows the place where the Goodby house stood. This section was originally granted to James Goodby by the Spanish Crown as was confirmed by Carlos Trudeau, surveyor general, on January 8, 1798. Reference B indicates the place where Freeman George's house stood; reference C is the Sharp house and reference D is the place used for a burying ground.

The Morgan map indicates for the first time the original "Road to Covington" cutting through the land tract and crossing Chinchuba Creek where it intersected with an East-West "Road to Bayou Lacombe." West of the Covington road is located the house of Delisle de la Barthe, an early settler of the area. On the eastern side of the Goodby tract, close to where the Covington road crosses Chinchuba Creek was the house of Thomas Spell and Elizabeth Goodby.

Field notes were made by surveyor David B. Morgan on September 27 and 28, 1827, of the lands in controversy between Letchworth and

Wife and Bartle and Wife. These notes and the survey map were made in conformity to the order of survey by the court. These two items were filed in open court on April 15, 1828, on time for the opening of the spring session.

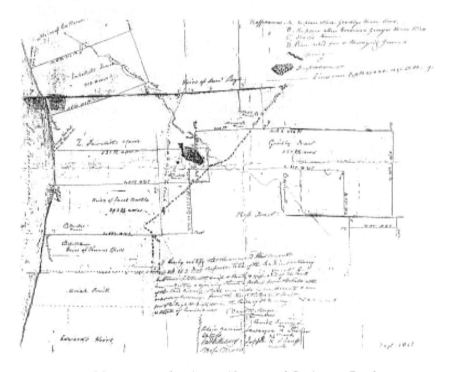

Morgan map showing residences and Covington Road

NOTES

1. McDermott, John Francis, Editor, *Frenchmen and French Ways in the Mississippi Valley*, Champaign, University of Illinois Press, 124.
2. Spanish Documents, Box 45, doc. 1073-3 no. 14, LSM.
3. Dates of concessions were confirmed on the survey map drawn by Gilberto Guillemard in 1798.
4. Campeau, Anita R. and Sharp, Donald J., "British and Spanish Land Grants: From Bayou Castin to the Tchefuncte," New *Orleans Genesis*, Volume XLVII, April 2009, No. 186, 130.
5. A microfilm copy of the Guillemard map can be found at Historic New Orleans Collection. The original copy is in the Library of Congress, Manuscript Division, Pintado Papers, Container 18, Washington, D.C., 20540.

6. Giardino, Marcio, Ph.D., and Guerin, Russell, "Surveying in West Florida," Online essay dated February 15, 2010.

7. Boagni, Ethel, *Madisonville, Louisiana*, St. Tammany Historical Society, 1981, 23.

8. Hugo Ernest Krebs had a first marriage to Marie Simon dite Lapointe.

9. Letter of David B. Morgan to Adam Comstock of Greenfield, in the State of New York, dated December 4, 1804.

10. File I.D. number is 2011.0313. The date of the letter is December 4, 1804, and is addressed to Adam Comstock of Greenfield, New York.

11. Bradley, Jared William, Interim Appointment, *W.C.C. Claiborne Letter Book, 1804-1805*, edited with biographical sketches, 2001, 14.

12. Ibid., 14.

13. Ibid., 14.

14. Letter of David Morgan to Adam Comstock dated December 4, 1804.

15. Ellis, Frederick S., *St. Tammany Parish: L'Autre Côté du Lac*, Pelican Publishing Company, Gretna, 1998, 113.

16. Court Case No. 225, David B. Morgan testifying for the plaintiffs Joseph Letchworth and Wife.

17. Boagni, Ethel, *Madisonville, Louisiana*, 25.

CHAPTER 18

LETCHWORTH *vs* BARTLE: CONTINUATION OF SECOND TRIAL, 1828

Interrogatory earlier propounded to John Whitten, United States surveyor, a resident in the County of Adams in the State of Mississippi, and a witness on behalf of the plaintiffs Letchworth & Wife, was filed with his answers in open court for the 8th Judicial District on April 15, 1828. Questions and answers were as follows:

Q. Do you know the practices to the present suit or either of them?

A. I know Letchworth and Bartle.

Q. Were or were you not formerly a surveyor in the employment of the United States?

A. I am one of the Commissioners of the Land Office at St. Helena Court House.

Q. If you, or did you ever use the lines of a tract of land confirmed by the land commissioners to Alexander Faircloth?[1]

A. I know of no claims in the name of Bartle and wife in the district to Thomas Spell. There are two claims confirmed: one a derivative title for a donation of 640 arpents, the other in the name of Thomas Spell for 360 arpents in the Parish of St. Tammany and reference being had to these papers or to the surveyor's plat of the same will give more definite information on the subject of the location than I can until the township plans are returned to this office.

Q. Where was said land located?

A. The claim of Thomas Spell for 360 arpents that stands confirmed in this office is definitely bounded on the original plat now in possession of the heirs.

In cross-interrogation, Mr. Whitten says his knowledge arose from the list of confirmations in Commissioners Office where he is one of them. Attorney Hennen, for Bartle, the defendants, dispensed with any other proof of the official character of this witness.

Filed on April 15, 1828, was the map and field notes made by David B. Morgan, St. Tammany Parish Surveyor, dated 27 and 28 September 1827, for the 8th District Court with regard to the suit titled Court Case No. 225.

The first trial ended in October 1825 with an appeal made to the Superior Court of Louisiana by Elizabeth Bartle through her attorney Alfred Hennen. No action with regard to this suit was taken until September 24, 1828, when the Honorable Clark Woodrooff, Judge and

Justice of the Peace, and a resident in the County of Adams, State of Mississippi, was appointed for the purpose of hearing the suit between Letchworth and Wife, the plaintiffs, *vs* Bartle and Wife, the defendants. Continuation of the second trial was set to begin during the October Term of the year 1828.[2]

On Saturday, October 4, 1828, Deputy Sheriff James Daniel went to General David B. Morgan's house in Madisonville to serve him with a subpoena for the forthcoming trial. Mr. Morgan was not home at the time of delivery, but later during the day, Sheriff Daniel ran into him. He was told by General Morgan that it would be impossible for him to comply with the subpoena since he had scheduled a business trip to Pensacola to meet with his brother-in-law, Jean Baptiste Baham, (Marie Constance's brother).[3] Morgan's intent was to develop a brickyard. He needed to purchase the Baham property, a tract of land situated south of Ponchitolawa Creek on the east bank of the Tchefuncte River.

Jean Baptiste Baham, familiar with the brick-making industry, removed earlier to Escambia County, Florida, to compete in the fast growing brick industry. The U.S. Navy facilities in New Orleans were closed, in 1823, and were relocated to Pensacola. The city had a fine harbor and, for this reason, the government made it a naval depot. The U.S. government was building a major facility in the area and needed all the bricks it could obtain from suppliers. Several major forts were to be built in the area, and because of the brick shortage, engineers had to make purchases as far away as New Orleans. Eventually the property purchased by General Morgan for the sum of $1,000.00 became known as Morgan's brickyard.[4] Seventy-five slaves worked there.[5]

Within a few years, Jean Baptiste Baham returned from Florida and, he too, operated a brickyard on the West bank of the Tchefuncte. The 1,600 acre tract of land was known as the Ferry Tract, today's present Flowers Estates.

On Wednesday, October 22, 1828, at the Claiborne Court House, Elizabeth Bartle being duly sworn deposes a statement through her attorney that Macklin Lloyd, a resident of St. Tammany Parish, has been subpoenaed as a witness for her case. "That the Sheriff reports the said witness to be sick and unable to attend court and, by that witness, this deponent intends to prove that the plaintiff, Mrs. Letchworth, declared that she had no claim to the land south of Ambrose's old field; that the defendants might cut wood down the land between said field and Lake Pontchartrain, to the west of Bartle's land, and that she, the plaintiff, could not and would not make any objections thereto. That this testimony is material without the benefit thereof this deponent cannot safely go to trial, as deponent does not know that she can prove the whole of the same parts by any other witness. This affidavit was not made for delay. That Lloyd's testimony can be obtained if time is granted for the purpose. That due diligence has been to obtain the attendance of Lloyd as a witness."

This statement was sworn before James B. McCoy, District Deputy Clerk, in open court on October 22, 1828. It was signed by Elizabeth Bartle with an X, her usual mark.

On the same day, the plaintiffs offered evidence of the title under which they claim the land in their petition mentioned. To the introduction of this evidence the defendants objected because, under the pleadings, the same could not be given in evidence for no allegations of the titles having been set forth therein. But the court overturned this objection and admitted evidence of title to which decision the council for defendants "excepted." Know this by "bill of exceptions" signed in open court by L. Esmault, Judge of the 4th District, holding sessions in the 8th District.[6] When the counsel for the plaintiffs offered to give evidence, the following documents were presently on file, to wit: Report of Commissioners dated 19 January 1820 for a section of land in favor of Zachariah Faircloth, marked A.

The order of survey dated 11 March 1825, marked B.

The survey of David B. Morgan dated 27 August 1825, marked C.

The appraisement and inventory of the estate of Thomas Spell, marked D.

The Certificate of the parish Judge marked E, and the proceedings before the parish Judge for putting Martha Faircloth, the wife of plaintiff, in possession of the estate of Zachariah Faircloth; also the proceedings before the Parish Judge adjudging the estate of Thomas Spell to his widow.

Counsel Hennen objected on the ground that it was illegal and irrelevant testimony and inadmissible. But the court permitted the demand to go to the Jury, and to this decision the counsel for defendants excepted. This, his bill for exception, was signed in open court by L. Esmault, Judge of the 4th District, holding sessions in the 8th District.[7]

A commission to take testimony was directed to John A. Ragan on the 24th day of October 1828. By those present, Ragan was given the authority to diligently examine all witnesses in the suit of Letchworth and Wife, plaintiffs, and Bartle and Wife, defendants, as well on the part of the plaintiffs as of the said defendants. Therefore "we desire you at a certain time and place by you to be appointed for that purpose you cause the said Witness to come before you; that you then and there examine said witness upon his corporal oath first taken before

254

you upon the Holy Evangelists; that you reduce his examination to writing and when you shall to have taken it, that you send the same closed up under your seal to us in our said District Court at the Court House in said parish without delay and have them there this writ."

Commission to take testimony was witnessed by the Hon. L. Esmault, Judge of the 4th District Court, holding sessions in and for the Parish of St. Tammany, this 24th day of October 1828.

An original document dated February 24, 1816, filed in the Court of Probates, stated that on that day, John Spell sold and conveyed to Sanders Spell all his rights and title and claim to a certain parcel of land containing four hundred acres, more or less, lying on the north side of Lake Pontchartrain and bounded south by the said lake, west by Madam O'Brian's now occupied by Jacob Bartle, north by vacant lands and east by Uriah Smith being the tract of land whereon Mrs. Elizabeth Spell, widow of the late Thomas Spell, now resides for and consideration of five hundred dollars paid in hand cash. "The receipt being acknowledged before the signing and delivery of these presents which said tract of land I do hereby warrant and defend unto the said Sanders and his legal representatives from my heirs."[8] Executed in the State of Louisiana. The foregoing document was certified as a true copy of the original petition and order on file in the Court of Probates by Jesse R. Jones, Parish Judge, who affixed the seal of his office on the 24th day of October 1828.

On Thursday, October 23, 1828, Mr. John Lanier sworn to say whether General Morgan is gone to Pensacola or not says he thinks he is. When did he go? In cross-examination, he replied: "Last Sunday, week was 8 days from Sunday."

Renez Baham introduced as evidence and asked whether General Morgan had gone to Pensacola, says he did not know, but thought he had. He did not see him start, but had seen him on Wednesday last and was told by Mr. Morgan that he should start as soon as the mail arrived. He believes the mail arrives at Madison on Wednesdays. He was not told when he would return.

Mr. Raymond, presently living at Madisonville, says that he saw General Morgan last Sunday, 19 October.[9] General Morgan told him that he had received a letter informing him it was necessary for him to go to Pensacola and that he would be going to New Orleans to take passage for that place. He saw him go on board the vessel.

James Daniels, examined, says that he is the Sheriff of the Parish. He went to Morgan's home to deliver a subpoena for him to be present at the court house. That shortly after, on the same day, he met the General who told him he would be unable to attend. On October 23rd, he called at the house of General Morgan and inquired of his daughter if the General was home. She said he was gone to Pensacola, and believed he had left home last Sunday. This corresponds to the information given by Mr. Ramon.

General Morgan's former testimony is allowed to be read in this case by the Court, followed by the previous testimony of John Edwards which is also read by the Court. In cross-examination by Counsel Hennen, John Edwards noted that he knew nothing of the corner boundaries of the tracts and neither knew of the Goodby tract in controversy. He was there when Mr. Guillemard made the survey of the Goodby tract and that he saw the corner post then put up, and they existed many years afterwards to his knowledge.[10]

Edwards states that Freeman George's house was near the line, but he doesn't know on which side it was situated. He explains to the court that Mr. Guillemard, the Spanish surveyor, came to run his father's tract, including the whole of the lines of that tract. He first run the front of the Geoffigon tract giving the bearings, then the Smith tract, then the Spell tract in front giving the bearings. He did not enclose the lines as far as he knew. He then runs round the tract of Mr. Francis Meeks which has since proved to be the O'Brian tract.[11] He thinks there were nine arpents in front. He knows of no other survey to the westward to his knowledge. A few days later, Guillemard made the Goodby survey. Edwards says Guillemard may have made other surveys but he has no knowledge of any. He remembers Guillemard coming here but once, but that he may have been here before and afterward.

When they went on the Goodby tract, he was in the company of Mr. Guillemard. Said Edwards, "Mr. Guillemard was backward and forward two weeks more or less. He may have stayed three weeks." Edwards says the survey was made in 1798 or 1799 and he would not know Guillemard's handwriting.

John Edwards says he knew Freeman George, knew him when he lived on Chinchuba Bayou, on the east side, a short distance from where Mr. Faircloth lived. He first knew James Goodby who is the brother of Mrs. Bartle, the defendant in this suit. He then knew Thomas Spell living in the same house afterward and Freeman George who married Thomas Spell's daughter. Goodby lived there several years and did so when Guillemard made the survey. Doesn't know Faircloth's of his having any Spanish survey, but might have had one. He knows Ambrose's old field and saw Faircloth cultivating a part of it raising

256

corn, 6, 8, or 10 acres. This field lies southerly of the house where Letchworth now lives.

John Edwards was not able to say when the bark was cut but asked for the price of the bark to Sanders Spell. Witness states that Thomas Spell left several children at his death, that some of them are now residing in this parish.

Witness says that Thomas, the former attorney general for the Territory of Orleans, and his wife, lived in the house where Freeman George had lived. Thinks he has heard Mr. Faircloth speak of a British grant to Ambrose but the particulars of the conversation, he does not know. He never heard of any opposition to Freeman George's building his house there or of enclosures or cultivating the land made by Faircloth or any other person.

In cross-examination by Branch W. Miller for the plaintiffs, Edwards says there was a little branch that ran between George's house and Faircloth's house. That on one side of the branch next to George, Faircloth had a Negro that lived there. There was a fence between the Negro's house and the Goodby house. Mr. Faircloth had erected fences and pens around his house as other farmers. That he never knew Mr. George, Mr. Goodby, Mr. Spell or Mr. Thomas to cultivate the land in controversy southerly to Faircloth's house.

The house that Mr. Goodby made was of round logs and the house that Mr. George lived was built with trim logs. He knew the place when Mr. George and Mr. Richardson were living on it. He had a farm and was cultivating it. He has known Mr. Faircloth to live on the same opening and cultivated it. He believes for the convenience of walk, he built another house on the same opening. Mrs. Faircloth resided there after Faircloth's death, and that she and Mr. Letchworth continued to reside upon it after their marriage. Edwards states that he never knew any person to cultivate on the disputed land to the southerly of Faircloth's house except Richardson, Faircloth, and the Letchworths. Mrs. Letchworth was the daughter of Richardson, and that she always lived on the place since Faircloth lived on the place. He does not recollect whether the Goodby tract or the Richardson tract was first settled.

Edwards, questioned by Hennen for the defendants, says that he knew Henry Sodon and his mother living on the lake west towards the tract called "Paradise."

Then, questioned by Miller for the plaintiffs, Edwards says that Henry Sodon lived 3 or 4 hundred yards from the improvement of Paradise. It may have been more or less.

Major John Baham's testimony was introduced by the counsel for the plaintiffs and read to the court and jury.

Questioned by Hennen, the defendant's counsel, witness says he knew the father of Thomas Spell, who was John Spell, who lived and cultivated land between the Castein Bayou and Chinchuba. There were no other persons living there except his family and the Edwards family that he knew of, and that he passed there frequently at that time.

Lawrence Sticker's former testimony was introduced and read by the plaintiffs. He says that Jacob Bartle's tract of land as run by the plat of General Morgan now filed, and marked A, runs to the eastern of Ambrose's old field and in sight of the opening that crosses the field now grown up with bushes and saplings and small trees. The line, which runs to the large live oak, runs to the eastward of the place where Sodon lived and does not touch any part of the improvement. Richardson made a turnip patch there and cultivated the place before Sodon went there. The line does not go in sight of it.

Witness Sticker thinks that Sodon only made corn there one year on this turnip patch of Mr. Richardson's. He supposes that it was in 1809. Mr. Sodon followed the lake after that year and never lived there afterwards. Witness has never known it to be cultivated since that period. Sticker says he married a daughter of Richardson, the sister of Mrs. Letchworth.

Mr. William Sharp is called and sworn to answer questions by the attorney for the defense. Sharp's former testimony was read by the plaintiff's attorney. There were no explanations given as to why only a part of that testimony was found.

Questioned by Miller for the plaintiffs, Sharp says he married a daughter of the defendant by her former husband. When he was first married, he built a house on what was said to be the Goodby tract. Whether it was on it or not, he does not know. He settled on it by permission of his mother-in-law. He supposed that he was building that house on the Goodby tract at that time and that he had no intention of building on any other tract, and that he had no intention of taking possession of any other tract of land but the Goodby one, and that he did not know the lines.

He was a chain carrier when Mr. Whitten, the United States surveyor, run the lines of that tract, and found his house to fall upon the Faircloth tract, agreeable to that survey, and that his house was 70 or 80 yards from the line. He had a conversation with Mr. Letchworth on the subject of his house and, in reply, was told that he might stay there as long as he wanted to, and when he left the place, he left Letchworth there.

In reply to Hennen's question, Sharp said he never had this conversation with Letchworth until after Whitten's survey which he believes was subsequent to the institution of this suit. Witness says Mrs. Bartle has eleven children living, and two or three are still minors.

He does not know of any previous surveys made previous to the survey of 1825, but witnessed General Morgan's. With regard to the date o the survey, he does not have the learning to remember the days, months and years.

Witness says he saw a Mr. Gibson living at the place where he last lived; say two or three months ago. That Mr. Letchworth has not cultivated the place since I left it and never resided in the house to my knowledge. Witness says he has no fear of being sued by Letchworth for his residence on the place above mentioned. Examination closed.

On Friday, October 24, 1828, Joseph Sharp's former evidence is read by plaintiff's counsel, Branch W. Miller. Under oath, Joseph Sharp said he was brought up from a child by Mr. Faircloth and lived as his family. He has always resided in the neighborhood since a child. He was well acquainted with Mr. Thomas Spell, was frequently at his house, has seen the Negros of Mrs. Bartle cutting wood frequently for two or three years at the west of the O'Brian tract, but cannot specify which years they were. He cannot state that he saw them cut any wood there in the year 1824, neither in the year 1825 or either of those years.

He has seen an improvement, about one quarter of a mile from the lake, made by Mr. Thomas Spell at the west of the O'Brian tract. He has seen the big live oak tree on the lake marked with X111 being the same to which General Morgan ran a line to the west of the Bartle tract. He thinks the line was a little eastward of the improvement, not more than 30 or 40 yards. He has no recollection of Thomas Spell ever making any claim to the land west of the Bartle tract; that he was young when Thomas Spell died in the year 1815. He recollects Thomas Spell, the son of Mrs. Bartle, cutting bark to the westward of the Bartle tract at the time Mr. Berry was overseer, which was before she married to Jacob Bartle.[12] Thomas Spell was shipping bark for more than a week, perhaps two. He had with him three or four hands, and they passed by his house every morning. He was living at the time at Jacob Bartle's place. This was during the life time of Faircloth that he passed by accidentally and saw them at work stripping bark.

He does not remember ever seeing Faircloth passing by and seeing Spell at work stripping bark, but no doubt Faircloth both saw and knew of it. He believes there was only one cart employed in carrying the bark; he knows that the bark was carried off from the land, and frequently hauled rails from there and passed by the house of Jacob Bartle. He never heard of Faircloth and Spell having any difficulty about their cutting wood or working on this land. He never heard of Faircloth state to Spell or any of the family that he claimed the land where they were cutting wood, except the time, subsequently, which he has already mentioned. Joseph Sharp never knew or heard of Mr. Faircloth having any permission to settle there either from the Spanish, British, or American Government, and he never heard him to have any title to his land from the Spanish or British Government.

Examination in chief resumed, Joseph Sharp says the improvement was about one half acre, more or less cut down into brush crops, no cabins on it, and can't say that any of the Spell's family ever lived there, and thinks it never was enclosed. It was in Thomas Spell's life time. He knew Thomas Spell to have lived in two different places: one was where Mrs. Bartle now lives and the other at Chinchuba. At the time of his death, Mr. Spell was residing at the place where Mrs. Bartle now lives, at the eastward of the O'Brian tract. The heirs of Thomas Spell continued to reside on that tract after his death, and have continued to reside there ever since, excepting as some of them grew up and went off. The Chinchuba tract is the same known by the name of the Goodby tract.

Questioned by Plaintiff's Counsel Miller: Did or did not Mr. Faircloth after the confirmation of the Land Commissioners say that he had a right to all the land marked on Morgan's map between the heirs of Bartle and Labatut's tract? Sharp answered: "I think he did."

This question is excepted to by the defendant's counsel.

Cross-examination resumed. Mr. Sharp says that Thomas Spell died at the Navy Yard on Tchefuncte River and was buried at the place marked D on Morgan's map.[13] The family of Mrs. Spell was residing in Covington while her husband resided at the navy yard. They came there to attend him on his death bed.

Joseph Sharp says, to his knowledge, that Spell never cultivated the land, but he saw a fig tree growing there, which tree does not grow in this Parish without being planted. As a witness he has heard Mrs. Bartle and her heirs claim the land since the death of their father and long prior to the said deliberations of this suit. He has heard Joseph Spell, one of the heirs of Thomas Spell say quite frequently that the land was intended for him, but none of the other heirs. This statement is excepted to by the plaintiff's counsel.

Joseph Sharp has seen the oak tree west of Jacob Bartle's tract marked on General Morgan's map, seen ever since he can remember. It has had the mark of an X on it ever since. He can remember the 111, but he does not recollect to have ever remarked prior to General Morgan's survey. These 111's appear to have been made a great while ago from the looks of them.

Examination in chief resumed. Joseph Sharp says there is but one grave yard on the Goodby tract, and two on the Faircloth tract. Mr. Spell was buried in the grave yard in the Goodby tract nearest to the Chinchuba Creek, which he supposes to be about 60 or 70 yards from the creek.[14]

Cross-examination of Joseph Sharp resumed by Hennen for the defendants. There is now a man by the name of Gibson who lives in the house built in a field where his brother William Sharp formerly lived, a little south of the field where Freeman George lived. This place was enclosed when he last saw it.

Joseph Sharp says he carried the chain for General Morgan when he surveyed the tract west of the Jacob Bartle tract and carried the chain from the northwest corner post of the Bartle tract all around to the live oak tree on the lake. Went north of all the fields and houses which he has above stated to be on the Goodby tract which takes in all the fields and houses except a small piece to the west. They crossed the creek Chinchuba on running this line twice, once running west and once running south in running the north line from the east to west. At the northwest corner of this tract they came within 150 or 200 yards of Thomas Spell Junior's field where he now lives. This line takes in the burying ground where Thomas Spell is buried. Examination closed.

The former evidence of Henry Cooper Senior is introduced and read by counsels for the plaintiffs. In reply to Hennen's question, Cooper says the tree which Mr. Thomas Spell pointed to was a pine tree at the corner of the Goodby tract and the O'Brian tract.

Q. Did Mr. Spell ever show you the lines between Mr. Faircloth and Himself?

A. He showed me the lines of the Goodby tract, a pine tree standing near to a dry Branch where the spring which Mrs. Cloth uses empties into this Goodby tract. I suppose was the tract which Spell then claimed as I understood from him that he had purchased it.

Q. How far was this corner to the north of Faircloth's house?

A. It stood to the eastward and it run to the westward the way he pointed for the line and it run by either by Lewis House or shop, I cannot say which; this house was a little house which Mr. Cloth or his Negro built over the Branch.

Q. How far to the North of Faircloth's house did this line run?

A. It run near and the line appeared to divide the interval between the openings of Spell and Faircloth.

In cross-examination, Miller asked:

Q. By who did Spell state that this line was run?
A. I do not know. I understood that they were old British lines.

Examination closed.

General Morgan's former testimony is introduced and read by plaintiff's counsel. The plaintiffs now offered a document that had been heretofore introduced and filed by the defendants to wit: "a certificate of the land survey marked a confirmation of 400 acres land to Jacob Bartle."

General Morgan was introduced by the plaintiffs and was called on the part of the plaintiffs under an agreement of counselors that all documents on file were to be considered as read to the jury, subject to all legal certificates whether filed by plaintiffs or defendants. The defendants introduce Melon's survey which the plaintiffs "excepted to".

Uriah Smith's former testimony is introduced and read by the defendants. In reply to Alfred Hennen's question, Uriah Smith says that Thomas Spell resided on a British grant tract. He knew him except for a short time, and believes he resided on the Goodby tract. Uriah also states that he knew John Spell, a brother of Thomas, who lived in the pine woods. He believes that he might have lived for some time on that British grant. He believes that John Spell died before Thomas. He thinks that William McDermott died since his return from New York. He cannot say whether Richardson or Goodby settled first on the Chinchuba. He recollects a field called Ambrose's old field when he was quite young. He knew a family by the name of Ambrose who were good hunters but lived here and there. He never knew of any man by the name of Ambrose living on the old field. Examination closed.

Testimony of John Edwards is read by the defense. Witness says that Thomas Spell Jr. showed him a place where he intended to live to the west of O'Brian's line and near the lake since the survey was made by General Morgan. He went to see the live oak mentioned in the plat as the corner. It bears the ordinary mark of a corner tree being marked with a chop and three chops. He says the statement by Spell, of his intentions of living on the tract, was made six or eight years before his death. This spot was about a quarter of a mile south of Ambrose's old field. He and Spell were hunting hogs and Spell went and showed him the spot described where he intended to live. He remembers Faircloth, north of Ambrose's old field and south of where Faircloth lived, when he remarked to Faircloth it was a pity his land did not extend to the lake. Faircloth told him there was land enough between where they were and his house for him during his life time. He did not wish any after his death. This question he put to Faircloth in consequence of the statement made by Spell of his intention to settle the land heretofore described. Faircloth has no heirs within his knowledge. This testimony was excepted by the plaintiffs counsel, Branch W. Miller. Cross examination: William McDermott died before the invasion.[15]

The former testimony of Abraham Penn is introduced and read. Penn states that as he returned from making the survey he was pointed out Ambrose's old field by someone of the company in the presence of Mr. Letchworth. He says on the lines of Guillemard's plan filed on the 20th of October 1825: In this case the lines run 14 degrees west and that the two lines should be parallel if correct, and that they are undoubtedly incorrect as laid down in the plans of Guillemard.

Joseph Letchworth was with them when they discovered the marked oak tree before spoken of, and Letchworth said he did not believe that there was such a tree. He had never seen the marks on the tree before. Surveyors generally denoted this mark of a corner tree with an X and three 111. That mark would not have been made within 3 or 4 years from its appearance. Examination closed on the part of the defendants.

Plaintiff's counsel, Branch W. Miller, cross-examines Penn:

Q. Whenever surveyors mark out plats, is it not the usage to make out the new plat on the same seal?

A. It is.

Q. Will you please Mr. Penn calculate in a direct line the distance from Chinchuba Creek to Spell's lower tract as laid down by Guillemard's plan marked E as nearly as you can assuming the one line of the upper tract to be 400 perches?

A. There is a little difference in the difference on the two plans by not more than 10 or 15 perches on the plans of Guillemard.

In cross-examination, Uriah Smith says he never saw the mouth of the Chinchuba, but thinks it runs into a swamp on the lake.

William Bowman after being sworn says that he has been all along the lake from the O'Brian tract to the mouth of the Tchefuncte. He has crossed a place called the mouth of Chinchuba and crossed it without wetting his shoes, at other times it is up to his knees. It comes into the lake west of the Labatut tract, about one mile.

Bowman further states that he heard Mr. Joseph Sharp say after one of the trials of this cause that he had sold his 200 acres of land to Letchworth. That he might be a witness in this case, the 200 acres being part of the tract claimed by Letchworth. He further states that Sharp had his note for 200 dollars which he intends to make Letchworth pay or he says that he would not take back his land. Examination closed.

We have seen that Joseph Sharp was given, by donation, from his uncle Zachariah Faircloth, 200 acres bordering on the Bartle tract. Joseph Letchworth played a waiting game with Martha's nephew about buying his 200 acres. Possibly on the advice of their lawyer, the sale took place on the Saturday before the first trial in 1825. Without ownership of that land, the plaintiffs, Letchworth and his wife Martha, would have had no legal basis to launch a suit of trespass against Jacob Bartle and his wife.

John Powell, in cross-examination by Miller for the defense says he became acquainted with Mr. Faircloth about 17 years ago and saw him frequently afterwards. In a conversation he had with Faircloth sitting in his own house, Faircloth directed him to two trees at about forty yards distance from the house which he told me was where Mrs. Ambrose lived. Testimony closed for the present.

John Sodon is sworn in, and in cross-examination by the defense says he went on the tract of land by permission of William McDermott which is about ¼ of a mile to the edge of the Labatut tract. This was in 1808. He cleaned it up and built a house and made a crop on it. He says he does not know such a place as Chinchuba Bayou. He has seen a little area by that name. At times you may cross it dry foot, other times waist deep. While living there Faircloth came past and asked by what permission he was working there. He told Faircloth that William McDermott told him to go there. Faircloth told him that it had been claimed by John Richardson.

In cross-examination by Hennen, Sodon says the nearest part of the Chinchuba Creek was ¼ of a mile to where he lived or a little better. No swamp lay between where he lived and the lake. He thinks the stream before spoken of is 2 miles more or less from the place he lived.

The evidence given at this court is now closed on the side of both parties. The members of the jury were next charged by Judge L. Emault, attending judge, in the eighth district. After due deliberations by the jury, judgment is rendered in favor of Joseph and Martha Letchworth. Elizabeth Bartle brought this down on herself and she would have to pay a heavy price for her actions.

On October 25, 1828, in the office of the 8th District Court, Elizabeth Bartle, once again, not satisfied with the outcome of the verdict, by her attorney Alfred Hennen, immediately files a petition of appeal from the final judgment that had just been rendered against her in the suit. The appeal reads as follows:

"At the trial of this cause, the defendant's counsel requested the court to charge the jury: that the plaintiffs had no such legal possession of the premises claimed by them, prior to the putting of the widow of Z. Faircloth in possession of his estate by the Parish Judge, as to enable them to maintain any action of trespass done to the same prior to such possession.

That prior to the order of the Parish Judge to put the widow in possession of Faircloth's estate, she had no legal title thereto - that an actual and legal quick possession of property is necessary to maintain an action of trespass.

That until a survey of land granted by the American government as a donation for settlement right, under the Act of Congress of the 3 March 1819, has been made through an authorized surveyor, the donee has no right to maintain an action of trespass committed on any part directly not in the actual possession of the donee. That such donee's possession could only extend to the portion of the land in his actual possession prior to a survey by an authorized surveyor under the donation from the land commissioners; that without a location by the surveyor no boundaries could be claimed by the donee. That the location is necessary for the donee to maintain an action of trespass; that the title to a donation is not complete so as to maintain an action of trespass until after a survey of location of the claim.

That is there is a claim to land under the second section of the Act of 3 March 1819 filed before the Commissioner's, no donation could be made under the third section of the same land claimed by another individual to the person claiming under the third section. That if a person claims land under the second section of the Act of 3 March 1819, the same land cannot be granted as a donation to another person claiming the land under the third section.

That an action of trespass could not be sustained by the heirs of the person against whom it was committed at the time of instituting this suit; that when this suit was instituted an action of trespass did not pass against or to the heirs of anyone.

But this charge the court refused to give, whereon before the jury retired the counsel for defendants excepted to the charge, and this, his bill of exception thereto is now signed in open court of 25 October 1828."[16]

The court charged the jury that the legal document, resulting of, was a good title and was sufficient to maintain an action of trespass.

Alfred Hennen wrote to the Honorable Judge of the District Court of the 8th Judicial District with regard to the petition of Elizabeth Bartle: "The petition shows that she was advised there was an error in the judgment of the Court in the suit instituted by Letchworth and Wife vs. Bartle and Wife. That she is aggrieved thereby and therefore prays an appeal to offer security to stay execution."

It was agreed that the appeal would be returnable on the first Monday of January 1829. The record of appeal was to consist of the proceedings, papers and evidence only on file since the last appeal now in the Supreme Court to form a supplement to said record of appeal. All the original plans of papers required by either party may be sent up to the Supreme Court on the appeal.

L. Delisle is accepted as security on the appeal for twenty-five dollars to stay execution. Petition was signed by Attorney Hennen on October 25, 1829. A copy sent to W. Ripley, Attorney for the plaintiffs.

Endorsed, the appeal is allowed returnable for the first Monday in January next 1829. Delisle is received as security. The appellant Elizabeth Bartle is to give security with said Delisle as security for twenty-five dollars to stay execution, 25th October 1828. Endorsement was signed by Judge L. Esmault, Judge of the 4th District, holding service in 8th District. Document was filed on the 25th of October 1828.

James B. Coy, Deputy Clerk, certified that the foregoing was a true copy of the original petition and affixed his seal of office on November 10, 1828.

The citation was recorded by James Daniels, sheriff, on November 10, 1828, and served the same day with defendant's petition to each of the plaintiffs, Letchworth and wife. They were advised that Elizabeth Bartle, by her attorney, filed on the 25th of October 1828 in the office of the 8th District Court a petition of appeal from the final judgment rendered in the said Court against her, in their suit. The appeal was returnable in the Supreme Court of the State of Louisiana on the first Monday of January 1829. They are cited to appear in person or by attorney in the said Court on the last aforesaid to answer to the said appeal. Witness, the Honorable C. Woodruff, Judge of the 8th District Court on November 10, 1828.

This appeal by Elizabeth Bartle claiming an error in the October trial would be the final event in her legal battle in fighting the Letchworths. It was scheduled to take place on the first Monday of January 1829. Would Elizabeth's determination and stubbornness in winning her case make her the author of her own misfortune?

NOTES

1. Alexander is possibly the middle name of Zachariah Faircloth.
2. Clark Woodruff was officially appointed Judge of the 8th District on April 14, 1828. He replaced Judge Henry H. Pattillo who was deceased by December 15, 1827.
3. "Brickyard, Profession and Morgan History," *St. Tammany Historical Society Gazette*, Madisonville Issue, Volume 4, March 1980.
4. Boagni, Ethel, *Mandeville, Louisiana*, St. Tammany Historical Society, 25.
5. Ibid., 25.
6. Filed October 24, 1828, by James B. McCoy, Deputy Clerk.
7. Filed on October 24, 1828, by James B. McCoy, Deputy Clerk.
8. Court of Probates, Judge Jesse R. Jones, October 24, 1828.
9. Mr. Raymond is identified as Juan Ramon, an immigrant from Spain, who arrived in Madisonville in 1819. He had property on the river front, and later was a store owner. He died July 5, 1855, leaving considerable property.
10. James Goodby lived on his tract from 1790 until 1798 or 1799.
11. The O'Brian tract was registered with Carlos Trudeau, the Spanish surveyor, in 1788. Francis Meeks settled on already claimed land. This shows that Abel Geoffigon's tract started in back of Morris Smith's tract.
12. After the death of her husband, Elizabeth Goodby hired a Mr. Berry to be her overseer. This would have been between the years 1815-1819.
13. The grave yard on the Goodby tract today is the Sharp, Spell, Strain graveyard and a historical site for Mandeville.
14. The grave yard on the Goodby tract today is known as the Tom Spell Memorial Cemetery, also known previously as the Chinchuba Cemetery. The Cemetery is located approximately one half mile from the intersection of Louisiana Highway 22. On U.S. 190, turn right on Chinchuba Cemetery road.
15. Reference made to the War of 1812 and the Battle of New Orleans in 1815.
16. The document was signed by L. Esmault, Judge in the 4th District, holding service in 8th district, on October 25, 1828.

CHAPTER 19

APPEAL BY ELIZABETH BARTLE GOES AWRY

On January 3, 1829, the Honorable Clark Woodrooff (sic), Judge of the District Court, St. Tammany Parish, commanded Sheriff James Daniels that he demand from Elizabeth Bartle the sum of twenty five cents debt, plus six hundred and nine dollars and fifty eight and a half cents costs for a judgment in which Joseph Letchworth and wife recovered in the Court House of the 8th district in October 1825. Should she not pay the same then he, as Sheriff, was given the authority to cause the said sum to be made of the real estate, or the slaves of Elizabeth Bartle, in the succession of her husband, the late Jacob Bartle, when they were joint owners on the 25th day of October 1825. His duty, as Sheriff, was to have the monies before the said Court in order to render judgment on the 6th day of April 1829.[1] Added were the Sheriff's costs of $100.00 to be received by February 21, 1829.

That same day, Judge Woodrooff (sic) commanded Sheriff James Daniels with a writ, to collect the amount of money above-mentioned and to appear in court with the money and writ in order to render for the judgment aforesaid on the twenty-third day of April 1829, and the 53rd year of the independence of the United States.[2]

Received on Wednesday, February 4, 1829, were the costs owed by Elizabeth Bartle: debt of twenty-five cents and costs exclusive of sheriff's costs amounted to one thousand and nine dollars and fifty-eight and a half cents.

What follows is that Elizabeth Bartle, not satisfied with the court's verdict given on February 26, 1829, filed in the Clerk's Office a petition of appeal from the final judgment rendered in the District Court against her in which appeal was returnable in the Supreme Court of the State of Louisiana on the first Monday of April next. Because of this appeal, Joseph Letchworth and his wife were cited to appear in person or by attorney on Monday, April 6, 1829, to answer to the said appeal.[3]

Unexpectedly, Elizabeth Bartle's appeal hits a snag! Clerk LeBreton, of the Louisiana Supreme Court, certified by letter dated February 14, 1829, that no record of the proceedings held in the district court for the eighth judicial district in the suit of Joseph and Martha Letchworth, plaintiffs, and Elizabeth Bartle, defendant, had been filed in his office. At the bottom of the missive was a note requesting $1.59 for costs. This certificate of the clerk of the Supreme Court was filed on the 19th of February by Samuel Mallory, Clerk for the 8th District.

Elizabeth Bartle, not the subdued type of person, blames the deputy clerk, Samuel Mallory, for failing to get her transcripts to the Louisiana Supreme Court. Why so inefficient? Was Mallory purposely trying to sabotage her case in favor of Joseph Letchworth and his wife? Her complaint is addressed to the Honorable Judge Clark Woodrooff through her attorney, Alfred Hennen, who requests action on behalf of his client:

"Elizabeth Bartles defendant in this case respectfully bequeaths to your honor that at a session of the District Court for this parish held last October, she obtained of the honorable court the benefit of an appeal to the Supreme Court, and the said Honorable Court ordered, and demanded that the transcripts in said suit should be transmitted to said Supreme Court by January last. Your petitioner further more represents to your honor, that she applied in due time, and several times by herself or persons acting by her directions, but owing to illness or other indisposition in the person of the clerk of your honorable court, she failed in the attempt to have said transcripts before the Honorable Supreme Court of this State in the time prescribed by this Honorable Court.

Therefore your petitioner prays for a new order for said transcripts to be sent to the Supreme Court, and your petitioner will forever pray." The complaint is signed by Elizabeth Bartle who uses her usual mark, an X.

Judge Woodrooff attested that Elizabeth Bartle who made oath in his presence attested that all the material facts set forth in the foregoing petition were true, and that the appellant made her mark in his presence on February 25, 1829.

Underneath Elizabeth's attestation Judge Woodrooff wrote: "Let the appeal be made returnable to the Supreme Court on the first Monday of April next."[4]

To Elizabeth's advantage, Judge Jesse R. Jones formally accuses the court clerk of the 8th judicial district of being drunk and not filing the appeal made by Elizabeth Bartle. Sworn on the part of the defendants, the Honorable Judge says "that Samuel Mallory, the clerk of the District Court, has for the last six months been in a state of intoxication for two thirds of the time. He had two deputies and has always found them ready to attend to any business in the office which he required."[5]

Mr. Delisle, also sworn, says that he called on Mr. Mallory several times to make out the appeal in the case. He, as a witness, acted as agent of Mrs. Bartle, and told Mr. Mallory, the clerk, that Mrs. Bartle wanted to pay him. He expressed himself satisfied and never asked for money from her for the costs. After the first of January, Mr. Mallory had told him, the witness, that they would have to apply for a new order of appeal as the return day had passed.[6]

Likely exhausted and fed up with all the court delays experienced since 1825, plus the appeal now granted to Mrs. Bartle, Joseph Letchworth somehow manages to get a writ of execution of the judgment from Samuel Mallory, the Deputy Clerk. Sheriff James Daniels and Joseph Letchworth, who now has an edge over Elizabeth Bartle, venture out to Elizabeth's home to seize four of her slaves.

Elizabeth Bartle, in an avenging spirit, now complains that even though she appealed the last court decision, Joseph Letchworth and wife Martha obtained a "writ of execution" from clerk Samuel Mallory to seize some of her slaves. Events have now turned ugly, not only for Elizabeth, but mainly for the poor innocent slaves who will have to sit in jail until auctioned off at a sale advertised to be held on April 7. But, we have to give Mrs. Bartle some credit for reacting to the most unusual of situations. She needs her slaves, and she expects to have them returned to her!

On March 10, 1829, Elizabeth petitions the court to get back her slaves that were "seized illegally" by Sheriff James Daniels and Joseph Letchworth. Her petition shows that during the last October term a judgment was rendered against her, the petitioner, in favor of Joseph Letchworth and his wife Martha Letchworth. She regularly appealed from the said judgment and that pending the appeal, Letchworth and wife applied to Samuel Mallory, the clerk of the honorable court for the Parish of St. Tammany and "obtained from him a writ of execution against the property of your petitioner." That James Daniels, the Sheriff under this writ of execution, illegally seized and took in his possession four Negro slaves belonging to her. To wit, Abraham a black man aged about forty-five, Bishop a black boy aged about 12 years, Sarah a Negro woman aged about forty years and her child aged about six months.

"Petitioner further avers that the said writ of execution was null and void and was wrongfully and illegally issued by the clerk aforesaid and the sheriff aforesaid was not justifiable in executing the same because it was issued contrary to the provisions contained in the articles 589 & 590 of the code of practice. Petitioner further states that she has sustained damages from the trespass of the said Letchworth and wife and said James Daniels to the amount of two thousand dollars in as much as the four slaves have been illegally taken out of the possession of your petitioner which she could not hire the same as she had done at the rate of nineteen dollars per month, for the slaves Abraham and Bishop. Petitioner further avers that the health and character of said

270

slaves have been deteriorated by the illegal acts of said James Daniels and Letchworth and wife by imprisonment in the public jail of the parish all to the damage of your petitioner for two thousand dollars as aforesaid.

Petitioner further shows that said James Daniels has advertised for sale on the 7th day of April next and as your petitioner verily believes, he will sell the same unless prevented by an injunction. Therefore your petitioner prays that Joseph Letchworth and Martha Letchworth, his wife, and the Sheriff James Daniels all residing in the Parish of St. Tammany in the State of Louisiana be cited to appear and answer this petition and that after due proceedings of Law in this case had, they may be ordered by judgment to restore to your petitioner the said four slaves and to pay the sum of two thousand dollars damages sustained by your petitioner in consequence of the trespass aforesaid. Your petitioner also prays for an injunction against the sale aforesaid, and that in the meantime the said slaves may be delivered to us, and your petitioner prays for all other equitable relief and as in duty bound."[7] Signed by Elizabeth Bartle with her usual mark.

Labarthe Delisle, the agent of the plaintiff, being duly sworn doth depose and says that "all and singular the material allegations as the petition above contained were just and true." This statement was sworn and subscribed before Clark Woodrooff, Judge of 8th District, on March 10, 1829.

Elizabeth Bartle, through Counsel Hennen, had succeeded to put her point across to the Judge. The verdict: "Let an Injunction issue as prayed for upon the petitioner giving bond and security according to law." Signed by C. Woodrooff, 8th District, on March 10, 1829. The injunction issued and filed on March 18, 1829, by Court Clerk Samuel Mallory, is titled "Elizabeth Bartles *vs* James Daniels & Joseph Letchworth & Wife."

Following the injunction that was issued in her favor, Elizabeth Bartle had the following letter written by J. Evans and witnessed by Obed Kirkland, a merchant, and father-in-law of Judge Jesse R. Jones, Justice of the Peace. The letter was addressed to the State of Louisiana and the Parish of St. Tammany:

"Know all Men by these presents that we Elizabeth Bartle and Delisle Labarthe are held and firmly bound to Joseph Letchworth and Martha Letchworth, his wife, in the sum of one thousand and sixty three dollars and fifty cents for the payment of which will and truly to be made to the said Joseph Letchworth and Martha Letchworth, their heirs, executors, administrators or assigns, we bind ourselves, our heirs, executors, and assigns, jointly and firmly by these presents. In witness whereof we have hereunto subscribed this 18th day of March, A.D. 1829.

Whereas, the above bound Elizabeth Bartles has this day sued out from the 8th District Court held in and for the Parish of St. Tammany an Injunction for four Negro Slaves taken by execution from the said Elizabeth Bartles. Now if the said Elizabeth Bartles shall prosecute her said injunction with effect, or in default thereof shall pay all such damages as may be adjudged for the wrong suing thereof, then the above obligation to be void, else to remain in full force and virtue."[8]

To this letter, in my office, "In testimony whereof I have set may hand and affixed the seal of said Court this 19th day of March A.D., 1829," was signed by Wesley Mallory, Deputy Clerk.

The citation received on March 23, 1829, was served the same day by delivery of a copy with the Defendant's Petition to Martha Letchworth in person. It was signed by James Daniels, Sheriff.

On Wednesday, the 15th day of April 1829, James Daniels was commanded by Judge Clark Woodrooff to demand of Elizabeth Bartle the amount of money she was previously asked to remit in the judgment that had been rendered against her. These were to be before the court on Monday, June 20, 1829. The writ was witnessed by Wesley Mallory, Deputy Clerk.

The counsel for the plaintiffs, on that same day, April 15, moved for an execution against the defendants, but the same was opposed by counsel Hennen for Mrs. Bartle, defendant.

"Whereon the evidence offered by the defendants taken down by the judge and reading part of this bill of exception was heard. But the court over ruled the objections of the defendants and ordered the execution to pass.

Whereon the counsel for the defendant excepted to the opinion of the court, and this, his bill of exception thereto is signed in open court that it may appear of record."

Signed by Charles Bushnell, Judge of the 3rd District holding session in the 8th District.

Received April 15, 1829, and served on the same day, was an order levied on four slaves as the property of defendant named as follows: Abram 40 years of age, Bishop about 12 years, and Sally aged about 35 years and her child. "This Execution was satisfied by the Defendant having paid the cash." James Daniels, Sheriff.

Litigation fee: Debt of 25 cents; Cash exclusive of Sheriff's fees one thousand and nine dollars and fifty-eight and a half cents, Sherriff's costs one hundred dollars. Litigation was filed on the May 9, 1829, by Wesley Mallory, Deputy Clerk.

No official receipt issued in the name of Elizabeth Bartle was found in the court documents to show that she had paid the sum of money as above mentioned. The records come to a dead end about her injunction against Joseph Letchworth and Sheriff James Daniels for the illegal seizure of four slaves as was cited in the petition under sections 589 and 590 of the code of practice mentioned in her appeal. Was an agreement made to resolve the case out of court? Possibly! Was Elizabeth Bartle compensated for the illegal seizure of her slaves? We have no clue, as there were no records to attest as to what transpired in court on that day. Elizabeth Bartle had a case, so why did the procedures stop there? Our conclusion: there was no trial on record at the Court House. Having followed Elizabeth Bartle through four long years of litigations, we know she was not the type of person to torpedo her own pirogue. Somehow, it would have to be to her advantage!

Elizabeth Bartle always held firm to the belief that the land in dispute was hers because of her Spanish grant. The Zachariah Faircloth (Letchworth) property had originally been a British grant, and according to the old British survey, Faircloth first owned the parcel of land. But, the Goodby tract had been a Spanish tract, and according to the Spanish survey, Elizabeth Bartle now owned it. The quick sale of the two hundred acres by Joseph Sharp to Joseph Letchworth was sufficient to tip the scales in Letchworth's favor. But did the illegal seizure of the four slaves tip the scales in favor of Mrs. Bartle?

We are indeed fortunate to have copies of the many surveys made on the north shore of Lake Pontchartrain beginning with the early English period, the Spanish period with Gilberto Guillemard and Carlos Trudeau, followed by those made by the United States government in the mid 1820s when the old land grants were delineated and surveyed, according to the township system, by Whitten and Runnels, plus the two made by David Bannister Morgan for Court Case No. 225.

The picture of economic development in St. Tammany between 1820 and 1850 was one of constant growth and increasing prosperity. It came from her geographic location and her natural resources. Natural deposits of clay adjacent to navigable streams created the brick industry with David B. Morgan and John Baptiste Baham.

Elizabeth Bartle participated in the trend of depleting the limitless forest resources of the parish. She wasn't the only one, but with her slaves cutting wood, she too had relied on the economic dependence on trade with New Orleans. Economic progress equals population growth. Settlers were now coming in increasing numbers to Louisiana.

It was soon after the Letchworth-Bartle trial that Bernard Marigny de Mandeville, planter, politician, statesman, whose family once owned a third of New Orleans, conceived the idea of purchasing land along the lake shore and forest adjoining his property, the Fontainebleau plantation, until sufficient land had been acquired for his purpose, to have a town named in his honor.

Court Case No. 225 impacted on the small community located between Bayou Chinchuba and Bayou Castein. Some long standing friendships were shattered and wounds had to be healed. Sad in a way, since most families were related either by blood or marriage! A direct result of the changes brought to the community was that land was sold to satisfy the heirs in the successions of Jacob Bartle, Thomas Spell, Samuel Smith, and Morgan Edwards.

The social climate was set to destroy the community's integrity! It fitted in with the dream conceived by the ambitious Bernard de Marigny who, in 1829, turned his interests to land acquisition on the north shore of Lake Pontchartrain.

Grace King wrote that Marigny, the aristocratic gentleman, "was inspired to make a town as poets are inspired to make a poem. He gave himself over, as a poet should, to his muse, and she as a muse should, confided herself to him. Nature and art lent themselves kindly to the enterprise."[9]

The opportunity to buy land came with the successions that had to be settled. It was given to Marigny on a silver platter which he grabbed. From 1829 to 1831, he bought all the available land, some 2,856.4 acres, at approximately $4.06 per acre, at a cost of $11,600.00, on the north shore of Lake Pontchartrain.[10]

In 1834, he sought to subdivide a portion of the land he had acquired west of Bayou Castein. He drew up a town plan, had the land surveyed and auctioned off the lots in the new town he called Mandeville. The lots that were advertized in *The New Orleans Bee* would be conformed to the plan drawn by Louis Bringier, General Surveyor, on January 14, 1834.

NOTES

1. The Honorable Judge Clark Woodruff for the State of Louisiana 8th District Court in and for the Parish of St. Tammany, January 3, 1829.

2. Court Case No. 225, Louisiana 8th District, Costs exclusive of Sheriff fees received on February 21, 1829.

3. Citation to Joseph Letchworth and wife to appear in the 8th District Court by the Honorable C. Woodrooff dated March 23, 1829. Filed by Samuel Mallory, Deputy Clerk.

4. Signed by Clark Woodrooff, Judge of the 8th Judicial Court,

5. Attestation under oath of Jesse R. Jones with regard to Samuel Mallory dated February 25, 1829.

6. Mr. Delisle, agent for Mrs. Bartles, his mother-in-law, attests that he made contact with Samuel Mallory on February 25, 1829.

7. Petition of Elizabeth Bartles signed by her attorney Alfred Hennen on 10 March 1829.

8. Delisle de la Barthe signed as a witness to this letter on March 18, 1828.

9. King, Grace, *Creole Families of New Orleans*, Op. cit. 35 and 37.

10. Johnson, Clarence, L., from a map showing site of Mandeville bought by Bernard de Marigny in 1829-1831, *Louisiana Conservative Review*, Spring Issue, 1939, 25.

CHAPTER 20

THE PHILIPPE DE MARIGNY DE MANDEVILLE FAMILY

The history of the Philippe de Marigny de Mandeville family of Louisiana can be traced to a couple whose marriage is recorded in France: Pierre Philippe, Sieur de Marigny, married to Chrétienne Souart, about 1638, in the bishopric of Bayeux, Normandy.

Bayeux is a sub-prefecture of Calvados within the Lower Normandy region. It is located seven kilometers from the coast of La Manche (English Channel) and 30 kilometers north-west of Caen. The country is known for the Bayeux Tapestry which depicts the events leading up to the Norman Conquest of England. The tapestry was made to commemorate the events of the Conquest in 1066.

From the Marigny marriage to Catherine Souart was born a son named Jean-Vincent Philippe, Sieur du Hautmesny, who arrived in Montreal, in 1665, and was recorded there as 22 years of age in the 1667 census and 35 years in the 1681 census.

Chrétienne was the sister of Gabriel Souart (1611-1691) a Sulpician priest whose calling was a late one. Ordained in 1650, he came to New France in 1657 to minister to Ville-Marie.[1] He was the first parish priest of Montreal and superior of the Sulpician seminary, doctor in medicine which he practiced with permission while on missions, and schoolmaster. He also held the title of bachelor of canon law. He was priest of the parish of Ville-Marie during the settlement's most terrible years 1657-1666: the time of the exploits of Dollard des Ormeaux in 1660; and of the earthquake in 1663.[2] In his capacity as seigneur of Montreal Island, on December 26, 1665, Gabriel Souart created the arrière-fief of Hautmesny, between the St. Lawrence River and the Rivière des Prairies.[3] This corresponds with the arrival of his nephew Jean Vincent Philippe, Sieur du Hautmesny, on November 26, 1665.[4] The Hautmesnil concession was sold on December 4, 1687, to four teaching brothers.[5]

Father Souart invited his nephews and nieces to join him in New France. In 1681, Claude-Élizabeth Souart, Chrétienne's cousin, married Charles LeMoyne, seigneur and baron de Longueuil, the eldest brother of the Sieurs Iberville and Bienville. It is through this familial tie that the Marigny family became associated with the LeMoyne family.

Pierre Philippe, Jean Vincent's father, was ennobled as a member of the *Compagnie des Cents Associés* (the Company of One Hundred Associates) in 1654.[6] In the creation of this company, Cardinal Richelieu initiated an interesting and unique policy: any noble or ecclesiastic might join the company without prejudice to his order, and it was promised that twelve of the one hundred members would accede to the nobility.[7] Commerce might finally lead to nobility. The company was given the rights in perpetuity to all fur trading as well as a fifteen year monopoly on commerce, except fisheries, and was granted seigneurial rights to a vast domain that extended from Florida to the Arctic Circle and from Newfoundland to beyond the "fresh-water sea," being The Great Lakes. These claims for New France were based on discoveries of Verazzano, Cartier and Champlain.

Jean-Vincent Philippe married Marie Catherine Lambert de Baussy, daughter of Jacques, Sieur du Fresne, and Françoise Catherine Morel, on January 19, 1671, at St-Symphorien de Bayeux, France. She was listed as 30 years of age in the 1681 census in Montreal.

On March 16, 1671, the title of Sieur de Hautmesnil was conferred upon Jean-Vincent Philippe, the fur merchant, for services rendered, "en la Nouvelle France." Like other families who came from France to the new world to seek their fortune in the strenuous pioneer days of Canada, the Philippe family affixed to their family names titular designations: de St. Lambert, de Manteville, de Marigny and de Mandeville.

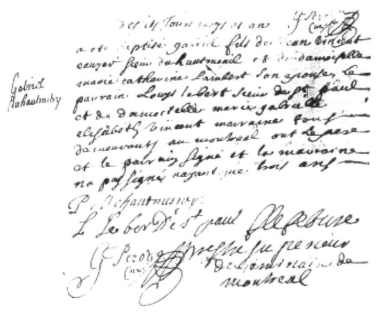

Baptismal Certificate of Gabriel du Hautmesny de St. Lambert

Thirteen children were issued from Pierre's marriage between the years 1672 and 1692. Marie Catherine died either in Montreal or in France after July 14, 1697. The couple left for France on September 13, 1693.[8]

Two of the Philippe names of whom we have any sure data in Louisiana are Gabriel-Vincent de Hautmesnil, Sieur de Saint-Lambert, the fifth child of thirteen, born September 5, 1677, Montreal. He was baptized there by the Sulpician priest, G. Perot, curé (pastor) of the *Séminaire de Montréal*, on May 9, 1677, Notre Dame Church. The sponsors were Louis Lebert, Sieur de St. Paul, a fur merchant, and *demoiselle* Marie Gabrielle Elizabeth Vincent, his sister. The father and godfather signed while the godmother, being 3 years of age, was unable to.[9]

The second, Jean-François, Sieur de Marigny, also de Manteville, the ninth child born to the Philippe couple, is the progenitor of the Marigny de Mandeville name in Louisiana. He was born June 21, 1685, in Montreal, and baptized there by E. Guyotte, *curé*, on June 21, 1685, Notre Dame Church. The sponsors were Jean François Charron, merchant, and Agathe Saint-Père, a business woman engaged in the textile and maple sugar industry, the wife of Pierre Legardeur, Sieur de Repentigny.

On May 13, 1702, Francois and his elder brother Gabriel, with whom he is often confused, joined the expedition of Sieur Charles Juchereau de Saint-Denys, trader, entrepreneur, founder of a tannery on the Ohio River.[10] Juchereau was a member of a network of important Canadian families. Saint Denys left with his party on May 18, 1702, and reached Illinois by way of Michilimakinac and the country of the Fox and Mascouten Indians late in the year. He secured the services of the Jesuit priest, Jean Mermet, as chaplain. The party quickly established communication with Louisiana and engaged Mascoutens, and possibly local coureurs de bois, as hunters. A fort was built about two leagues from the mouth of the Ohio, the exact site of which is not known. The concession granted to Juchereau carried several conditions. He was permitted to secure any skins for tanning or bleaching except beaver. Should he violate this clause, it would mean forfeiture of the concession.[11]

With the death of Saint-Denys, in 1703, perhaps from the epidemic that swept the Mascouten tribe as well as many people in Louisiana, the venture failed. François Philippe de Mandeville, one of the survivors, attempted to salvage the tannery and its products: an accumulation of several thousand of skins that included buffalo, deer, bear, roebuck, panther, and wolf. Unfortunately, many pelts were stolen by the Indians while others were damaged by moths, or lost in a sudden flooding of the river.

Life in Mobile in early September 1704 was indeed chaotic because yellow fever had spread to the village site, sixteen miles upriver. On the morning of September 4, Henri de Tonti, better known as the "Iron Hand," a man who had withstood onslaughts of climate and disease expended his last breath. No doubt, since his death occurred in the summer, he was quickly sealed into his coffin, and after brief rites was laid to rest in the cemetery up the *rue d'Iberville*.

Within a period of six days, Jean Baptiste LeMoyne Sieur de Bienville, (brother of Iberville) a lieutenant for King Louis XIV, from 1702-1706, had lost fifty percent of his high ranking command. Looking towards the future, he would shortly begin to groom a core of young replacements. Two Canadians of good family were on his list: Gabriel Philippe de Saint-Lambert and his brother François-Philippe de Marigny de Mandeville.

On January 28, 1705, Gabriel Philippe de Saint-Lambert and his brother Mandeville arrived at the fort at Mobile with a small force of Canadians after being forced to abandon the post on the Wabash.[12] After the departure of Mandeville, Louis Juchereau, brother of Charles, took charge of the tannery. Louis had accompanied Pierre Lemoyne, Sieur d'Iberville to Louisiana in 1697. After that date, Iberville made three trips to Louisiana, exploring the lower Mississippi Valley, building forts, and setting up colonies.

Jean Baptiste Lemoyne, Iberville's brother, who is better known as Bienville, in need of good officers, quickly assigned the command of Vaulezard's company at 480 *livres* per year to Gabriel-Vincent de Saint-Lambert, a post he diligently served for the next year and a half.[13]

Bienville always counted on his Canadians for support. He needed their backing for the growing opposition to his leadership. The principal reason, he wrote to the minister: that the Canadians could possibly survive without the colony, but the colony absolutely needed the Canadians at this point to see it through these early and difficult years. "I don't know what I would do without the Canadians," he later wrote. Taken as a whole, the Canadians were an asset to the new colony, and as far as Bienville was concerned, the colony should support them as far as possible.[14]

In 1706, the necessity was felt of removing Canadians from dependence on the king. Some who were more affluent were removed from the rolls while newcomers who had no other means of support were added to the list. A few who were personally favored by Bienville remained on the list. One who was removed from the roll was François Philippe de Hautmesnil, a twenty-three-year-old trader originally from Montreal.[15] He was on the colony's payroll at 360 *livres* per year, after having served for a short time in the Wabash country with Charles Juchereau de Saint-Denis.

François Philippe de Mandeville, not particularly an admirer of Bienville, was greatly angered when he was removed from the payroll in mid-June. A few weeks later, Gabriel Philippe de Saint-Lambert died on July 15, 1706, a fatality that stemmed from the fever brought by the *Aigle* from Havana. Mandeville was commissioned as an ensign in the Company of Vaulezard at Fort Louis de la Mobile below the present city of Mobile. He completed his brother's term at the same salary of 40 *livres* per month, or 220 *livres* for the 5½ months he served in 1706.[16] Bienville described Mandeville to Pontchartrain as "a man very suitable for such a position."[17]

On the first map of Mobile, next to the Market-Place, located in the south eastern section of town, there were allotments marked to Jean-François Philippe de Hautmesnil, François Philippe de Mandeville, and Gabriel Philippe de Saint-Lambert.[18]

Bienville always worried about the problems of defense or when the next supply ship from France would arrive. The arrival of boat builder Jacques Leroux made it possible for the country to free itself from isolation. While the ensign François de Mandeville engaged in some experiments on the qualities of wood capable of resisting the climate, Leroux began constructing some small ships which could navigate along the shore whose waters hid many sandbars.[19] Facilities could have been enlarged, but the support of France would have been needed to continue with the projects.

In early October of 1708, a vessel from Saint-Domingue anchored at Massacre Island in search of Indian slaves to take back to Cap-Français. Bienville saw the opportunity to send an envoy to Versailles to lobby in person for much needed supplies and put in a good word for him, since he knew that Pontchartrain would be seeking a replacement for Sieur Daneau de Muy.

Jean-François de Mandeville was the first to volunteer. For nearly a year he had been seeking compensation for supplies he had lent the colony during the expedition to aid Pensacola at the time of the 1707 siege. Bienville convinced him that a voyage to France would certainly result in his being rewarded by the crown. At the same time, he would render the colony a great service, and perhaps receive a promotion.

On October 16, 1708, Mandeville left Fort Louis for Massacre Island, along with twenty-five soldiers Bienville had sent to protect the ship while in port. Twelve days later, Mandeville was on his way to France *via* Havana. That fall of 1708, a shortage of food and gunpowder was felt. Officials bickered, plus the fear of a surprise attack by Indians served to demoralize the inhabitants. But, there was a glimpse of hope for the inhabitants instilled by Bienville with the reconstruction and enlargement of Fort Louis. With sufficient gunpowder, they could withstand an attack. There were approximately 345 Frenchmen in lower Louisiana by October 1708, double the number that were enumerated in 1704.[20]

From 1709 to 1711, Jean-François de Mandeville was in Paris. During his stay, he prepared a memoir on Louisiana. Dated April 29, 1709, written after his arrival in France, (place not given) he describes his voyage, and the condition of the colony: "...with the intention of informing the Minister Pontchartrain of everything he desires to know about that country, of the quality of the country, about what can be done there and about what can be derived from it, knowing it thoroughly and having been there for eight years, having traversed all the lands and rivers that flow to the sea, knowing and understanding the majority of the nations that occupy it because of the long period that he has been with them, he departed from Havana on the fourteenth of last January in the *Corvette Biche*...".[21]

In a letter dated July 11, 1709, to Bienville, Pontchartrain mentions having talked with the Sieur de Marigny. Pontchartrain to Bienville on May 10, 1710, writes: "I was greatly surprised to learn that you have appointed Sieur Blondel to fill the lieutenancy made vacant by the absence of Sieur de La Durantaye and that you have given the post of ensign of the former to Sieur Darroc. His Majesty has not all approved of what you have done in that and his intention is not that you should think yourself authorized to make appointments to the posts. He has given the lieutenancy of the said Sieur de La Durantaye to Sieur de St. Lambert."

For his services, Mandeville received a *lettre de garde de la Marine* and was made a lieutenant. He returned to Mobile on the *Renommée*, a voyage that suffered delay after delay from May 1710 to the end of November when it finally weighed anchor at La Rochelle and set sail for the West Indies. Once in the West Indies, it suffered further delays, and in the summer of 1711 the *Renommée* was still in the French Antilles while Mobile desperately awaited its arrival for supplies.

In early September, through a system devised by Bienville, by means of gunshots and smoke signals, sent between Massacre Island to New Mobile, messages could be relayed. The message received at Mobile set off a wild celebration, one long overdue. After three and a half years, the colony was once again to be supplied. The *Renommée* was in port. Amid the cheers, Bienville set out for the harbor accompanied by a number of officers and inhabitants in pirogues and small boats. The *Renommée*, after two weeks in Havana, had required 27 days to reach Massacre, usually a week's voyage.[22]

Returning as a lieutenant, Jean-François de Mandeville was accused by Bienville of having deceived the court, "by passing himself off as his deceased brother". From Port Dauphin, Bienville wrote to Pontchartrain on October 27, 1711: "Sieur de Mandeville has just arrived from France to whom your Lordship has given the lieutenancy of Chateauguay's company…I venture to tell you my lord, that he told me himself that he had deceived your lordship, by passing himself as his deceased brother." Should this be true, then his reputation as second in command of the Charles Juchereau de Saint-Denis expedition could be open to doubt.[23]

Governor Lamothe de Cadillac, the founder of Fort Pontchartrain *du détroit* in July 1701, recently arrived at Mobile, wrote to Pontchartrain on October 26, 1713, to inform him that he was sending the Sieur de Chateauguay "to command at Dauphin Island to relieve Sieur de Mandeville who has been there and who has been asking me for this for a very long time…"[24]

Jean-François de Mandeville is again mentioned by Sieur Lamothe de Cadillac, Governor of Louisiana, in 1716, as being one of the captains satisfactory to him and as not being included in the clique headed by Bienville which opposes the Governor.[25] For this reason, Mandeville's opposition to the controversial Bienville was termed an "exécration" (distasteful) by La Tour, a supporter of Bienville.[26] That same year, Marigny de Mandeville and his company were ordered to Dauphin Island and "to make themselves huts in rows of four, for the work on which they will be paid, to make the camp compact and to enclose it in pickets.[27] In 1717, Marigny and his company stationed at Mobile was ordered to the newly built Fort Toulouse near the confluence of the Coosa and Tallapoosa rivers, in the present state of Alabama.[28]

About 1720, presumably at La Mobile, according to the Canadian demographer René Jetté, François Philippe Marigny de Mandeville married Madeleine LeMaire, born in Paris, France, about 1702, the daughter of Pierre LeMaire and Marguerite Lamothe.[29]

His children included Antoine Philippe de Marigny de Mandeville and an illegitimate daughter of mixed blood.[30] In 1721, Mandeville was dismissed from service, the reason being "insubordination to the *Compagnie des Indes*, but he was restored to rank that same year.[31] He journeyed to France and, on June 4, 1721, arrived at Mobile on the *Ponteix*. He was given a commission as Commandant of Fort Condé and had received the title of *Chevalier de St. Louis*.[32]

The Company of Mandeville is mentioned among the military companies stationed at New Orleans in 1724. When the Mandeville family left Mobile, the engineer Mr. Devin writing from Fort Condé on August 29, 1724, to Mr. De Pauger, lamented that Madame Mandeville's departure was robbing the post of its "ornament," adding "There is, so to speak, no more society."[33]

By 1724, Bienville's ambition to see New Orleans as the capital of the province was realized. It was made the seat of government and the Superior

Council had been removed from Biloxi. Regular sittings were held in the Government Building facing the River. The site of New Orleans laid off by the Royal Engineers was progressing: a hospital and barracks and public buildings for the military had been erected. The Chapel of St. Louis had been built with the necessary quarters for a priest.

On December 2, 1724, the Council of War assembled at the residence of M. de Bienville, the Commandant General of the province. The council was composed of M. Bienville, M. de Chateauguay, the King's Lieutenant, M. de Mandeville, the first captain of the troops, M. de La Chaise, the Commissary, and Fazende and Perry, members of the Administrative Council.

Jean-François de Marigny de Mandeville had now risen in rank from ensign to a place in the Council of War in Louisiana and, subsequently, he was made *Major de Place* or Military Commandant of New Orleans from 1727-1728.

In the minutes of the Superior Council of Louisiana, New Orleans, dated May 2, 1724, we read that the home of M. de Mandeville "is of so little value that at most only the planks could be got from it." Also it is "not worth much, however, it would be well to demolish them [it and other similar ones] since they are too close to the fort, but we can wait until there are other quarters to afford lodging for these gentlemen." This is probably the house that M. de Marigny lived in with his wife and two children, 2 Negro and 1 Indian slave, on Chartres Street where they were listed in the 1726 Census.[34]

François de Mandeville received a land grant in St. Bernard Parish. It is a well-known site for it later formed a portion of the famous Chalmette Battlefield. The lowermost six arpents of the twenty-two-plus-arpent front plantation is traced directly to the early French Colonial Period under Bienville. It includes other portions of the Chalmette plantation. Unfortunately no direct chain of title remains to demonstrate the original land tenure from the French colonial period.[35]

Jean-François Philippe de Marigny died, cause of death unspecified, in New Orleans, November 4, 1728.[36] He was interred with honor in the Parish Church of St. Louis. The Marigny tomb, still to be seen, is situated on the left aisle of the church, at the foot of the altar of Our Lady of Lourdes. The tomb is marked by a large white marble plaque which bears the Marigny coat of arms and the inscription of three generations of them, all written in French.

The marble plaque indicates that François Philippe was born in Bayeux, Normandy, but his baptismal certificate indicates that he was born and baptized in Montreal.

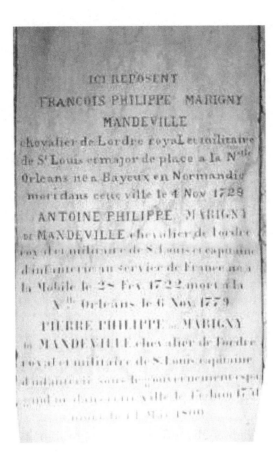

White marble plaque bearing the names of Bernard de Marigny's three ancestors, St. Louis Cathedral, Jackson Square, New Orleans.

Jean-François de Mandeville was the prototype of a frontier officer who explored and experimented. He lived in an era when life was harsh and often uncomfortable in an isolated society. His devotion to his king and country were never questioned, but what is important is that he was instrumental in bringing about internal improvements, was respected by the Indians and, by his services, he contributed to the peace and progress of the colony at a time when it was most needed.

Madeleine Lemaire, widow of Jean-François, remarried in New Orleans on September 2, 1729, to Ignace François Broutin, a royal engineer, who commanded the Natchez Post. The family divided their time between their home on Chartres Street and the "Habitation de Mandeville" below the city at Pointe St. Antoine, now Chalmette.

Two of the daughters issued from the Broutin marriage married: one to Jean Delfau de Pontalba and the other to Louis-Xavier de Lino de Chalmette. The real name of the Chalmette family was Martin, originating from France, going to Canada in the first half of the century, then to Louisiana. The name Chalmette is associated with the Battle of New Orleans which was fought on January 8, 1815. Chalmette's Field today is a national shrine.

Antoine Philippe de Marigny de Mandeville, son of François and Madeleine Lemaire was born at the *Fort Louis de la Mobile* on February 28, 1722.[37] His sponsors were the Sieur Le Moyne de Chateauguay, lieutenant of the king, and a brother of Bienville, and widow Marguerite Le Sueur, née Messier, presently the wife of Nicolas Chauvin de Lafrenière, the patriot who was executed by O'Reilly in 1769.

Reared under the tutelage of Ignace Broutin, stepson Antoine was educated from the funds of his deceased father's estate and received his military education in France.

Antoine Philippe de Mandeville married Marie Françoise Dupard Gaschet Delille, daughter of Pierre Joseph Dupard Gaschet Delille and Jacquemine Micaela Michel on January 8, 1748, New Orleans. Dupard was a wealthy colonist in early Louisiana. From Antoine's marriage to Francoise Dellile there were two children: Pierre Enguerrand de Marigny, born in New Orleans on June 15, 1750, and Magdeleine Philippe de Marigny.

Antoine made major improvements to the St. Bernard plantation he had inherited from his father. Pierre Enguerrand and Magdeleine spent much of their childhood on this concession. The 1770 census recorded Antoine Philippe's ownership of ten arpents of land, fifty slaves, sixty head of cattle, fourteen horses, one hundred sheep, twelve hogs, and two muskets.[38]

Antoine's name appears in the annals of Louisiana. He enjoyed the friendship of the Canadian born Governor Pierre Rigaud de Vaudreuil (1743-1753) who won the acclaim of the Louisiana colonists. Vaudreuil's greatest achievement or contribution to the colony's history was economic prosperity. His successor, Baron Louis Billiouart de Kerlerec (1753-1763), a naval officer originally from Quimper, France, with twenty-five years of service, was a contrast to that of the noble Marquis. He ruled differently, and New Orleans suffered greatly during his tenure. His administration suffered also due to lack of support from the French Government which was immersed in the French and Indian War.

During Kerlerec's tenure, Antoine Philippe de Marigny added by his explorations additional knowledge concerning the topography and the resources of his native province. In his *Mémoire sur la Louisiane*, written in 1759, this officer of distinction formed the design with the consent of the Governor of Louisiana, of making new discoveries towards the isle of Barataria, "of which we know the coasts but very imperfectly." With this intent he produced a general map of the Colony. He made it at his own expense, with the indefatigable zeal of a worthy citizen, who is always occupied for the glory of his prince, and the enlargement of his possessions. The Memoirs of this brilliant officer were printed at Paris, by Guillaume Després, in the rue St. Jacques in 1765.[39]

Kerlerec found fault and quarreled with all his subordinates. In less then six months after his arrival there was a sea of trouble and vexations rising against him from the part of officers who were discontented, plus the Capuchins, whom he had offended, who used their priestly influence against him. His contention with the colonial administrator Vincent de Rochemore broke all the official etiquette, and even brought in the participation of their wives. The two men were embroiled in a constant power struggle. So much so, that the social elite of New Orleans was divided in two hostile camps.

It seemed as if the bickering and scheming of Bienville's days had returned. Kerlerec and Rochemore, the Intendant Commissary, dispatched "copious epistles" to the King, accusing one another of corruption and disloyalty to the crown.

Gilbert Antoine de St. Maxent, a leading merchant of New Orleans, took the side of the Governor. He formed a committee of merchants, and made a formal protest to Paris, against the accusations of Rochemore's partisans declaring that there were no foundations to the charge that the Governor had disrupted commercial pursuits in which he and his colleagues were engaged.

Kerlerec granted St. Maxent the exclusive right to trade with the Native Americans of the Missouri River, as far north as Lake St. Peter and west of the Mississippi. Sieur Joseph Desruisseaux had held the monopoly from 1746 to 1750. It was Maxent's turn!

Antoine Philippe de Marigny incurred the wrath of Kerlerec for siding with Rochemore. This resulted in his being sent a prisoner with Rochemore and other supporting officers to France where they lingered for some time in the Bastille. At the same time was sent Jean-Baptiste Destrehan, the Royal Treasurer of the colony, described by Kerlerec "as being too rich and dangerous." "What if I send all the mauvaises têtes here," he wrote, "What would remain of the population?"

The *procuration* (power-of-attorney), Antoine Philippe de Marigny de Mandeville gave to his wife for the management of his affairs in Louisiana during his absence is dated July 15, 1762, in the morning. It shows proof of his marriage to Françoise Dellile and that he is a Lieutenant of the Colonial Troops. "He resides on his plantation, situated about one league and a half from New Orleans, on this side of the River below this city." He declares that he is the owner of several landed properties situated in the colony. In consequence of his absence, his interests could be in danger, therefore he appoints his wife to whom he grants full power to manage his properties and business.[40]

On his arrival in France, Marigny petitioned Choiseul to know the cause of his ill treatment, accusing Kerlerec of abuse of power and other violations of duty. To his petition, he annexed two certificates, one from Bienville and one from Vaudreuil, containing the highest commendations.

In 1763, Rochemore used his own political influence to have Kerlerec recalled, accusing him of violating the king's orders. On his return to France, Kerlerec was imprisoned in the Bastille, exiled from Paris in 1769, and ordered to remain at least 30 leagues from any royal residence. He was exonerated a year later, on September 3, 1770. He died on September 8, in Paris, a few days after clearing his name.[41]

Antoine Philippe Marigny de Mandeville, *chevalier de l'Ordre de St. Louis*, died after a lengthy illness in New Orleans on November 6, 1779. His name is the second on the family tombstone in the St. Louis Cathedral where he was buried. He was survived by his widow, a daughter who married Charles Honoré Olivier de St. Maurice, and his son, Pierre Enguerrand de Mandeville.

When you look at Antoine's portrait, from the Gaspar Cusach collection of the Louisiana Historical Society, he is wearing a peruque and queue. What you see is a refined, aristocratic, scholarly looking military officer. The two generations of Marigny families that lived in New Orleans since the early days were highly esteemed in the colony. Their descendants married in prominent families.

Antoine Philippe's widow sold ten arpents of land to Charles Antoine Reggio on July 13, 1794. Subsequently, Reggio sold six arpents of this ten arpent parcel to Ignace de Lino de Chalmet in 1805. The property conveyed was described as being located about 1.75 miles below New Orleans, bounded on the lower side by lands of Antoine Bienvenue and on the upper side by lands owned by Laurent Sigur.[42]

Pierre Enguerrand de Marigny followed in father's footsteps. He received his military education in France. Between 1765 and 1770, he served in the French military in Guyana and as a royal musketeer in France. He returned to New Orleans, and on July 14, 1772, he married

Jeanne Marie Destrehan de Tour, daughter of Jean-Baptiste Destrehan, royal treasurer in the colony during the administrations of Governors Vaudreuil and Kerlerec, and Jeanne Catherine de Gauvry.

Jeanne Marie had a sister married to Étienne de Boré, grandfather of historian Charles Gayarré and another to Favre d'Aunoy, the French Royal Commissioner at New Orleans. Her brother, Jean Baptiste Honoré Destrehan, a member of this prominent and wealthy Louisiana family, married Félicité de St. Maxent, daughter of Gilbert Antoine de St. Maxent and Elizabeth de La Roche, another prominent family who lived in opulence surrounded with household slaves and with all the comfort and luxury money could buy.

After her husband's death on October 20, 1773, Jeanne Marie married Colonel Bernardo de Galvez, Commander of the Louisiana Regiment, and second in rank to governor Unzaga, thus binding by marriage more of the prominent New Orleans families together.

Pierre Enguerrand de Marigny did not take part in the revolt against the Spanish Ulloa since he was too young, but as he grew to manhood he accepted and profited from the regime through his immediate connections with his brother-in-law, Governor Galvez. He had participated in various campaigns, as a musketeer in the French guard, and had been rewarded with the cross of the Royal Military Order of St. Louis.

In 1778, in accordance with the recommendation of Governor Galvez, Charles III, King of Spain, commissioned Pierre de Marigny to establish the Canary Islanders or "Isleños" families in Louisiana, four leagues below the city of New Orleans on land Marigny had donated to the king for their colonization. He participated in the campaigns of the Galvez Expedition: Fort Bute of Manchak and Baton Rouge in 1779; Mobile, where he commanded the Negro and free Mulatto troops in 1780; Pensacola, as adjutant or aide-de-camp of General Bernardo de Galvez in 1781. He was commandant of one of the detachments sent to capture the runaway Negro slaves, in 1784.[43]

The Galvez expeditions concluded victoriously, and Pierre Enguerrand returned to the St. Bernard Post where he initiated successful administrative policies that earned him respect. Governor Carondelet appointed Marigny commander of a newly militia regiment, "The Volunteers of the Mississippi," in 1792. The purpose of the regiment was to defend the "Lower Coast" below New Orleans, an area encompassing present-day St. Bernard and Plaquemines parishes. When Marigny resigned as commandant of St. Bernard, he appointed his first cousin, Denis de La Ronde, as his successor. In 1798, Pierre Enguerrand was promoted to the command of the Battalion of New Orleans with the rank of colonel.

From the marriage of Pierre Enguerrand de Marigny de Mandeville with Jeanne Marie Destrehan were born five children in New Orleans but only three survived to adulthood.

1. Antoine de Marigny de Mandeville, born April 27, 1773.
2. Jean Baptiste who was engaged to Azélie Delino Chalmette at the time of his demise.
3. Bernard Philippe de Marigny de Mandeville whose birth occurred October 28, 1785, died there February 4, 1868, is considered as a colorful character of New Orleans in ante-bellum days.
4. Marie-Céleste, baptized February 2, 1786. Her godparents were Etienne de Boré and Céleste Macarty, wife of Governor Miro. She married November 28, 1797, Jacques François Enould de Livaudais, captain of militia, later a lieutenant colonel in the colonial troops, and president of the state senate, during the American regime. He was the son of Jacques Enould de Livaudais and Charlotte Chauvin de Léry des Islets. He died in New Orleans April 9, 1850.
5. Antonia Marie called "La Perle" by the Duke of Orleans because of her ravishing beauty, died without issue.

Eulalie de Marigny de Mandeville is believed to have been an illegitimate daughter born to Pierre Enguerrand. She was freed from slavery at the age of five with her mother Marie Therese on the plantation on Bayou Terre-aux-Boeufs in eastern St. Bernard. In 1790, Pierre, through his agents, gave property to Marie Therese. In 1779, he gave about $15,000 to Eulalie.[44] Eulalie de Marigny de Mandeville; married Eugene Theodore Macarty in 1793; died October 20, 1848.

Pedro Marigny, as he was called by the Spanish, as an officer, was noted to be very intelligent and capable of command, whether political or military. He was known for his valor, good application, capacity and conduct. To concessions obtained from France by his father, he added the large concessions granted him by Spain. He was able to compete with Gilbert Antoine de St. Maxent, known as the "Merchant Prince" in New Orleans.

St. Maxent owned four plantations at one time: one was on Bayou St. John, and another was on the west bank used to run cattle. The third, later known as the Marigny plantation, was outside the town of New Orleans, on the other side of the Fort, known today as Faubourg Marigny.

The plantation house, of the earlier Louisiana type, built by St. Maxent was an imposing two-story mansion with upper and lower galleries on all four sides. Seven square white columns with elegant capitals framed the lower-floor façade and seven smaller rounded columns framed the upper. Two dormers, two chimneys, and a lightning rod protruded from a tall, double-sloping, hipped roof.

This palatial house was sold to Don Lorenzo Sigur, a Captain of the Militia, with the "tapestries which were fastened to the walls as well as the woodwork and mirrors above the fireplaces." There were two flights of stairs, twenty-eight feet long and sixteen feet wide. The frontage of the property measured seven arpents, one arpent being slightly less than two hundred feet.[45] Hard to believe, but this lavish house was too humble for St. Maxent who built an even grander one near one of his plantations, the largest at 34,500 acres on the Gentilly ridge.

In addition to the fur trade, St. Maxent had several other businesses including a saw mill and a construction firm. Over 200 slaves worked his plantations and businesses. He was lauded with a recommendation for promotion to brigadier-general on June 4, 1794. Unfortunately, he became ill in July and died, aged 70, on August 8, 1794, in the house he had sold to his friend Lorenzo Sigur, located just outside the old French Gate in New Orleans.

Shortly after St. Maxent's death, Pierre Philippe de Marigny acquired in a property exchange with Laurent Sigur the plantation that was later subdivided into the Faubourg Marigny.

The great conflagration of 1788 that wrought ruin and desolation to New Orleans was perhaps a blessing in disguise as the small homely French wood houses were replaced by stately edifices of Spanish architecture such as the Cabildo, the cathedral, the market, and the large courtyard houses with their cool alleys, verandas with large quantities of blooming plants in bright flower pots, great stairways and spacious living rooms, doors with decorative knockers and grill work enclosing their galleries.

Undoubtedly, one of the richest men of his day in New Orleans along with Antoine St. Maxent and the Almonaster, Pierre de Marigny entertained the elite on his plantation, located a little below the present Esplanade Avenue and the Champs Elysées, fronting on the river and extending almost to the woods.

The Marigny house was handsomely furnished with European furniture and objects of art. Beautiful ancestral portraits painted by noted French artists adorned the walls of all the rooms. This is where he is known to have entertained Louis-Philippe, a future king of France, and his two brothers in 1798. It was the execution of his father, better known as Philippe Égalité, in 1793, that made Louis-Philippe, Duke of Orleans, and he became the center of intrigues of the Orleanist party. Because of the Revolution, he was destined not to return to France for twenty years.

In 1796, the Directory offered to release his mother and two brothers who had been kept in prison since "the Terror" on condition that he went to America. He set sail for the United States. He settled in Philadelphia where he was met in February 1797 by his two brothers the Comte de Beaujolais and the Duke of Montpensier. The exiled royals spent the next two years travelling in New England, the region of the Great lakes, and the Mississippi. While in New Orleans, they were lodged with Governor Gayoso.

They were lavishly entertained by the most prominent citizens of the city who spared no expense in preparation of the many balls, banquets and luncheons. We can just picture all the carriages with the black footmen jumping down to unfold and fold up the hanging steps when all the invited guests arrived at the Marigny mansion to be entertained by Pierre and his wife.

That the Marigny de Mandeville family was infatuated with the royal presence in their home is not surprising since, according to family lore, one story recounts that special gold dinnerware made for the occasion of the duke's visit and was thrown into the river afterward "because no one would be worthy of using it again." It has been repeated that the princely fortune loaned to Louis-Philippe at the time he departed from New Orleans was never returned, nor was the royal sum generously contributed by Enould de Livaudais, his son-in-law, reimbursed. Contrary to popular belief, the 1,000 *piastres-fortres* borrowed were repaid to his son, Bernard, in 1813.

The character of Louis-Philippe was traced by Queen Victoria in a memorandum of May 2, 1855. She speaks of his "vast knowledge upon all and every subject" and "his great activity of mind." She also speaks of all of the "tricks and over-reaching" practiced by him, "who in great as well as in small things took a pleasure in being cleverer and more cunning than others." (*Letters*, 111, 122.)

Pierre Philippe de Marigny conferred upon himself the title of Marquis, since Louis-Philippe, Duke of Orleans, used to write: *Mon Cher Marquis.*

Still in the prime of his career, Pierre Enguerrand suffered an apoplectic seizure; he died at one o'clock in the afternoon, Wednesday May 14, 1800. His body was transferred in state to the home of Madame Don Andres Almonaster. His burial took place at 7 a.m., Thursday May 15, 1800. This is according to the funeral notices, tacked, as was the custom, on the door of the Cathedral or the corners of the streets.

One of them was preserved for posterity. His name is the last one recorded on the Marigny family tombstone in St. Louis Cathedral.

On the other side of the main aisle, short of the sanctuary, lie the remains of Andres Almonester y Roxas, the Spanish philanthropist, who died in 1798, after founding what would become the Charity Hospital.

With the closing of the coffin and the last duties of mourning, we bring the eighteenth century to a close. The nineteenth was heralded by Pierre Enguerrand's young heir, Bernard Philippe de Marigny, who would soon be a witness to the historic transfer of Louisiana from Spain to France, and then from France to the United States. He eventually became a key player in key events of the State of Louisiana.

NOTES

1. Rumilly, Robert, *Histoire de Montréal*, Édition Fides, Ottawa, Tome 1, 1970, 147-149.
2. Maurault, Olivier, "Gabriel Souart," *Dictionary of Canadian Biography Online*, 1000-1700, Volume 1.
3. The fief was land given by a seigneur for use by a habitant in return for certain services. A modified form of this French system determined the land use in New France.
4. Gabriel Souart, *Dictionary of Canadian Biography Online, 1000-1700*, Volume 1.
5. Jetté, René, *Dictionnaire Généalogique des familles du Québec des origines à 1730*, Les presses de l'Université de Montréal, 1983, 1910
6. Letter, patent of nobility, signed Louis and Phélipeau, dated Paris 1654, and registered "à la Cour des Aydes et Comptes de Rouen, 1656. "
7. Cornell, Hamelin, Ouellet, Trudel, *Canada Unity in Diversity*, Holt, Rinehart and Winston of Canada Ltd., Toronto-Montreal, 1967, 26.
8. Jetté, René, *Dictionnaire Généalogique des familles du Québec*, 910.
9. Archives Nationales du Québec à Montréal, May 9, 1677.
10. Contract by Notary Adhémar dated May 13, 1702. Massicotte, E. Z. "Repertory of Engagements Conserved in the Judicial Archives of Montreal," 1929-1930, 207.
11. Juchereau de Saint-Denys, Charles, *Dictionary of Canadian Biography Online*, Volume 2, 1701-1740.
12. Higginbotham, Jay, *Old Mobile: Fort Louis de La Louisiane, 1702-1711*, The University of Alabama Press, 1984, 220.
13. Ibid., 220.
14. Bienville to the minister, July 28, 1706, loc. cited f. 519-524.
15. According to his birth certificate, Jean-François de Mandeville would have been twenty-one years of age.

16. Higginbotham, Jay, Old Mobile: *Fort Louis de La Louisiane*, footnote 23, 272.

17. Jetté, René, *Dictionnaire généalogique des familles canadiennes*, 233, 300.

18. Mobile Public Library, Maps and Plans No. 120 B. Refer to Illustrations in *Old Mobile* by Jay Higginbotham.

19. Giraud, Marcel, *A History of French Louisiana : The Reign of Louis X1V, 1698-1715*, Louisiana State University Press, Baton Rouge, Volume 1, 172.

20. Dénombrement du 12 août 1708, par M. de La Salle, AC, C13A, 2, f. 225-27.

21. Rowland, Dunbar, and Sanders, *Mississippi Provincial Archives, 1701-1729*, 46-52.

22. Bienville to the Minister, October 27, 1711, loc. Cit., f. 584-92.

23. Fortier, John, "Philippe de Hautmesnil de Mandeville François," *Dictionary of Canadian Biography Online*, Volume 2, 1701-1740.

24. Rowland and Sanders, *Mississippi Provincial Archives, 1704-1743, French Dominion*, Op. cit., 2, 195.

25. Rowland and Sanders, *Mississippi Provincial Archives, 1704-1743, French Dominion*, 210.

26. Giraud, Marcel, *A History of French Louisiana, Years of Transition, 1715-1717*, Louisiana State University Press, Volume 2, 76.

27. Rowland and Sanders, *Mississippi Provincial Archives*, 214-215.

28. Martin, François-Xavier, *The History of Louisiana from the Earliest Period*, Printed by Lymann & Bradslee, 1827, 142.

29. No marriage record was found to attest that their marriage took place either at Mobile or in France. Cited as Mobile by René Jetté, in *Dictionnaire Biographique des canadiens-français à 1730*, 910.

30. Fortier, John, "Philippe de Hautmesnil de Mandeville François", *Dictionary of Canadian Biography Online*, Volume 2, 1701-1740.

31. Fortier, John, "Philippe de Mandeville," *Dictionary of Canadian Biography Online*.

32. Martin, François-Xavier, *The History of Louisiana from the Earliest Period*, 142.

33. Fortier, John, "Philippe de Hautmesnil de Mandeville François," *Dictionary of Canadian Biography Online*.

34. Maduell, Jr., Charles R., *The Census Tables for the French Colony of Louisiana from 1699 through 1732*, Genealogical Publishing Company, Baltimore, 1972, 68.

35. Wilson, Plantation Houses, Samuel Wilson Jr., "The Rene Beauregard House: An Architectural Survey Report," unpublished manuscript dated 1956, National Park Service Southwest Regional Office, Santa Fe.

36. Inscription on Tombstone of Marigny Family, St. Louis Cathedral, New Orleans.

37. Family Tomb in St. Louis Cathedral at New Orleans, Louisiana.

38. Voorhies, J.K. (comp), Some Late Eighteenth Century Louisianans: Census Records, 1758-1796, Lafayette: University of Southwestern University, 221.

39. Bossu, M., historian, *Travels through that part of America formerly called Louisiana*, English translation, London, 1771, 346.

40. The document was signed on the aforementioned plantation in the presence of the Royal Notary Broutin., and witnessed by the Sieurs Marin Bary and Pierre Chiron. Owner/Source: *The Louisiana Historical Quarterly*, Volume 24, i1, 231-232.

41. Adapted from Carl A. Brasseaux's entry for the *Dictionary of Louisiana Biography*, a publication of the Louisiana Historical Association in cooperation with the center for Louisiana Studies at the University of Louisiana, Lafayette.

42. P. Pedesclaux, February 9, 1794, New Orleans Notarial Archives.

43. Pedro de Marigny Service sheet, June 30, 1792, AGI, PC, leg. 161-a. The Pedro de Marigny record can be found in the Spanish Military Archives stored in *Archivo General de la India," Papeles procedentes de la Isla de Cuba* 161-a, in Sevilla Spain.

44. Martin, Alex, "Black revolt leader became a symbol to Louisiana slaves," *St. Bernard/Plaquemines* Bureau, December 2, 1984.

45. Coleman, James Julian, Junior, *Gilbert Antoine de St. Maxent: The Spanish-Frenchman of New Orleans*, Pelican Publishing House, New Orleans, 47-48.

CHAPTER 21

BERNARD DE MARIGNY: FOUNDER OF MANDEVILLE, LA.

Bernard Xavier Philippe de Marigny de Mandeville (1785-1868), the son of Pierre Enguerrand Philippe de Marigny and Jeanne Marie Destrehan, the fourth generation of the Philippe de Marigny de Mandeville in Louisiana, was destined to have a profound impact on the history of Louisiana, more so than many of his antecedents. His story echoes through New Orleans history where he is often depicted as a French–Creole,[1] nobleman, playboy, planter, land developer, politician, town councilor, Territorial Representative in 1810, serving in the legislature until 1838, President of the Louisiana Senate between the years 1822-1823, and Orleans Parish Register of Conveyances, 1843-1855.

What we read about Bernard de Marigny de Mandeville has not always been written accurately, but over the years people have enjoyed reading the romantic accounts where Bernard is portrayed as spoiled and undisciplined, "raised like a prince," squandering the fortune he inherited through his extravagant style of living and his gambling habits. He has been described as "the last great Creole gentleman, a relic of the golden era of his race, the epitome of their virtues and their faults."[2] Considered a polarizing figure, he was either admired or detested by those who knew him. He was a leading man not because of his inherited wealth, but because of remarkable natural and acquired abilities and his consistent political views for the benefit of his Creoles *concitoyens*.

Legends and myths about the Marigny family abound and were perpetuated by writers. One contends that Bernard's father, Pierre Enguerrand, poured 1,000 silver dollars into the melting pot from which his plantation bell was cast to give it a sweeter tone. True, it was the custom to cast silver dollars in the molten iron so that the finished product might have a more pleasing ring. The Bernard Marigny plantation bell was cast in 1825. Every plantation could boast of a large cast-iron bell to call the Negro slaves in from the field or to announce unusual events.

Another falsehood that was perpetuated is that when Pierre Enguerrand died, he left his 15 year old son a fortune of seven million dollars. True, Bernard's father was a very rich man who owned the Marigny Plantation downriver from the French Quarter plus other valuable properties, but documents relating to the amount of his estate should have been verified, rather than estimated. Remember, the *piastre fortres* was accepted as the medium of exchange during the Spanish period.

Considered "a reckless spender" and according to a tale about his prodigality, Bernard was reproved for lighting his cigar with a United

States green-back of high denomination, and had exclaimed "Bah! What of it? It is only a *bagatelle!*" A trifle! From this incident, Bagatelle Street in the Third District of New Orleans derived its name.[3] Once asked about the truth about similar money burning incidents, Bernard replied: "I know I have been a fool about money; but I was never fool enough to burn it."[4]

With so many reported extremes, we will accentuate the fact that Bernard Marigny was a prominent public servant who was friends and worked with the notables of his time: W.C.C. Claiborne, first Governor of Louisiana, General Andrew Jackson, Edward Livingston, David B. Morgan, the Marquis de Lafayette, Zachary Taylor, and other notables of his generation, thus dismissing the myths that he just squandered great sums of money when the gambling habit took hold of him and that he died "a pauper" as stated by many writers. Not true! Bernard did not live the final years of his life in "abject poverty." When you look at the records, you will find that he left a considerable estate for the time period in which he lived.

Bernard Marigny was fifteen years of age when his father died at age fifty years in 1800. He did inherit from his father a phenomenal estate consisting of the family plantation just below the city gates, east of New Orlean's *Vieux Carré*, parcels of property in New Orleans, concessions below the city in Plaquemines Parish, slaves, elaborate furniture, silver, and other movables. Since Bernard was a minor, his uncle Ignace Delino Chalmette, one of Pierre's first cousins, was placed in charge of the estate and named as his guardian.

Whether rich or poor, the death of a father at the tender age of fifteen leaves scars. It may explain why some writers claimed that "he became as wild and headstrong as an unbacked mustang." But in the aristocratic French bourgeois tradition of the period, "a man is not whole without an education." Following in the military tradition of his ancestors, he therefore trained as a cadet in the Spanish militia.

His guardian, Chalmette, then sent him to Pensacola to study business at the firm of Panton and Leslie, strict Scotsmen guardians. It was a short stay, since in April 1801, Bernard was sent to London to finish his business education. There, he frequented the coffeehouses and spent most of time at Almack's and other famous gambling places. It was reported that his escapades there soon resulted in his return to the family home. One of the things he brought back to New Orleans from England was the dice game Hazard which became popular in a simplified form.[5] Bernard was now fluent in English, although he kept his French accent throughout his life. He could have matured to some extent, although still a youth, he would soon begin to lead a long life of public service.

It is said that Louisiana first introduced the game of craps to the Nation. Edward Tinker Larocque states that Bernard Philippe de Marigny de Mandeville learned the game in London and introduced it on his return, but did he really? The game was Americanized into craps by the river men from the term "Johnny Crapeau" meaning "the frog" because of the hunched over position of the players, squatting like toads, as they threw dice on the ground.[6] Another theory emerged arguing that it was due to its popularity among the French Creole residents who were called "Frogs" (crapauds is French for toads) by the English-residents. The same dice game was known as crabs, krabs, or kreps, both in England and on the European continent at that time. Bernard's love of the game did lead to financial losses.

Bernard Marigny lived during the momentous period of the Louisiana transfer and worked with Pierre Clément de Laussat, the French commissioner, who arrived in New Orleans on March 26, 1803. Laussat was empowered by Emperor Napoleon Bonaparte to take possession of Louisiana from the Spanish authorities and turn it to the United States government. Having no regular troops, a company was formed from French citizens. Another company of Americans, under great favor with the Spanish government, was raised by Daniel Clark. Gabriel Villere and Bernard Marigny were selected by Laussat as his aides-de-camp and the two men remained in that capacity to the day that Louisiana was transferred by Laussat, to W.C.C. Claiborne and James Wilkinson, commissioners on the part of the United States Government.[7] Bernard's sister, Marie Céleste, was the hostess for the elaborate ball her brother gave to celebrate the Louisiana Purchase event.

During his brief tenure in Louisiana, Laussat resided in the home of Bernard de Marigny. The latter had vacated the upper floor of his gargantuan mansion and prepared it for the use of Laussat who was to use part of the quarters as his official base of operations and where he would transact his administrative duties. The main living area was on the second floor and other uses were found below. In 1803, Laussat had a watercolor plan of New Orleans prepared by his military deputy, Joseph Antoine Vinache, which remained in the Laussat family until it was acquired by the Historic New Orleans Collection. The map features an excellent rendering of the Marigny Plantation.

In his Memoirs, Laussat says on March 26, 1803, that "he proceeded to the house that had been reserved for him, that of Bernard de Marigny, near the eastern gate of the city. The governor, escorted by his officers, came shortly after to pay me a visit."[8]

On April 10-15, Laussat describes Marigny's home: "...as it is necessary to cross the least inhabited quarter of town to reach our house, people leave around after ten o'clock and after that hour nobody ever comes...but counting this drawback, our house is one most agreeable. The river shows itself to the best advantage: we are situated at a point in its crescent that dominates the port. One hundred ships, some of France, some of Spain, but mostly Anglo-Americans, stretch out in the distance as would a forest afloat and offer a perspective worthy of the most active settlement of the world."

"Mosquitoes and gnats are bad," wrote Laussat. "After sundown they take possession of the air, they prick with their stings, cover your arms and hands with some smarting pimples, which if you least scratch them they become just as so many sores. It is even impossible to read or to write; even in a drawing room, in spite of the diversions usually provided there by a numerous assembly, becomes a place of torture; the passion for gambling and the toughness of one's skin, secured from long habit can render these bearable at all."[9]

The place, according to Laussat, "is always called *hors de ville* (out of town), being near the gates, and thirty paces remote from the rampart." The Prefect appreciated the advantage of living in such a comfortable house, "so charmingly situated." His greatest pleasure was the library, "an entire collection of books, even to his favorite ones."

Laussat bade Marigny farewell in 1804, the two men having shared intimate confidences. Bernard de Marigny then became a member of the U.S. Army, as volunteer aid to General Wilkinson where he served until 1808.

Bernard was nineteen years of age when he married Mary Anne Jones on May 28, 1804, St. Louis Cathedral, in New Orleans. Nicknamed "Pomponne" by her family and her husband, she was the daughter of Evan Jones who was born August 17, 1739, in New York; died Monday, May 11, 1812, New Orleans, and Marie Verret, daughter of Philippe Nicolas Verret and Marguerite Cantrelle, Ascension, Donaldsonville, Louisiana, a descendant of early settlers at the German Coast.

Evan Jones was a former American consul in New Orleans. He came to Louisiana from Pennsylvania under the Spanish regime where he was popular with the Spaniards, and as a result became a wealthy merchant. His daughter's marriage contract refers to him as a "Négociant demeurant en cette ville" meaning that he was involved in some commercial enterprise in the city. The increase of the commerce of the United States had induced the appointment of a consul in 1799. President Adams commissioned Evan Jones as consul in New Orleans, and he was replaced in 1801 by Daniel Clark.

Bernard's marriage contract was executed before Peter Pedesclaux, Notary in New Orleans, May 19, 1804, at the home of the bride-elect's father. Bernard was represented by Solomon Prevost who was his guardian. Bernard's wealth had "a real and effective value of One Hundred Thousand Dollars specie."[10] This wealth consisted of, (1) a plantation situated near the Fort of St. Charles, and having seven arpents front on the river by eighty arpents in depth and adjoining on one side the ancient fortification of this city...the said plantation being valued in the sum of Eighty Thousand Dollars specie."[11] (2) "Twenty-eight heads of slaves valued in the sum of Fifteen Thousand Dollars Specie."[12] (3) "Five Thousand Dollars specie due him by the succession of his father."[13] ($1.00 worth of 1804 dollars is worth $19.61 in 2012.)[14]

The beginning of the American period in Louisiana coincided with slave insurrections in Haiti. During the period 1804-1809, Louisiana's free colored population more than doubled as free blacks fled the violence in Haiti. Louisiana benefited economically from a relatively large population of free people of color. A result of this wave of immigration was the creation of federal laws restricting free black immigration and manumission. Free men of color were forbidden to serve in the militia, and they were denied the right to vote or to hold political office. The free colored population continued to grow throughout the nineteenth century by manumission of slaves, immigration of free blacks from the West Indies and from natural production. The wealthy elite among the free men of color "espoused the ideology of the planter class." A few owned large cotton and sugar plantations where labor was provided by Negro slaves.

In 1805, Bernard de Marigny, possibly under the influence of his guardian, realized that the population of New Orleans would continue to expand under the American Regime. An act dated April 19, 1805, entitled "Enablement of Bernard Marigny" authorized him "jointly with his guardian" to "sell and lease all or any" of the lots to be laid out in his plantation adjoining the city. Furthermore the act stated that all the conveyances were to be binding "as if the same had been made by a person of full age."[15] As a result of this act, Bernard contracted with Barthelemy Lafon, surveyor, in 1806, and part of his plantation was subdivided creating the first suburb below the original city of New Orleans. The area grew rapidly, and the smaller the land parcels the more there was to sell. Lots were sold well into the 1820s. Since the development was popular, Marigny spent most of 1806 and 1807 at the office of notary Narcisse Broutin selling sixty-foot lots to prospective homebuilders.

In 1809, Marigny advertised 650 lots for sale in the Faubourg Marigny. They could be paid for over a period of 15 years with interest at 8%.[16] Many of the lots were later seized and sold by the Sheriff for non-payments of notes.

As Americans settled up-river, immigrants and free persons of color settled in Faubourg Marigny. The word "faubourg" is described in Webster Dictionary as a suburb of a French city or a city quarter. Many of the street names of the Faubourg Marigny are still retained: Champs Élysées was the main thoroughfare to his house. A colorful character with a sense of humor, Bernard was said after a gambling loss to have told his agent to sell off another street and name it *Rue du Craps*. The name stuck for fifty years and was changed to Burgundy since the street address was a source of embarrassment for the four churches located on that street.

Other street names were "D'Amour (presently Rampart) where white Creole gentlemen set up households for their mistresses of color, and their offspring, in separate cottages, and "Bons Enfants" or "Good Children" (presently St. Claude).

This first experience in real estate speculation proved advantageous. Marigny later sold his lots not only to his fellow Creoles, but to French-speaking "gens de couleur" to whom he was related through his half-sister, Eulalie Mandeville Macarty, an accomplished businesswoman who had a plantation near Poydras and owned slaves which she bought and later freed. Records are sketchy for the early 1800s. St. Bernard Parish judicial records reveal that Eulalie Mandeville freed 11 of her slaves in 1819. Over the years she bought slaves from other planters in St. Bernard Parish, retained them for two years, the period prescribed by law, and then released them.[17]

Unfortunately because of fires and neglect in the care of parish records, we don't know how many she freed and if 1819 was the first time she freed any. At the time of her death Eulalie owned property in New Orleans and in St. Bernard, St. John the Baptist, St. Charles and St. James parishes.

In "Creoles of Louisiana," George W. Cable has a good illustration of the old Marigny mansion after it had been fenced in, once the plantation had been cut into city blocks. Of the French Colonial style, Gilbert Antoine Maxent's architect was influenced by the buildings of the West Indies and blended it in with the French, Native American, Spanish and African culture. This is the beginning of the Creole style of housing suited to the hot, humid and rainy climate of Louisiana. The raised basement, high off the ground, protected against flooding. The large umbrella-like double pitched roof covered in cypress shingles and dormers extended over the two stories with wrap around double galleries and wooden balustrades on the sides. The wooden mantels had columns and the door frames and window casements were substantial but simple in design. The windows were of the French style: double-glazed door arrangement, which opened inward while heavy solid batten shutters opened on the outside.[18]

Courtesy of Ray Samuel

Marigny plantation house

The second house depicted in the picture, next to the Marigny residence, was rented to Master Commandant David Porter after he arrived in New Orleans in June 1808. From his house he could view his gunboats anchored on the opposite shore at Algiers Point. He would communicate from his house to the gunboat Commandants with signals from a flagpole. He attempted to establish a telegraph system to reach his gunboats at the mouth of the Mississippi river. If the system had been completed, he could have received or send messages to Balize in five minutes. Construction was stopped, being too expensive. Sailors of each gunboat would come to his house and practice shooting with their rifles.

The once fabulous Marigny mansion became hedged in by Bernard's faubourg. Hidden by a brick wall and to the rest of the city, at the time of Bernard's death in 1868, the patrimonial dwelling in which Marigny once lived and lavishly entertained, "like his person formed the landmark of the soil and a link between the present and former generations."[19] The building was still standing near the river on Levee Street, opposite the "Marigny Buildings" within a few yards of the Pontchartrain Railroad depot. It was now used as an asylum for the insane, having long since passed out of his hands.[20] Eventually it fell into ruins and was torn down. The power plant on Elysian Fields Avenue is now on that site.

The Territorial Legislation on June 7, 1806, emancipated Bernard Marigny, now in his 21st year, and in an Act stated that Bernard Marigny "be, and is hereby authorized from this day forward to administer and take care of his estate by himself, and to do all and singular the civil acts which are and may be done by all persons who have arrived at the age fixed by law for attaining the rights of majority."[21]

Mary Anne Jones, Bernard's wife, died in Philadelphia June 4, 1808, in childbirth. The body was later brought to New Orleans and buried on August 6. Little is known about Mary Anne, except that Bernard chose to be buried with her in St. Louis Cemetery #1, tomb number 106.[22]

From their union was born a daughter and two sons, which are named as follows:

(1) Clémente born March 28, 1805, baptized May 16, 1805, St. Louis Cathedral, died May 23, 1805 and was buried the same day, New Orleans.

(2) Prosper François de Marigny born March 6, 1806, (although the inscription on tomb in St. Louis Cemetery No. 2 says March 17, 1807); he later became the husband of Marie Céleste Destrehan, August 1826, St. Louis Cathedral, New Orleans. He died October 23, 1836, Natchez, Mississippi. Celeste Destrehan died 01 December 1886, Lyon, France.

(3) Gustave Adolphe, born in Philadelphia, June 15, 1808, was killed in a duel October 26, 1830, according to Cruzat and Tinker. Another source says he succumbed to a wound received in a duel with Mr. Lanus."[23]

His father then fought in the state legislature to stop the practice of dueling. In 1855 the police began to enforce the laws against dueling, but it continued for many years despite arrests and prosecutions. By 1890 dueling was history.

Benjamin Latrobe gives an insight into Mary Anne's personality where he records the following account in his *Impressions Respecting New Orleans*, in reference to women who abused their slaves: "The first Madame Marigny was a beast of the same kind. I was a horrified witness, as I watched her strap a Negro servant to a ladder, whipping him unconscious."[24]

At that period, Bernard was unable to follow General Wilkinson to Washington City. He resigned his commission since his wife Mary Jones was on her death bed. "She died and with her death, my hopes of a brilliant military career vanished," he wrote later.

On September 9, 1808, Bernard advertised for the sale of a superb plantation, known by the name of the *Plantation Dupard*, situated about five leagues from the city and on the opposite side of the river above the city, and in the environs of the Cannes Brulées. This "superb plantation" belonged "to the community which existed between Bernard and his deceased wife.[25]

In late 1808, the young dejected widower left to visit Pensacola, seat of the Spanish Government in West Florida. He was 23 years of age and the father of two living children. While attending to his business, he was encouraged to attend a ball in Pensacola. He escorted a very beautiful young woman named Mathilda Morales, and he held her attention during the whole evening, much to the displeasure of other young gentlemen. Warned by friends, the young Bernard did not heed the message that he could be challenged to a duel. Marigny himself was a duelist.

The next morning, at breakfast, it was said that he received seven challenges. He announced that he would take them one by one. At the right opportunity, when he thrust his sword through the body of his first opponent, it was reported that the other men offered their apologies. Other writers contend that he met them all, and one by one, they fell under his expert swordsmanship.

Still popular at the beginning of the nineteenth century, dueling was an old European custom brought to America to settle insults and differences while Americans in the colony settled theirs with pistols. Bernard had trained in the art of fencing, and among his contemporaries, he gained a legendary reputation.

He is credited with exercising his fencing skills at numerous times, and according to legend, he would have fought 15 duels without a scratch beneath the "dueling oaks", a favorite setting where you could settle *les affaires d'honneur*. On one occasion, when Bernard challenged a blacksmith and gave him a choice of weapons and place, the challenged man, over six feet tall, chose Lake Pontchartrain in six feet of water and sledgehammers as the weapons. Bernard, about 5 feet 10 inches, who saw the humor of the reply, gracefully apologized and bowed out of the competition acknowledging defeat, and with a smile ordered drinks for all present.

Bernard found a companion in the youthful Anna Mathilde Martina de Morales Hidalgo, born November 12, 1789, and baptized September 3, 1794, aged 4 years, New Orleans.[26] Mathilde was the daughter of Marie Catherine Guesnon and Don Juan Ventura Morales Hidalgo, the last Spanish Intendant of Louisiana and Contador for Louisiana at New Orleans from April 1796, to the time of The Cession to France by Spain, except for a few months. After the transfer of Louisiana to the United States, Morales lingered in Louisiana. His intrigues and political machinations and land sales made him *persona non grata* to Governor Claiborne, who on January 25, 1806, ordered him "to leave The Territory in the course of the present month." He departed for Pensacola on February 1. He held the same office at Pensacola and later in Puerto Rico.[27]

The marriage contract Between Bernard and Ana Mathilda was executed on March 21, 1809, before Francisco Maximilien de Maxent, commandant of The Province of West Florida and "performing the duties of Notary," at Pensacola. With this contract Marigny was binding himself to still another vast fortune. His father-in-law awarded him several land grants in the vicinity of Pensacola, which amounted to thousand of acres, but these were not confirmed by the United States Congress.

Bernard Marigny and Anna Mathilda Morales

In September of 1809, Bernard Marigny was elected one of the six representatives of the County of Orleans in the Territorial Legislature.[28] To his *concitoyens* (fellow citizens) Marigny says: "In 1810 I was under the Territorial Government elected a member of the Legislature." Though the Legislature did not meet until 1810, the election was held in 1809. Thus began his colorful political career of twenty-six years of service in the Territorial and State Legislature.

Bernard was elected to the Constitutional Convention of the Territory of Orleans in 1811. The aim was to prepare a constitution for the New State of Louisiana. The convention sat in New Orleans from November 4, 1811, to January 28, 1812. At this time Bernard was also a member of the Territorial Legislature from the County of Orleans,[29] and a member of The City Council of New Orleans.[30]

In 1812, Marigny a member of the convention help draft the first constitution of the State of Louisiana, thus erecting the Territory of Orleans into the State of Louisiana. Louisiana was admitted to the Union by an Act of Congress dated April 8, 1812, which went into effect April 30, of the same year, with the following boundaries:

> Beginning at the mouth of the river Sabine; thence by a line to be drawn along the middle of the said river, including all islands to the thirty-second degree of latitude; thence due north, to the northernmost part of the thirty-third degree of north latitude; thence along the said parallel of latitude, to the river Mississippi; thence down the said river to the river Iberville; and from thence, along the middle of the said river and Lakes Maurepas and Pontchartrain (sic), to the Gulph of Mexico; thence bounded by the said gulph to the beginning; including all islands within three leagues of the coast...[31]

The territory between the Mississippi River and Pearl River and bounded on the North by the Mississippi Territory, which is still known as "the Florida Parishes" was added to the state by an Act of Congress of April 14, 1812. During the Constitutional Convention, Marigny on two occasions voted against the inclusion of the Florida Parishes in the State of Louisiana.[32]

In the sitting of the Council of New Orleans of September 22, 1812, Marigny was elected one of the aldermen of the Fifth district or Ward.[33] He emerged as a powerful leader of the Creole population, and exerted all his influence to preserve the civil code in this state. As the zealous defender of the rights of the *anciens habitants* he soon became the foe of the *nouveaux habitants*, the new Americans who were flooding into Louisiana creating tensions between them and the settled Creoles. It irritated him to see them make political inroads following the Battle of New Orleans. He did praise the courageous and industrious nature of the Americans, which he said was "characteristic of their race," but on the other hand he felt that "they wanted to take it all and share nothing."

When two American developers approached Marigny about two future development of the city in the area of the Faubourg Marigny, he first agreed, then reneged thus killing the deal. This act was not well received by the two developers. As a result of this act, housing development grew uptown instead of east of the city. The American feeling of dislike for Marigny eventually affected his finances and political career, and when he became a candidate for the governorship of Louisiana, they refused to support him.

On July 5, 1814, Bernard Marigny was elected a Representative from the County of Orleans.[34] The First Session met on November 10, in New Orleans, and did not adjourn until February 6, 1815. This special Session to meet was in compliance with Governor Claiborne's Proclamation of October 5, to consider "great and weighty matter."[35] Marigny acted as Chairman of the House of Representatives Committee of Defense. In 1848, Marigny wrote a pamphlet *Réflexions sur la Campagne du général André Jackson en Louisiane en 1814-1815*. His aim was to make known his line of conduct in New Orleans at the time of the war.

While in Pensacola, General Jackson met Governor Morales, Bernard's father-in-law. The latter gave the General a letter for Bernard, in which he bestowed great praise on Andrew Jackson. Arriving at Bayou St. John, the General handed the letter to Inspector Davis of the Tennesseans, to hand deliver to Bernard. The Inspector was accompanied by Mr. Laneuville, an old officer in the army of the United States, the Adjutant General of the State of Louisiana. Wrote Bernard: "I was speaking with Mr. Nathan, who is still at New Orleans – we were standing at the corner of Chartres and St. Louis streets, when Inspector Davis handed me the letter of which he was the bearer. General Jackson was asking "if it would be agreeable for him to descend at my home on the morrow and to establish there his headquarters."

Marigny's reply to Inspector Davis was that "I would receive him at my home with great pleasure, the Conqueror of the Floridas, and of Colonel Nicholls (sic), who had maltreated my old compatriots in Pensacola and had carried away a great number of their slaves. Finally I told him that I would receive the General the next day after the review that he proposed to make of the *Battalion d'Orléans* and of the Militia of the city on Esplanade Street, and that breakfast would be awaiting him. I entered at once in my home and commanded it. The drawing room of my house was spacious and nothing was neglected, in order that the reception should be worthy of the General and the officers who accompanied him."

Bernard waited and waited for the General, but it was a no-show. By midday not seeing him come, he went to the rampart of Fort St. Charles, which dominated the Esplanade. Describing the day, Marigny writes, "The rain was pouring down and all present were wet and muddy and uncomfortable."

Mr. Pelletier, an Attakapas Dragoon, told Bernard that the General had changed his mind and that he would remain at Dr. Kerr's on Esplanade Street.

Marigny felt it was his duty to pay a visit to the one who had been destined to be his guest. He went immediately to the General, to whom he was presented by his old friend Colonel Peire "who should remember all these circumstances." He was received cordially by the General. Marigny was now 29 years of age, and if the General had come to his house and offered him service in his staff, he would have accepted. Marigny decided to enter the staff of Governor Claiborne, who commanded the militia of the state and there he found himself with Messrs. Octave LeBlanc, L.B. McCarty, Laneuville and others.

During the campaign of 1814 and 1815, Marigny acted as chairman of the Committee of Defense, appointed by the House of Representatives, to place at the disposal of General Jackson, all the available resources of the State. He was instrumental in enlisting the services of Jean Lafitte and the Baratarians. In one of his Memoirs, written in 1853, entitled *Bernard de Marigny à ses Concitoyens*, Bernard describes his role in securing the services of the Baratarians for the defense of New Orleans. He recalled his role, and had told the General that that he had announced in his proclamation, issued at Mobile, that he would not accept the services of the inhabitants of Barataria, whom he qualified as pirates calling them "hellish bandittis." The General then got excited, and told the committee that those men were under the ban of the United States laws, and he declared that he could not enroll them under the American flag. Knowing that the General was of a violent and excitable temper, Marigny did not insist but called on Judge Dominic Hall of the U.S. Admiralty court who took the matter into his hands and drafted some resolutions for Marigny to offer to the House of Representatives.

The intent of those resolutions was that the Judge would be requested by the Legislature to suspend all proceedings against those men for the term of four months. Said Hall, "As soon, as those resolutions are adopted, I shall order the U.S. District Attorney to suspend all proceedings against them; and if they assist our cause bravely and faithfully, I have no doubt that the U.S. Government will pardon them… The resolutions were offered by me in the lower House and passed there, and in the Senate unanimously."

In this Memoir, Bernard recalled the role he played during the War of 1812-1815. On December 23, 1815, he was in the company of Governor Claiborne when the militia received the order to advance to first meet the British army. Arriving at the Macarty Plantation, Colonel Chambord came to say to Governor Claiborne that the General had changed his mind and that he must go to Marigny Canal on the Gentilly Road where he would find Lt. Bosque with the artillery. They met at the corner of Rampart and Bayou Streets; the Orleans Battalion coming to meet the English. Arriving at Canal Marigny, the first shot of the cannon from the U.S. ship *Carolina* was heard.

Marigny told Macarty: "We were expected to be in the battle, do you wish us to go there?" He agreed, however the distance from Canal Marigny to the Lacoste Plantation was at least three leagues, so they arrived at the end of the battle that had lasted some two hours. Under an oak tree by the side of the road that goes through the length of the Laronde Plantation were seen a number of wounded who he thought belonged to the 7th Regiment commanded by Colonel Peire. Marigny met Major Gabriel Villeré, and shortly afterwards, Colonel Peire, told Marigny that he had been struck in the hand by a spent ball. Peire conducted Marigny to General Jackson who inquired as to what was happening in the City. He was told that all the citizens were under arms and that General Carroll with his soldiers were in battle order on the Levee of New Orleans. Jackson reported that "the affair" had been very hot.

Marigny left to return to the City while Mr. L.B. Macarty took the road to Gentilly to go and give the news to Governor Claiborne. As for Marigny, he had to make it known in the City that neither General Jackson nor those of his army had been wounded, which was good news.

A few days later, Governor Claiborne handed over all the militia to General Jackson where he placed them in different commands. As for Marigny, he remained with the Legislature as President of the Committee of Defense named in the Chamber where he remained in contact with the General-in-Chief to assist him in the best interest of the country. For his role, Bernard felt "that he might like many others wear the blue ribbon on great occasions, but not having been in the fire of the enemy, neither on the 23rd or the 8th of January, I think differently."

Marigny praised the Lafittes and the Baratarians: "Those men behaved bravely and gallantly during the war. Five of the pieces of artillery used in the campaign, were manned and directed by Dominique You, Cadet Bouteille; the brothers Lafitte, Gamby and Beluche. It is an incontrovertible, historical fact, that the artillery was most efficient in the memorable campaign of 1814 and 1815." The Lafittes supplied powder, shots, flints and canon and dexterous men to fire them.

On Jackson's recommendation the Baratarians received a free pardon, and all indictments outstanding against them were discounted. Most of them returned to piracy. They lost everything in the raid carried out against them by Patterson and Ross, and their first action had to be to succeed in their defense against the official claim to the ships and merchandise taken from Barataria Bay. Their case dragged on, and no quantity of testimonials or Presidential pardons would be likely to effect the restoration of their property. The Lafittes were bankrupt! To the younger brothers, Pierre and Jean Lafitte, like Dominique "had found patriotism a poor investment."[36]

Several reputations were enhanced by the New Orleans campaign, but curious to reflect, that to a certain extent, Andrew Jackson later owed his election as President of the United States to the aid of the Lafittes and their band of Baratarian pirates. The special attention given to the artillery shows that Jackson was fully aware of his debt to gunnery. But the richest beneficiary of the campaign was the city of New Orleans for the British attack had drawn the attention of the Western world to the importance of the Mississippi trade through New Orleans.

The following public notice, December 1815, is of special interest not only as an example of advertisement of Slaves for sale but mainly for the use of the word "Creole" used by Bernard Marigny in which he signs in an uncommon manner as "A Creole."

NOTICE: The public are hereby informed that on the 1st of February next, at 11 o'clock, A.M. at Maspero's Coffee house will be sold, 100 slaves:

> Belonging to the undersigned, and who are now on the plantation sold by him to Mr. Joseph Decuir. Those slaves are too well known to need any further details about them; suffice it to say that there are among them ninety Creoles from 15 to 32 years of age, a great number of whom have trades – Their qualities and vices will be made known.
>
> Conditions: Payable in March 1817, in notes endorsed to the satisfaction of the seller, with mortgage until final payment. The deeds of transfer to be at the exchange of the purchasers.
>
> Signed B. Marigny.[37]

The Supreme Court of Louisiana ruled in 1822 that all *procès-verbaux* (official reports) of family meetings written in French were null and void. Elected that year to the presidency of the State Senate, Senator Marigny sponsored legislation, known as The French Bill. This piece of legislation permitting the continued use of French in legal documents passed the House and Senate with overwhelming majorities. Marigny was proclaimed Defender of the French Language by his *concitoyens.*

Marigny became embroiled in the controversy involving the riverfront batture of Faubourg Ste. Marie that developers wanted to develop.[38] Marigny contended that it was public domain, and that it been from the onset of the city. The battle against Edward Livingston and his partisans continued for several years, until the defection of men such as Pierre Derbigny and Joseph Roffignac to Livington's cause.

On January 8, 1822, Marigny was elected president of the Senate of the Louisiana Legislature.[39] On March 16 of that year he addressed the Gentlemen of the Senate in view of his visit to Europe. He and his family had been invited to come to France and take up their residence at Louis-Philippe's Court.

Mr. Marigny felt it was his duty to inform the honorable members so as to avoid inconveniences in his absence.[40] Two days later, on March 18, Mr. Julien Poydras was elected to the presidency of the Senate and the following resolution was adopted: "Resolved unanimously by the Senate of the state of Louisiana that the justice and impartiality which mark the conduct of the honorable Bernard Marigny while exercising the high duties of president, entitle him to the esteem and respect of the Senate, and the expression of their individual regard for him and wishes for his happiness."[41]

Marigny continued in the senate until it adjourned on March 23, 1822, as is shown by his vote on several bills.[42]

The friendly invitation being accepted, the Marigny family crossed the ocean and presented themselves at the French court where they were received at the court of Louis-Philippe XVIII, known as *l'Inévitable* (the Unavoidable), the Bourbon King of France and of Navarre from 1814 to 1824, omitting the Hundred Days in 1815.

Louis-Philippe had spent 23 years in exile, in Prussia, the United Kingdom and Russia, from 1791 to 1814 during the French Revolution and the First French Empire, and again in 1815, for 111 days, upon the return of Napoleon I from the island of Elba. Louis-Philippe ruled as king for slightly less than a decade. Louis XVIII was the last French monarch to die while reigning. Since he had no children, upon his death, the crown passed to his brother, Charles, Count of Artois.

It was Louis-Phillippe, then Duke of Orleans, and his two brothers who were exiles in the United States that were entertained lavishly in 1798 by Bernard's father. They were received with all the kindness which the Marigny had extended in Louisiana to the exiled royals. In return, during their stay, they were treated as members of the King's family.[43]

During this trip, Marigny met and became friends with the Marquis de Lafayette, a young French aristocrat and military officer, who joined Washington's army and served as general in the American Revolutionary War. He later helped import American revolutionary ideas to France and was a leader of the *Garde Nationale* during the French Revolution. The fact that he and Thomas Paine repeated their American exploits in France emphasized the kinship of the two struggles.

Marigny returned to Louisiana in 1823 and continued in the pursuit of his political dreams. When Lafayette visited New Orleans in 1824, it was Marigny who assumed the important role of receiving and entertaining the General.

By 1824, Marigny's political ambition was to become governor of the state of Louisiana. He had served as President of the Louisiana Senate, and as there was no Lt. Governor, he was next in line of succession to Governor Thomas B. Robertson. He was a candidate and received 1,420 votes running third in the race, Henry Johnson being elected. In his second attempt, in 1828, he was defeated by Pierre Derbigny whom he had supported in 1820. On January 21, 1830, *Le Courrier de la Louisiane* announced the candidacy of Bernard Marigny for Governor.[44] The election was called early due to the death of governor Derbigny and the resignation of the next two acting Governors. The election was described as tumultuous, and although Marigny employed every conceivable approach by touring the state, staging elaborate shows with hired bands, dancers and singers to woo the electorate, to no avail, it was A.B. Roman who was elected in July.

Marigny's 1822 prophecy that "Virginia will exhaust herself before another Louisianan is made governor in his country" was fulfilled as the following paragraph appeared in *Le Courrier de la Louisiana* for June 1824.[45]

"We read this morning in the *Louisiana Gazette* a very mean paragraph, from a very mean writer, BERNARD DE MARIGNY, candidate forever and ever for the office of Governor, which he shall *never* get, notwithstanding all his journeys, and the handsome Spanish songs and *Boleros* with which he treated the voters of the upper Fourche; his promises to some, and his threats to others, in short those delicate means which excited a feeling of pity in the mind of everyone."

In 1828, General Andrew Jackson visited New Orleans and was entertained by the city. On January 8, the anniversary of the Battle of New Orleans, a public dinner was given to honor the general at the Orleans Ballroom. Marigny presided over the dinner. *The Louisiana Courrier*, reporting the dinner, said "General Jackson arose, before taking leave of the assembly, and gave the following toast: To B. Marigny, president of the Banquet."[46]

Marigny never accepted defeat, and he remained persistent. He was the outstanding Creole in the state and he carried the predominantly Creole Parishes, but he received scant support from the upstate Parishes. Once again on December 15, 1831, he was defeated at a special election for the seat of Mr. Freret who had resigned from the House of Representatives.[47] Nine days later, Marigny was a candidate at another special election for the seat vacated by W.C.C. Claiborne, Jr. in the House of Representatives by resignation[48] and was defeated by S.O. Dixon by one vote.[49] The election was immediately contested and on January 23, 1832, declared void by the House of Representatives.[50] In the new election Marigny won by a majority of 130 votes.[51]

In the 1832 regular July election Marigny was elected one of the seven State Representatives from Orleans Parishes.[52]

Marigny's main aim was always to preserve the French language for the old French population. Perhaps he was too much of a visionary, but in 1822, he did succeed in making it possible for the legislature to debate in both French and English, and for the proceedings to be recorded in both languages. The clerks in both Houses had to be bilingual. The legislation he sponsored known as "The French Bill" passed the House and Senate with overwhelming majorities, permitting the continued use of French in legal documents.

In the 1833 State Legislature, Marigny introduced a bill to incorporate the Citizens Bank of Louisiana. With the stroke of a pen, he helped create the monster that would later claim a large part of his fortune which he held in mortgages. The economic depression of 1837 was catastrophic for many Louisiana planters, including Bernard Marigny. Economic conditions continued to worsen leading to the bubble burst in 1842, when the Citizens Bank, along with other banking institutions, stopped specie payments. The result was over $150,000,000 of bankruptcies and failures. Bernard was nearly ruined, but so were others. Hoping to recover his losses, he managed to get a prolongation of time on the terms of his mortgages. His lucrative sugar plantation in Plaquemines Parish and his brickyard at his Fontainebleau estate in good times should have kept him afloat, but it was not to be. Landed property and slaves declined fifty per cent in value, plus the price of bricks and sugar fell. The Fortier Crevasse that occurred in April 1849 on the right bank of the Mississippi about 13.5 miles above New Orleans, followed by the Gardanne Crevasse in 1851, totally devastated Bernard's Plaquemines property.

The Citizens Bank and the Bank of Louisiana would no longer wait for their money. Bernard was compelled to liquidate a large portion of his estate in 1852.

During the waning days of his political career, Bernard continued to assert leadership. He did have a voice in the formulation of laws governing Louisianans in the state's second constitutional convention in 1844 and 1845. To his credit, he introduced a clause which protected the French language, requiring the secretary of the Senate, and the clerk of the House of Representatives to be familiar with the French and English languages. Another clause allowed members of both houses the privilege of addressing themselves either in French or English. Another important contribution he made was the giving of equal political rights for naturalized, as well as native citizens.

Contrary to several published accounts Bernard de Marigny did not inherit Fontainebleau from his father's estate nor did his father ever own property in St. Tammany Parish or that he died at Fontainebleau. There are no notarial, judicial and congressional records to establish conclusively that he did, nor in the funeral notice to indicate such a rumor. The death announcement clearly states *dans sa maison*.

The home referred to must be the one near the fortifications of the city. The error may have been perpetuated by Cruzat who wrote that "Pierre Enguerrand Philippe died at his country home, May 14, 1800," and this would be the basis for the perpetuation of the story that he died at Fontainebleau.

Clément Laussat stayed at the Marigny plantation in 1803 and says: "Our habitat being near the gates....is always called out of town (*hors de ville*). Then it follows that "out of town" would be in the country and would be referred to as a country home. But then Cruzat also says "among the estates left by his father, Mr. Marigny owned the charming property of Fontainebleau near Mandeville."[53]

Then there is Grace King who further writes on Bernard Marigny that his second marriage not proving a happy one, "he passed more and more of his time at his father's old summer home of Fontainebleau, on the north shore of Lake Pontchartrain, not for the sake of seclusion and quiet it offered after the excitement of American politics and financial speculations, but for the greater liberty it granted for the enjoyment of his favorite pleasures – the table and convivial intercourses with friends."[54]

Tinker also says that Louis-Philippe, Duke of Orléans, and his entourage were entertained at "Fontainebleau," beautiful plantation at Mandeville and that visits were made there by Laussat in 1803.[55]

Tinker also wrote that after the War of 1812 "Louisiana soon took to her natural life … and Marigny was pursuing pacific designs, improving his Fontainebleau Plantation and to call his slaves to labor ordered the biggest bell which the State had ever known." The quotations just cited could be multiplied, but the ones given are typical of the legends that have been firmly implanted in the public mind throughout the years. All activities that allegedly took place at Fontainebleau by the Marigny family are not founded on facts. To set the record straight, it was Antonio Bonnabel who became owner of the land through decrees of 1790, 1797, and 1798, of the land later known as Fontainebleau. From 1829 to 1852, this area was operated by Bernard Xavier de Marigny as the Fontainebleau Plantation. It has been reported that the plantation bell, ornamented with scroll and figure work could be heard, under favorable conditions, in New Orleans. Tradition has it that the bell, showing almost human loyalty to the Old South, crashed to the ground the morning Lincoln signed the Emancipation Proclamation.[56]

Bernard de Marigny, from his second union with Ana Mathilde Morales, had two sons and three daughters. They are, as follows:

1. Antoine Jacques Bernard de Marigny was born in New Orleans in 1811. He attended and graduated from the French military academy of St. Cyr in the 1830s before briefly serving as a lieutenant in the French cavalry, fought a duel, retired and came back home to operate his father's plantation. His wife was Sophronia Claiborne, daughter of William C.C. Claiborne, first American governor of Louisiana, and Cayetana Susana Bosque y Fangui. He built a home near what is now the north shore town that bears his father's name. Their three children died without issue.

Another real estate promotion that went up about the same time was Jeffersonville, on the Tchefuncte River just above Madisonville. The property was purchased by Benjamin Hart and Antoine Bernard de Marigny de Mandeville, Bernard's son, but Hart later bought him out. The 1,600 arpents tract was subdivided into squares, which were put up for sale at public auction at the New Exchange Coffee House, on the corner of St. Louis and Chartres streets in New Orleans on

November 7, 1836. Although many lots were sold, there is no sign today that such a division ever existed.[57]

During the Civil War, Jacques was a Colonel of the 10th Louisiana Infantry Regiment (French Brigade) and served at the Battle of Fredericksburg. He resigned, July 23, 1862, and returned to planting after the war. He died 30 June 1890.

2. Rose de Marigny de Mandeville, born in 1813, married Mr. Sentmanate y Sayas of Havana on June 20, 1831. He was executed in Mexico for conspiring against President Santa Anna.[58] After the death of her husband, Rose married Adolphe Esnould de Livaudais, a Louisiana state senator but had no children from him.

3. Angela de Marigny, born January 19, 1816, married F. Peschier, Swiss consul, in New Orleans, with whom she had seven children.

4. Armand de Marigny de Mandeville was not married.

5. Mathilde de Marigny born January 21, 1820, married Albin Michel de Grilleau, son of a French consul in New Orleans.

Bernard's marriage to Ana Mathilda Morales was not a happy one. She filed for a separation of property in 1852, which the court granted her in 1853. She remained at the Marigny family home where she occupied the lower floor while her husband occupied the upper story and it was reported that they never exchanged one word in conversation. Bernard saw it as his duty to feed and clothe his estranged wife, even paying all of her medical expenses until the day of her death.

The inscription on her tomb in St. Louis Cemetery No. 2, New Orleans reads as follows: *"Anna Mathilde Morales Épouse de Bernard de Marigny Décédé le 1er août 1859, à l'âge de 69 ans."*

Bernard remained active in the civic and social life of New Orleans. From 1816 to 1868, he always presided over commemorative celebrations held in Jackson Square in observance of the Battle of New Orleans. In the face of adversity, Bernard always maintained the façade of an aristocratic gentleman for he was a man of the finest manners and of the greatest courteousness. He was a generous man, one who could also afford the luxury of being eccentric. He possessed immense resources and devoted his income to the gratification and entertainment of his friends. He was well versed in history and other subjects. Even in adversity, he manifested his customary gaiety or disposition. He enjoyed conversing with friends, and indeed possessed rare conversational talents. For a long time, he was an orator most loved by the public. His voice was well-suited for this art. He was graceful, confident and well-known for his puns which he would let fly at random, so many at times others were at loss for an answer. W. H. Sparks who served with Marigny in the Legislature once said that Bernard's wit and satire were his most dreaded weapons, and ridicule was his forte.

Bernard Marigny was often misrepresented by historians as well as by his contemporaries during his lifetime. His greatest aim in life was to preserve Louisiana's French cultural heritage, a legacy that would distinguish her from its other sister states in the union.

Bernard maintained a cottage in Mandeville facing Lake Pontchartrain in the square bounded by Lake, Gerard, Claiborne and Lafitte streets. It was Edmond, a former Marigny slave, who diligently took care of the property. In this cottage, Bernard was said to have spent the happiest moments of his life where he continued to receive family, friends and his contemporaries. He last visited his cottage less than six weeks before his death.

Bernard lived nine years after the death of his estranged wife. It happened suddenly on the afternoon of February 3, 1868, at the age of eighty-three years, on one of his daily walks up Royal Street, when he slipped and stumbled on an icy patch in front of the residence of Mr. d'Hémécourt. The blow on his head produced almost immediate death.[59]

Bernard's Will was dated July 8, 1865. He especially requested that his body be placed in the tomb with his first wife. His grandson, Gustave de Marigny, being the son of Prosper de Marigny, by his first marriage with Maria Jones, was named as the head of his family. His testamentary executor was to remit to him all family portraits, the engravings representing the New Orleans Marigny family, family papers, letters of his ancestors, and correspondence, particularly with the Duke of Orleans, who became King Louis-Philippe, and the letters of that King.

The solemn services of the Catholic Church, for the repose of the souls of the dead, were performed at the residence of the deceased, on Frenchmen street, opposite Washington Square, and at the graveyard.[60]

He was buried on a cold, wet and dreary day, but in spite of the weather the procession of mourners "was of a magnitude that showed the esteem in which the deceased was held and the high respect entertained for the family."[61] The pallbearers were W.C.C. Claiborne, Jr., William Hepp, Gabriel de Feriet and Melcourt Bienvenu.

316

The greatest of tribute came from his former slaves and their descendants who were among the mourners, showing that in their change of status they remembered the kindness and sympathy of this venerable gentleman.

In a ponderous mausoleum, in St. Louis Cemetery Number 1, the chivalrous Bernard lies beside his first wife and other members of his family. He did not die a pauper, he left an estate valued at more than $20,000, including $5,000 cash in the Citizens Bank and unimproved property in New Orleans and Mandeville. ($1.00 worth of 1868 dollars is now worth $16.13 in 2012, and $25,000 of 1868 dollars would be worth $403, 225.81 in 2012).[62]

A representative of the *ancien régime*, Bernard Marigny witnessed the breaking up of old ties, the wrecking of old estates, but saw hope in the future. Being born in 1785, in 1868 he was considered of a past generation. For his generous nature and courtly manners, we consider and admire him as a *chevalier* of the olden times.

Throughout his life Bernard remained the perfect gentleman, a man who gave himself to public service, a man who strived to preserve Louisiana's cultural legacy and a man who will forever remain the representative of a forgotten society. His ancestors were present at the founding of the Louisiana colony while he saw the flags of Spain, the United States and the Confederacy fly over the city.

NOTES

1. "Creole" is identified as descendants of families who were in the Province of Louisiana before the Purchase of 1803. "Creole" has to do with time and place – not with race.
2, "Did You Know?" *Reader's Digest*, Volume XXIV, April 15, 1974, No. 48.
3. Familiar to Bernard de Marigny, the Château de Bagatelle is a small neo-classical château with a French landscape in the Bois de Boulogne, initially a small hunting lodge near Paris.
4. King, Grace, *Creole Families of New Orleans,* Macmillan, New York, 1921, 20,
5. Tinker, Edward Larocque, *The Palingenesis of Craps*, New York Press, 1933, 1-3.
6. *Louisiana, A Guide to the State*, Hasting's House, New York, 1941, 146.
7. Cited by Bernard Marigny *à ses Concitoyens*.
8. *Memoirs of Pierre Clément de Laussat,* photo static copy of original available at Howard Memorial Library. Original published by M. Vignanjour, Paris, 1851. A translation made through the courtesy of Stanley Clisby Arthur, in an article by Clarence L. Johnson, "The Family of Marigny de Mandeville and the

Fontainebleau Plantation 1700-1938, Part 3," *Louisiana Conservation Review*, Winter 1939, 49.

9. Ibid., 49.

10. Notarial Archives, New Orleans, Peter Pedesclaux, Notary, Book 3333, Act No. 534, May 19, 1804.

11. Ibid., Article 3.

12. Ibid., Article 4.

13. Ibid., Article 5.

14. Inflation Calculator 2012 Online.

15. *Acts of the Louisiana Territorial Legislature*, Session of 1805, Chapter 36, 352.

16. Martin, Alex, "Black revolt leader became a symbol of Louisiana slaves," St. Bernard/Plaquemines Bureau, December 2, 1984.

17. Ibid., December 2, 1984.

18. Seebold, Herman de Bachelle, *Old Louisiana Plantation Homes and Family Trees*, Pelican Publishing Company, Gretna, 1971, Volume 1, 55.

19. Obituary Notice, Bernard Marigny, *L'Abeille/The New Orleans Bee*, February 4, 1868, Page 1, Column 7.

20. Ibid., Page 1, Column 7.

21. *Acts of the Louisiana Territorial Legislature*, 1 Session, 1806-1807, Chapter 27.

22. St. Louis Cathedral Archives, New Orleans.

23. *The Times Democrat*, November 15, 1885, Page 3, Column 3.

24. Hyland, William de Marigny, "A Reminiscence of Bernard de Marigny, founder of Mandeville," Delivered before a meeting of Mandeville Horizons, Inc. May 26, 1984, Online article, p. 12.

25. Le *Courrier de la Louisiane*, September 9, 1808, page 3, Column 1.

26. *Sacramental Records of the Archdiocese of New Orleans*, Volume 5.

27. Gayarré, Charles, *History of Louisiana*, 3rd Edition, 125-131.

28. Le *Courrier de la Louisiane*, September 22, 1809, Page 3, Column 1.

29. Ibid., February 1, 1811, Page 3, Column 1.

30. Ibid., May 20, 1811, Page 3, Column 3.

31. Ibid., May 25, 1812, Page 3, Column 1.

32. Gayarré, Charles, *History of Louisiana*, Volume 3, 1866, *Op. cit.*, Volume 3, 272-273.

33. Le *Courrier de la Louisiane*, September 25, 1812, Page 3, Column 1.

34. Ibid., July 5, 1814, Page 3, Column 1.

35. Ibid., October 7, 1814, page 3, Column 1.

36. Reilly, Robin, *The British at the Gates: The New Orleans Campaign in the War of 1812*, Putnam Publishers, 1974, 322.

37. Le *Courrier de la Louisiane*, December 29, 1815, Page 3, Column 5.

38. Derived from the French, to beat. Alluvial land built up beyond the levee by the silting action of a river and exposed during low-water stages.

39. *Journal of the Senate*, Second Session, 5th Legislature, State of Louisiana, New Orleans, 1822, Volume 3, 265.

40. Ibid., 57.

41. Ibid., 59.

42. Ibid., 67-68.

43. *L'Abeille/The New Orleans Bee*, February 4, 1868, Page 1, Column 7.

44. *Le Courrier de la Louisiane*, January 21, 1830, Page 1, Column 1.

45. Ibid., June 20, 1824, Page 1, Column 2.

46. Ibid., January 18, 1828, Page 3, Column 4.

47. Ibid., December 6, 1831, Page 3, Column 3, and December 15, 1831, Page 3, Column 1.

48. Ibid., December 24, 1831, Page 3, Column 1.

49. Ibid., January 5, 1832, Page 3, Column 1.

50. Ibid., January 23, 1832, Page 3, Column 1.

51. Ibid., February 2, 1832, Page 3, Column 1.

52. Ibid., July 6, 1832, Page 3, Column 2.

53. Cruzat, *Op. cit.* 45

54. King, Grace, *Op. cit.* 35 and 37.

55. Tinker, *Op. cit.* 301 and 307.

56. *Louisiana, A Guide to the State*, Hasting House, New York, 1941, 440.

57. Ellis, Frederick, *St. Tammany Parish, L'Autre Côté du Lac*, Pelican Publishing Company, 1971, 111.

58. *Le Courrier de La Louisiane*, June 24, 1831, Page 3, Column 3.

59. Obituary Notice of Bernard Marigny, *The New Orleans Bee*, Page 1, Column 7.

60. Obituary Notice of Bernard Marigny, *New Orleans Daily Crescent*, February 5, 1868, Page 1, Column 3.

61. Ibid., Page 1, Column 3.

62. Inflation Calculator 2012 Online.

CHAPTER 22

BERNARD DE MARIGNY'S LEGACY

Bernard de Marigny de Mandeville, considered as one of the grandest Creoles of his time, should be remembered for establishing the first suburb of New Orleans. Beginning in 1805, with the subdivision of his plantation, he gave his name to the Faubourg Marigny which has survived to this day. It was his answer to the newly created American sector on the other side of Canal Street. The natural antagonism that existed between the American and Louisianan citizens of New Orleans had developed into a fierce rivalry of business competition. Bernard's development was an instant success, and as early as 1836 Faubourg Marigny was chartered as a separate city governed by its own council. In 1852, the three cities now known as le Vieux Carré, Faubourg St. Mary and Faubourg Marigny were again consolidated into a single government. The area developed by Marigny has survived to become one of the most intact Creole neighborhoods in the city. In the issue of New Orleans Magazine, March 2001 issue, Faubourg Marigny was named one of the four great neighborhoods of New Orleans. The faubourg is on the National Register of Historic Places. Two streets of New Orleans, Mandeville and Marigny, carry Bernard's family name.

On June 25, 1829, Bernard de Marigny bought magnificently wooded tracts of land where he and his family would later spend the hot summer months to enjoy a temperate climate amid a lush canopy of oaks and towering pines, where wildlife, fish, numerous species of birds and water fowl were abundant throughout the area. This vast land became known as Fontainebleau, which Bernard named after the palace and former royal Hunting Park and forest located 55 kilometers outside of Paris, an area he had visited and admired. Renowned as a symbol of grandeur, it was the setting of the Second Empire Court of Napoleon III.

Tracing the history of Bernard Marigny's Fontainebleau, it all began with Don Antonio Bonnabel, a prominent New Orleans merchant, who acquired three tracts, under land grant, from Spanish Colonial Government. Situated to the east of Bayou Castine, in the Parish of St. Tammany, facing Lake Pontchartrain, it was sold by Marcellin and Amelia Bonnabel, heirs of Antonio Bonnabel, for 1,200 dollars. The three concessions amounted to a total of four thousand and twenty superficial arpents, according to a plan drawn on January 15, 1799, by the late Charles Carlos Trudeau, then Surveyor General for the province of Louisiana. The plans as well as the titles were delivered by the vendors to Sieur Marigny, the purchaser. The sale also included a master residence, other outbuildings and possibly the sugar mill already on it.

On March 15, 1832, the Congress of the United States met to confirm Marigny's claim to the two tracts of land bought on June 25, 1829, from the Bonnabel heirs.[1] Titled An Act for the relief of Bernard de Marigny of the State of Louisiana, it was enacted by the Senate and the House of Representatives of the United States of America in Congress assembled, so that Bernard de Marigny as assignee of Antonio Bonnabel be confirmed in his land grant of four thousand superficial arpents situated in the Parish of St. Tammany, in the State of Louisiana, bounded on the southwest by Lake Pontchartrain, and on the northwest by lands formerly owned by the heirs of Lewis Davis.[2]

The tract to be confirmed, by this section, is the same which was surveyed by Carlos Trudeau for Antonio Bonnabel on January 15, 1799, and granted to Bonnabel by Manuel Gayoso De Lemos, Governor General of the provinces of Louisiana and West Florida; and for which a claim was filed in the name of Bonnabel, in the land office at St. Helena court house, under the act of Congress of April 25, 1812.

Claim had first been presented to the Commissioner at St. Helena court house under the act of 1812, in the name of the heirs of Lewis Davis; "but no report was ever made to the Commissioner. The omission seems to be accidental, as no reason has been assigned for not reporting on it."[3] The claim was marked on the plat with the name of Pedro Piquery, to whom Bonnabel had sold it, and who retroceded it to him, not having been able to pay the price. It was understood that a portion of the land sold could be the object of reclamations by Mrs. Ford, or the Etourneaux (Letourneau) heirs. If the claimants were to succeed, Bernard Marigny would have nothing to exact from these vendors.

The Committee was satisfied that the title to this tract of land was complete and valid in the heirs of Lewis Davis; that if the transfers and conveyances from the heirs of Lewis Davis through Antonio Bonnabel, down to Bernard Marigny were genuine, "of which they have no doubt, it should be confirmed to the petitioner."

In Section 2, it was further enacted that Bernard de Marigny be confirmed in his claim to a tract of land of seven hundred and seventy-four superficial arpents, situated in the State of Louisiana and Parish of St. Tammany, bounded on the southwest by Lake Pontchartrain, on the north side by Castin Bayou, and on the southern side by the lands confirmed in the first section of this act; the said tract of seven hundred and seventy-four arpents being the same which was granted on January 20, 1777, by Peter Chester, British Governor at Pensacola, to Lewis

Davis, whose title to the same was afterwards, to wit, on June 11, 1788, confirmed by decree of Estevan Miro, Spanish Governor of the provinces of Florida and Louisiana, and for which a claim was filed in the name of the heirs of Lewis Davis, in the land office at St. Helena court house, under the Act of Congress of April 25, 1812: "Provided that the said two tracts of land shall be considered as confirmed, in the same manner, and under the same regulations, restrictions, and provisions, as if the same had been recommended for confirmation in the reports of the commissioner for the district west of Pearl River and east of the island of New Orleans, which was confirmed by the act of Congress, approved on third day of March, one thousand eight hundred and nineteen, entitled "An Act for adjusting the claims to land, and establishing land offices in the districts part of the island of New Orleans."

It was also provided that the claim of Antonio Bonnabel, embraced in the said commissioner's report, as of four hundred arpents, to be considered as comprised in the forming part of the tract of four thousand and twenty arpents confirmed in the first section of this act. This Act was approved on March 15, 1832.[4]

It was there at Fontainebleau that Marigny would spend much of his leisure time and where he engaged in many of the pastimes that earned him a somewhat "notorious reputation." At his estate in Fontainebleau, he entertained his friends with the elegance for which his family was noted. Friends were treated to regal parties of fine dining, drinking, hunting and fishing. It was not only Bernard's north shore retreat to relax, entertain and hunt, but a working sugar plantation. Then, a brick-making facility and other structures were added.

Marigny's sugar plantation, a questionable business plan to begin with, was not successful, easily explained if one looks at the land at Fontainebleau; it does not compare to the growing of sugar cane as in the Cajun country to the west. Unable to harvest enough to make the operation pay, Marigny had to resort to transporting cane grown at his two plantations in Plaquemines Parish by steamboat across the lake for processing in the Fontainebleau mill.

The 1837 economic downturn was a hard blow for Louisiana planters. A cause of the financial distress in Louisiana was the tariff which had depreciated the value of American sugar in proportion as the duty had been reduced on the foreign article. Taken from the *Annals of Louisiana*, one hundred and thirty-six sugar plantations were given up in 1837; numerous bankruptcies followed. Lands could no longer be sold; therefore fortunes based on them were devalued and fell even more suddenly than they had risen.

Bernard's private explanation of financial loss and failure was only too well known in Louisiana: "a road to failure well trodden by sugar planters in the past."

"Certain persons, "writes Marigny, "have often asked the question: 'How did Mr. Marigny lose the fortune he possessed, of five or six hundred thousand dollars?' To which he replies: "The answer to the question is as easy to make as to understand – it disappeared under the influence of events and circumstances which I could not control."

At the time of his departure for France in 1839, Bernard had an appraisement prepared of all his property. The amount of his fortune was fixed at nine hundred and fifteen thousand dollars and his debts amounted to three hundred and twenty thousand dollars, two hundred and eighty thousand of which represented a debt to the Citizens Bank.[5]

Writes Bernard: "I had a sugar plantation and a brickyard, but to develop the sugar plantation I needed to construct buildings, dig canals, provide equipments, and put in necessary machinery. To meet such great expenses, crops were needed. They failed in consequence of a crevasse in 1850, followed by another in 1851. That is not all: bricks fell to their lowest price."

Even though Marigny had received a prolongation on the terms of his mortgages, believing that he could retrieve his losses, his lingering credit problems of 1837 caused him the loss of Fontainebleau when the Citizens Bank and the Bank of Louisiana compelled Marigny to liquidate the majority of his estate in 1852 or they would seize it.[6] He was forced to sell at a very moderate price being "The Citizens Bank, naturally." Fontainebleau was then sold to H. Griffon on February 23, 1852, Adolphe Boudousquie, Notary.[7]

In the late 1800s logging operations came to the pine forest of St. Tammany, and in the early 1900s, the property was acquired by the Great Southern Lumber Company who operated one of the largest sawmill in the world between 1908 and 1938.

Bernard Marigny's Fontainebleau plantation was later referred to as the Tchefuncte State Park, followed by a major park which grew out of the Fontainebleau Marigny tract on Lake Pontchartrain, in the 1930s, when the Louisiana state park system was created and the 2,800 acres for the current park was acquired. De Marigny's Plantation is now beautiful Fontainebleau Louisiana State Park, a tribute to Bernard de Marigny. It is located 45 minutes from New Orleans on the north shore of Lake Pontchartrain near Mandeville, the resort town developed by Marigny in 1834.

Readily visible today in the park are parts of the walls and chimneys of the sugar mill near the Visitors Center. The Fontainebleau wooden cottage, of the New Orleans type, no longer exists. Foundations and remnants of other buildings continue to be uncovered.

The Bernard Marigny plantation bell is in the Cabildo Museum, property of the Louisiana State Museum. It was given by Mr. George William Nott who purchased the plantation in 1881. The following inscription appears on one side of the bell in raised letters: "J'appartiens à Monsieur Bernard Marigny." (I belong to Mr. Bernard Marigny). On the other side is inscribed "Sous la gestion [*sic* Gestion] de Monsieur H. Turpeau." (Under the management of Mr. Turpeau). Around the rim at the bottom is, "Fondue à l'atelier de Thiac Maignan Durand Nouvelle Orleans le 2 juillet 1825. (Cast at the workshop of Thiac Maignan Durand New Orleans 2 July 1825). Around the top of the bell are twenty-three raised stars, lower down are twenty-three eagles.

The real estate developer, Bernard de Marigny, did not begin to purchase property on the north shore of Lake Pontchartrain until twenty-nine years after the death of his father. He had subdivided his plantation next to the French Quarter in New Orleans to create a neighborhood still named after him. His aim, in 1829, was to buy, then subdivide and sell with similar success part of his extensive holdings that lay west of his plantation, the area known as Bayou Castein, in St. Tammany Parish. The village founded in 1834 by Bernard de Marigny de Mandeville was made up from the following tracts of land.

On January 22, 1829, Marigny purchased three different parcels of land which devolved to the said five children of the late Morgan Edwards. The first parcel contained seven hundred and seventy five arpents fronting on the Bayou Castein and having a front on the Lake Pontchartrain. The first parcel is now Section 51, T.8S. R.11E and Section 46 in T. 8S. R.12E.

The second parcel contained eight hundred arpents, formed a parallelogram and lay contiguous to the first parcel. The description on the plot of survey was made by Charles Laveau Trudeau, Surveyor General, on January 8, 1799. The second parcel is Section 38, T.8S. R. 11E. and Section 45 in T.8S. R.12E.

The third parcel, 5 arpents frontage, on the margin of the Lake, more or less, lay contiguous to the lands of Uriah Smith, and was bounded on the east by the two parcels first described with all the improvements on said lands. The third parcel is Section 50 of T.8S. R.11E.

The sale was made for four thousand dollars. The three parcels of land are all in the Greensburg District of Louisiana. Most of this property was later subdivided and became part of the town of Mandeville.[8]

On November 17, 1829, Marigny bought the property described below from William Bowman: "…part or parcel of land situated in the Parish of St. Tammany measuring ten arpents front on Lake Pontchartrain (between Bayou Tchefuncte and Castein) by forty arpents deep be the same more or less, bounded on the west by land belonging to Joseph Letchworth, and on the east by land belonging to the heirs of Thomas Spell, being the same which the said William Bowman acquired by purchase from the heirs of the late Jacob Bartles….on December 20, 1826."

The property known as Section 47, T.8S. R11E of the Greensburg District was later subdivided and became part of the town of Mandeville. The purchase price was $1,200 payable one-half cash and the balance secured by a note for twelve months.[9]

signatures of Bernard de Marigny, Parish Judge Lyman Briggs, and witnesses Obed Kirkland and W. P. Mortee

On December 24, 1830, personally appeared before Judge Jesse R. Jones, Uriah Smith, brother of Samuel Smith deceased, and Margaret Edwards, wife of Thomas Tate, daughter of Margaret Smith, deceased, the sister of the said Samuel Smith, deceased, and who has been the widow of Morgan Edwards, deceased, and afterwards widow of Hugh Sheridan, deceased, said Margaret Edwards is authorized and assisted by her said husband. Also appeared John Edwards, Daniel Edwards, Robert Edwards, and Charles Edwards, sons of the said Margaret Smith by her first marriage and Samuel Sheridan, the son of the said Margaret Smith by her second marriage, and Jacob Wood, the son of Margaret Edwards, deceased, Daughter of said Margaret Smith by her first marriage; and Charlotte Sheridan, the daughter of the said Margaret Smith by her second marriage.

The said above-named persons, being the heirs of the said Samuel Smith, deceased; declared that they have bargained, sold, conveyed and delivered to Bernard Marigny of the city of New Orleans present and accepting for himself and his heirs a certain tract or parcel of land lying and being situate in this parish on the margin of Lake Pontchartrain bounded on the East by lands formerly belonging to the Edwards and now owned by present purchaser, on the South by Lake Pontchartrain and on the West by lands occupied by Mrs. Elizabeth Bartle supposed to contain two hundred superficial acres, the same having been confirmed by the government to Samuel Smith as appears by the certificate of the Register and Receiver of the Land Office at St. Helena Court House.

The said Vendors declare that they and their ancestors have been in peaceable possession of said land for upwards of thirty years, and that they put the purchaser in their place and stead, and subrogate him to all their rights upon the said tract of land, but without any guaranty of title or quantity. This sale is made for and in consideration of the sum of sixteen hundred dollars all in hand paid, the receipt whereof is hereby acknowledged. It appears that the certificate of the Register of mortgages for this parish of this date that this property is free of any mortgages registered against the present vendors. Thus done and passed and the parties have signed their names in presence of James B. McCoy and Wesley Mallory; witnesses who have also signed with the Judge aforesaid, Jesse R. Jones.

signatures of interest

On July 12, 1830, Bernard Marigny bought the property of Martha Richardson, wife of Joseph Letchworth: "A parcel of land situated in

326

the Parish of St. Tammany, bounded on the South by Lake Pontchartrain, on the East by the Obner tract, now owned by the present purchaser, on the North by Chinchuba Creek, and on the West by the Labatut tract, now owned by Judge Lewis, containing six hundred and thirty one acres."[10]

This property had been acquired by inheritance from Zachariah Faircloth, her former deceased husband who died leaving no heirs but his surviving wife, the said Mrs. Martha Richardson. This property now Section 46, T.8S. R.11E. of the Greensburg District was sold for $3,200.

signatures of interest

Marigny, the purchaser, made two promissory notes of even date payable to Joseph Letchworth: the first for two thousand dollars payable on the first day of November next, at which time possession of the property to be given. The other for twelve hundred dollars payable November 1, 1831.

On August 6, 1834, no other heir having appeared to contest the sale it was ratified and confirmed before Jessie R. Jones, Notary Public. The Bond previously given by Martha Richardson and by William Cooper on August 6, 1825, was cancelled and annulled on July 28, 1838.[11]

On September 6, 1830, in the presence of Judge Jessie R. Jones, appeared Joseph Sharp, the bearer of a power of attorney, for John, Aaron and Thomas Spell of Madison county, Mississippi, and Sarah Spell, wife of Joseph Sharp, who sold and conveyed to Bernard Marigny of the city of New Orleans, a tract of land containing 640 acres lying and being situated in the Parish of St. Tammany, twenty acres from the lake, at the back line of the Thomas Spell tract now occupied by Mrs. E. Bartle and running back of the Smith and Edwards tracts the same distance of the lake, for quantity having been acquired by the present sellers by inheritance of their father, John Spell, deceased.

The sale was made for the sum of three hundred dollars. Witnesses were David B. Morgan and Daniel Edwards.

Marigny acquired additional property in the Parish of St. Tammany. Jesse R. Jones on September 5, 1831, in pursuance of a judgment of the Court of probates for said parish, pronounced in the case of Hortense Delisle vs. Thomas Spell's heirs, after the legal advertisements and all the formalities required by law proceeded to the sale of a tract of land situated in this parish fronting on the Lake Pontchartrain and bounded on the other sides by lands belonging to Mr. Bernard Marigny. No record was found to indicate that Marigny bought Section 39 to the north of this tract, thus it would appear that he owned land on two sides only. According to certificate it contained 360 acres, but according to the surveyor's return, it contained only 220 acres.

After various offers and bids, Bernard Marigny of the City of New Orleans, being the highest bidder, said tract of land was adjudged to him, for the price of $1,620.00.[12] This property, now Section 48 of T.8S. R11E, of the Greensburg District later became part of the town of Mandeville.

The early site of Mandeville, comprised the William Bowman tract, purchased by Marigny, November 17, 1829; the three tracts of the heirs of Morgan Edwards purchased January 22, 1829; the tract of land from Martha Letchworth, the widow of Zachariah Faircloth, July 12, 1830; the purchase from the heirs of Samuel Smith, December 24, 1830; the purchase from the heirs of Thomas Spell, September 5, 1831, and the additional property in the Delisle *vs* Thomas Spell's heirs.

The total cost of the above property amounted to $11,620., or approximately $4.06 per acre. Based on a survey approved 8/12/1852, the total acreage for the above property amounted to 2,856.4 acres.[13]

During the early 1830s, the population and the economy of New Orleans had flourished as never before. By 1834, the north shore was beginning to prosper economically as Mississippi River traffic increased and more people traveled north *via* Lake Pontchartrain to Covington and Madisonville, the only two towns in St. Tammany Parish, while en route to other destinations.

In 1805, Marigny had succeeded handsomely in his real estate speculations in New Orleans. With all the land recently acquired, he decided that the year 1834 was the most propitious time to pursue a new development across the lake. John Davis, entrepreneur, his business associate and friend, encouraged him to establish a small resort community for wealthy New Orleans to visit in the summertime in order to escape the summer heat and seasonal outbreaks of Yellow fever.

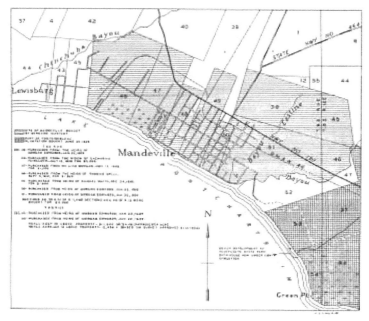

Map showing site of Mandeville bought by Bernard Marigny in 1829-1831:
Greensburg District T.8S. –R.11E

On January 1, 1834, Marigny published an advertisement in *L'Abeille de la Nouvelle Orléans* (*The New Orleans Bee*).

Valuable Property for Sale[14]
Quartier de Mandeville

Will be sold at public auction at Hewlett's Exchange, as soon as the plan shall be made, the wide space of ground divided in large lots, laying in front of Lake Pontchartrain, opposite the Railroad and at seven leagues distance from New Orleans: situated between Casting Bayou and Judge Lewis' plantation; it measures 5,000 arpents; previously to the sale a prospectus shall be published, which will give some particulars of the advantages of the place and the beauty of the trees which over-spread it, and in order that the purchaser may convince himself of the facts mentioned in my prospectus, he shall be allowed to refuse the sale within one month after the day of sale, provided he will go and visit the lot adjudicated to him and will declare to my agent on the premises that he does not accept the adjudication; the purchasers shall be afforded the facility of repairing to Quartier Mandeville, on appointed days at the house of Mr. Coquillon, who is a resident there.

December 7th   B. Marigny

Subsequently, an additional announcement was published in *L'Abeille de la Nouvelle Orléans* on February 5, 1834:

"The steamboat Black Hawk, Captain Hofffman, will leave the railroad, Sunday next, at 9 o'clock A.M. for Mandeville and will on the same day leave Mandeville at 4 o'clock P.M. Persons desirous to visit the lots of ground offered for sale, are to meet at the railroad near the river at 8 o'clock A.M. – the departure will be at 8½ A.M. Steamboat expenses will be paid by the subscriber."[15]

B. Marigny

A few days later *Le Courrier de la Louisiane* carried the following item: "The sale of a small portion of the lands at Mandeville, situated over the lake, belonging to Mr. Marigny, and, which took place yesterday, February 24, at Hewlett's Exchange brought $55,000 (it should be $40,975). The part of the lots sold does not constitute the fourth part of the whole. The sales continue today and will not probably be completed under two or three days."[16] Other lots were sold from time to time but as late as 1842, all were not sold.

The conditions attached to the sale of the lots were to be payable in one, two and three years credit, in notes endorsed to the satisfaction of the seller with special mortgage until full payment. The acts of sale were by Felix de Armas, at the costs of the purchasers.[17]

The sale lasted for three days (February 24-26 inclusive). The auctioneers were T. Mossy, Garidel and F. Dulillet. Sales on the first day amounted to $40,975, on the second day to $27,975 and on the third day to $11,050, a total of $80,000 for the three days.[18] A total of 426 lots were sold and the price ranged from $1,275 for Lot No. 3, Block 25 on the Lake to $40 per Lot No. 6, Block 18 (fourth Block from the Lake between Madison and Monroe Streets). Considering that the entire property cost only $11,620 dollars, and that much of it was still unsold, Marigny made quite a profit on his investment.

The lots were sold conforming to the town plans drawn by Surveyor General Louis Bringier for Marigny's *Quartier de Mandeville*, and were notarized January 14, 1834.

Louis Bringier first began making maps about 1808. He was made surveyor of the Parish of St. James by governor Villeré about 1822, and was made surveyor general of Louisiana in 1825.[19]

Marigny, a forward thinking-developer, attached several conditions to the sale preserving the right of public domain:

* That the area between the lake and Lake Street was to remain free and common ground in perpetuity.
* All streets to the lake were to remain open.
* All streets required to have a width of fifty feet with the exception of Marigny and Jackson streets, which were to be one hundred feet in width and Lake Street which was to be sixty feet in width.
* Marigny prohibited the obstruction of "Little Bayou Castaing" and the destruction of the shell ravines which apparently lined the banks of the bayou.
* Marigny obligated himself to complete a wharf extending into Lake Pontchartrain and to construct a bridge over Bayou Castaing, but stipulated the future maintenance of these structures would be the responsibility of the property owners in Mandeville.
* The steamer the *Blackhawk* would be provided for transportation to and from New Orleans, and the fare would not exceed one dollar. This service under succeeding ownerships continued.

The development was an instant success. The street names given by Marigny were less colorful than the ones used in Faubourg Marigny. Names of presidents, war heroes and statesmen such as Jackson, Monroe, Galvez, Carondelet, Claiborne and Lafitte were used.

A gambling casino and many hotels were built in the newly established resort town. In July 1837, the steamboat *Pontchartrain,* built in St. Tammany, began running to Mandeville, Lewisburg, Madisonville and Covington landing three days per week with regular Sunday excursions.[20] Regular steamboat excursions carrying passengers from New Orleans to Mandeville became popular. The scenic lakefront beach, the fresh air and cool breezes were all promoted and as a result the town flourished as a popular resort.

Mandeville was an instant success, but many families were forced to give up their properties during the depression of 1837. Bernard

Marigny lived long enough to see the community evolve into one of the most popular resorts in nineteenth century Louisiana. He also maintained a cottage in Mandeville facing Lake Pontchartrain in the square bounded by Lake, Gerard, Claiborne and Lafitte streets. Edmond, a loyal and former slave of the Marigny family, lived in Mandeville and was caretaker for Bernard's property there.

Few people inhabited Mandeville during the Civil War. Union troops under the command of Major F. H. Peck occupied the town. By the late 19th century, Mandeville's lakeshore resort town increased in popularity.

The north shore of Lake Pontchartrain is known as the oldest inhabited locality in St. Tammany Parish. It was first visited by pioneers who crossed the lake, then by British settlers who fled to escape the Revolution. Further development came with Bernard de Marigny. Today's Mandeville, after Madisonville and Covington, can be considered as the third oldest town in what is now St. Tammany Parish where it sits amid wild woods and encroaching swamplands.

Bernard Marigny is memorialized by Marigny and Mandeville streets in New Orleans; St. Bernard Avenue, Mandeville, Louisiana; Faubourg Marigny, a suburb of New Orleans, and the Fontainebleau State Park.

Many historians on both sides have distorted or misrepresented their recollections of the Battle of New Orleans. Marigny's 1848 Historical Memoir, *Réflexions sur la campagne du général André Jackson en Louisiane en 1814 et 1815* has received little if any attention in contemporary accounts. In his 1853 pamphlet entitled *Bernard Marigny à ses Concitoyens*, he describes his role in securing the services of the Lafittes brothers and the Baratarians.[21] As chairman of the legislative defense committee, he dealt with the responsibility of making available all the state's resources available to Andrew Jackson to win the war. He deserves credit in that he successfully managed to have the Lafitte pirates decriminalized by the legislature and the court. Had it not been for the artillery used in the campaign, manned and directed by the Lafittes and their men, the course of history could have been changed dramatically.

As the leader of the Creole population, Marigny exerted his influence, fighting to preserve the continued use of French in legal documents. He was a supporter of the public school system and equal political rights for naturalized as well as native citizens.

Bernard Marigny, a key player in most state events in the first decades of the nineteenth century, described his life as one given to public service, "and no one doubts that this has cost me considerable expenditures. These expenditures I have borne, for I have never solicited or obtained a lucrative office. I have contributed my efforts that my compatriots should not be entirely dispossessed of their language, their customs and their laws."

The use of his money, he wrote "has always been honorable, by my household standards as well as by the assistance I have been able to give to the needy, to the poor mother of the indigent family, and to the unfortunate soldier. Have they not always found me willing to give a helping hand?"

As a politician and statesman, Bernard served with dignity and integrity. He embraced the principles of the Democratic Party of which he remained a faithful partisan. At the time of his death, it was said that for fifty years he had presided at every mass meeting of the party.

Generous and extravagant, he was more practical than he has been portrayed. He and the Philippe de Marigny de Mandeville ancestors are a living symbol in the history of Louisiana. In our eyes, Bernard de Marigny de Mandeville was and will always remain "an honorable man."

NOTES

1. Laws of the United States Passed at the First Session of the Twenty Second Congress, Private No. 37.
2. Laws of the U.S. Treaties, Regulations, and other Documents Respecting Public Lands, No. 756, Volume 2, entitled "An Act for the Relief of Bernard de Marigny."
3. Reports of Committees of The House of Representatives at the Second Session of the Twenty-first Congress (Begun and Reed) at the City of Washington, December 6, 1830, printed by Duff Green, 1831, 106.
4. Johnson, Clarence, L., "The Family of Marigny de Mandeville and Fontainebleau Plantation, 1700-1938, Part 4, *Louisiana Conservation Review*, Summer 1939, 41-42.
5. A description of Fontainebleau Plantation, in mortgage to Citizen's Bank of Louisiana by Bernard Marigny and wife in *Notarial Archives*, New Orleans, Theodore Seghers, Notary May 12, 1837. Document 235, also in Act of Sale by Marigny in 1852 to H. Griffon. Notarial Archives, New Orleans, Adolphe Boudousquie, Notary, February 23, 1852. Book No. 3105, Document 37.
6. One may refer to the description of Fontainebleau Plantation, in mortgage to Citizen's Bank of Louisiana by Bernard Marigny and his wife, Anna Mathilde

Morales-Marigny, in *Notarial Archives*, New Orleans, Theodore Seghers, Notary, May 12, 1837, Document 235.

7. *Notarial Archives*, New Orleans, February 23, 1852, Book No. 3105, Document 37.

8. *Notarial Archives*, New Orleans, Felix de Armas, Notary, March 4, 1834, Document 84, Deposit of Document by Bernard Marigny. See also Carlisle Pollock, Notary, January 22, 1829, Book 949, 33.

9. *Notarial Archives*, New Orleans, Hugh K. Gordon, Notary, November 17, 1829. Document No. 940. Act was signed by all the parties and witnesses excepting the Notary who died sometime between November 17, 1829 and February 4, 1830. On the latter date the same act was notarized by Hugh Pedesclaux, Notary, Book No. 3389, Page 106. No Document Number. See *Deposit of Documents* by B. Marigny, September 1, 1834 with Felix de Armas, Notary, Document No. 483. Boman signs his thus, but it is usually spelled Bowman. *This Deposit of Document* gives the date of the sale of the property by the heirs of Jacob Bartle, also spelled Bertell, to Bowman.

10. *Notarial Archives*, New Orleans, Felix de Armas, Notary, dated September 6, 1834. Document No. 489. Deposit of Documents by B. Marigny. On August 6, 1834, no other heir having appeared to contest the sale it was ratified and confirmed by Jesse R. Jones, Notary Public, St. Tammany Parish.

11. Court of Probates for the Parish of St. Tammany, under the signature of Lyman Briggs, Parish Judge, August 8, 1834.

12. *Notarial Archives of New Orleans*, Felix de Armas, Notary, March 4, 1834. Deposit of Documents by Bernard Marigny, Document 5.

13. Map showing site of Mandeville bought by Bernard Marigny in 1829-1831.

14. *L'Abeille de la Nouvelle Orléans*, January 1, 1834, Page 1, Column 6.

15. Ibid., February 5, 1834, Page 2, Column 3.

16. *Le Courrier de la Louisiane*, February 25, 1834, Page 3, Column 1.

17. *Notarial Archives*, New Orleans, Felix de Armas, Notary, March 4, 1834.

18. *Notarial Archives*, New Orleans, Felix de Armas, Notary, March 4, 1834, Document 84. *Deposit of Documents* by Bernard Marigny.

19. Reports of the Committee of the Senate of the United States for the First Sessions of the Thirty-Sixth Congress in Two Volumes, Washington: George W. Bowman Printer, 1860, Volume 1, 89.

20. Ellis, Frederick S., *St. Tammany Parish: L'Autre Côté du Lac*, Pelican Publishing Company, Gretna, 1998, 111.

21. This pamphlet was privately printed in French.

CHAPTER 23

CHANGING TIMES ON THE LAKE FRONT

During the period, 1820-1840, immigration rapidly increased as the concept of *manifest destiny* swept the nation. Thus, the massive emigration west pushed white settlement even further west into the American wilderness. In 1834, the north shore of Lake Pontchartrain entered an era of progress with easier means of transportation to get in and out of Madisonville, Mandeville and Lewisburg. Steamer access proved essential to the development of Mandeville which traces its roots to Bernard de Marigny de Mandeville, the New Orleans developer, who gave his family name to the new resort town, and for the development of Lewisburg named in honor of Joshua Lewis.

The Labatut tract, an early English land grant, often mentioned in Court Case No. 225, has an interesting history. Haden Edwards (no relationship to Morgan Edwards Huett) was a businessman from a wealthy and political family in Kentucky, his father being the first Senator when it became a State. Haden came down to Louisiana around 1817 for business interest. He had a family of twelve children. Soon after his arrival, two of his children died of yellow fever. He wanted out of New Orleans because of his children. He bought the old Paul and Peter Labatut land grants on the lake-front from sailing master Jonathan Ferris who had purchased the land from William Dewees who had gone to Washington, District of Columbia.[1]

The tract was purchased after 1830 by Joshua Lewis, a prominent gentleman and lawyer by profession, and a graduate of Washington College. From Virginia he removed to Lexington, Kentucky, to practice his profession. He was elected to the state legislature of Kentucky. Six of his children were born in Lexington. When Louisiana was purchased in 1803, he was sent to New Orleans by President Jefferson, together with Edward Livingston and James Brown to receive the purchase territory from the French.

In 1806, he was appointed judge of the Superior Court of the Territory of Orleans, and when the state was admitted into the Union, he was made judge of the first judicial district, a position he retained, until his death in 1833. He served under General Andrew Jackson in the second war with Great Britain, and participated in the night attack on the British, December 23, 1814, as the captain of an organized military company composed of Americans.

At the second election after the admission of Louisiana to the Union, Judge Lewis being a prominent citizen was placed in the gubernatorial field against Jacques Villeré. Owing to the intense rivalry between the Creole and American elements, he was defeated by a small majority. He died in 1833. Members of the bar desired to erect a monument in his honor, but his children refused. Their father had requested that he be buried with his wife who had departed this world, three years prior. He was entombed with her in the cemetery just above Madisonville, on the west bank of the Tchefuncte River. The lake front of his country seat, lying immediately west of Mandeville, was laid out, then sold in town lots. Named Lewisburg in his honor, the town was dedicated in 1834.[2] It has remained to this day a quiet residential area.

The first two towns in St. Tammany Parish were Madisonville and Covington. Madisonville was founded in 1800 as the town of Coquille because of the abundance of shells in the area, at the site of the Native American village of Chiconcte. In 1810 it was renamed in honor of the President of the United States James Madison.[3]

Jacques Dreux, who received a Spanish land grant on the west bank of the Bogue Falaya River, laid out a small town as early as 1805 and called it St. Jacques (St. James). The Dreux tract was acquired by John Wharton Collins who on July 4, 1813, dedicated the Town of Wharton. By a Legislative Act adopted March 11, 1816, the town was incorporated and the name changed to Covington.[4]

The isolated community where Elizabeth Bartle and Martha Letchworth, worthy adversaries in Court Case No. 225, lived during the Spanish period, when it was known as Pontchartrain Post, and the early American period, was now attractive to New Orleanians. Three days per week, with regular Sunday excursions, steamboats began regular service from New Orleans to Covington, Madisonville, and Mandeville. A large hotel was built in Mandeville and excellent dining became an attraction of the new community.

Court Case No. 225 took its toll on the small Bayou Castein community. To settle estates, over five thousand acres of land, the old English land grants along the lakeshore, were sold to Bernard Marigny. Within a few years, the two new settlements that began in 1834 had filled up with new residents lining the lakeshore with fine new homes.

What happened to Elizabeth Bartle and Martha Letchworth, the two *grandes dames* of Bayou Castein? What legacy did they leave? Elizabeth Bartle remained on the 320 acres known as the Goodby tract, land on which the Tom Spell Memorial Cemetery is presently located. Elizabeth's son, Thomas T. Spell, Junior, and his wife, Mary Sodon, purchased, for $200 dollars, the Goodby tract of 320 acres and improvements at the public auction sale in the partition of his mother's estate in 1844.[5] Joseph Letchworth had property between Bayou Chinchuba and Covington and this is where he lived until he sold to Bernard Richardson. Short changed of 75 acres, Richardson sued Letchworth.

Today, we can only visualize how life was different for Elizabeth Goodby when she was young and involved in raising a large family. The land that had been for many years more wilderness than anything else needed much optimism to make the going possible on a day to day basis. Friends and neighbors supported themselves through their endeavors, their trials, their joys and their sorrows. Zachariah Faircloth was not the type of man who would have sued a neighbor. Had he lived, Court Case No. 225 would never have taken its toll on the small community since they were all related by blood or marriage. Times were changing. Young couples were leaving the area to settle on homesteads that were readily available in the state of Mississippi or Washington Parish. Elizabeth's daughter Eleanor Helen married to Freeman George had left to settle in Texas. They were with the "Original 300" that settled in the "Steven F. Austin First Colony." Those who sold their land to Bernard Marigny did so at the right time for within a few years land prices had dropped drastically.

Elizabeth Bartle may have been Jacob's and Elizabeth Goodby's only child, but she was issued from a long line of children, twelve Spell siblings. Elizabeth and her first husband, Thomas Spell, left a large progeny. Their descendants today are too numerous to count! Martha Faircloth did not have any children with either Zachariah Faircloth or Joseph Letchworth, but she raised her two nephews as her own, Joseph (line of Donald Sharp) and William Sharp. The Sharp family and their descendants have been a part of the North Shore of Lake Pontchartrain for more than two hundred years.

Widow Elizabeth Bartle died January 10, 1844. She was between 70-72 years of age. Martha Letchworth, about 63 years of age, died at Strawberry Bluff on November 14, 1844, and was buried there.

Elizabeth Bartle was buried near her first husband, in the Tom Spell Cemetery. Her coffin was made by John Fontini, an Italian immigrant, husband of Sarah Charlotte Sharp, eldest daughter of Joseph and "Sally" Spell, for the sum of five dollars. Fontini, a local carpenter, was paid to construct with select pieces of wood kept on hand, pine or cypress lumber, the wedge shape, simple six-sided coffin in accordance with the measurements of the deceased, wide at the shoulders and narrow at the feet.[6]

Charles Morgan, son of David B. Morgan, surveyor and Justice of the Peace, was the administrator of the Estate of Elizabeth Bartle. Joseph Sharp and William Strain were the appraisers of the property belonging to the deceased. The major share of Elizabeth's estate consisted of 320 acres and the four slaves described below:

Amount derived from the sale of the Negro girl named Belle:
$595.00
Amount derived from the sale of the Negro woman named Sarah:
66.00
Amount derived from the sale of the Negro man named Philip:
170.00
Amount derived from the sale of the Negro man named Abraham:
126.00

Abraham and Sarah were the faithful slaves that were illegally seized and jailed in 1829 by Sheriff James Daniels and Joseph Letchworth. Belle appears to be Sarah's child who was listed "about aged six months." Abraham was now about 60 years old and Sarah about 55 years of age. Unfortunately, the names of the purchasers are not known.

The Succession of Mrs. Elizabeth Bartle and the Petition, Accounting and Tableau of Distribution were filed on May 2, 1845, by Lyman Briggs, Parish Judge.[7] Interest on $847.00 for one year at 8% was $67.70. Total of estate amounted to $1,866.00. Debts, expenses and administrative commissions amounted to $324.00. The balance to be distributed among the twelve Spell heirs amounted to $128.00 dollars per person.

Joseph Letchworth was a man of several trades during his life time: a mariner, a ship captain, carpenter, and ferryman.

In September 1831, Judge Jesse R. Jones, William Bagley, George T. Gilbert, Commissioners appointed by the Police Jury of St. Tammany gave a contract to Joseph Letchworth and another man to build the first wooden bridge over the Bogue Falia at or near where the military road crosses the same.[8] Because of the description, it appears to be an error on the part of Jesse R. Jones, the composer of the contract. What is likely meant is the Bogue Chitto River. Reference made to the Washington Parish map prior to 1825.

The bridge was to be built of good light wood or heart pine and finish the same in a workmanlike manner with good hand tools. It was to be high enough to pass whenever the Road can be passed through the swamp to the bridge. The bridge was to be delivered on or before the first day of December 1832, and to be built in conformity to the plan deposited in the parish bridge office, except in such parts as may be changed with the consent of the Commissioners.

"Commissioners on their part agreed to deliver to Letchworth a subscription list which amounts to upwards of the three hundred and fifty dollars, and to authorize him to forthwith collect the amounts there subscribed, and on completion of the bridge, to give him a draft on the parish Treasury for the sum of one hundred dollars and to authorize him to receive from Messrs. John W. Hyde and Martin G. Penn, the sums in their hand, arising from road fines to the order of the Police Jury. Letchworth agreed to pay Commissioners five dollars per day for any day that shall pass after the first day of December next, until said bridge to be completed. Letchworth was to keep bridge in good condition for three years after the first of December. Letchworth as principal and Charles R. Hyde as security bind themselves in the final sum of five hundred dollars for the faithful performance of the conditions of the contract. Contract made in single and deposited in the office of the Parish Judge where each party shall be entitled to have access to it, and to use is in evidence when necessary." Covington, September 28, 1831.

[Signed] Jesse R. Jones, Geo. T. Gilbert, Wm. Bagley, Joseph Letchworth, Chas. R. Hyde.[9]

An 1804 survey depicting a 25, 830 arpents grant made to Don Enoul Felipe Dugues, shows two roads intersecting just south of the Bogue Chitto River. The one that runs northwest is called the road from Pearl River to Natchez. The other, which runs about north and south, crossing the Bogue Chitto, is called the road to Buck Falia. From other surveys of the period, we find that the Barrio of Buck Falia encompassed the Covington area.[10]

Strawberry Bluff was settled about 1808. In the St. Tammany Census of 1812, Richard S. Chappel had a settlement at Strawberry Bluff. It is of historical importance because on his way to New Orleans, in November 1814, General Andrew Jackson followed the overland route which led from Mobile to the Pearl River, just above the Louisiana state line, then southerly to Madisonville. It is located very close to where the Military road crosses the Bogue Chitto.

On November 29, 1814, Major H. Tatum in his diary details the route saying that Strawberry Bluff was 24½ miles from Alston's to Madisonville, and he allowed 8 miles from Madisonville to Wharton, narrowing it down to 16½ miles from Covington to Strawberry Bluff.[11]

"Alston" is Absalom H. Alston whose property was sold to Richard S. Chappel, on June 9, 1819, located at Strawberry Bluff. As early as 1821, there is an indication of heavy traffic on the Military road. An exclusive franchise was granted by the legislature to Richard S. Chappell on January 13, 1821, to operate a ferry across the Bogue Chitto on the main road from Covington to Jacksonville Springs, "at a place called the Strawberry Bluff."[12]

The John C. Seaman St. Tammany Ward Map, 1906, is a good drawing of where Strawberry Bluff and the Military road were, from Bogue Chitto, all the way down to Covington.[13]

The dividing line in Washington Parish was not made until 1820. It went around the Chappel property, which makes the property still in St. Tammany Parish. The John Spell property is adjacent to the Chappel property, but north of it and in the new Washington Parish. When Washington Parish was created it was in the description of the dividing line between the two Parishes: "beginning at David Robertson's on the Tangiphoa, then a direct line to Daniel Edwards on the Tchefuncte, thence a direct line to the Strawberry Bluff on the Bogue Chitto, from thence, a direct line until it strikes the Pearl River.

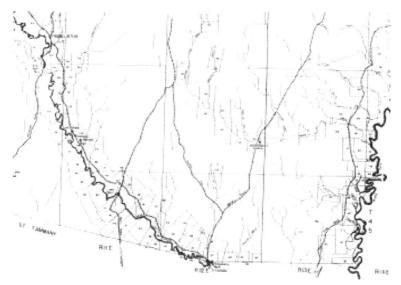

Lyman Briggs noted that the Bank of Louisiana acquired Strawberry Bluff from Richard S. Chappell who held a mortgage on the place until the Sheriff of St. Tammany Parish seized the property and returned it to the Bank. There is no specific date of Chappell's acquisition or the seizure noted in the document.[14]

The Bank of Louisiana having foreclosed on Richard S. Chappel, on June 30, 1835. Joseph Letchworth bought the 640 acre tract of land with Martha's money.[15] This purchase, bought for $1,042.00, was arranged before notary Charles W. Crawford in East Baton Rouge Parish. Lyman Briggs wrote and recorded it in St. Tammany Parish on February 15, 1836.

Seaman's map shows the location of Strawberry Bluff listed under R. S. Chappell under D. Porter. The neighbors are John Tally, Judge "Bushesel" Warner, and the Bogue Chitto River. To the north is John Spell, formerly of Bayou Castein.

On September 30, 1839, Joseph and Martha Letchworth, for unknown reasons, jointly mortgaged the Strawberry Bluff property in the sum of $1,300.00. Nothing about a bridge is said in this mortgage.

The 1843 Civil Suit #590, Parish Court, Benjamin Richardson *vs* Joseph Letchworth is about an unpaid note. Letchworth owes

Richardson $284.86 with some interest. Richardson is listed as residing in Washington Parish.

In a court order signed May 26, 1843, Judge Lyman Briggs instructs Letchworth to pay up. Abraham Penn, Sheriff, serves the order to Letchworth on June 3, 1843. Sheriff Penn seized the tract of land known as Strawberry Bluff, with all the buildings and improvements thereon, plus 140 heads of stock cattle, an unnumbered stock of hogs, and two young horses.

Penn also seized the exclusive privilege of keeping a bridge across the Bogue Chitto River for the term of ten years, part of which time had expired. Rights had been granted to Letchworth by the Louisiana Legislature in an Act approved March 14, 1836.

In Court Case No. 225, Joseph Letchworth appeared to be the driving force behind the suit. Reminiscent of Elizabeth Bartle, Martha Richardson now takes a stand against her husband and demands a Separation of Property.[16] The object of her claim is to recover the $3,370.00 of her funds and belongings. Martha alleges that Civil Suit # 590, Parish Court, was unsupported. She states that Benjamin Richardson is attempting to deprive her of her rights to own property; that her husband owes her in the first place.

Specifically, the 100 head of cattle belonged to her before her marriage. She considers they were in joint ownership with Joseph, but no one had the right to seize them. Martha maintains her rights to mortgage the whole place herself, if she wanted to, for that amount of money, or for a different amount.

It appears from some tiny notes in the file that some kind of public auction was held July 1, 1843: some cattle were sold, but at least 75 remained. No one bid up to 2/3 of the value of the other items, so nothing else really changed hands that day.

Judge Jesse R. Jones, familiar with Court Case No. 225, signs an order telling Sheriff Penn to stop any further proceedings of seizure, and/or stop any sales of Mrs. Letchworth's property. Martha demands a re-negotiation of the debt with Benjamin Richardson, giving herself until July 17, 1843, to pay off the remainder of the $284.56. The response does not appear until an Answer was filed November 6, 1843.

A small affidavit included in the previous mentioned file was signed by Joseph Letchworth on November 7, 1843. Joseph states that Bernard Marigny paid him $3,200.00 dollars. No date specified, but he says he converted these funds to his own use and purposes. This is the amount that was paid by Marigny when he purchased the land that Martha had inherited from her deceased husband, Zachariah Faircloth.

Benjamin Richardson filed an Answer in November 1843, alleging that Martha's affidavits were insufficient; that she filed her suit in the 8th District Court, whereas his seizure was ordered in the Parish court. Next, he requested Martha pay him an additional 20% on his notes as damages, and $100.00 as "Special damages." It is not known if he collected these additional monies or not, but the situation seems to have dragged on into the spring of 1844.

It does appear that some kind of private mortgage or assurance was secured by Martha before March 1844. On March 9, 1844, she bid for, and bought her own Strawberry Bluff property at auction. That same day, Sheriff Abraham Penn gave Martha $706.65 which was the exact proceeds from the sale held that day liquidating assets, not described, at the home of Joseph Letchworth.

Eli Baker, a neighbor, witnessed Penn giving Martha the money. On that same day, she paid off her mortgage in the amount of $706.65. There is no record of Martha taking out a formal mortgage at the Clerk's office.

In a civil suit titled Joseph Kirkland *vs* Joseph Letchworth, March 21, 1843, the Sheriff tried to attach Strawberry Bluff for non payment of a debt. Kirkland said Letchworth borrowed $249.16 from him on April 24, 1841. The money had not been repaid in the spring of 1843, and Kirkland pointed out Strawberry Bluff to the Sheriff, so Letchworth could be served. It appears that Letchworth was instructed to bring 100 heads of cattle forward to be auctioned. There were no further actions about a sale, but on June 3, 1843, W. H. Kirkland wrote a note to the Sheriff, stating that no further action was necessary, and there was no need to sell any property to settle the debt.

Jacob Bartle may have judged right when he said that Letchworth "was a contentious and cankerous old man."

On September 16, 1844, being weak and feeble in body but sound of mind, Martha Letchworth, at her residence in St. Tammany Parish, on the Bogue Chitto River, proclaimed her last Will and Testament. At the request of Lyman Briggs, Parish Judge, it was Mr. G. Penn who wrote Martha's Will.

After the usual opening formalities, Martha clearly states that she is the owner of Strawberry Bluff, and having no forced heirs, gives her husband Joseph a usufruct to enjoy and reside at the place for the remainder of his life. At his death, the property is to be divided between her nephews Joseph Sharp, William Sharp, Martin L. Sticker, her niece, Martha Sticker, wife of Henry Cooper, Drucilla Raiford, niece, the widow of William Raiford, deceased, and Elizabeth, wife of Ambrose White, niece.

The Will was done in the presence of Charles Magee, Israel Mayfield, William Galloway who made his mark, William Galoway, Martin G. Penn, and Lyman Briggs, Parish Judge.

Martha Letchworth died November 14, 1844, at Strawberry Bluff. The property remained in the hands of Joseph Letchworth until his death in August 1851.

In the 1850 St. Tammany Census, Joseph Letchworth is listed as being 69 years of age, born in Virginia. Sarah Letchworth, 59 years of age, is possibly his third wife. Living with them is Abigail Purce, 19 years of age, born in Mississippi. It is not known if this is Sarah's daughter or hired help. Joseph gives his occupation as ferryman. The value of real estate owned is given as $1,700.00 dollars. His son Stokeley, farmer, lives next to him, with his wife Nancy and 6 children ranging in ages between 11 years and 1 month. A young girl, A.C. Bartles, 10 to 12 years of age, is listed as living in the household.

It is not known what happened to Sarah, Joseph's third wife, or how he provided for her after his death.

To settle Martha's estate, Alexander Cooper was named administrator.[17] Notice for an inventory to be made was in the hands of Paris Childress, Notary Public, dated August 6, 1851. By order of the 8th District Court, the heirs were notified that the inventory of Martha's property would be held on August 22, 1851.[18] Welcome Penny and George B. Miller, the appraisers, were duly sworn before Paris Childress, Notary Public, on August 22, 1851. It was Charles Magee who would point all the property belonging to Martha's estate, having it in his possession as keeper.[19]

Martha's tract of land was situated in St. Tammany Parish on the East side of the River Bogue Chitto, "containing 640 acres, more or less, known as the Strawberry Bluff, with the buildings, improvements, rights ways, privileges, and appurtenances, whereon the deceased resided at the time of her death." Appraisal of Martha's estate amounted to $1,081.10.[20]

Through Court Case No. 225, a historical gem, Elizabeth Bartle and Martha Letchworth left the people of present-day Mandeville a record of its early history. The two women, through their personal trials and the losses they endured, gave us the importance of their extensive family connections. Martha had no forced heirs, but Joseph and William Sharp left large progenies.

The story of these two valiant women, Court Case No. 225, and the early history of Bayou Castein under British and Spanish rule, could have remained dormant in the Covington Archives had it not been for an old family Bible that led Donald J. Sharp Senior discover his Mandeville roots.

The story begins in 1936, when Joseph "Dolly" the last living Sharp, son of Marshall Sharp and Virginia Moss, died in Mandeville. Clarence Sharp, Donald's father and his uncle Edmund Daniel from Sheridan, Wyoming, were part of the heirs of Dolly's estate.

Shortly after the burial, the two brothers went to Dolly's house as it was being cleaned out. In a trash can, in the backyard, they found the family bible ripped in half. Considering that the spine had come apart, it was in relatively good condition. Interesting to note that someone may have thought, "Why should we hang on to this old thing when we don't even know who these people were?" How sad! This bible could have ended in the local dump. Luckily, at the right time and the right place, and with 20/20 hindsight, Edmund Sharp retrieved the bible and took it back with him to Sheridan to have it restored. After his death in 1955, Edmund's family donated the bible to Clarence Sharp.

The page for the date of publication is missing but it is believed to be *circa* 1850. The Bible is an English translation of the King James Version.

To answer his father's questions, Donald Sharp took the Causeway that opened in 1956 to get to the Covington Court House. His research on his family and the early families at Bayou Castein has been a labor of love that has to be passed on to future generations. Their stories had to be told since they form the nucleus for the development of Mandeville!

NOTES

1. E-mail from Donald Sharp to Anita Campeau sent January 7, 2008.
2. Louisiana: Comprising Sketches of Parishes, Towns, Events, Institutions, and Persons, Arranged in Cyclopedic Form (Volume 3), 256-259. Edited by Alcée Fortier, Lit. D. Published in 1914, by Century Historical Association.
3. Madison Historical Marker.
4. Ellis, Frederick S., *St. Tammany Parish: L'Autre Côté du Lac*, Pelican Publishing Company, 1998, 88.
5. Campeau, Anita R., & Sharp, Donald J. "The Tom Spell Memorial Cemetery, Part 1," *New Orleans* Genesis, Volume XLVII, No. 189, 28.
6. Campeau, Anita R., & Sharp, Donald J., "The Tom Spell Memorial Cemetery, Part 1," *New Orleans Genesis,* Volume XLVIII, No. 189, 28.
7. Probate Court of St. Tammany, Louisiana, No. 169.

8. Jesse R. Jones Document No. 1980, Covington Court House.

9. Transcript of Jesse Jones, Document # 1980, dated September 28, 1831. Courtesy of Robin Leckbee, deputy clerk and archivist, Covington Court House, Louisiana.

10. Ibid., 66.

11. Ellis, Fredrick, *St. Tammany Parish: L'Autre Côté du Lac*, Pelican Publishing Company, 1998, 95.

12. Act of Louisiana Legislature, January 13, 1821.

13. Map is a document held in the Covington Court House, through the courtesy of Robin Leckbee, deputy clerk and archivist.

14. Lyman Briggs, Document #2803.

15. St. Tammany Conveyance Book E-1, pages 282-283. Our thanks to Robin Leckbee for the information she gave us on the land sale arranged in the presence of notary Charles W. Crawford of East Baton Rouge Parish.

16. Civil Suits #651, June 5, 1843, and #654, July 27, 1843, 8th Judicial Court titled Martha Richardson *vs* Joseph Letchworth and Abraham Penn, Sheriff. Our thanks to Robin Leckbee for her information on that court case.

17. 8th Judicial Court, St. Tammany Parish, 50½ #203.

18. Paris Childress, Notary Public, Covington, Louisiana, August 12, 1851.

19. Sworn and subscribed in the Parish of St. Tammany in the presence of Paris Childress on 22 August, 1851.

20. Succession of Martha Richardson, deceased, No. 288, 8th District Court, also 288 Probate, copy filed September 8, 1851.

EPILOGUE

During the early 1830s, the economy of St. Tammany Parish blossomed as never before. Bernard de Marigny, the successful entrepreneur from New Orleans, who had acquired large tracts of land across the lake in St. Tammany Parish, in 1834, in a booming economy, saw it as the propitious moment to pursue a new development across the lake. In their summer retreats constructed along the Lake Pontchartrain shoreline, the fortunate people of New Orleans could now enjoy an exquisite landscape in a water-front and water-oriented community.

The country's speculative boom brought about from the sale of public lands that were paid with the notes of insecure Western banks prompted President Jackson to order the public-land offices in the future to accept only specie in payment for lands. The "Specie Circular" played havoc on an already unsound economic situation. The crash held off until after the election of 1836. Elected president, Martin Van Buren, reaped the whirlwind of depression. The 1837 panic, as it was called, swept the country. Economic conditions continued to decline and when the banking institutions stopped specie payments, the result was bankruptcies and failures. Due to the depression, a number of people were forced to give up their properties. Growth of Mandeville remained at a stand still for a number of years.

Marigny did provide land for a Church, a cemetery and a school. Our Lady of the Lake Parish Church celebrated 150 years of history in 2000. The first baptism was in 1850 and the first slave to receive the sacrament was Elisa, daughter of Rosalie, a slave of Joseph Pujol. Margaret Blany was the first person buried there when the Reverend Joseph Outendirck, a native of Belgium, the first pastor of the church of Mandeville, performed the first funeral on January 26, 1851. The Archdiocesan Archives in New Orleans have an alphabetical list by surname of the five funerals that occurred between the years 1858-1859 while Father Lamy was pastor. Four of the five were buried in the cemetery of Our Lady of the Lake while the Reverend Victor Privet was buried in the sacred sanctuary of the church.

From information gathered in the 1850 Census for the St. Tammany Parish there were two Methodist Preachers, one Baptist Preacher, one Episcopal Minister and two Roman Catholic Priests who attended to the spiritual needs of the parishioners.

Secession from the Union by the Pelican State in 1861 and the Civil War that followed proved devastating for the citizens of the north shore. Mandeville was inhabited by very few people during the War since Union troops under the command of Major F. H. Peck occupied the town. The period of Reconstruction, characterized by corrupt governance and widespread violence left a painful legacy in the area. People on the north shore were faced with a shattered economy and war ravaged infrastructure associated with so many years of warfare.

Mandeville came into prominence in the late 1800s primarily as a resort town. It was regarded as a health and vacation resort, and a safe refuge against yellow fever that came to New Orleans each summer with alarming regularity. As the need for hotels and other services grew, so did the population. The north shore area continued to grow. Lake steamers, commuter trains, enabled development of the area. Bridges and highways encouraged more development.

The Benedictine Fathers took over Our Lady of the Lake Parish in the early twentieth century and would establish the parish school under the Reverend E.J. Lavaquery. The first religious teachers were the Sisters of Christian Charity. Due to conflicts with the sisters, Reverend J.C. Schmitt would ask the Benedictine Sisters at St. Scholastica Convent to teach the students, but as the school grew, a lay faculty was needed.

The history of Mandeville would not be complete without details of *Père* Adrien Rouquette, a frequent visitor. Reared as a youth in his Creole parents' home on Bayou St. John (near *Bayou Sauvage*), this missionary priest, naturalist, poet and romanticist, crossed the lake from New Orleans to work with the Choctaw Indians. Beginning in 1845, he gave them twenty-nine years of faithful services. He became their Chahta-Ima, "like a Choctaw," by living with them and administering to them from his five hermitages on the northern shore of Lake Pontchartrain.

One small chapel, built of pine logs, was near the Tom Spell family cemetery on the east banks of the Chinchuba Creek, a thousand feet south of present-day Highway 190. Spell was the owner of 500 acres in 1790 that include present day Chinchuba Gardens as well as the church property. Père Rouquette's log cabin was located on the present "Little Terry" or "Little Tory" property off Highway 190. Another chapel known as "Chuka-chaba" or "The Night Cabin" was on Bayou Castine near the lake.

In regard to the dead Christian Indians under his care, oral tradition is that Father Rouquette buried his dead on high knolls on both sides of the creek. According to Mr. Edgar Sharp, in an article written under the pseudonym of "The Old Pelican," no markers have ever been found to show their last resting place.

Chinchuba, a corruption of Hachunchuba (Indian alligator) was an institution for the deaf maintained by the Sisters of Notre Dame so named for the bayou that ran near the school. L'Abbé Rouquette's small square log chapel known as "The Cabin in the Oak on Chinchuba Creek" was moved to the school grounds for safekeeping. It was covered with boards to protect it from the weather.

In the 1940s, the deaf institute was closed and the Kildare Chapel fell in disrepair. People were now breaking up the building for wood and grazing sheep used it as a shelter. The door was hanging by its hinges. Edgar Sharp, who had worked at the Deaf Institute, called the Archbishop in New Orleans and told him of the situation. The church dignitary was not interested in the old Chapel, so he and his son, Darryl, brought the altar to their garage. It remained there for a long time, used as a wood saw table and work bench. About 1985, Edgar Sharp donated the altar to the monks at St. Joseph's Abbey, in Covington, where it remains today in display in the Rouquette Library. "Ah! So this is why the altar has saw marks and drill holes in it," exclaimed Father Dominic Braud when Donald Sharp recently told him the story. [Father Braud, a monk of St. Joseph Abbey, wrote the introduction to Blaise C. D'Antoni's *Chahta-Ima*].

The old oak tree where Father Rouquette preached is no longer there. It was removed when the land was cleared to make way for a modern highway.

Were it not for the missionary work of Father Rouquette among the Choctaws and the narratives of François Rouquette on the history of the Choctaws and the *History of the Chickasaws*, we would have much less understanding on the history and the ethnology of the region. These men were the specific products of their time and their society, and probably their most profound expression.

The date of a community cemetery in Mandeville is obscure. We were unable to find the year of the first burial in Mandeville's Cemetery. The size of the cemetery is two blocks square and one half of a square is swampy. About 3 acres in size, rectangular in shape, it fronts on Villere with sides of Foy and Jackson Streets and in the back that of Montgomery. The cemetery if full of remarkable graves, upwards of 300 with some over a hundred years old. This cemetery is home to the many persons responsible for the rise and the success of Mandeville.

Chinchuba where Thomas Spell, Elizabeth Goodby's husband, was buried in 1815 definitely falls in the category of the oldest family and privately owned cemetery in the area. Now known as the Tom Spell Memorial Cemetery, with its first burial in 1815, it is an important historical site in Mandeville.

This majestic site, characterized by its natural and exceptional beauty, is a habitat of local flora, and is a peaceful refuge from the world. Prior to 1980, according to the markings in the Cemetery, half of the area was still wooded with pine and hardwoods, such as cedar and oak. Today, only a few large oaks remain. Modern Highway 190, with all the traffic and business runs today through the land where *Père* Rouquette had his Chapel and close by is the once Sharp, Spell, Strain Cemetery enclosed by a fence because of encroaching new homes.

Today we can celebrate the rich and sophisticated history, in a frontier country, of captivating and energetic personalities set against the background of a romantic region.

The research recorded in *The History of Mandeville from the Revolutionary War to Bernard de Marigny* was pursued with a twofold interest: that of contributing to the local history of Mandeville in its formative years and to give as broad a view as possible of the people involved on the North Shore of Lake Pontchartrain.

BIBLIOGRAPHY
ARCHIVAL SOURCES

A. Canada
Archives Nationales du Québec à Montréal, May 9, 1677. Presently
housed at La Grande Bibliothèque, 475 Blvd. De Maisonneuve,
Montréal, Québec, H2L 5C4.
Massicotte, E.Z., Repertory of Engagements Conserved in the
Judicial Archives of Montreal, 1670-1778.
Archives Paroissiales de Notre-Dame de Montréal:
*Registres des baptêmes, mariages et sépultures, Notre-Dame de Montréal,
1642-1708.*
Census, Montreal: 1677, 1681.

B. Cuba
Cooper to Folch, Legaho 1568, *Papeles de Cuba.* September 12, 1810.

C. England
Minutes of the Council, February 26, 1776, Colonial Office 5/634.
Governor Johnstone's instruction relating to granting of land in C.O.
5: 44-56; 5: 201, 131-177; CO 5/608.
C.O. 5/595, Memorial of Proprietors of Land, Planters, Merchants –
undated.
Grant Book A, as extracted in An Index to English Crown Grants,
1755-1775.
British Florida Land Claims, Book 2, part 2. MS. 976.3 (396.13)
Special Collection, Tulane Library, Louisiana.
Memorandum by Queen Victoria on the character of Louis-Philippe,
May 2, 1885. (*Letters 3*, 122).

D. France
Letter, Patent of nobility, signed Louis and Phélipeau, dated Paris
1654, and registered "*à la Cour des Aydes et Comptes de Rouen, 1656.*"
Bienville to Minister Jérôme Phélypeaux, Comte de Pontchartrain,
July 28, 1706; October 27, 1711, loc. Cit., f. 584-592.
Census : 12 August 1708 by M. de la Salle. AC, C13A, 2, f. 225-227.
Mandeville, Jean François. *Mémoire sur la Louisiane*. Paris, April 29,
1709. Printed by Guillaume Després. Paris, rue St. Jacques, 1765.
Pontchartrain to Bienville, July 11, 1709.

E: Spain
Index to the Archives of Spanish West Florida, 1782-1910.
Pedro de Marigny Service Sheet, June 30, 1792, AGI, PC. Leg. 161-a.
Pintado Papers. Microfilm Reel #SARS-2. Survey of Federal Archives
in New Orleans Library.
Spanish Documents, Box 45. Doc. 1073-3, No. 14. LSM.

F. United States
Acts of Louisiana Territorial Legislature: Session of 1805, Chapter 36;
Session 1: 1806-1807; April 24, 1811.
Acts of Louisiana Legislature, March 25, 1813; March 11, 1816;
February 18, 1817; January 13, 1821; March 6, 1819.
Reports of the Committee of the Senate of the United States for the
First Sessions of the Thirty-Sixth Congress in Two Volumes.
Washington: George W. Bowman Printer, 1860, Volume 1.
Notarial Archives, New Orleans: Peter Pedesclaux, Notary, Book
3333, Act No. 534, May 19, 1804; Felix de Armas, Notary, March 4,
1834, Document 84, Deposit of Document by Bernard de Marigny.
New Orleans Notary Archives. Acts of Juan Batista Garic, Volume 9,
April 6-8, 1778, ff. 02-224.
Rowland, Dunbar and A.G. Sanders, *Mississippi Provincial Archives,*
1763-1766. English Dominion, Volume 1, Nashville, 1911.
——-*Official Letter Books of W. C.C. Claiborne, 1801-1816,* Jackson, State
Department of Archives and History, 1917, Volumes 5, 6.
United States Federal Census, 1850, Wharton County, Texas.

SACRAMENTAL RECORDS

Hebert, Donald J. *Southwest Louisiana Records,* 1770-1783, Volume 2.
Inscription on Tombstone of Marigny Family. St. Louis Cathedral.
New Orleans.
Sacramental Records of St. Louis Cathedral: 1786-1796. Volume 2. Act No.
547; 1548.
Sacramental Records of St. Louis Cathedral: 1802-1806. Volume 4. Act
No. 601.

ST. TAMMANY 8th JUDICIAL DISTRICT COURT

Archives, Clerk of Court, St. Tammany Parish.
Archives, St. Tammany Historical Society.

Civil Suit #651, June 5, 1843, and #654, July 27, 1843: 8th Judicial
Court titled Martha Richardson *vs* Joseph Letchworth and Abraham
Penn, Sheriff.
Court Case No. 225: Letchworth & Wife vs. Bartle & Wife, 1825-1829.
Index to Court Records: St. Tammany Parish Courthouse, Covington,
Louisiana.
Jones, Judge of the Parish of St. Tammany, dated October 15, 1819.
Notarial Record Book A. Parish of St. Tammany and State of Louisiana.
Notarial Record Book B. Parish of St. Tammany and State of Louisiana.
Petition of Amelia Morton and her husband John Morton to the
Honorable Jesse R. Petition filed by Samuel Mallory, May 21, 1825.
Probate #38, Elizabeth Middleton, Probate B. Morgan, 1848.
Succession of Thomas and Mary Spell, December 20, 1848.
Suit No. 519-B of the 8th District Court, St. Tammany Parish.

ABSTRACTS

Peterson, Mary A. "British West Florida: Abstracts of Land
Petitions," *Louisiana Genealogical Register.* December 1971; March
1972; June 1972; September 1972; December 1972.
Watson, Joseph W. *Abstracts of Early Deeds of Edgecombe County, North
Carolina, 1772-1778*, Volume 2, 1967.

DICTIONARIES

Fortier, John. "Philippe de Hautmesnil de Mandeville François."
Dictionary of Canadian Biography Online. Volume 2, 1701-1740.
Jetté, René. *Dictionnaire Généalogique des familles du Québec des origines à
1730.* Les Presses de l'Université de Montréal, 1983.
Juchereau de Saint-Denys, Charles. *Dictionary of Canadian Biography
Online*, Volume 2, 1701-1740.
Maurault, Olivier. "Gabriel Souart," *Dictionary of Canadian Biography
Online, 1000- 1700,* Volume 1.

PUBLISHED SOURCES

Burns, Francis P., "The Spanish Land Laws of Louisiana." *The
Louisiana Historical Quarterly.* Volume II 1928: 579-581.
Calhoun, Robert Dabney. History of Concord. Louisiana Historical
Quarterly, XV, 1932, 44-67.

Campeau, Anita R. and Sharp, Donald J. "The United States Navy and the Naval Station at New Orleans, 1804-1826." The *New Orleans Genesis,* Volume XLVII. No. XLIX, April 2009: 243-284. "British and Spanish Land Grants: From Bayou Castein to the Tchefuncte." *The New Orleans Genesis.* Volume XLVII. No. 186, April 2009, 101-141. "Land Records Helpful in Research." The *New Orleans Genesis.* Volume XLVII. No. 185, January 2009: 1-37. "The Tom Spell Memorial Cemetery, Part 1." *The New Orleans Genesis.* Volume XLVIII. No. 189, January 2010: 1-37. "The Tom Spell Memorial Cemetery, Part 2." *The New Orleans Genesis.* Volume XLVIII. No. 190, April 2010: 101-147. "The Tom Spell Memorial Cemetery, Part 4." *The New Orleans Genesis.* Volume XLVIII. No. 192, October 2010: 351-395.

Casey, Powell A. "Military Roads and Camps in or near Covington and Madisonville, Louisiana." *St. Tammany Historical Society Gazette,* Volume 2, 1977. "Military Roads in the Florida Parishes of Louisiana." *Louisiana History,* Volume XV. "Louisiana in the War of 1812." *Louisiana History,* 1963: 10.

Caughey, John Walton. "Willing's Expedition down the Mississippi." *The Louisiana Historical Quarterly,* January 15, 1932: 57-83.

Coles, Harry L. Jr. "The Confirmation of Foreign Land Titles in Louisiana." *The Louisiana Historical Quarterly.* No. 38, October 1955: 1-22.

Giardino, Marcio, Ph.D. and Guerin Russell. "Surveying in West Florida." Online essay dated February 15, 2010.

Hyland, William de Marigny. "A Reminiscence of Bernard de Marigny, founder of Mandeville." Delivered before a meeting of Mandeville Horizons Inc., May 26, 1984. Online article.

James, James Alton. "Oliver Pollock, Financier of the Revolution in the West." *Mississippi Valley Historical Review* 16, 1929: 67-80.

Johnson, Cecil S. "The Distribution of Land in West Florida." *The Louisiana Historical Quarterly.* Volume 16, No. 4, October 1933: 539-553.

Johnson, Clarence L. "The Family of Marigny de Mandeville and the Fontainebleau Plantation." *Louisiana Conservation Review.*

Jordan, Terry G. "Antecedents of the Long-Lot in Texas." *Annals of the Association of American Geographers.* March 1974: 70-86.

Maurault, Olivier. "Gabriel Souart." *Dictionary of Canadian Biography Online, 1000- 1700.* Volume 1.

Morgan, H.G. Jr. "Tammany, Origin of name." *Publications of the Louisiana Historical Society.* Volume 5, 1954: 54.

Mulloney, William F. "Oliver Pollock: Catholic Patriot and Financier of the American Revolution." *Historical Records and Studies of the U.S. Catholic Historical Society,* 1937: 164-236.

Padgett, James A. ed. "Official Records of the West Florida Revolution and Republic." *Louisiana Historical Quarterly*, Volume 21, July 1938: 688-731.

Prichard Walter, Kniffen Fred, and Brown Calir A. (eds.) "The Journal of James Leander Cathcart." *The Louisiana Historical Quarterly*, XXVIII, July 1945: 850-851.

Rae, Robert R. "A Better Fate! The British West Florida Seal." *Alabama Historical Quarterly*. Winter 1981: 288.

Simoneaux, N.E., and Clarence L. Johnson. "The Family of Marigny de Mandeville and the Fontainebleau Plantation, 1700-1938." *Louisiana Conservation Review*. Autumn 1938; Winter, 1938-1939; Spring, 1939; Summer, 1939. Louisiana Department of Conservation.

Sloane, William M. "The World Aspects of the Louisiana Purchase." *American Historical Review*. Volume 9, No.3, April 1904: 507-521.

Smith, Gene A. "Our Flag Was Displayed Within Their Works: The Treaty of Ghent and the Conquest of Mobile." *Alabama Review* 52. January 1999: 3-20.

Sterkx, Henry E. and Brooks, Thompson E. "Philemon Thomas & the West Florida Rebellion." *Florida Historical Quarterly*. Volume 39, No. 2, April 1961.

Tate, Albert Jr. "The French in Mobile, British West Florida, 1763-1780." *New Orleans Genesis*. Volume 22, No. 87, July 1983.

Watson, Alan D. "Orphanage in Colonial North Carolina: Edgecombe County as a Case Study." *North Carolina Historical Review*. Volume 52, No. 2, April 1975: 105-119.

JOURNALS

A Century of Lawmaking for a New Nation: U.S. Congressional Documents and Debates, 1774-1875. *Journal of the Continental Congress*, Volume 17.

Bassett, John Spencer and Sydney Bradshaw, eds. *Major Howell Tatum's Journal while Acting Topographical Engineer (1814) to General Jackson*. Smith College Studies on History, Volume VII, October 1921 to April 1922. Northampton: Department of History of Smith College.

Clark, Morgan, and Crawford. "Naval Documents of the American Revolution." *Journal of the Continental Congress*. June 17, 1776.

John Halley's Journal...of His Trip to New Orleans...1789 and 1791 taken from Judge Samuel Wilson's photo static copy, collection number 49W31 copied from the Original Journal. Manuscript

Collections and Archives, Service Center, Margaret I. King Library, University of Kentucky, Lexington, KY.
Journal of the Senate, Second Session, 5th Legislature. State of Louisiana, New Orleans, 1822, Volume 3.

NEWSPAPERS

Thompson, Ray. "Oliver Pollock, Unsung Hero of the American Revolution." *Times-Picayune*, New Orleans. Volume 7, No. 3. December 14, 1972.
McLellan, Tara. "Group restores marker dedicated to Battle of Lake Pontchartrain." *The Times-Picayune*. November 14, 2008.
Mangiapane, Erin. "The Forgotten Courthouse, Parish's first courthouse unearthed." *News Banner*. Sunday, October 18, 1998.
L'Abeille/The New Orleans Bee. Obituary Notice for Bernard de Marigny, February 4, 1868, p.1, col. 7.
Le Courrier de La Louisiane: Sale of the Dupard Plantation by Bernard de Marigny, September 9, 1808, p. 3, col.1.
Martin, Alex. "Black revolt leader became a symbol to Louisiana slaves." *St. Bernard/Plaquemines Bureau*, December 2, 1984.
New Orleans Daily Crescent. Obituary Notice of Bernard de Marigny, February 5, 1868, p.1, col. 3.
"Did You Know?" *Reader's Digest*. Volume XXIV. April 15, 1974, No. 48.
St. Tammany Farmer. "Obituary Notice for Judge Jesse R. Jones." March 27, 1880.

PRINTED PUBLICATIONS

Appleton's Encyclopedia of American Biographies and Company, 1900.
Arthur, Stanley Clisby. *The Story of the West Florida Rebellion*. Baton Rouge: Louisiana Classic Series Reprint, Claitor's Publishing Division, 1975.
Barr, Chidsey Donald. *Louisiana Purchase*. Crown Publishers Incorporation. New York, 1972.
Boagni, Ethel. *Mandeville, Louisiana*. The St.Tammany Historical Society Inc., 1980.
Bossu, M. *Travels through that part of America formerly called Louisiana*. English Translation. London, 1771.
Brasseau, Carl A. *Dictionary of Louisiana Biography*. Publication of the Louisiana Historical Association in cooperation with the center of Louisiana Studies at the University of Louisiana, Lafayette.

Candler, Allen D. *Colonial Records of the State of Georgia*. Volume 1. Atlanta, Georgia: The Franklin Printing and Publishing Company, 1904.

Caughey, John Walton. *Bernardo de Galvez in Louisiana, 1776-1783*. Gretna: Pelican Publishing Company, 1972.

Coleman, James Julian Jr. *Gilbert Antoine de St. Maxent: The Spanish-Frenchman of New Orleans*, New Orleans: Pelican Publishing House, 1968.

Conrad, Glen R., ed. *The First Families of Louisiana*, 2 Volumes. Baton Rouge, 1970.

Cooke, John Esten. *Virginia: A History of the People*. Houghton: Mifflin and Company, 1883.

Cornell, Hamelin, Ouellet, Trudel. *Canada: Unity in Diversity*. Toronto-Montreal: Holt, Rinehart and Winston of Canada Ltd., 1967.

Cox, Isaac Joslin. *The West Florida Controversy, 1795-1818: A Study in American Diplomacy*. Baltimore: John Hopkins Press, 1918.

Crane, John Door. *Annotated Genealogical Listings of the Southern Bickhams*. Second Edition, 1992.

Dalrymple, Margaret Fisher, ed. *The Merchant of Manchac: The Letter boos of John Fitzpatrick, 1768-1790*. The Baton Rouge Bicentennial Corporation. Louisiana State University Press, 1978.

Dieler, Hanno J. *The Settlement of the German Coast of Louisiana and the Creoles of German Descent*. Philadelphia: German Historical Society, 1909. Reprint. Baltimore: Genealogical Publishing Company, 1970.

Du Pratz, Le Page. *History of Louisiana*. 1774. Reprint. Baton Rouge: Claitor Publishing Division, 1972.

E. Wade Hone. *Land and Property Research in the United States*. Salt Lake City: Ancestry, 1997.

Ellis, Frederick S. *St. Tammany Parish: L'Autre Côté du Lac*. A Firebird Press Book. Pelican Publishing Company: Gretna, LA., 1998.

Fortier, A.L.C. *Louisiana comprising sketches of parishes, towns, events, institutions, and persons arranged in encyclopedic form*. Volume 3, 1799-1800.

Gayarré, Charles. *History of Louisiana*. Volume 3, 1866.

Gaspard, Elizabeth. *The Rise of the Louisiana Bar: The Early period, 1813-1839*. Louisiana Historical Society, 183.

Giraud, Marcel. *A History of French Louisiana: The Reign of Louis X1V, 1698-1715*. Translation by Joseph C. Lambert. Louisiana State University Press. Baton Rouge: Volume 1, 1974.

A History of French Louisiana: Years of Transition, 1715-1717. Louisiana State University Press, Volume 2, 1974.

Hamilton, Peter J. *Colonial Mobile*, 1897; reprint, *Mobile, Alabama* : First National Bank, 1952.

Hayden, Horace E. *A Biographical Sketch of Oliver Pollock*. Harrisburg: Pennsylvania, 1883.

Haynes, V. Robert. *The Mississippi Territory and the South West Frontier: 1795-1817.* University Press of Kentucky, 2010.

Higginbotham, Jay. *Old Mobile: Fort St. Louis de La Louisiane, 1702-1711.* The University of Alabama Press, 1984.

Holden, Doris E. Martin. *Descendants of John Spell and Cecilia McLemore.* Dogwood Printing Company, MO., 1992.

James, James Alton. *Oliver Pollock, the Life and Times of an Unknown Patriot.* New York and London: D. Appleton-Century Company, 1937.

Johnson, Cecil S. *British West Florida, 1763-1783.* New Haven: Yale University Press, 1943.

King, Grace. *Creole Families of Louisiana.* New York: Macmillan, 1921.

Latour, A. Cacarriere. *Historical Memoir of the War in West Florida and Louisiana in 1814-1815.* Gainesville: University of Florida Press, 1964.

Lebreton, Dagmar Renshaw. *Chahta-Ima.* Baton Rouge: Louisiana State University Press, 1947.

Louisiana, A Guide to the State. New York: Hasting House, 1941.

Maduell, Charles R. Jr. *The Census Tables for the French Colony of Louisiana from 1699 Through 1732.* Baltimore: Genealogical Publishing Inc., 1972.

Marigny, Bernard. *Réflexions sur la campagne du général André Jackson en Louisiane en 1814-1815, Nouvelle Orléans,* 1848. *Bernard de Marigny à ses Concitoyens.* Privately printed in French, 1853.

Martin, François-Xavier. *The History of Louisiana from the Earliest Period.* Lymann & Bradsley, 1827.

Martinez, Raymond J. *Rousseau: the Last Days of Spanish New Orleans.* Pelican Publishing Company, 1964.

McGinty, Garnie Williams. *A History of Louisiana.* Exposition Press. New York City, 1949.

McMichael, Andrew. *Americans in Spanish West Florida: 1785-1810.* University of Georgia Press, 2008.

Pénicaut, André. *Fleur de Lys and Calumet,* edited by R.G. McWilliams. Louisiana State University Press: Baton Rouge, Louisiana, 1953.

Reilly, Robin. *The British at the Gates: The New Orleans Campaign in the War of 1812.* Putman Publishers, 1974.

Robichaux, Albert J. Jr. *Louisiana Census and Militants, 1770-1789.* Volume 1. Polyanthos: New Orleans, 1977.

Rumily, Robert. *Histoire de Montréal.* Ottawa: Édition Fides. Volume 1, 1970.

Sanders, Mary Elizabeth. *An Index to the 1820 Census of Louisiana's Florida Parishes and 1812 St. Tammany Parish Tax List,* 1972.

Schwartz, Adrian D. *Sesquicentennial in St. Tammany: The Early Years of Covington, Madisonville, Mandeville and Abita Springs*. Auspices of City Council, 1963.

Seebold, Herman de Bachelle. *Old Louisiana Plantation Homes and Family Trees*. Gretna: Pelican Publican Company, 1971, Volume 1.

Starr, J. Barton. *Tories, Dons and Rebels*. University of Florida Presses, 1976.

Thwaites, Reuben Gold, and Kellogg, Louise Phelps, eds. *Frontier Defense on the Upper Ohio, 1777-1778*. Madison: Wisconsin Historical Society, 1912.

Tinker, Edward Larocque. *The Palingenesis of Craps*. New York Press, 1921.

Whitaker, Arthur Preston. *The Spanish-American Frontier: 1783-1795: The Westward Movement and the Spanish Retreat in the Mississippi Valley*. Boston: Houghton Mifflin Company, 1927.

White, Joseph M. *A New Collection of Laws, Charters, and Local Ordinances of the Governments of Great Britain, France and Spain: Relating to the Concessions of Land*, 2 Volumes, 1839.

Wolfram M. Von-Maszewski, ed. *Austin's Old Three Hundred: Histories of the First Anglo Colonists*. Eakin Press, First Edition, 1999.

Louisiana Books from Cornerstone

In Camp and Battle with the Washington Artillery of New Orleans
by Wm. Miller Owen
6x9 Softcover 500 pages
ISBN 1613422083

Gravier's Bookshop
A Breslin Family Tale of the Supernatural
by Evelyn Klebert
6x9 Softcover 190 pages
ISBN 1613421400

Lafitte of Louisiana
by Mary Devereux
6x9 Softcover 434 pages
ISBN 1613421311

A New Orleans Cookbook from Momma's Kitchen
by Eulalie Miscenich Poll
7.5 x 9.25 Softcover 396 pages
ISBN 1934935379

Social Life in Old New Orleans
by Eliza Ripley
6x9 Softcover 350 pages
ISBN 1613420374

The History of Mandeville:
*From the American Revolution
to Bernard de Marigny de Mandeville*
Anita R. Campeau & Donald J. Sharp
6x9 Softcover 394 pages
ISBN 1613420706

Cornerstone Book Publishers
www.cornerstonepublishers.com

Louisiana Books from Cornerstone

The Louisiana Book
Edited by Thomas M'Caleb
6x9 Softcover 430 pages
ISBN 1613420552

Strange True Stories of Louisiana
by George W. Cable
6 x 9 Softcover 360 pages
ISBN 1613420536

A History of Louisiana 4 Vols.
by Alcée Fortier
6x9 Softcover Four Volumns 1226 pages
ISBN 1613420382

Louisiana: its Colonial History and Romance
by Charles Gayarré
6x9 Softcover 548 pages
ISBN 1613420021

New Orleans - The Place and the People
by Grace King
6x9 Softcover 426 pages
ISBN 161342000-

Treading on Borrowed Time
by Evelyn Klebert
6x9 Softcover 198 pages
ISBN 1613420226

Louisiana Folk-tales
by Alcée Fortier
6x9 Softcover 140 pages
ISBN 1613420706

Cornerstone Book Publishers
www.cornerstonepublishers.com

Louisiana Books from Cornerstone

Sanctuary of Echoes
by Evelyn Klebert
6x9 Softcover 330 pages
ISBN 1934935891

The Creoles of Louisiana
by George W. Cable
6x9 Softcover 334 pages
ISBN 1456506048

Old Street Names of New Orleans
By Sidney P. Lafaye
6x9 Softcover 40 pages
ISBN 1-456500-42-2

History of the Louisiana Purchase
by James Q. Howard
6x9 Softcover 172 pages
ISBN 1613421265

New Orleans As It Was
by Henry C. Castellanos
6x9 Softcover 370 pages
ISBN 1613420706

Creole Families of New Orleans
by Grace King
6x9 Softcover 480 pages
ISBN 1456486829

New Orleans Desserts from Momma's Kitchen
by Eulalie Miscenich Poll
6x9 Softcover 182 pages
ISBN 1613421680

Cornerstone Book Publishers
www.cornerstonepublishers.com

Louisiana Books from Cornerstone

The Settlement of the German Coast of Louisiana and the Creoles of German Descent
by J. Hanno Deiler
6 x 9 Softcover 146 pages
ISBN 1613422032

Code of Practice in Civil Cases for the State of Louisiana
by Thomas Gibbes Morgan
6x9 Softcover 382 pages
ISBN 1613421842

Handbook of the Carnival
by John W. Madden
6x9 Softcover 148 pages
ISBN 1-887560-72-6

Cornerstone Book Publishers
www.cornerstonepublishers.com

Made in United States
North Haven, CT
01 April 2022

17744854R00236